ALSO BY STEVEN STOLL

The Great Delusion: A Mad Inventor, Death in the Tropics, and the Utopian Origins of Economic Growth

U.S. Environmentalism Since 1945: A Brief History with Documents

Larding the Lean Earth: Soil and Society in Nineteenth-Century America

The Fruits of Natural Advantage: Making the Industrial Countryside in California

RAMP HOLLOW

RAMP HOLLOW

The Ordeal of Appalachia

STEVEN STOLL

 HILL AND WANG   A division of Farrar, Straus and Giroux I New York

Hill and Wang
A division of Farrar, Straus and Giroux
175 Varick Street, New York 10014

Portions of chapter 5 first appeared, in slightly different form, as "Nowhere, Fast: George Inness's *Short Cut* and Agrarian Dispossession" in *Environmental History* 18 (October 2013): 786–94. Portions of chapter 6 first appeared, in slightly different form, as "The Captured Garden: The Political Ecology of Subsistence Under Capitalism" in *International Labor and Working-Class History* 85 (Spring 2014): 75–96.

Library of Congress Cataloging-in-Publication Data
Names: Stoll, Steven, author.
Title: Ramp Hollow : the ordeal of Appalachia / Steven Stoll.
Description: First edition. | New York, NY : Hill and Wang, [2017] | Includes
    bibliographical references and index.
Identifiers: LCCN 2017017082 | ISBN 9780809095056 (hardcover)
Subjects: LCSH: Land tenure–Appalachian Region–History. | Mountain
    people–Appalachian Region–History. | Farmers–Appalachian
    Region–History. | Appalachian Region–History. | Appalachian
    Region–Economic conditions. | Appalachian Region–Social conditions.
Classification: LCC HD210.A66 S76 2017 | DDC 333.3/174–dc23
LC record available at https://lccn.loc.gov/2017017082

Designed by Richard Oriolo

www.fsgbooks.com
www.twitter.com/fsgbooks • www.facebook.com/fsgbooks

10   9   8   7   6   5   4   3   2   1

For Leslie

The social order is a sacred right . . . Yet that right does not come from nature and must therefore be founded on conventions.

—Jean-Jacques Rousseau, *The Social Contract* (1762)

For since we are the outcome of earlier generations, we are also the outcome of their aberrations, passions and errors, and indeed of their crimes; it is not possible wholly to free oneself from this chain. If we condemn these aberrations and regard ourselves as free of them, this does not alter the fact that we originate in them. The best we can do is to confront our inherited and hereditary nature with our knowledge, and through a new, stern discipline combat our inborn heritage and implant in ourselves a new habit, a new instinct, a second nature, so that our first nature withers away.

—Friedrich Nietzsche, "On the Uses and Disadvantages of History for Life" (1874)

CONTENTS

	MAP	x
	PREFACE	xiii
1.	**Contemporary Ancestors**	3
	FROM DANIEL BOONE TO HILL-BILLY	
2.	**Provision Grounds**	37
	ON CAPITALISM AND THE ATLANTIC PEASANTRY	
3.	**The Rye Rebellion**	90
	WHY ALEXANDER HAMILTON INVADED THE MOUNTAINS	
4.	**Mountaineers Are Always Free**	127
	ON LOSING LAND AND LIVELIHOOD	
5.	**Interlude: Agrarian Twilight**	176
	THE ART OF DISPOSSESSION	
6.	**The Captured Garden**	212
	SUBSISTENCE UNDER INDUSTRIAL CAPITALISM	
7.	**Negotiated Settlements**	244
	THE FATE OF THE COMMONS AND THE COMMONERS	
	NOTES	291
	BIBLIOGRAPHY	343
	ACKNOWLEDGMENTS	387
	INDEX	391

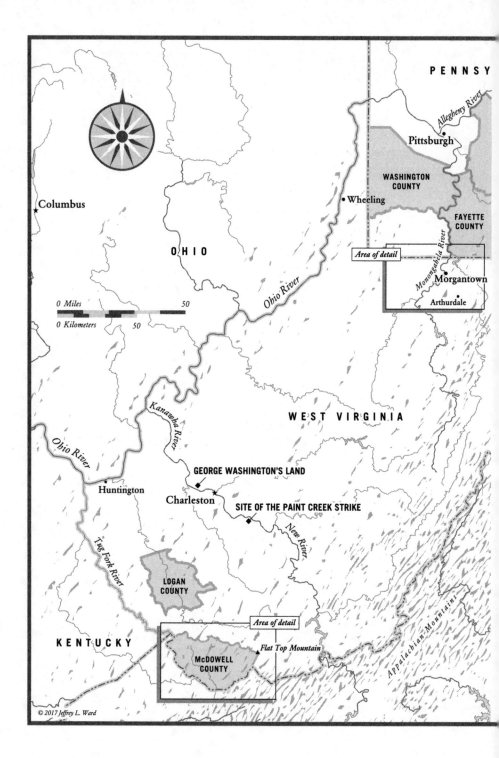

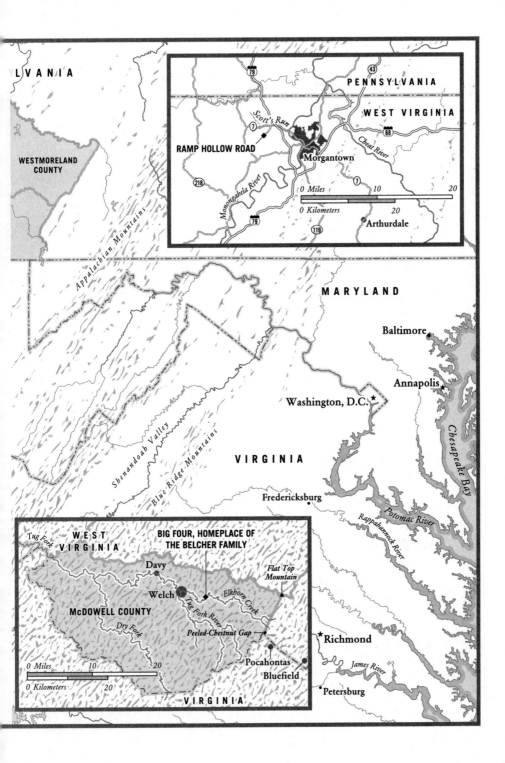

PREFACE

THIS IS A BOOK ABOUT an American settler culture, how its people hunted, foraged, farmed, and gardened, and how they lost their land. We all learned a version of American history that emphasizes the widening possession of land. That version tells of the brave women and men who voyaged into the wilderness. They did build homes in the wilderness, and they were brave, but in making homes for themselves they took homes from others. Their possession caused the *dispossession* of Shawnee, Cherokee, Munsee, Creek, and other nations. Many other Americans lost their lands and livelihoods during the last two centuries or were prevented from gaining access in the first place: African-Americans coerced into sharecropping throughout the South after the end of slavery and Mexicans evicted from their ranchos after the takeover of

California. Even the descendants of those pioneering settlers were forced to leave their gardens and woods after little more than a century.

I am interested in how people get kicked off land and why we don't talk about them. Americans tend not to think of ejectment and enclosure as central to the history of the United States. In the decades after the pioneers arrived in the mountains, they established families and communities and propelled their sons and daughters into households of their own. Yet when they weren't moving westward anymore, they no longer advanced the American Empire. Their story no longer coincided with the one about a nation destined to embrace a continent. They no longer served a particular role in the version of American history we all learned. They continued to grow maize in narrow hollows and graze their cattle in forest openings. But for some reason their persistence became a problem. They entered a period of conflict and decline that is the shadow of another story we've been told, about the Industrial Revolution. The central event in *Ramp Hollow* is the scramble for Appalachia, or the rapid onslaught of joint-stock companies to attain the rights and ownership needed to clear-cut the forests and dig out the coal. How this happened and what was lost is the subject of this book.

This book is also about country people throughout the Atlantic World over the last four hundred years. By *country people* I mean *settlers, peasants, campesinos,* and *smallholders,* all of whom make their livings by hunting, foraging, farming, gardening, and exchanging for the things they cannot grow or fashion themselves. The general word for them is *agrarians.* My purpose is to unite the experience of backcountry settlers of the southern mountains with that of agrarians elsewhere, to demonstrate that English peasants in 1650 and Malian smallholders in 2000 shared a similar fate and encountered similar sources of power as Scots-Irish farmers in 1880. My method is to create a thick context around the particular story I tell.

It can be difficult to understand people who live close to their environments. While preparing these chapters, I found critics who said either that agrarians work interminably for little gain or that they don't work hard enough. Both can't be true. The apparent contradiction between futile drudgery and laziness has nothing to do with how much time households spend in their gardens. Instead, these are two ways of saying that such people waste their time and labor no matter what they do. We tend to see settlers, peasants, campesinos, and smallholders as relics of the past. I ask the reader to look at them differently, as inhabiting the same planet and the same moment in time as everyone else. There are no primitives, savages, or backsliders. There are only humans in various social arrangements. I present their way of life, not as unfit or doomed but as functional and legitimate, though often riven with hardship. Yet in the years I spent traveling to libraries and archives where I read all sorts of documents, I often came across an idea that amazed me but that I could not understand, the idea that historical progress required taking land away from agrarians and giving it to others.

〰️

RAMP HOLLOW IS A TRIBUTARY of Scotts Run, once a profitable but now an abandoned coal seam just outside of Morgantown, West Virginia. A few years ago I traveled there with H.R. Scott, an agent for the West Virginia University Agriculture Extension Service. We'd been visiting sites in the area all day when H.R. stopped at a neighborhood that followed a road up a gentle grade. I stepped out of the truck where a trickling branch emptied into a larger creek. While H.R. rested, I walked unhurriedly in the afternoon humidity, after the sun had fallen just below the rim of the tiny valley. It narrowed and steepened, with each house at a slightly different elevation. Behind the houses, trees and brush covered the abrupt inclines that rose to a height of about 150 feet. The bottom of the hollow was just as wide, making it seem like I was walking in the rut of a giant wheel.

Halfway up I came to an abandoned house, older than the others. White windowpanes stood out against red tar paper. A metal roof extended over a pocket-like porch. The windows on one side had fallen in, and I could see things left behind by the last residents. This was a miner's shanty, circa 1900. I imagined a man walking out in the morning, a woman with children inside, smoke from the chimney floating to the canopy. An outhouse stood a few feet away, almost over the branch. It reminded me that humans packed close together become intimate with each other's waste.

The coal miner who earned the money that supported the family who lived in the tar paper dwelling might have been William Fulmer or Ross

Spicer or John Raketsky—names from the Census of 1940. Everyone in Scotts Run was a miner or married to one or the child of one. They lived fairly well when wages covered food and rent, but many reported no income for at least one week in 1939. I wondered whether they had once had their own farms or if they had been brought up in Scotts Run. I wondered how they lived when the money stopped. I kept a photograph of that house on my desk while writing this book, next to one of a different house.[1]

The day before, I visited the dairy farm belonging to Charles Hunter, on the spine of a hill twelve miles from Ramp Hollow. We stood a little awkwardly in the barn as H.R. and Charles shot glances at each other before asking me what I wanted to see. I wasn't sure. I suggested a garden that H.R. had told me about. We set off in that direction, when the wreck of a log cabin came up on the left. I asked Charles to stop the truck. The roof had caved in, making it impossible to get inside. Charles told me that John Hoard had acquired the land by grant from the last colonial governor of Virginia, John Murray, 4th Earl of Dunmore. Hoard died in 1778 while a captain in the Virginia militia and is buried next to the cabin, along with other members of his family. The last Hoard on Hoard Road had been born in that very cabin. He fought in the Second World War and then returned to live there the rest of his life. He died in 1984.

But that's not the cabin that made the greatest impression on me. Charles mentioned another one, half a mile up a muddy cow path overlooking the Monongahela River. It stood on one side of a hilly clearing with everything but the roof intact. A two-sided hearth and chimney (for cooking inside and outside) survived in almost perfect condition. Straw, stones, bark, and grass still filled the gaps between beams cut from large trees. The floorboards had rotted away, and a great willow presided over the middle of the only room, draping the house in a tent of leaves. I picked at fragments of newspaper stuffed around a window frame for insulation. It was the *Toledo Weekly*, dated 1903. It told of the goings-on three hundred miles away to the northwest. Clapboard and wallpaper still covered the walls here and there. All these touches reminded me that I was in someone's home, where members of the Stewart family had lived for two hundred years. People had slept and cooked in this room. Babies had crawled on this floor. Jessy and Anabelle Stewart lived here into the 1940s, though both were over the age of seventy by then. They described themselves to a census taker as retired farmers with some other source of income. They did odd jobs for the Hunters and lived in the cabin until they died in the 1970s. I took a picture.[2]

The log cabin in the high meadow and the tar paper shanty in the industrial hollow form a pair of sorts, a unity of apparent opposites. In one sense, they stand for two moments in Appalachian history. The cabin gave way to the shanty, just as a free and robust set of subsistence practices gave way to impoverishing wage labor. But history does not offer us neat formulations. By the time extractive industry had reordered the landscape, the people who inhabited both houses lived almost the same way. Husbands and sons spent their days in the mines, while wives and daughters tended gardens. The distinction between cabin and shanty had collapsed into Appalachian poverty.

*

I SET OUT TO BROADEN and deepen the narrative of dispossession in the southern mountains. I read the works of historians, anthropologists, literary scholars, and sociologists. I read corporate records, private correspondence, popular magazines, government reports, and novels. The result is episodic. My exact setting is southern Pennsylvania to southern West Virginia, but every chapter excavates a different stratum. The first considers Appalachia itself and how Americans have thought about it from the seventeenth to the twentieth centuries. The second explains the history of enclosure as part of the history of capitalism, contrasting that with peasant economy. The third reinterprets the Whiskey Rebellion by renaming it the Rye Rebellion, a conflict I see as arising from tensions over what served as money and the uses of land. The fourth takes up the destruction of the Appalachian forest and how the elimination of this ecological base contributed to the dependency of mountain households.

An interlude follows, in which I think through artistic depictions of dispossession in nineteenth-century America, including paintings by Winslow Homer, Thomas Hovenden, and George Inness. The sixth chapter explores the transfer of subsistence production from mountain cabins to coal camps, where garden vegetables reduced the wages paid to miners. The seventh and final chapter explains the persistence of peasant economy in the thinking of anthropologists and economists involved in economic development during the twentieth century. This book closes with land grabbing in Africa in the twenty-first century, suggesting that the story I tell is not done and over with, not really past at all.

RAMP HOLLOW

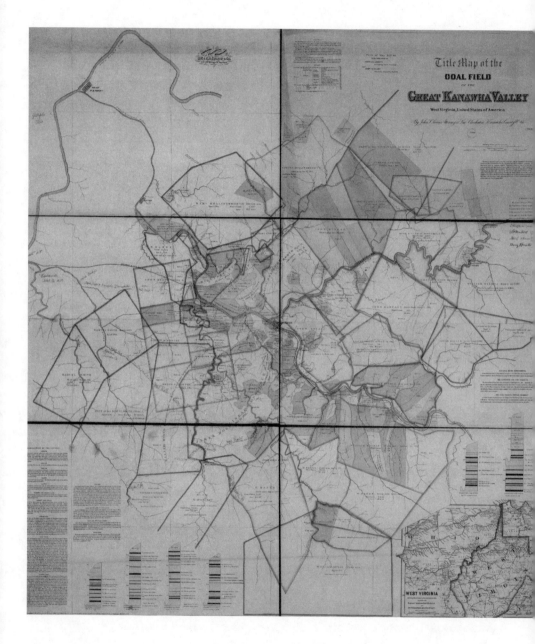

Title Map of the
COAL FIELD
OF THE
GREAT KANAWHA VALLEY

West Virginia, United States of America

WEST VIRGINIA

1. Contemporary Ancestors

FROM DANIEL BOONE TO HILL-BILLY

In all societies there are off-casts. This impure part serves as our precursors or pioneers.

—J. Hector St. John de Crèvecoeur, *Letters from an American Farmer*, Letter III (1782)

I**T IS AN ORDINARY MAP** of southern West Virginia, adorned with shapes representing private property. Some of the shapes adhere to watercourses. Others run ruler straight, throwing squares and trapezoids across innumerable hills and hollows. Distant investors consulted the *Title Map of the Coal Field of the Great Kanawha Valley* for its cross-section diagrams, which reveal the depths and strata of bituminous minerals. They learned the exact distances by river and railroad from these deposits to factories in Cincinnati, Richmond, and New York City. But their two-dimensional aspirations did not match three-dimensional reality. Thousands of people hunted and gathered, planted beans and maize, and raised livestock beneath the ownerships of the men whose names mark each survey. Looked at in this way, a mundane illustration of cadastral boundaries, "fixed by litigation or otherwise," posed a threat in carto-graphic form, a lit fuse in an ongoing war over the control of subsistence in the southern mountains.[1]

There are many other maps like this one, each a fragment of a region known better by myth and legend than by history. The named investors believed that the best use of the Kanawha Valley was to remove its trees and dig its coal. They believed that these commodities enriched not only them but West Virginia, the United States, and even the world—that imposing private property over these mountains enlisted a neglected land and a for-gotten people in an inevitable movement. They also believed that nothing stood in their way. As they saw it, the Kanawha Valley lay within a propi-tious region where wealth multiplied without social or environmental ob-stacles. For their part, the people on the ground had never paid much attention to lines demarcating private property or to landowners who often lived far from the mountains. Together, the investors and residents created a region, not by cooperating or by participating as equals in a political process but by the outcome of their conflict. We know the geographical location of this region as the southern extent of the Appalachian Moun-tains. The industrial invasion that took place there gave it another name: Appalachia.[2]

Where is Appalachia? Is it a province of eastern North America, locat-able on any map? Or is it a set of cultural characteristics, not entirely limited to elevation or topography? West of Washington, D.C., the traveler makes a gradual ascent, rising 328 feet in forty miles to the undulating plain of the Piedmont. The Blue Ridge comes into view, topping off at 1,100 feet outside of Harpers Ferry. The landscape then slopes into the northernmost point of the Shenandoah Valley. The Civil War battlefield Antietam lies on the eastern bank of the Shenandoah River. On the other side begins a physiographic formation known as Ridge and Valley, includ-ing Spruce Mountain (4,863 feet), Cheat Mountain (4,848 feet), and Back Allegheny Mountain (4,843), features of an escarpment called the Alle-gheny Front. Crossing over, the countryside extends west and south as the broad, highly eroded Appalachian Plateau. A forester writing in the 1880s described rivers with myriad tributaries, each opening to still smaller forks and branches. "What renders the topography of this region most remarkable is the extraordinary narrowness of its numberless watersheds, the different creeks and brooks taking rise in the immediate neighborhood of each other."[3]

We could just leave the question there and say that Appalachia consists of these uplands, including southwestern Pennsylvania, a sliver of Virginia, all of West Virginia, the eastern thirds of Kentucky and Tennessee, and the elevated counties of Georgia and the Carolinas. But physical features are not always enough to define a place as distinctive. One government report concluded that the various counties and corners often referred to as Appalachia "have only one feature in common—an elevation higher than that of the surrounding country." There is also a wider conception that draws in all of western Pennsylvania, the bottom tier of counties in New York, parts of Ohio, a third of Alabama, and a bite of Mississippi. Not all of these areas are particularly elevated. The first use of the name *Appalachia* offers no clarity. While wandering in what is now northern Florida, the survivors of a disastrous Spanish expedition heard the name of a village as *Apalachen*. A map from 1562 has the word hovering over a vague northern territory.

Nor does Appalachia have a specific or unique ethnic identity. Shawnee, Mingo, Delaware, and Cherokee all lived there at different times, but none of them exclusively. Many among the descendants of the white settlers who found their way to the mountains after the American Revolution kept on moving, generation after generation. Before the end of the nineteenth century, they had arrived in the Ozark Mountains, the Illinois prairie, the Great Plains, and the Willamette Valley of Oregon. Whether highland whites composed a separate subculture of the South or a slight variation in the foodways, music, and lore found in the lowlands depends on whether we choose to emphasize minor differences or major similarities. As late as 1900, a Cherokee in northern Georgia, an African-American in North Carolina, and a Hungarian recently arrived in Kentucky would not have thought that they lived in the same region.[4]

There might be no reliable way of defining a cultural region. But consider that human patterns in tandem with landscapes create lived experience. People change their boundaries, migrate to escape drought or cold, and enlarge their presence through trade and conflict. We could construct a region entirely from the mental maps of its inhabitants, keyed to seasonal work or the burial grounds of ancestors. If this is right, then a region is a set of defining events, process unfolding in place. Every region is based on a theory.

There are plenty of theories. In the nineteenth century, geographers began to think of regions as clusters of interactions within spatial limits. In particular, they asked how markets located in cities changed surrounding landscapes. A German named Johann Heinrich von Thünen came up with a model in which a town at the center of a uniform agricultural plain influenced what farmers planted over the entire territory. He expected to find perishable products close to market and hardier ones farther away because strawberries, unlike wheat, would not survive days in transit. For Thünen, city and country worked together to create a geographical division of labor in which both merchants and farmers benefited. Every exchange took place between equals and every outcome served the greater good, without a hint of class conflict or asymmetric power. He assumed the universality of capitalist rationality, in which everyone acted to maximize profit.

A century later, historians, anthropologists, geographers, and political economists rejected most of Thünen's ahistorical and socially simplistic model. They asked different questions. How did the financial power emanating from cities reorganize people and environments in its image? What happened to households and communities, as well as the landscapes they depended on, when everything took on monetary values? Have different forms of economy—peasant and capitalist—existed together at the same time? How can we use these relationships to understand the capitalist world? And instead of thinking only in terms of city and country, they broadened their thinking to include the various ways networks of capital allied with governments dominate resource peripheries and frontiers. In other words, rather than limit themselves to regions and nations, they saw the world itself as a division of labor, in which regions and nations created certain commodities. Rather than imagine exchanges between individuals on an equal footing, they discovered political power operating within and between markets.[5]

But while these ideas are good to think with, I don't hold them too close. They aren't flexible enough to absorb the depth and detail of actual people in actual places. Exactly when the southern mountains became a resource periphery is not entirely clear and not very important. Was it when the first colonial governor of Virginia granted the first tract of mountain land or when the first joint-stock corporation opened the first coal mine?

Yet grand theories offer us something worth carrying into the following pages. They construct the world *historically*. New geographical entities emerge from corporate strategies, leaps in transportation infrastructure, and other events that change the relationship between people and environments. All of which has helped me to understand a region called Appalachia. *The southern mountains are half a billion years old, but Appalachia did not exist before the industrial invasion of those uplands during the nineteenth century.* It appeared as a location within the capitalist world when its coal and labor ignited the American Industrial Revolution. It was created and constantly re-created by hunters and farmers of every ethnicity who employed the landscape for subsistence and exchange; by land-engrossing colonial elites; by corporate attorneys scheming to get hold of deeds; by investors wielding cadastral maps; by coal miners resisting company managers and starving on strike; by the social engineers of the New Deal; by the Appalachian Regional Commission; and by brokenhearted citizens watching beloved hollows buried by mountaintop-removal mining. Appalachia consists of these contextual identities and events and their continuing fallout between the Blue Ridge and the Ohio River.[6]

This book is about the ordeal of greater West Virginia, regarding that state as exemplary for the region as a whole. It takes place in the Pennsylvania counties that gave rise to the Whiskey Rebellion; in Scotts Run, a long industrial hollow near Morgantown; and in the coalfields near Flat Top Mountain, up against Kentucky and Virginia. It is predicated on the collision between two forms of economy: one represented by corporations, the other manifested in families and farms and as old as agriculture itself, if not older.

WE KNOW THE PEOPLE who lived in the mountains by various names: *highlanders, mountaineers,* or settlers of the *backwoods.* We also know them as individual frontiersmen, soldiers, and statesmen. William Henry Harrison led Kentuckians into the Old Northwest against forces commanded by the Shawnee brothers Tecumseh and Tenskwatawa. Andrew Jackson's parents arrived in the mountains of South Carolina from Ireland in 1765. By 1814, Jackson had turned from fighting the British to fighting the Red-Stick Creeks. Two soldiers who would become backwoods legends served in Jackson's Tennessee militia at Horseshoe Bend: Sam Houston (born on Timber Ridge in the Shenandoah Valley and reared in Tennessee) and David Crockett (born in Greene County, Tennessee). The Confederate general Thomas "Stonewall" Jackson grew up west of the Blue Ridge. Abraham Lincoln came from the same people, from Sinking Spring Farm in Hardin County, Kentucky. In 1832, in his first political address, Lincoln said, "I was born and have ever remained in the most humble walks of life."[7]

No other son of the southern mountains commanded more cultural gravity than Daniel Boone. He was born in 1734 on the Pennsylvania frontier, soldiered for the British Empire during the French and Indian War, and arrived in Kentucky in 1767. He moved in and out of the region over the next decade, hunting and trapping for a living, fighting and negotiating with Shawnee and Delaware. In 1775, a North Carolina judge and merchant hired Boone to blaze a trail through the Cumberland Gap and northward into central Kentucky. It became known as the Wilderness Road. Boone established Boonesborough at its northern terminus on the Kentucky River and brought his family there.[8]

Boone became famous during his lifetime, but few among the eastern elite spoke a good word about anyone else who lived in the same places and in the same way he did. John Murray, 4th Earl of Dunmore, the last British governor of Virginia, considered mountain people dangerous to administrative order. "They acquire no attachment to Place . . . wandering about seems engrafted in their Nature." A group of squatters went so far as to promulgate their own laws, sneered Dunmore, nearly declaring themselves "a separate State . . . distinct from and independent of his majesty's authority." In October 1780, Major Patrick Ferguson terrified his loyalist militia with this description: "Unless you wish to be eaten up by an inundation of barbarians . . . if you wish or deserve to live and bear the name of men, grasp your arms in a moment and run to camp . . . The Back-water men have crossed the mountains." Ferguson reported that these vipers had cut up a boy in front of his father. Days later, backwater men killed Ferguson and 150 of his soldiers in the Battle of Kings Mountain.[9]

"The *first* settler in the woods is generally a man who has outlived his credit or fortune in the cultivated parts of the State," claimed the Philadelphia doctor and essayist Benjamin Rush. He said that every pioneer lives in filth and rags, enduring privation and hunger. He lives and thinks like an Indian. Most of all, he hates "the operation of laws." At best, thought Rush, these reckless and irredeemable people prepared the way for husbandmen who paid taxes and furnished the cities with food. Whether wilderness outliers would ever submit to constitutional authority remained the greatest question. They were, wrote J. Hector St. John de Crèvecoeur, "a kind of forlorn hope." The French-born author of *Letters from an American Farmer* scorned if he did not outright fear them. Along "our extended line of frontiers . . . many families exhibit the most hideous parts of our society." In this view, no one who preferred hunting to farming could be relied upon as a civilizing force.[10]

Castoffs living in anarchy haunted the Federalists who came to power during the 1780s, but a different kind of migration brought the southern mountains into the Atlantic World. By grant and purchase, the Revolutionary elite came into millions of acres. None of the owners moved to western Virginia or eastern Kentucky. Properties the size of major watersheds belonged to men who would know them only as metes and bounds described on parchment. Most of the land was too steep to be cultivated in cotton or tobacco and too far from cities to have any other commercial use. Owners filed their deeds and forgot about them, unaware that a frontier society took shape on their property. The first census of the United States revealed that 56,000 whites, blacks, and Indians inhabited the area that became West Virginia, a density of 2.3 per square mile. Each household tended to claim around four hundred acres by squatting or "tomahawk right," but others claimed much more, with the expectation that Virginia or Kentucky would acknowledge their titles. A two-tiered land system took shape. The first consisted of state-endorsed absentee ownership. The second appeared when cabin-building, cattle-grazing, bear-hunting households moved in.[11]

By the end of the Revolution, fear of the woodsmen at higher elevations had given way to a kind of admiration. To some, they exemplified national independence more vividly than planters or merchants or the farmers of New England. In 1805, a theater in Charleston, South Carolina, staged a performance of *Independence; or Which Do You like Best, the Peer, or the Farmer?* In the play, Lord Fanfare attempts to re-create an English manor in the mountains. There he encounters Mr. Woodville, a perplexing commoner who refuses to play the part of serf or servant.

> LAWYER WITTINGTON: That beautiful, romantic farm of the valley, is situated in the very centre of your lordship's estate, and no sum whatever could tempt the now proprietor, Mr. Woodville, to part with it. He is one of the queerest animals I ever came across—an eccentric, by this light; celebrated for glorying in, and boasting of, his INDEPENDENCE, and declaring, that an honest farmer knows of no dependence, except on heaven . . . I had a presentiment 'twould be agreeable to you to possess Mr. Independence's farm, so offered him three thousand pounds for it, on your lordship's account; but he told me, by way of answer, he intended, God willing, to live fifty years, and would, in the course of that term, make five times the sum I proffered him, off of it—Ergo, 'twould be bad policy in him to sell it.

> LORD FANFARE: Why didn't you make the plebeian acquainted with my rank and fortune? He certainly would not have dar'd refuse to accommodate a peer of the realm!

> LAWYER WITTINGTON: I did, my lord, I did, tell him, what a monstrous great man you were; and he then, strutted about, like a beau 'fore a church porch, or a monkey, with the king's evil, and swore, by the dignity of a man, he would not sell a single furrow! No, not a pound of earth; to gratify the caprice of any mortal; be him peer of the realm, or peddler of the highway, and that he would retain his to be envied INDEPENDENCE, pure and unsullied, in spite of you and all the peers and aristocrats in Christendom.

Woodville mocks Fanfare and outwits Wittington. The conflict between aristocratic rank and the anarchy of the backwoods is funny because Fanfare doesn't understand that Woodville is not his subject. The audience recognized the misplaced lord. But Wittington introduces Woodville as "one of the queerest animals I ever came across." The key to Woodville's political and economic independence is his ability to seize land and subsist without regard to Fanfare. And while Fanfare represents feudal rules and obligations, Woodville is free in a way almost unintelligible to the aristocrat. He is disdainful of and unaccountable to power, more of a trickster than a clown.[12]

Politicians of the 1830s and 1840s praised these *pioneers*—a word that originally referred to an advance infantry of laborers who prepared for the regular army by digging fortifications and repairing roads. Representative Charles Faulkner of western Virginia promoted them: "Our native, substantial, independent yeomanry, constitute our pride, efficiency and strength; they are our defense in war, our ornaments in peace; and no population, I will venture to affirm, upon the face of the globe, is more distinguished for an elevated love of freedom—for morality, virtue, frugality and independence, than the Virginia peasantry west of the Blue Ridge." Senator Thomas Hart Benton of Missouri spoke of them in world-historical terms. To him, they were the vanguard of a racially defined society. In 1846, Benton recalled the Proclamation Line established by Great Britain after the French and Indian War to keep colonists out of the backcountry. "Where is that boundary now? The van of the Caucasian race now top the Rocky Mountains, and spread down to the shores of the Pacific . . . Civilization, or extinction, has been the fate of all people who have found themselves in the track of the advancing Whites."[13]

Faulkner and Benton celebrated a mountain folk who crossed borders with little regard for those who governed from afar. As long as political elites pretended not to see the flaunting of private property and constitutional authority, they could continue to believe that the interests of the backwoods aligned with those of the nation-state. For a time, their interests did align. In every skirmish with Shawnee, in every frontier battle, the pioneers made visceral claims to territory. By defending and dying for their own homes, they fought the wars of the American Empire. In fact, the specific pioneers whom Benton exalted were not in Tennessee or Kentucky. They were a few miles from the Pacific Ocean, in territory disputed between Britain and the United States, where they founded the Provisional Government of Oregon. Senator Levi Woodbury of New Hampshire demanded forts and supply lines to protect them from Indians and Redcoats. He called the Oregon settlers defenseless, by which he meant stateless. "But they are American citizens no less than we—they are on American soil no less than we." This is how a fierce and mobile people served the interests of the United States. Their unsanctioned seizure of a contested frontier justified the expansion of American authority.[14]

Washington Irving turned to the backwoods for a relevant symbol of national identity. In 1839, the lifelong New Yorker searched for a more rational nomenclature of citizenship than the one he had inherited. "United States citizen" seemed to him "a clumsy, lumbering title." An American? "There are two Americas, each subdivided into various empires." Irving found a new term in "one of the grand and eternal features of our country . . . I allude to the Appalachian or Alleghany mountains." This grand feature stood in the middle of everything, separating the northern farm from the southern plantation, the Atlantic Seaboard from the Mississippi River Valley. Thus he announced the "United States of Appalachia."[15]

Twenty years later, the relentless expansion of the United States had left the southern mountains behind. Texas had exploded into national politics, first as a borderland of cotton and slavery, then as a republic after its war of independence with Mexico. Its admission to the Union as the twenty-eighth state set off the Mexican–American War, in which the United States seized 529,000 square miles of arid territory. The California Gold Rush of 1849 and the discovery of the Comstock Lode in 1859 ignited emigration to the Far West. A political crisis ensued. Congress, riven by conflict over slavery, found it impossible to integrate the Mexican Cession as well as the unorganized remnants of the Louisiana Purchase. When the locus of territorial struggle shifted, expansionists no longer recognized their own aspirations for control of the continent in the settlers of western Virginia. The admiration of mountaineers marked a particular geopolitical moment. By 1860, that moment had ended.

The pioneers went from the present to the past. One way to explain how their fortunes changed is to look at one of the first biographies of Daniel Boone, published by a Connecticut journalist named George Canning Hill in 1859. What makes Boone's story (in Hill's telling) so important for understanding the fate of Appalachia in the nineteenth century is that Boone's life did not conform to that of other mythic heroes. He didn't die in a ritualistic battle between good and evil. He never made it back home. Between the American Revolution and his death in 1820, Boone endured a tangle of financial missteps and hardships having to do with land. All this matters because what happened to Boone mirrors what was happening in Appalachia. Hill's story displays nearly every aspect of the declining cultural significance of the southern mountains.

After the Revolution, the Commonwealth of Virginia granted millions of acres in its far-distant counties to soldiers, politicians, and financiers. The owners often turned around and sold their holdings, setting off a frenzy. The thought that wilderness land might be valuable sent all sorts of people into the mountains to grab it up. Kentucky was part of Virginia until 1792, and Boone joined in the rush. He bought and sold warrants, which conferred the right to make a claim that might result in title (meaning ownership). But if another claimant proved that he had made the first survey or demonstrated a superior right in some other way, all competing warrants became void. This made buying a warrant like placing a bet. The process required tenacity, a touch of mendacity, and a smattering of legal knowledge. Between the early 1780s and the early 1790s, Boone bought warrants to at least thirty-nine thousand acres, resulting in about twelve thousand acres in his name.

Soon after, Boone lost almost all of it, leading his biographer to write about the wealthy men who bought the ground from under him.

How was he doomed to the bitterest of disappointments! The title, however it might have been concocted, was put before the occupancy! The speculator could drive out the brave and self-sacrificing pioneer! . . . And this the law permitted. There seemed to be no help for it. The authority of the original pioneer and discoverer was not accounted equal to that of the man who held cunningly drafted instruments in his hand, and could quote nice technicalities in his favor . . . Boone was turned out of his home, and his farm became the property of another!

Hill's morality tale is much simplified, but it isn't wrong. Boone loaned money without security. He sold to people who never paid him. He bought land for his children at significant cost. To raise money, he sold pieces of his holdings at a discount, then invested in additional warrants that never turned into titled property. Plaintiffs sued him, called him a liar, and won judgments against him. He stopped defending himself and failed to show up in court. In 1798, a judge ordered him taken into custody, but the pioneer of Kentucky had fled to Missouri. The mythic journey of the most American of all American heroes began in wilderness and ended in petty lawsuits over real estate.[16]

The frontier hero plays a distinctive historical role. He might be born in the woods, but he dedicates his life to the destruction of the very forces that create him as a hero. The first cut for civilization requires a touch of savagery. Only Boone's colossal moral strength allows him to maintain his mission, though he is continually exposed to moral danger. But the schemers finally get him. In Hill's account, they defeat the hunter without the blade-and-gunpowder contest he always won. Title overcomes occupancy; technicalities undercut self-sacrifice. Most of all, *there seemed to be no help for it.* Cunningly drafted instruments represent the way of the world. They indicate that Boone has lost his grip on the times. "Settling up a new country is not civilizing it." Boone knows how to find a path through the woods and seize territory—not how to develop it into governed, productive space.[17]

Hill wrote about Boone's ineptitude and bankruptcy at the very moment that the plain folk of the southern mountains had entered their own eclipse. Hill's interpretation of Boone has nothing to do with what actually happened in the mountains or how the people who lived there responded to change. Instead, it reflects a shifting mood. In 1860, approximately 150,000 households lived in the American highlands. Members of Congress no longer celebrated them. Charles Faulkner, who had wrapped them in poetry in 1832, spoke of them obliquely in 1876: "Ours is a mountain country. Its population is thinly scattered through its hills and valleys." He told the House of Representatives that West Virginia might overtake Britain in coal and iron production but not if its treasures remained "unused in the bowels of the earth." The best that Faulkner could say about the peasantry he once called Virginia's pride and strength was that they posed no impediment to what was coming.[18]

The cultural slide seemed to pause during the Civil War. Northerners praised those southerners who fought on their side. West Virginia seceded from Virginia during the war and joined the Union. Kentucky also refused to join the Confederacy. To northerners, loyal mountaineers seemed to prove the justness of their cause. A writer for the *Saint Paul Press* compared the cotton-bound coastal plain to an infested swamp. But liberty lived in the mountains. "Freedom has always loved the air of mountains . . . The sky-piercing peaks of the continents are bulwarks against oppression: and from mountain valleys has often swept most fearful retribution to tyrants." *The New York Times* consistently looked upon them favorably, as "loyal mountaineers," "simple-hearted and faithful mountaineers," and "brave mountaineers who have trusty rifles, and, if attacked, there will be some rebel blood left there to pollute the mountain soil." But this esteem did not outlast the war. The ongoing struggle for control of the continent changed locations and took a different form in the 1870s. The conflict shifted to the Great Plains, where the Union fought the Sioux. Investors created wheat fields the size of counties, harvested them with steam engines, and employed armies of immigrants. The locomotive overtook the frontiersman as the paramount symbol of progress.[19]

Before outright disdain came fascination. Edward Pollard, a Baltimore attorney born in Virginia, took a jaunt into the mountains in 1869. No one told him it had been done before. "The Author comes before the public . . . bearing what may be described to many readers in America as the discoveries or revelations of a *New World*!" He described the inhabitants as the sturdy poor: "There is nothing of the squalor or wretchedness of poverty in the mountains," chirped Pollard. "The poverty of the mountain is picturesque; it is hardy, healthful; it is a school of rude but independent manners." The giddy sophisticate went cabin to cabin in search of some kind of aesthetic sublime. What, exactly, did he mean by a "delicious sensation, with contrasts in it of bodily discomfort only sharp enough to increase the zest"?

Pollard jumped up and down and clapped his hands at the rustic interiors. One evening after watching as his host (a stoic dude in homemade clothing) filled pipe after pipe for an hour, Pollard cleared his throat. "Look here . . . old man . . . why do you smoke so much?" Stoic dude responded, "Well, sir, I live *here* . . . I has my pleasure in whatsoever I is at for de time I am at it." This only deepened the mystery. Another highlander seemed "a splendid specimen of his class—a stalwart son of the forest, of Herculean stature." Pollard also noticed the landscape. Tazewell County (soon to become McDowell County) offered crystal springs and romantic views, ideal sites for spas and hotels. He advertised the place: "At present we are firmly persuaded that there is no field of investment in Virginia that presents such opportunities as does the already awakened improvement of springs property." He found sulfur springs pouring with cool tonic water and had a gallon of it analyzed. Perfect for invalids![20]

Travelers continued to emphasize local color, but others wrote in a more menacing voice. An article appeared in *Lippincott's Magazine* that seemed to mark a new conception of the region and its people. Its opening is benign. "We were journeying over the mountains in the autumn of 1869. Our camp was pitched in a valley of the ascending ridges of the Cumberland range, on the south-east border of Kentucky." The author arrives at a cabin door. An African-American woman answers, revealing "the sordid interior . . . sickly with the smell of half-eaten food and unwashed dishes; the central figure a poor, helpless old man sitting on a stool." The man was white, and the author supposes him a deposed slaveholder, rotting in some unspecified immorality among his former property.

For the author, that moment set off a torrent of scorn against the poor whites of the mountains, some of it strange and shocking. "The natives of this region are characterized by marked peculiarities of the anatomical frame. The elongation of the bones, the contour of the facial angle, the relative proportion or disproportion of the extremities, the loose muscular attachment of the ligatures." This racialized condemnation, perhaps more than any other insult and degradation they received, most indicates the extent to which they had fallen down a cultural gradient, from the formidable owners of their material world to curiosities—at best the makers of homely quilts and rough-hewn furniture, at worst moonshine-distilling insurgents and violent slackers against the social order. The disparaging writing about the poor whites of the southern mountains tends to assert or imply their incapacity for historical change. It accuses them of stagnation amid opportunities for wealth. Rather than admit that they did not understand the people they confronted, the journalists, social scientists, and tourists who produced this writing often castigated and dismissed them.[21]

The writers expressed three attitudes, sometimes in combination. Some, like Pollard, delighted in cultural difference. They regarded the mountaineers as the survivors of a pure Anglo-Saxon culture that should be preserved. Others diagnosed degeneracy. In this view, the descendants of the bold pioneers became wretched in isolation and failed to live up to their supposed Anglo-Saxon potential. Another group held either of the first two views and also tried to figure out where the mountaineers had come from as a way of diagnosing their problem. This last group is the most interesting, since they claimed to be doing social science.

Nineteenth-century social science came into being in order to categorize so-called backward and changeless people. "Let students of sociology leave their books," advised one authority, "and at first hand in the Cumberlands deal with the phenomena of a social order arrested at a relatively early stage of evolution." The historian Frederick Jackson Turner made a similar pronouncement in 1893. "Among isolated coves . . . the frontier has survived, like a fossil, in a more recent social formation." Two broad explanations emerged, one environmental, the other racial. Some theorized that geology and geography influence certain qualities or characteristics. In other words, the left-behind posterity of the first settlers eventually succumbed to isolation; they became stunted by the hollows. Another line of investigation attempted to trace the mountaineers to an originating ethnic group. In this view, degeneracy could be passed from generation to generation as an inherited trait.[22]

Several of these ideas appear in the writings of William Goodell Frost and Ellen Churchill Semple. Born in Buffalo, New York, the son and grandson of New England missionaries and abolitionists, Frost presided over

Berea College in Madison County, Kentucky, for almost thirty years. He believed that the highlanders composed a forgotten colony of Anglo-Saxons, unchanged by the times, like air bubbles trapped in Arctic ice. "The mountaineer is to be regarded as a survival," wrote Frost in 1898. "In his speech you will soon detect the flavor of Chaucer; in his home you shall see the fireside industries of past ages . . . in a word, he is our contemporary ancestor!" Frost's oxymoron contains a theory of regionalism. He defined Appalachia as the place where physical isolation preserved the cultural traits of a frontier society.

Frost also expressed an environmental theory of cultural formation, an idea popular among the northeastern elite. Along with Theodore Roosevelt and Frederick Jackson Turner, Frost believed that the struggle and strain of frontier life provided an experience of conquest that produced the American character. According to Turner, the end of the frontier as a place of conflict and a process of state formation marked the end of an epoch. Appalachians stood apart from the relentless technological change of the late nineteenth century, and for Frost, Turner, and Roosevelt that wasn't necessarily a bad thing. With other metropolitans they certainly advocated for locomotives and electricity, but they also thought that white mountaineers represented certain barbarian virtues worth preserving. The highlanders' steadiness offered a polestar—"a fixed point which enables us to measure the progress of the moving world." How or whether these noble savages in their redoubts would withstand industrial capitalism no one could say.[23]

To the geographer Ellen Churchill Semple, the wayward mountaineers composed a seed bank, the stored germ plasm of Anglo-Saxon Puritans, "as if they had disembarked from their eighteenth-century vessel but yesterday." She knew that just yesterday the reeking scum of Europe had disembarked from their nineteenth-century vessel. *Irishmen* patrolled the streets of New York City and Boston. By the 1880s, their political machines had supplanted the genteel influence of the Astors and the Lowells. The ongoing invasion of Italians and Jews sent the guardians of Anglo-Saxon culture into anxious fits of racial conservation. They invented eugenics, spread chapters of the Daughters of the American Revolution, and gated Plymouth Rock. The people of upland Kentucky gave Semple strange solace. They had been tainted by a smidgeon of French and German but were otherwise pure. "The stock has been kept free from the tide of foreign immigrants." But what proof did she have for the pure blood of the hollow folk?[24]

Frost and Semple both believed that they heard Elizabethan English spoken in West Virginia and Kentucky. Words like *afeared*, and *learn* (for *teach*, as in "Learn me how to lose a winning match," from *Romeo and Juliet*) are among the few cited as evidence. *But there is no evidence.* These words were common all over the South. They did not "survive" in the mountains. It isn't clear why mountaineers would speak like Shakespeare anyway, given that they had stronger ties to Scotland and Ireland than to England. Neither Frost nor Semple knew of the Swedish and Finnish origins of the backwoods settlement culture or that the ancestors of the log-cabin folk had spent the seventeenth century at or near the seaboard, mixing with Delaware Indians. The contention that Appalachian dialect originated in early-modern England, writes the linguist Michael Montgomery, "cannot withstand even a little objective scrutiny."

What Frost and Semple thought they knew turns out to be less important than what they assumed. They believed that certain people *created* culture; others *received* it. In this view, Appalachians exhibited inherited traits, having invented nothing themselves. Other examples of the same thinking also involve mountain dwellers. In northern Luzon, the largest island of the Philippines, smallholders cultivate wet rice in terraces. Anthropologists once believed that the practice of terrace construction had arrived from China in about 1500 B.C. False. Recent studies show that the terraces date only to the seventeenth century, when lowland farmers sought refuge at higher elevations from the Spanish colonial military. Within a relatively short time, in other words, highland Filipinos developed practices that observers could not conceive of as having come from them.[25]

It isn't the falseness of these ideas that makes them interesting but the problems they appeared to solve. A few old English words here and there, a comforting assertion about elevation and culture, simplified matters too complex for the prevailing models of reality. Some of the same geographers who invented Appalachia advocated environmental determinism, or the idea that climate and geography generate human differences and drive history. Ellsworth Huntington, the best-known determinist of the twentieth century, claimed to have cut a clarifying path through the messiness of human events. "Maps of what we may call climatic energy are practically identical with maps of health, crop yields, transportation, income, wages, education, and a host of other economic and social conditions . . . Therefore the only logical conclusion is that the main geographical pattern is set by climate." Huntington invented "climate energy" out of thin air and then confused correlation with causation. He didn't really practice social science at all. Climate didn't pose questions for his investigation. Instead, it provided simple answers to historical problems he did not understand.[26]

The two broad explanations of highland degeneracy often appeared in the same works. The basic premise was that a class of northern Europeans (either sturdy Anglo-Saxon pioneers or Scots-Irish criminals) found their way into the mountains and became trapped by topography, stagnating in their remoteness and turning into the grotesque mountaineers of the 1890s. It should be clear that none of this came from what we would recognize as ethnographic fieldwork. Frost, Semple, and Huntington made what they wanted of their subjects. No one asked them to justify their faulty methods because their so-called findings reinforced the Atlantic elite's most versatile sociological category: race.

Race emerged as the self-serving ideology at the center of social science. It's a spectacular fabrication in which one group collects the qualities of another group (speech, skin color, geography, social status, or foodways) and casts them as inferior under an inviolate authority (God, Nature, or Progress). As the historian Jacqueline Jones argues, "Race signifies neither a biological fact, nor a primal prejudice, and it lacks the coherence of a robust political ideology; rather, it is a collection of fluid, contingent mythologies borne of (among other imperatives) fighting a war, assembling a labor force, advancing the designs of demagogues, organizing a labor union, and preserving voting and public schooling as privileges reserved for some, rather than as rights shared by all." We know that white slaveholders began to prefer African to English indentures for a variety of reasons and only later justified African slavery on the basis of skin color. Once *black* became synonymous with *slave* in the Atlantic

World, planters could deploy a circular argument for bondage, torture, and rape.[27]

Poor whites also became a despised race defined by their own circular argument. Descriptions of mountaineers emphasize their supposed degeneracy and grotesqueness, which came from their isolation, causing moral depravity, resulting in . . . degeneracy and grotesqueness. Once a racial type is in place, any worsening of a subject people's condition reinforces the type, providing proof after proof. Racialization has often gone along with ejectment and enclosure, offering an intellectual tool for taking resources away from people said to be incapable of progress or change. This is what we find in the southern mountains. The knowledge that wood, coal, and other minerals existed there came first, soon followed by the technical capability and political organization necessary to extract them. Between the 1860s and 1900, metropolitans accused struggling households, many in tenuous legal possession of the land they farmed, of unfitness for the modern world. The writer James Lane Allen fired a shot for speculators and shareholders. "For, within a hundred years, the only thing to take possession of it, slowly, sluggishly overspreading the region of its foot-hills, its vales and fertile slopes—the only thing to take possession of it and to claim it has been a race of mountaineers, an idle, shiftless, ignorant, lawless population." Aspersions of stupidity, backwardness, primitivism, and volatility coincided with the seizure of the environment.

Inventing a race of people and depriving them of land not only required the force of law, it required a story. The writer Allen told it dramatically. Once upon a time mountaineers lived in high-and-away Kentucky, "a zone of almost inaccessible hills with steep slopes, forests difficult to penetrate, and narrow jagged gorges . . . a virgin wilderness, a vast isolating and isolated barrier." The author lived to see the fortress of the Cumberlands fall before the world-historical movement of extractive industry, "bringing into it the new, and letting the old be scattered until it is lost." The people, like the landscape, are redeemed to a higher purpose. "Old manners and customs, old types of character and ideals of life, old virtues and graces as well as old vices and horrors," are obliterated.

Isolation appears often in these stories. No one who lived in Kentucky thought that they lived behind "inaccessible hills . . . a vast isolating and isolated barrier," as Allen called it. Merchants and farmers there sold cattle to Baltimore, floated logs to Ohio, and shipped whiskey down to New Orleans. They acquired consumer products from all over. And yet, the slant of the ranges favored commerce in certain directions and not others, northeasterly in the Blue Ridge, northwesterly on the Plateau. Getting around wasn't like galloping through Kansas over a hundred miles of good road. The mountains made travel difficult much of the year and at times impossible. But industry had no trouble finding what it wanted and removing it. Corporations lay track into thousands of hollows and pulled billions of dollars in lumber and coal from the region over the following century. Still, those searching for the causes of poverty in Appalachia—throughout the twentieth century and even today—blame its *isolation*.

As recently as 2007, the Appalachian Regional Commission used a boilerplate that could have been written a century earlier. "These . . . mountains have stood throughout history as nearly impenetrable barriers to socioeconomic interaction, commerce, and prosperity . . . Appalachia is a place apart, a place where people have long-suffered the chronic economic consequences of physical isolation." Isolation, as it is used in this sense, doesn't really describe location. It describes an unholy remove from civil society, an outlier status. Like race, it doesn't really exist, but the story requires it. It defines the thing to be overcome.[28]

For foresters, missionaries, and businessmen, the thing to be overcome was the very cultural distinctiveness that travelers and geographers admired. When they said that mountaineers were different from other white citizens of the United States, they meant that highlanders wasted the resources under their control. They meant that older ways of being and doing things would never blend with twentieth-century needs and opportunities. They meant that folk religion deviated from institutional Protestantism. They meant that a people who used common lands for common uses lived within a deviant economic culture. By the late nineteenth century, they meant that industrial agriculture would not work in Appalachia. Sloping, rocky, narrow, inaccessible fields could not be modernized. A vast monoculture for export would never be planted there. Credit from financial institutions would never flow there.[29]

Racialized qualities and geographical theories culminated in a single sentence. In 1900, a journalist for the *New York Journal* described a person he had never seen before. "A Hill-Billie is a free and untrammeled white citizen of Alabama, who lives in the hills, has no means to speak of, dresses as he can, talks as he pleases, drinks whiskey when he gets it, and fires off his revolver as the fancy takes him." Hill-Billie was threatening for being free from hierarchy and unassimilated into Atlantic capitalism. But we cannot understand Billie without his historical setting. The mountains at that time were under full-scale assault. The landscape that sustained him by providing him with food at all seasons and commodities for exchange was vanishing. Writing in 1904, an engineer condemned highlanders with unusual ferocity. He called them "forlorn and miserable in appearance and behavior; but, never having known or dreamed of anything better than the wretched surroundings of their everyday life, they are supremely unconscious of their own misery." The engineer mistook Hill-Billie's condition for the historical process that had created him as poor and cast it back upon him.

This is how a story that begins with Daniel Boone arrives at Hill-Billie, how admiration for frontier independence and tenacity turned into racialized condemnation and hatred within twenty or thirty years. The period of admiration might have been the exception. Plenty of people distrusted backwoods people before Boone's career. It appears to have coincided with a certain moment in which settlement did not violate administrative authority but furthered American expansion. Nonetheless, it's still remarkable how quickly the shift happened. The chapters that follow explain the events and methods that resulted in an astonishing process of dispossession, as well as the changes from within mountain ecology and economy that played a part in it.[30]

And yet, some of the people most involved in extractive industry had another way of talking. They used a romantic language of light pathos and wistful regret. The president of the West Virginia Coal Mining Institute addressed assembled executives in 1912. He recalled his early career as a "mineral man," climbing into hollows looking for coal. "I count it as a bit of rare good fortune that professional duties called me into the mountains while the men and women there were still natural, the spinning wheel in use, handmade rifles in service, good old sorghum served in coffee." One night at twilight, "traveling a strange trail in a strange land," he heard cowbells in the woods and smelled bacon from a nearby cabin. The inhabitants welcomed him in for "a long hour's talk before a big log fire with all the family present." The speaker did not wish to see those "natural" men and women again in possession of the mountains. In his mind, they now belonged to memory. And though he himself contributed to the demise of their way of life, he implies that a transcendent force of progress controlled events. Yet something else is striking about the speaker's description of "natural" men and women, their homely ways, and their inevitable and necessary downfall. He could have been talking about American Indians.[31]

⁂

NO TWO DISPOSSESSIONS are the same. The white settler culture of the southern mountains did not share the same fate as the Cherokee, Choctaw, Chickasaw, Seminole, and Creek. The compulsory removal of these five nations in 1838, known in Cherokee as the Trail of Tears, would seem to have no connection to the coming of corporations to West Virginia. Still, these events bear a resemblance. They rhyme. In both instances, a privileged commercial class depicted the members of a target group as a despised race before taking their land.

Forty years before, the United States favored a policy of assimilation. When Georgia planters and speculators tried to sway George Washington to help them eject the Creek from their homeland, the president snubbed them. If Creek men and women dressed, spoke, farmed, and worshipped like white southerners, Washington would commit the United States to protecting them. In the summer of 1790, he invited a Creek delegation to New York City. It was the beginning of an unprecedented pact with their vibrant leader, Alexander McGillivray. The son of a Scottish trader and a Creek mother, McGillivray had been commissioned a British colonel during the Revolution. He wanted to bridge the two worlds and the two peoples to whom he belonged. Weeks of negotiation and heavy drinking resulted in a treaty that established permanent borders to be enforced by the United States.

On the twentieth of July, McGillivray and Washington stood at 39 Broadway. Said Washington, "I am glad you have come, Colonel. I have long felt that we had much in common." Responded McGillivray, "I cannot flatter myself that much, Mr. President, but it has long been my ambition to shake your hand in friendship." Their meeting held the promise of territorial sovereignty and Indian citizenship. Under the terms of the treaty, McGillivray became a brigadier general, suggesting a place for him within the nation-state. Over the following twenty years, many members of the five southern nations accepted certain aspects of white American culture. They became Christians and planted cotton. Some owned slaves. The Cherokee published a newspaper in their own language and ratified a constitution in accordance with the Constitution of the United States.

None of these concessions or adaptations, however, made them more secure. Washington never enforced the treaty with McGillivray. The army never arrived to protect the Creek against speculators who instigated confrontation by fraudulently offering Creek land for sale. McGillivray repudiated the treaty in 1792 and died the next year. The electoral defeat of the Federalists in 1800 left Indians subject to Thomas Jefferson, an expansionist with little commitment to tribal sovereignty. Instead, Jefferson thought up ways of dispossessing the Chickasaw by predatory lending and foreclosure. Let the Indians come and trade, he said, and the army would furnish them "with all the necessaries and comforts they may wish," encouraging them "to run in debt for these beyond their individual means of paying." Once the scam was running, "they will always cede lands to rid themselves of debt." A general sense that Indian claims throughout the South would soon be open to whites inspired a popular ditty: "All I ask in this creation / Is a pretty little wife and a big plantation / Way up yonder in the Cherokee Nation."

With the election of Andrew Jackson in 1828, planters and speculators believed that they had accumulated the political influence necessary to eject every last Cherokee, Choctaw, Chickasaw, Seminole, and Creek and send them to the far side of the Mississippi River. Georgia's political leadership declared the Cherokee Constitution null and void (though its legislature and governor had no authority to do so) and passed a series of laws asserting their rights over the Cherokee homeland. The Supreme Court seemed to come to the defense of the Cherokee by ruling that no state could claim jurisdiction over any Indian nation. The Court affirmed, however, that the United States did possess that authority. In other words, the Court threw the entire question into national politics. The same forces and interests so intent on puncturing Cherokee autonomy immediately appealed to Jackson. He responded by giving them everything they ever wanted.

The Indian Removal Act of 1830 authorized the president to make some unnamed location available for those Indians "as may choose to exchange the lands where they now reside, and remove there." But no offer ever conveyed a more blatant threat. Nothing prevented Jackson from using extralegal means to enforce this "exchange," which really required people to leave the only home they had ever known for one they never wanted. But what makes the lead-up to the Trail of Tears so important is that justification for this policy of dispossession required public argument. It called for definitions and explanations from every branch of government.

Removal began with an intellectual process, a rhetorical attack intended to erase the long-standing relationship between the nations and the United States. Representative Lewis Cass of Michigan, a former governor of the Michigan Territory, attempted to undermine any notion that Indians and whites could share the same social space. He said that missionaries had tried for decades to teach Christian morality to the Cherokee, "but there seems to be some insurmountable obstacle in the habits and temperament of the Indians." As for the assertion that many among the Cherokee had conformed to the expectations of whites, Cass lied that only "half-breeds" did. Instead, "the great body of the people are in a state of helpless and hopeless poverty," improvident and indolent. "We doubt whether there is, upon the face of the globe, a more wretched race than the Cherokees." Cass recast their desperate attempt to find stability and gain acceptance as shallow mimicry.[32]

Andrew Jackson dismissed the Cherokee as a failed race. He expressed a mystical ideology of white supremacy, in which the white settlement of North America necessarily supplanted Indians. Addressing a delegation in 1835, Jackson revealed the sham of a voluntary exchange. "Listen to me . . .

while I tell you that you cannot remain where you now are. Circumstances that cannot be controlled, and which are beyond the reach of human laws, render it impossible that you can flourish in the midst of a civilized community." Some Cherokee fled to Indian Territory (now Oklahoma) in advance of the policy. Some hid high in the mountains and evaded expulsion. But sixteen thousand found no way to hold out, part of an estimated sixty thousand Indians throughout the South who were ripped from their farms by marshals and made into refugees. Jackson promised to ameliorate any suffering that might ensue during the forced migration, but in December 1838 he did nothing while four thousand died of starvation, hypothermia, and sickness.[33]

This forced exile differed entirely from the departures of the Scots-Irish from their homes in the hollows. Even under similar aspersions of degeneracy, mountain whites had a different relationship with those in power. Unlike the Creek and Cherokee, the Scots-Irish did not claim a collective identity in a sovereign territory. The five nations had engaged in treaty negotiation with the United States as *nations* since the end of the Revolution. Then, when the United States extinguished that sovereignty, it ejected the Indians *as Indians*. This collective ethnic identification made the Removal Act and the Trail of Tears different from the slow violence that brought an end to agrarian autonomy in places like West Virginia. No act of Congress or appeal to the Supreme Court or disavowal of treaties characterized the industrial invasion of Appalachia.[34]

But the similarities also matter. Both groups were cast as degenerate races with no capacity for historical progress. Neither Scots-Irish cattle herders nor Chickasaw maize gardeners could be brought into the circulation of capital without shedding their rootedness in locality and their household sufficiency. Indian territorial sovereignty conflicted with the expansion of cotton and slavery. Mountaineer kinship made some of the same kinds of claims on the landscape as homeplace. Neither group made much sense to an emerging conception of land as commodity. Most of all, perhaps, both underwent an intellectual dispossession that preceded the one that actually took away their land. "Assaults on a nation's environmental resources frequently entail not just the physical displacement of local communities, but their imaginative displacement as well," writes the scholar Rob Nixon. By the time marshals arrested those Cherokee who refused to go peacefully, the five nations had already become notional refugees, "uncoupled from the idea of both a national future and a national memory." Mountain whites lost their land under the same assumptions, if not the same tactics, deployed against Indians. Neither vanished, but rather they resisted and endured. They shared one other thing in common: their displacements made them poor.[35]

⋙

ALL AGRARIANS PRACTICE SOME VERSION of the same kind of economy. Anthropologists call it the *household mode of production*. It describes people who grow their own food and the ways they organize themselves to do so. A mode of production is not a particular way of making something. It is the making of something within all its social, environmental, and historical relationships. Think of someone working a plow. Is it an English peasant behind a horse, c. 1200? Or is it a worker under the direction of a district manager riding a tractor, c. 2000? Looked at one way, all plowing is the same. It opens the earth for planting. But to think of farmers in all places and times as doing the very same thing is a mistake. The peasant sustains his village and his lord, to whom he owes rent. He lives within webs of local obligation and religious devotion. The manager lives in a suburban community and regards agriculture as a source of income. He produces commodities for a remote corporation and is paid for his time. Each operates under differing conceptions of his place in the world. A mode of production describes the entire context of making something, including cultural cues and forms of authority. Thinking this way leads us to ask who benefits by any new tool and who doesn't.

As a mode of production, the household unites Daniel Boone with every African-American slave, each English peasant, and most of the humans who have ever lived. The words I will use to describe this form of economy (and explain later, along with the household itself) are *subsistence*, *makeshift*, and *self-provisioning*. Urbanized people of the twenty-first century tend to know little about the household mode of production, and often approach it with misconceptions and prejudices. Peasants, campesinos, and smallholders provoke two typical responses. They represent either a past of deprivation and suffering from which the people of the industrial world have escaped, or they exemplify lost simplicity, mutuality, and natural community to which we must return. They're either brutish or noble, stupid or wise. We have seen this in the way outsiders to Appalachia looked at the people who lived there during the nineteenth century (loyal and brave during the Civil War, ignorant and degenerate after). The same thinking is common among whites toward American Indians. Yet neither way of thinking helps us to see people for who they are. It might be that the persistence of peasants and smallholders violates our implicit belief in progress, not the progress that we experience in working toward completing a task but the world-historical progress we think we see in technological innovation.

This sense of progress is embedded in *capitalism*, a social system that demands constant expansion into new environments, absorbing new people in order to increase its rate of profit. Since expansion brings wealth to those who own and invest in production, they conceive of it as progress in the world-historical sense. Tens of millions of people link their identities, the trajectory and meaning of their lives, to a social system with all sorts of destructive tendencies, associating it with the highest aims of society itself. But if the perpetuation of capital is the same thing as progress, where does that leave smallholders all over the world, up to their shins in muck day in and day out? Though they buy and sell into the global economy (as I will explain), they have a different sense of progress. They thus appear to exist in some other universe, outside the dominant way of seeing and being. As the sociologist Teodor Shanin has written, "The real peasantry does not fit well into any of our concepts of contemporary society." This is one of the problems at the center of this book.

The peculiar thing about our way of thinking is that it conditions us to see peasants and others who live in "traditional" societies as inherently poor, awaiting the redemption of modernity. We compare their daily labor and stock of food to the abundance we experience on automotive gathering expeditions to the supermarket. Peasants sometimes don't have enough to eat, though they might work at little else. Periodic shortages of food can happen because of drought, flood, or a fast-growing population. But smallholders with sufficient access to the landscape rarely go hungry. The diversity of their environments and occupations provide safeguards and fallbacks.

Nonetheless, we've all seen images of villagers starving, desperate mothers clutching gaunt and listless babies, older children with bellies distended by kwashiorkor.[36] Journalists detail the suffering, and we are sometimes left with an impression of perennial misery. One argument of this book is that whenever we see hunger and deprivation among rural people, we need to ask a simple question: What went on just before the crisis that might have caused it? We can escape false assumptions and dichotomies by understanding a people's history.

An example will make my point. In 1940, an anthropologist named Allan Holmberg spent a number of years in the rainforest of eastern Bolivia studying a people called the Sirionó, in a region known as the Beni. Their culture seemed remarkably simple. They used few words, played no games or music, and seemed to lack mythology, medicine, and rituals. They had almost no tools but their longbows. They feared dogs, built poor shelters, and were strangely unfamiliar with their own environment. Holmberg said that they scrambled for food every waking moment and bickered over what little they found. He declared them among "the most culturally backward peoples of the world," regarding them as primitives in the earliest stages of social evolution. Holmberg's report, *Nomads of the Longbow* (1950), became essential reading for students of anthropology for more than forty years.[37]

And yet, almost everything Holmberg wrote about the Sirionó turned out to be wrong. He noticed that they planted informal plots, which they abandoned and revisited at harvest. But he didn't ask why. In addition to their food plants, they grew cotton and tobacco. When did they acquire these seeds and from whom? Why didn't they garden more and hunt less when game ran short? The answers would have provided clues to their recent experience. By concentrating intently on what the Sirionó lacked and all the ways they failed his test of civilization, Holmberg hardly saw them at all.

Holmberg mistook condition for culture. In fact, the Sirionó lived in close proximity with whites during the end of the nineteenth century.

They sometimes raided colonial rubber plantations for metal tools. They had absorbed Africans or African-Americans, as well as individuals from other Indian groups. As late as the beginning of the twentieth century, they lived in grasslands, before being driven out by smallpox and enemies. White ranchers discovered them and tried to coerce them into peonage. Those who evaded capture lived a furtive existence in the rainforest. This might be why Holmberg found them always on the move, never dwelling long enough for seeds to sprout. Perhaps worst of all, though he knew that smallpox had killed many in the late 1920s, reducing the population to 150 individuals by 1945 from perhaps as many as 2,000, Holmberg learned nothing more about the epidemic. Yet this explains their cultural simplicity better than anything else. Toolmakers died before transmitting their skills to the next generation. Elders and ceremonial leaders vanished, making certain rituals impossible to perform. Groups winnowed to small numbers have simplified divisions of labor.[38]

Like Holmberg, we will fail to ask the right questions if we are deceived into thinking that some people have no history, that their poverty is inherent, its causes self-evident. Without knowing history, we might conclude that the 1 billion people who live in slums have always picked through garbage for food. Seeing the world without the past would be like visiting a city after a devastating hurricane and declaring that the people there have always lived in ruins.

Here is another example. An economics textbook published in 1985 begins a discussion of "late-developing countries" with this statement: "No one has produced a definitive list of causes of the poverty of the LDCs." The authors have their own list, including "lack of physical capital, rapid growth of populations, lack of education, unemployment," and so on. This might look like an entirely plausible set of explanations. But a historian sees their list differently—as effects, not causes. European colonizers took over the best farmland, cordoned off forests, and trapped indigenous people in wage dependency or slavery, thus undermining every structure of authority. The end of colonization often left these nations in ecological and financial debt.

Consider Haiti. Once slaves freed themselves and took over the island, their French tormentors threatened to invade with a massive force if the struggling society did not pay for its freedom. France wanted an amount equal to all former plantation property, including the lost value of the people themselves. France enforced this indemnity between 1825 and 2010, declaring it void only after an earthquake killed thousands in Port-au-Prince. The total amount charged against the country would be worth somewhere between $20 and $40 billion today. It sapped Haiti's national income and stifled its development. The point is that economists rarely consider that poverty on such a scale is only comprehensible historically. Neither the United States nor a single country in Western Europe had to overcome the same obstacles. If poverty on such a scale is so misunderstood, if it appears to have no historical origin, then it can only be cast back upon the poor as their own failure.[39]

Every resident of every slum (or her parents or grandparents) once lived in an environment that sustained her most of the time. When the government sold off her woods and enclosed her land and relegated her and her family to the worst soil around, when she had nothing to exchange for money and the army arrived in the village, she found it impossible to remain. She saw her village combined into industrial latifundia under government or corporate control. Harvests from these giant fields now travel in containers from trucks to ships to trucks to big-box stores in the United States. As for her, she migrated to informal settlements of extraordinary density where she lives without sewers or clean water. She makes her living by washing car windows or by collecting metal from discarded computer parts or by prostituting herself. This explains the contradiction of more food *and* more hunger than ever before in human history. But it says something else—that the poverty of so-called underdeveloped countries is of recent origin.[40]

My purpose is to take a group of people who have been alternately praised and despised and open up their material history. The story of the industrialization of the southern mountains has been told before, but I see it in a wider gaze. Here are a few contentions. The people I am concerned with practiced household food production and vigorous exchange. The form of their economy likens them to peasants in other places and times. They traded close to home and far away, in two transactional realms. They depended on an extensive landscape that sometimes did but often did not belong to them. Governments attempted to capture the value they created through taxation (the United States) and by offering up the landscape to corporations (the state of West Virginia). The takeover of the landscape and the industrial cutting of the forest brought an end to their autonomy. Some semblance of their old economy survived into the twentieth century. It did not disappear when the mountains became real estate in the eighteenth century or when coal mining began in the nineteenth. All of this happened between the 1790s and the 1930s.

Most generally I say that the past occupants of hollows and ridges lived in a manner typical of humans all over the planet. They attained sufficiency, a makeshift existence, not always thriving but rarely starving. Mountain people ran into trouble for their own reasons. Their land use was too extensive to be maintained amid the changes they confronted. They had trouble modifying how they did things to compensate for their own increasing population. But they were never poor until they lost the forest, their *ecological base*. This is a vast renewable fund of resources that provides spaces for fields, food for gathering, fodder for cattle, and habitat for wild game. The base gives everything but costs nothing. It only needs to be taken care of within its own dynamics. Nothing else compares to the loss of this commons. Without the woods to provide them with commodities for exchange, they depended on wages for the money that connected them to the rest of the world. Yet dependence on wages meant subjecting themselves to corporate authority, the vagaries of coal markets, and other things out of their control. Some pronounce the coming of industrialization as necessary and even inevitable. I reject this mysticism. If we see it from the vantage of the people with the most to lose, it looks different. Nothing about the history of the southern mountains can be explained as social evolution.[41]

Yet I do not venerate the nineteenth-century social ecology of Appalachia as exemplary for some postcapitalist future. The settler culture and their descendants did not inhabit an Arcadia without conflict or change. Their entire history from the eighteenth to the twentieth centuries is one of conflict and change. I am under no illusion that they lived abundantly or easily. They sometimes wrote eloquently about the hardships they faced, but their sense of fairness and justice often did not extend to

African-Americans or Native Americans. I do not believe that they always tended their land well or that they could have maintained themselves for another century. But the virtues of their makeshift have been largely erased and the historical causes of their poverty are little known to the reading public. I describe their ecological practices as fragile but *legitimate*. If I gloss over some of their social problems, it is because I have my eye on other things.[42]

Readers interested in a global history of the southern mountains might not find it here. It all depends on what *global* means. Perhaps a global history would trace the capital that launched coal and railroad companies to banks and bankers in Philadelphia, New York, London, and Edinburgh. It would place Appalachia at the center of a transnational migration of dispossessed peoples. If global history consists of this, then the following book is not an example of it. Yet I assume that generating capital requires combinations of labor and environments. Commodities go to sale. The rendered value takes the form of money, drips into distant accounts, and ends up spawning another circuit somewhere else. This book tells of one place where that process touched ground. Appalachia appears to be the epitome of locality, and much of what follows takes place in the folds of the mountains, between households and within counties. But in another sense, Appalachia's key industrial product was unlike any other. Coal from Pennsylvania, Kentucky, and West Virginia powered the American Industrial Revolution. Almost everything manufactured on the Atlantic Seaboard after 1850—all the steel forged in Pittsburgh, all the cotton milled in North Carolina, all the steam-powered ships carrying all the guns and clocks made in New Haven—required the burning of coal. This is not a global history, but it is a history with global implications.

※

PERHAPS NO ONE WHO CONDEMNED mountain people spoke with the authority of Arnold Toynbee, the British historian and diplomat. Toynbee spent the majority of his career as a professor at the London School of Economics, where he wrote one of the most successful books of the century, *A Study of History*, published in twelve volumes between 1939 and 1961. Toynbee believed in *civilization* as an intellectual and moral stage. Some people arrive there, he asserted as self-evident; some don't. "Man achieves civilization, not as a result of superior biological endowment or geographical environment, but as a response to a challenge in a situation of special difficulty which rouses him to make a hitherto unprecedented effort."[43]

With these foggy lenses, Toynbee reviled the struggling farmers of the American highlands as "no better than barbarians." Actually, he considered *barbarian* too kind a word for them. Toynbee defined Albanians and Kurds as categorical barbarians, ancient holdovers, never roused out of backwardness. People who had never known anything other than mud huts and goat milk didn't bother him. "The Appalachians," on the other hand, "present the melancholy spectacle of a people who have acquired civilization and then lost it." How curious that Toynbee gave no thought to the historical causes for such a precipitous decline. At least it simplified his task. Not all those among the Atlantic elite wrote with Toynbee's arrogance, but they tended to see the Appalachians the same way he did.[44]

The people of the southern mountains told their own stories. Emma Bell Miles's "The Common Lot" (1908), William Zinn's *The Story of Woodbine Farm* (1931), Hubert Skidmore's *I Will Lift Up Mine Eyes* (1936), G. D. McNeill's *The Last Forest* (1940), James Still's *River of Earth* (1940), and Florence Cope Bush's *Dorie: Woman of the Mountains* (1992) reveal the fierce desire for dignity and stability in circumstances forced upon them. Consider this passage from an obscure chronicle written in 1927 by a West Virginia farmer and civic leader named David Idleman: "We are sometimes conscious that in the past we have . . . been cheated out of our natural inheritance. It was necessary first for the homemaker to build up a civilization before the natural wealth of our community[,] here in coal and timber[,] could be developed. This being done[,] this wealth in a greater degree should have been the common heritage of our people." Instead, Idleman lamented, "this great natural wealth went into the hands of syndicates for a nominal sum and [was] lost to the people." Such eloquence, such historical nuance, surpasses anything that Toynbee wrote.

But the categories that Toynbee relied upon are worth thinking about. He filtered everything he learned about cultures and nations through a ready-made set of developmental stages. And although these stages tell us nothing of any value about the history of recent times, to him and others they explained everything.[45]

2. Provision Grounds

ON CAPITALISM AND THE ATLANTIC PEASANTRY

Every savage has the full enjoyment of the fruits of his own labours.
—Adam Smith, *Lectures on Jurisprudence* (March 29, 1763)

The modern is that subject which measures any distance from itself and redeploys it against an unlimited space of imagination.
—Michel-Rolph Trouillot, "North Atlantic Universals" (2002)

THERE IS A STORY that overhangs the history of modern times. No monarchs or militaries figure in the plot. It is not a myth of peoplehood or national origin. Yet many people have told it—philosophers and merchants, geographers and presidents, schoolteachers and ministers. It recounts change in the past but lacks the specificity of events. The story moves through stages that mark the various ways that humans found food and accumulated wealth. In this purposeful fable, things happen on cue, under some unnamed force of change. One of the most important things to happen is that people stop growing their own food.[1]

The theory of stages begins with skin-clad hunters alone in a misty wilderness, with nothing but their bows to feed and protect them. In the

Savage State, humans know perfect freedom but also relentless privation. They possess heroic virtue (in Jean-Jacques Rousseau's version), but they live by the chase. As far as the political economists were concerned, scattered hunters roaming around the mythical landscape demonstrated one distinguishing quality: they fulfilled all their own needs. The social theorists of the eighteenth century asserted that such people generated no surpluses; sustained no divisions of labor. To the political economists, *savage* itself did not really refer to particular ethnic groups but to any people who used everything they made and made everything they used.[2]

According to the story, humans increase in the passage of time. They eat up most of the wild animals and begin to coax the more docile ones into domestication. They become herders or nomads, with cattle and sheep providing the economy of what theorists regarded as a middle stage between savagery and civil society. Some defined it as *barbarism*, others as *Arcadia*, somehow actual and mythical at the same time. Virgil launched the mythical Arcadia with his description of the earthly one, a rocky upland region southwest of Athens on the Peloponnesian Peninsula. There he found simple shepherds with simple wants. Arcadia is not Eden. It's not where you have anything you desire but everything you need. It's a dream of sufficiency, not of hedonism.

This is why Rousseau called this moment the happiest for humankind. Painters and poets longed for the freedom it represented from rents, taxes, and other instruments of organized power. The American painter Thomas Cole depicted it in *The Pastoral or Arcadian State* (1834), the second of five canvases in his series *The Course of Empire* (1834–1836). (It is preceded by *The Savage State* [1834].) Smoke rises from a Stonehenge-like temple while Pythagoras sketches out his theory of right angles in the earth with a stick. Others invent dance and music. At the very center of the scene, a young herder tends a flock. Between the seventeenth and twentieth centuries, the intellectual class of Europe and North America commemorated this stage as a time of rustic virtue, when people thrived in innocence, enjoying the freedom of savagery without its privations and the benefits of civility without its threat of tyranny and exploitation.

The emotive power of Arcadia comes from its ephemeralness. It exists as a kind of sacrifice, doomed by progress that might increase wealth but perhaps not virtue. The destruction of Arcadia is essential to this narrative. In this sense, Daniel Boone's flight from the Kentucky wilderness he tamed but did not own is comparable to Moeris's lament in Virgil's *Eclogue IX*:

> *O Lycidas, we've lived to see the time when a stranger,*
> *Owner of our land, could say (as we never thought could happen):*
> *"These lands are mine: you old tenants move on."*[3]

But what cause did Cole attribute to dispossession and the end of Arcadian freedom? He might have identified the source as merchant or planter wealth. He might have painted slaves in cotton fields or country women bound to oppressive mills, churning out cloth. Instead, Cole painted the insidious cause lurching minutely at the left edge of the canvass. It's a man behind a plow.

We can hear Cole's anxiety in Thomas Paine's pamphlet *Agrarian Justice* (1797), where Paine begins by acknowledging the cultivation of the earth as the greatest human invention. But great inventions have unforeseen consequences: "The landed monopoly that began with it has produced the greatest evil. It has dispossessed more than half the inhabitants of every nation of their natural inheritance, without providing for them . . . and has thereby created a species of poverty and wretchedness that did not exist before." Cole depicted this gross inequality and the decadent imperium that he saw emerging from a subordinated countryside in *Consummation of Empire* (1836), the third painting in the series.[4]

The series reaches its own consummation with *Destruction* (1836), followed by *Desolation* (1836). Rather than bless empire as the apex of power, if not human achievement, Cole condemned it to a violent death. Technological innovation only enabled the accumulation of wealth, the enslavement of labor, and the monopoly of land. An invasion of fur-clad barbarians wrecks the state. Cole makes the point symbolically by painting the decapitated statue of a warrior standing over a massive stump (a decapitated tree). In the last scene, everything is restored to the stable state, the deep order of things. The moon rises in silence over a single vine-enveloped pillar standing before a tranquil sea. Everything was going just fine, he seems to say, before the farmer showed up.

Few social thinkers thought of agriculture as leading to domination and tyranny, as some romantics did. Most saw it as the catalyst of civilization. "By the labor of the husbandman," according to John Quincy Adams, "the means of subsistence are multiplied; as the earth yields its increase, population thickens." Most of all, farmers produced more food than they needed, making possible cities, governments, and nation-states. Adams put it like this: "The fourth stage of society, may perhaps better be considered *as a necessary appendage* to the third, than as by itself a separate and distinct condition. The congregation of men in cities, which forms the basis of civilized life, naturally follows from their assemblage as husbandmen." Yet Adams's confident narrative says nothing about the troubled relationship between farmers and the state bureaucracies and financial institutions concentrated in cities. Nor does it explain why farmers became city dwellers involuntarily. But the theory of stages cannot embrace that kind of complexity. Its appeal comes precisely from the way it makes a certain kind of change seem natural when it really hides the exercise of power.[5]

In the happy version advanced by Adams, and every political economist at the time, the final stage brings expanding wealth. Fed by farmers, cities surge in population. Occupations multiply and subdivide. No resident of the town produces her entire existence. She consumes the product of everyone else's labor, exchanged through money. For those who told the story, the argument did not need proving. The commercial streets of Glasgow, London, and New York City displayed a proliferating division of labor: ironsmiths, mechanics, druggists, glassblowers, general merchants, grocers, coopers, leather cutters, shoemakers, stonemasons. The Scottish theorists declared the attainment of this form of social organization a world-historical event. And with that, the fable ends. No other stages follow. History continues as quantitative, not qualitative, change: more transactions, greater efficiency, rising wealth, and the geographical expansion of the division of labor itself.

As simple as a child's bedtime story, and lacking any evidence to support it, the theory of stages nonetheless served as the commonplace representation of material progress for centuries, exerting enormous influence over how elites in the Atlantic World thought about history, political economy, and race. It is the basic historical assumption in the thought of Adam Ferguson, Lord Kames, David Hume, Adam Smith, and Karl Marx, who gave it credit as the first attempt "to give the writing of history a materialistic basis." And think of one of the most popular novels of all time, *Robinson Crusoe*, endlessly cited as a work of social science after its publication in 1719, in which Crusoe, marooned on an island off the coast of Africa for twenty-eight years, recapitulates all the stages of material progress. He evolves from a screaming savage on a desolate beach, to a wandering herdsman, to a prosperous farmer. He finally presides like William of Orange over a tiny civil society, in which his three subjects enjoy the freedom of religious conscience.

The theory infused the writings of innumerable American thinkers, especially Benjamin Rush, the political economist Henry Carey, and the historian Frederick Jackson Turner, whose "Frontier Thesis" merely recast the same stages as a pageant of American expansion. "Stand at Cumberland gap," Turner asserted, "and watch the procession of civilization, marching single file." Economists have clung to it. W. W. Rostow enshrined it in his *Stages of Economic Growth* (1960). More recently, Jeffrey Sachs has argued that the purpose of development is to move the billion or so residents of the world's villages from "subsistence farming" to the next "stage," in which people live by the market and stop growing their own food.[6]

Thinking in terms of stages not only structured the way the Atlantic elite saw the world, it gave them a tool for intervening in societies. The purity of the stages, their lack of historical specificity, allowed them to be projected onto any people. The result has been a muddle. "The fundamental error of ahistorical social science," according to the theorist of world systems Immanuel Wallerstein, "is to reify parts of the totality . . . and then to compare these reified structures." In other words, intellectuals began with a mistaken history of their own societies, subdivided this narrative into stages, and then universalized the stages. They judged the people they colonized as "stuck" in this or that stage and called the whole wreck social science. Michel-Rolph Trouillot captures the mentality: "As soon as one draws a single line that ties past, present, and future, and yet insists on their distinctiveness, one must inevitably place actors along that line, either ahead or behind." Placing these actors meant sorting out all the peoples of the world into one or another of the stages, resulting in the simpleminded and manifestly false distinctions that Toynbee made about Appalachians. Never has there been a model of reality so utterly divorced from reality.[7]

The consequences of these ideas for people supposedly "behind" cannot be overstated. An "advanced" society can justify moving a "backward" one along the line connecting past and present. Extraction becomes progress. Taxation becomes training in civilization. Disaster (or "shock") becomes an opportunity for change. Dispossession becomes integration. Stage theory makes it possible to recast taking something away from people as giving them something they never asked for. Most spectacular of all, no degree of suffering on the part of the subject group, no death by famine or descent into wretchedness, invalidates the model. The stages function as a self-contained, self-referencing vision. An idea that comes into being without argument or evidence cannot be defeated for lack of them.

But here is the larger point for the fate of smallholders in general and the residents of Appalachia in particular. *Farmers occupy an awkward position within the theory of stages.* Like hunters and herders, they belong to a stage before modernity, but unlike the others their work remains essential to modernity. The progress of civil society depends on them. Who but farmers raise the wheat and wool that generate commerce, merchant wealth, and population? Hunters and herders offer little or nothing to civil society, but farmers pull the entire enterprise. Beginning in the seventeenth century, some asked if the country people whose fields fed the towns and filled the hulls of trade were equal to the task. Only those farmers who turned out more wheat and wool than they needed could be said to have entered the final stage. As I will argue throughout this book, no people who grew their own food lived without exchanging things. Nonetheless, political economists accused them of refusing to join the great, burgeoning division of labor. The key distinction, they said, between plodding in stagnation and flowing down the torrent of history lay in the complete alienation of the product from the producer. In civil society, people did not live like savages, fulfilling their own needs. They sold everything they made.[8]

There are two divisions of labor. In the first, or *social* division, everyone is a buyer and seller of commodities. It's what we see in the diversity of occupations and businesses on city streets. The second is sometimes called the *technical* division. It describes workers who sell their daily capacity to hammer and heave in exchange for money. They labor for the benefit of someone else, never owning the commodities they fashion. Adam Smith begins his *Inquiry into the Nature and Causes of the Wealth of Nations* (1776) at this juncture. Break the manufacturing of pins into eighteen operations, and the result is many more pins per day, "and a general plenty diffuses itself through all the different ranks of the society." Smith sensed the dangers and ambiguities, as well as the promise, of a life spent in the pin factory. Wedging humans into world-changing productivity had moral consequences. Every buyer and seller on Commercial Street receives full value, whether for a haircut, a pound of apples, or a necklace. But a factory worker receives a tiny fraction of the value she creates. In the absence of protective laws, she has no recourse for twelve-hour shifts and starvation wages.[9]

Even worse, Smith said, the work itself extracts life from the worker in the same proportion that it creates wealth for others. "The man whose whole life is spent in performing a few simple operations . . . has no occasion to exert his understanding or to exercise his invention . . . He naturally loses, therefore, the habit of such exertion, and generally becomes as stupid and ignorant as it is possible for a human creature to become. The torpor of his mind renders him not only incapable of relishing or bearing a part in any rational conversation, but of conceiving any generous, noble, or tender sentiment, and consequently of forming any just judgment concerning many even of the ordinary duties of private life." Smith grossly overstated his case by asserting that such workers lacked the capacity for generosity, tenderness, and courage. But even before ranks of operatives stood before clattering looms, breathing the sooty air of Manchester, he perceived the physical and moral cost of wealth—the contradiction between human degradation and economic progress. "In every improved and civilized society this is the state into which the labouring poor, that is, the great body of the people, must necessarily fall, unless government takes some pains to prevent it."[10]

All sorts of writers condemned the division of labor on view in any factory for creating more poverty than wealth. David Williams, a dissenting priest, argued that commercial societies imposed despotism different from that of the ancient empires, "in complicated and oppressive forms; by arbitrary inequalities, and by divisions of labor, which degrade the general mass of the community below the condition of brutes." David Urquhart, an outspoken Scottish diplomat and member of Parliament, once considered himself a disciple of Smith but grew to detest the factory system. "To subdivide a man," Urquhart wrote in *Familiar Words* (1855), "is to execute him, if he deserves the sentence, to assassinate him if he does not.–The subdivision of labour is the assassination of a people." Yet the fracturing seemed to be identical to modernity itself. The view of an American speaker came closer to the majority: "This division of labour is so essential to civilized man, that whenever we abandon it we must return to barbarism."[11]

Agriculture appeared to resist both divisions of labor. Farming favored people who could perform many tasks, not one. And because farmers could sustain themselves, they exchanged what they wanted, when they wanted, not because they needed to for survival. As Smith explained, husbandry did not work like other trades. "The nature of agriculture, indeed, does not admit of so many subdivisions of labour, nor of so complete a separation of one business from another, as manufactures. It is impossible to separate so entirely, the business of the grazier from that of the corn-farmer, as the trade of the carpenter is commonly separated from that of the smith. The spinner is almost always a distinct person from the weaver; but the ploughman, the harrower, the sower of the seed, and the reaper of the corn, are often the same." Smith admired farmers, but he also regarded them as inscrutable and problematic. With a new order in the offing, where workshops pointed the way to a kind of production in which everyone depended on everyone else, country people seemed to insist on making their own pins.[12]

Smith didn't leave it at that. A brilliant observer of the material world, he had an eye for dichotomy and the dual natures of things. He must have seen cattle chewing their cuds and excreting all day, leading to an insight. If a farmer pays a worker to plant and harvest, resulting in salable products, then does he not also "pay" a cow to perform the labor of filling its udders? The farmer presides over a division of labor after all, for "not only his labouring servants, but his labouring cattle, are productive labourers." By "productive" Smith meant something very specific. The cattle's labor could be alienated in the form of commodities that when sold brought the cow into relation with the rest of society as a producer. The implications go deeper, because by defining cattle as part of the division of labor, Smith implicitly defined everything that *sustained cattle* as monetized workers as well: grasses, soil microbes, worms, even the dew that settled lightly on the clover at dawn. Each performed specific tasks in the making of milk.[13] So while the farm might function as an undifferentiated unit in one sense, its various functions resulted in distinct commodities, making it look more like an ecological workshop. Every animal gave (or amounted to) the product of its labor.

The farmstead combined elements of divided and undivided labor, and from where Smith stood it must have looked perplexing. Plowman and harrower were sometimes the same person, sometimes not. He entirely missed the sexual division, in which women and girls turned wool into textiles or preserved foods, while men and boys cut hay and stacked it in barns. Yet the labor of a peasant household served a collective purpose. Smith did not acknowledge collective economic forms—like households, kin groups, guilds, trade unions, benefit societies, and the communal experiments of radical ministers and priests. Instead, he built his argument on the individual as the basic unit of analysis. So instead of parsing the interior world of the peasant family, with its own logic and pooled resources, he subsumed it into a single identity—the farmer.[14]

Smith's description of agriculture leaves all kinds of questions unanswered. A farm that turns out wheat, fruit, vegetables, milk, hay, and eggs can sustain a family, but one that grows wheat alone is like a pin factory. Which farm does Smith describe? England had experienced two centuries of enclosure by the time he wrote. With the help of Parliament, lords were extinguishing peasant rights and taking the common lands for themselves. Why didn't Smith mention this? Did he consider it so obvious to the progress of civil society that he assumed it? No one knows.[15]

Political economists far more blunt than Smith took up these questions. No writer argued with the same dark brilliance of James Steuart. In 1767, nine years before the publication of *The Wealth of Nations*, Steuart completed his *Inquiry into the Principles of Political Economy*, the first comprehensive work of its kind. With an iciness that makes his thought incomparably fascinating, Steuart asserted that the new order did not need the farmer, only the farm. Agriculture forms the basis of wealth and population, he said, "the most essential requisite for the prosperity of a state," but it can't be independent. "That would be inverting the order of things, and turning the master into the servant."[16]

Steuart thought that country people who managed to exist without turning all their labor into money inverted the order of things. He really hated vinedressers, or a certain hypothetical vinedresser. A vinedresser earned some money by pruning grapevines and tilled his own "spot of ground for subsistence." Steuart said that the time the vinedresser spent planting his garden produced no commodity for anyone else. But whenever he worked for wages, he proved himself useful. Steuart even believed that only when the vinedresser got paid did he become a member of society, only then did he exist. "Consequently, were it not for his trade, the state would lose nothing, though the vine-dresser and his land were both swallowed up by an earthquake." Steuart didn't hesitate to draw out this point. "If we can suppose any person entirely taken up in feeding himself, depending upon no one, and having nobody depending on him, we lose the idea of society." Our notion of progress, of history, and of people who do not work within the global economy owes much to Steuart. This idea comes back again when we get to Appalachia. When Alexander Hamilton tried to tax the distillers of western Pennsylvania, provoking the Whiskey Rebellion, he had the same idea in mind.

Steuart didn't believe in evolution toward a final stage, driven by self-interest or some mystical historical force. He saw a scaffolding of power, not just human propensities, beneath the social order. He favored the calculated ejectment of parliamentary enclosure in order to create workers out of peasants, even if that meant that people starved. Remove the vinedresser from his meager spot of ground and he does great things. He converts his worthless puttering into money. Steuart praised manufacturing for the same reason. It promised to "purge the lands of superfluous mouths," and those "purged off, must begin to gain their whole subsistence at the expense of those who employ them." By living on money, they finally belonged to society.[17]

Steuart was not alone in this view. Hunger had its defenders. "When hunger is either felt or feared," wrote Joseph Townsend, "the desire of obtaining bread will quietly dispose the mind to undergo the greatest hardships, and will sweeten the severest labours . . . In the progress of society, it will be found, that some must want." Only by this threat did beast-like peasants put in a day's work, said Townsend. Patrick Colquhoun blessed poverty as an engine of affluence. Without it, "nations and communities could not exist in a state of civilization. It is the lot of man. *It is the source of wealth*." Peasants who became wage earners maintained the logic of household survival. Cheap grain allowed them to stretch wages for weeks. They often quit work until their shillings ran out. William Temple recommended keeping them hungry. "The only way to make them tempered and industrious is to lay them under the necessity of labouring all the time they can spare from meals and sleep, in order to procure the necessaries of life."

The moralizing writer Hannah More praised poverty itself as a great motivator and moral instructor. She condemned Thomas Paine's *Rights of Man* (1791 and 1792), especially Paine's thundering demand that government come to the aid of the poor. More wrote fables about the contentedness of the indigent. In one story, a gentleman named Johnson encounters a shepherd and asks if he is hungry. "'Sir,' said the shepherd, 'poverty is a great sharpener of the wits.'" The shepherd goes on to explain that he sends his children to collect the wool torn from browsing sheep clinging to bushes and brambles. They loom these bits into their own socks. "Mr. Johnson lifted up his eyes in silent astonishment, at the shifts which honest poverty can make." In More's view, keeping the poor intent on their survival kept them from sin. It made no sense for the rich to relieve this blessed condition. These are some of the ways that political economists construed hunger as improvement and poverty as progress.[18]

Subsequent theorists attacked peasants and smallholders in the same voice, calling them redundant, lazy, wasteful, isolated, outside the boundaries of civil society, beneath the market, and bystanders to history. Friedrich List argued that hunters and herders made no dent in the earth, employing not a "hundredth part" of their natural advantages. Problem was, said List, certain farmers produced little more. "In the case of a people in a primitive agricultural condition, a large portion of the existing natural resources lies yet unutilized, and man still continues limited to his nearest surroundings."

As List saw it, as long as indolent farmers had rights over the countryside, waterpower languished, minerals remained buried, trees stood in the forest, and rivers flooded the lowlands rather than providing navigation and trade. Indolent peasants held the state and its progress hostage. Anne-Robert-Jacques Turgot warned that husbandmen could live without other kinds of workers, "but no other workmen can labour, if the husbandman does not provide him wherewith to exist."[19]

Karl Marx liked peasants no better. He saw them as set apart from all the action and tumult of the century, the flow of historical change going on around them. "Each individual peasant family is almost self-sufficient, directly produces most of its consumer needs, and thus acquires its means of life more through an exchange with nature than in intercourse with society." This is what baffled him about the apparent indifference of French country people to the coup led by Louis-Napoléon Bonaparte in 1851. It is why he called them politically inert and socially disconnected, "much as potatoes in a sack form a sack of potatoes." And it explains his mistranslated phrase, "the idiocy of rural life," in the *Communist Manifesto*. One scholar finds that the German word is closer to the Greek for *idiom* or *idiosyncratic*. It refers to one withdrawn or isolated. As Marx saw it, when it came to the great political events of the times, peasants had no skin in the game. "Small property in land creates a class of barbarians standing halfway outside of society." Marx denounced enclosure, revealing the starvation and poverty that resulted from it as essential to the beginnings of capitalism. But he also saw it from within his own overdetermined narrative. Only by losing their wherewithal would peasants ever become revolutionary proletarians who would seize the means of production. In this way, Marx didn't differ from other political economists. His story merely culminated in a different final stage.[20]

Marx showed that under capitalism, only labor that takes the form of commodities possesses social value. So any people who labor for themselves are outliers yet to be absorbed into capitalism. Just as the Scottish philosophers believed that any savage could travel the distance from backwardness to productivity, development agencies hold the same view. As the World Bank put it in the 1970s, "Development is concerned with the modernization and monetization of rural society and with its transition from traditional isolation to integration with the national economy." But "traditional isolation" was the invention of the modernizers. They invented isolation as a malady and offered fully monetized commodity production as the cure.

The modernizers spoke a utopian language. Capitalism portrays itself rationally and scientifically, but it is no less utopian than communism in the sense that both permit the suffering they cause in obedience to an ideal. Whereas Soviet communism exposed people to the unbridled power of the state, American capitalism exposes people to the unbridled market. For our purposes, capitalism demands that every form of production result in capital. That has meant the relentless modernization of food and farming. The peasant garden, the village field, the diversified landscape of products and employments, must everywhere become fully monetized, integrated, engineered, and subordinated.[21]

Political economists had different names for the final stage. By about 1850 they called it capitalism. It did not emerge from an evolutionary process. We cannot find the New York Stock Exchange inchoate the first time our Natufian ancestors corralled a pair of sheep. Capitalism came into being like anything else, from the way people in a certain place at a certain time responded to events. The way back to Appalachia leads through the history of capitalism in Great Britain. The reason is that English lords established the idea and legal procedure of enclosure. We can understand much about what happened in the southern mountains by looking at this first instance. Americans might not think that capitalism on these shores required the seizure of land, but it did.

THE HISTORY OF the most extraordinary social system ever invented is like an ever-forming algorithmic fractal landscape. Comprehending it requires us to see the grand patterns that emerge from its repeating yet chaotic capillary structures. One reason for a brief history of capitalism is to make the point that it *has a history*. It cannot be understood as the outcome of evolutionary stages. It did not dwell for millions of years in the human brain like a dormant virus. It is no better a reflection of human nature than any other social construction. Just a few hundred years ago, it didn't exist. The people of that not-so-distant past were not *precapitalists*, nor did they live in *precapitalist* societies, no matter how deeply engaged they might have been in trade or commodity production. These terms presuppose the thing to be explained. There is another reason for going through the turns and events of early capitalism. It reveals that trade, exchange, money, and markets do not account for it. It came from a new set of relationships having to do with the control of land and labor.

All of this has to do with the transformation of nineteenth-century Appalachia, because while conditions there differed in all sorts of ways from seventeenth-century England, capitalism arrived in the southern mountains with many of the same assumptions and replicated many of the same patterns. We can't really appreciate the similarities or see Appalachia as fully part of an Atlantic and global expansion of capitalism without a brief history of capitalism itself. The theory of stages functioned as its software. Its hardware consisted of woods and fens and villages—the ecological space and human labor that capitalists combined into a new system. But history is not a series of simple causes and effects. Things that seem to come from out of nowhere can change everything in an instant.[22]

For thousands of years before very recent times, people were rich if they could command large quantities of food. *Piers Plowman* is a fourteenth-century poem about a peasant by that name. Piers daydreams about "beans and baked apples . . . by the lapful," cream and curds, the best brown ale, white bread, and fresh baked meat. The aristocracy and the clergy demonstrated their power any number of ways, but one of the most remarkable was the giving of feasts. They reinforced the obligations that kept them powerful by feeding plowmen like Piers. The archbishop of York celebrated his appointment in 1467 by banqueting perhaps two thousand lords, barons, ladies, bishops, their servants, and other commoners. They ate in shifts, and the menu included thousands of animals—oxen, calves, sheep, deer, pigs, peacocks, pigeons, partridges, and other birds.[23]

Lords and peasants might have gone on like this for another thousand years. Money would have become more abundant as a means of exchange. Traveling fairs offered opportunities to buy things from far away and sell local crafts for gold and silver. Some merchants became rich from international trade, but they had great trouble finding ways to invest their money at interest. It's not obvious how the feudal system could have morphed into something else. It did change, but not from within itself. Instead, change arrived on an October day in 1347, and no one welcomed it.

Twelve galleys heavy with trade from Jaffa sailed into the port of Messina. The Genoese crew groaned in the hold, suffering in sickness. At least one staggered onto the wharf. The first Sicilian he greeted received a bacterial infection from a sneeze, a cough, or maybe a fleabite. Three days later, the sailor was dead, along with every Sicilian who had stood close enough to smell his breath. The afflicted buckled with fever and hard, bleeding ulcers—the first European victims of the Black Death. Over the next four years, as many as 50 million people perished from the plague—representing between 30 and 50 percent of all the inhabitants of Italy, Hungary, Lithuania, Germany, France, Spain, Ireland, Scotland, England, Norway, Sweden, Syria, and Palestine, as well as parts of Egypt, the Ottoman Empire, and Azerbaijan. So many Italians died so quickly that rotting corpses lay for days and weeks until neighbors noticed the smell. Entire families needed to be dragged to doorsteps so that undertakers could carry them away. "No tears or candles or mourners" ushered off the dead, wrote Giovanni Boccaccio; "in fact, no more respect was accorded to dead people than would nowadays be shown toward dead goats." Bodies were dumped in shallow trenches, "stowed tier upon tier like ships' cargo."

The dead left entire towns empty, fields unharvested. The social order came apart. People became scarce. One region in southern France did not regain its pre-plague population until the nineteenth century. Marginal places like mountainsides and wetlands, some settled as early as the eleventh century, lost their human presence altogether. Ruined drainage canals on the coast of Lion hummed with malarial mosquitoes. Wild game, including bears, boars, wolves, and partridges, returned to the upland plateau that borders the Rhône Valley. Sheep filled some of the ecological niches left vacant by the deceased.[24]

Political turmoil, as well as disease, contributed to the crisis of the old order. English peasants rebelled against another source of misery. In June 1381, Richard II, then fourteen years old, decreed a flat tax that charged the poor the same rate as the rich. Wat Tyler refused to pay it and raised an army of fifty thousand to take London. After crossing London Bridge, they confronted and executed the archbishop of Canterbury and the lord treasurer. The boy-king sent a message to the peasant-rebel. He wanted to talk. Tyler rode into the meeting alone and unarmed. No one knows what he said to Richard, but he might have drawn a dagger. The lord mayor of London ran his sword through Tyler, who bled to death in the street. Richard addressed the insurgents soon after, allegedly yelling, "You shall have no captain but me!" Yet he had also written a series of letters that promised reform and asked the peasants to meet his agents in Kent to work out the details. When eight rebel leaders showed up, royal officers tore up the letters. Then they executed the rebels.[25]

Richard put down the Peasants' Revolt, but he couldn't prevent the collapse of the medieval labor system. The tens of millions dead changed the balance between a few lords and many bondsmen into something more like a smallholder's Arcadia. There were abundant vacant acres and too few people to cultivate them. Those who survived the demographic implosion challenged the terms of work. Peasants walked away from ruined manors and coerced higher wages and fresh meat from desperate nobles. Food flourished. Married couples could be sure of their own farm with minimal obligations. One lord grumbled about country people, "A short time ago one performed more service than three do now." Yet this only meant that peasants had gained a modicum of leverage over their material lives. But if Richard's victory says anything, it is that although feudalism did not survive the Great Mortality, the landed aristocracy did.[26]

Capitalism emerged out of this enormous crisis. The Black Death should be seen as related to if not identical with the Little Ice Age, the period between 1350 and 1850 when falling temperatures upset long-standing patterns. Outbreaks of plague did not cease after its first visitation. It struck throughout the cold and rainy sixteenth century. In 1575, it killed sixteen thousand people in Milan and one-third of Venice. By then, the disease hit populations weakened by successive harvest failures. A merchant class and some farmers benefited from higher grain prices, but living conditions deteriorated for everyone. In Languedoc, France, people enjoyed relative prosperity (1460–1504), then periodic harvest failure (1504–1526), followed by a decade of famine (1526–1536). Spring rains spoiled the crop of 1527, when bishops commandeered wheat off the highway on its way to the pope. No social system can survive centuries of epidemic, climate volatility, and starvation.[27]

This is how feudalism died, but in order for capitalism to have been born, a degree of stability needed to return. Science might well have arisen from out of the disorder as a way of finding rational explanations for the triumph of death and chaos over every existing institution. By the end of the seventeenth century, Isaac Newton and John Locke had demoted God, revealing that people could calculate the motion of planets with their own minds and organize themselves politically without divinely ordained monarchs. Inventors and improvers drained bogs, rotated crops, and devised new animal breeds. The last famine in England ended in 1624. The last instance of epidemic plague ended in 1666. Better prospects for survival were cause and consequence of intensified exchanges and more circulating money. An infusion of food and other resources from the American colonies changed the horizon, suggesting the possibility of return on investment. The gentry had their own plans. They decided that profit in money would replace the tribute and mutual obligations between vassal and bondsman. Even as the dreary cold lingered over Britain, lords moved to restore the control over laborers they had lost in the demographic disaster and take advantage of commercial opportunities. But doing all or any of these things demanded that they redefine the foundation of the entire social order: land.[28]

Before the sixteenth century, no one in England owned land, not even Richard II. It existed within a bewildering index of tenures and estates, defining who could use it, what could be done with it, and for how long. It did not slide from hand to hand in the alienable form that we know. It was wrapped and bundled in customary rights that cascaded downward from king to knight to peasant. They all lived off a complex commons. A commons is any set of resources that is used or controlled by a village, town, nation, or some other group. It is a managed environment, with households or individuals possessing specific rights to plow, hunt, or gather. A commons is not free for all but exists under certain rules.[29]

English peasants and lords each had different kinds of rights to the commons, called tenures. Some of these arrangements (like *copyhold*) gave peasants something very close to private property. In others (*at will*), a lord exercised absolute power over how *villeins* and *serfs* farmed. Most peasants lived as smallholding tenants who paid a fee in food, labor, or money to the manor. But the real point is that lords and peasants adhered to the customs of the commons. Village associations—not lords themselves—often determined what could be planted and where, even to such minutia as what portion of a certain field would be pasture rather than tillage. These governing bodies made the landscape a collective undertaking. They also made doing anything new with it nearly impossible.[30]

This is what began to change in the sixteenth century. By then, the British lordly class had lost its military purpose. English knights no longer jousted in armor or bashed their enemies over the head. They also no longer extracted tribute by threatening peasants with violence (though extreme brutality and imprisonment awaited anyone who refused). Instead, peers of the realm lent the use of violence to an increasingly centralized state. The one thing still under lordly control was land. But the demographic shift and their vanished power of coercion left them with only *economic* means of extracting value. They did not want that value paid to them in quantities of food or days of labor but in money. In attempting to solve these problems and maintain their wealth and power, they created a new social system. Making money by extracting value from land required new techniques, new commodities, and new relationships.[31]

Enclosure began with wool. Throughout the middle of England, for example, including the counties of Gloucestershire, Northamptonshire, Nottinghamshire, and Oxfordshire, food for a rebounding population ran up against the extent of land. Tension emerged between how much area would be allotted to crops like oats and wheat and how much for raising sheep. Peasant and lord alike favored sheep. Wool emerged as the most significant export commodity of late medieval England, a trend that intensified in the following centuries. Along with meat, leather, and tallow, wool required lighter labor and sold for higher prices than grain. But the lords saw a greater potential. They looked past the domestic market to a North Atlantic trade. They knew of experiments in converting fields from grasses like timothy to fodder crops like turnips. This sophisticated husbandry increased the numbers of small livestock that could be sustained in a given space. But no improving lord or tenant farmer could do any of these things as long as common-use rights reigned over the English countryside.[32]

Enclosure was just what it sounds like. Lords secured the places where peasants had planted, herded, mowed, gathered wood, and hunted, and then literally surrounded them with hawthorn hedges or stone walls. They made claims in local courts and eventually in Parliament in order to create a new and shocking category of land use: private property. It was new because it had never existed before in England or anywhere else. It was shocking because never before had individuals possessed an exclusive right over land. The process of transferring the English countryside into real estate took centuries and reflected regional differences, like the power of lordship and traditions of use. It sometimes proceeded by public agreement (though probably accompanied by private threat). Enclosure's appearance in any given place often depended on whether arable crops grew in proximity to markets or whether pasturing predominated.[33]

But wherever the nobility enclosed common fields and pasture, they transformed much more than legal rights and definitions. They turned subdivided strip fields into consolidated sheep walks. They built farmhouses and elaborate mansions where none had been before. Old tracks and paths vanished. They amalgamated the peasant world from a mosaic of assorted shapes into much larger pieces made of corners and straight lines. Said the Board of Agriculture, "The first great benefit resulting from an enclosure is contiguity." The more square, the better.[34]

The English common lands also consisted of fens, marshes, and other marginal environments known as *wastes*. Lords created real estate when they ordered these wetlands drained, though nearby villages had engaged in peat and hay gathering for centuries. If the enclosing gentry had only seized active fields, they might have left peasant livelihood intact. But the agrarian economy depended less on fields than one might think. It was not where peasants planted grains but where they gathered mushrooms, which mattered more to them. One-third of the peasantry (in one sample) farmed fewer than five acres. Another third lived on more than five but fewer than nineteen. Households with only a little ground in garden or tillage survived by externalizing the greater portion of their needs to the wider landscape. They found the core of the makeshift economy in such places—fuel and lumber, grasses for animal, roots, mushrooms, nuts, fish, berries, game for hunting, and medicinal herbs. Livestock fattened in marshes and woods cost nothing yet produced milk and meat and other marketable commodities. We will return to this idea.[35]

More typically, enclosure narrowed the uses of land. An act of 1773 helps to clarify the logic. It condemned the use of two common fields in Oxford totaling five thousand acres. Lawyers for Philip Wenman, 7th Viscount Wenman of Tuam, insisted that the fields combined too many functions in too many divisions, "intermixed, and dispersed in small parcels," and "inconveniently situate[d]." Viscount Wenman didn't see a complex assortment of products and cycles at work in the fields. He saw a stagnant, incoherent mess, "incapable of improvement" without his control. The lawyers summed up their brief: "So long as the same lie open and unenclosed, will produce but little Profit." This is how agricultural improvement served the justification for enclosure.[36]

Midland peasants revolted against this logic. According to one historian, "One hundred and twenty-five enclosure riots occurred during the reign of James I and Charles I alone. It seems that the pattern of social protest was keeping apace with the pattern of social change during the transition towards . . . capitalism." In 1607, at least one thousand rioters in Northamptonshire tore up hedges and filled in ditches that demarcated land claimed by Sir Thomas Tresham. The peasants made a statement: "Wee, as members of the whole, doe feele the smarte of these incroaching Tirants, which would grind our flesh upon the whetstone of poverty, and make our loyall hearts to faint with breathing, so that they may dwell by themselves in the midst of theyr heards of fatt wethers." James I didn't flinch from the whetstone. His forces killed forty or fifty insurgents and hanged the peasant general John Reynolds.

The threat of violence had not subsided by 1649 when Gerrard Winstanley placed his name atop a list of forty-five of "the poor oppressed people of *England*, and the whole world." They demanded the return of the common lands to those who "labor the Earth to cast in seed," and castigated with Biblical invective lords who held "the Treasury of the Earth, locked up in your Bags, Chests, and Barns."

> The main thing we aym at, and for which we declare our
> Resolutions to go forth, and act, is this, To lay hold upon, and
> as we stand in need, to cut and fell, and make the best advantage
> we can of the Woods and Trees, that grow upon the Commons, To
> be a stock for our selves, and our poor Brethren, through the land
> of *England*, to plant the Commons withal; and to provide us bread
> to eat, till the Fruit of our labors in the Earth bring forth increase;
> and we shall meddle with none of your Proprieties (but what is
> called Commonage) till the Spirit in you, make you cast up your
> Lands and Goods, which were got, and still is kept in your hands
> by murder, and theft.

Winstanley demanded sufficiency ("To be a stock for our selves"), commodities for exchange ("and make the best advantage we can"), and a dignified existence without becoming intertwined with the owners of properties. Rebels against enclosure spoke for a feudal order that cannot be understood as dysfunctional or backward. Maybe one reason we assume it to have been is that our received story justifies the demise of older social forms, especially if they provided a realm of peasant autonomy averse to the wants of lords and tenants, the inventors of what came next.

And yet, sometimes peasants gained rights within the tumult. They remained in villages and evaded enclosure. One lord was so strapped for money that he sold the manor lands of Winston Magna to its inhabitants in 1606. The common fields survived. The village became free of any lord. Winston Magna is just one case, but it indicates something important. Historical events never have simple or obvious implications. Some people thrived by using the very instruments intended to dispossess them.

Still, by 1850, the grasping lords had enclosed all of the South Midlands (2.8 million acres), along with 75 to 80 percent of all the farmland in England. Enclosure annihilated the peasant economy. It removed the capacity of tens of thousands of people to meet their own needs. In this way, it satisfied those who argued, along with James Steuart, that labor and land were wasted that did not contribute to the accumulation of capital. English peasants sometimes ended up with land after enclosure, as tenants or cottars, but without the wastes they became dependent on money, a representation of value over which they had no control. Take note of this. A century or so later, nearly the same thing happened in the southern mountains of eastern North America.[37]

Enclosure solved a problem much grander than increasing pasturage for sheep. It transformed people who had always decided when or whether to sell the things they made into wageworkers whose every motion created a commodity for their employers to sell. "As long as people can lay their hands on the means of production," explains the anthropologist Eric Wolf, "there is no compelling reason for them to sell their capacity to work to someone else. For labor power to be offered for sale, the tie between producers and the means of production has to be severed for good." Enclosure severed labor from land and made both available for other uses. Smallholders who once owned the entire value of their labor, wrote one observer in 1812, "will be converted into a body of men who earn their subsistence by working for others, and who will be under a necessity of going to market for all they want . . . There will, perhaps, be more labour, because there will be more compulsion to it." Marx compared enclosure to a scissors. "The first blade served to undermine the ability of people to provide for themselves. The other blade was a system of stern measures required to keep people from finding alternative survival strategies outside the system of wage labor." For all their differences, Marx and Steuart would have agreed that capitalism is not well described as the *freedom* to sell one's labor.[38]

Dependency always travels with its shadow, a depth of poverty unknown before the sixteenth century. The word *pauper* first appeared in 1516, meaning someone with no home but the poorhouse and no means of livelihood. In the 1770s, a Welsh minister wrote of the shattering dislocation going on before him. "The depriving the peasantry of all landed property has beggared multitudes." He had seen "an amazing number of people . . . reduced from a comfortable state of partial independence to the precarious condition of hirelings, who, when out of work, must immediately come to their parish." A dispossessed army of labor could be hired at prices "below its proper level," resulting in a destitution he had never seen, the starving "crowded together in decayed farm-houses, with hardly ground enough about them for a cabbage garden." Cast out of work, they ran out of food. The minister continued, "This new mode of life has been the fruitful source of numerous evils . . . it has spread the vices of the capital over the whole kingdom."[39]

Writers expressed the brutality of enclosure in poetry and prose. Oliver Goldsmith witnessed a village being torn down during the 1760s in order to construct a garden, probably at Nuneham Courtenay in Oxfordshire. Lords delighted in paintings of Arcadian landscapes. They liked actual landscapes even better and sometimes transformed their estates into symbolic renderings of rural life, with anything unsightly excised from the frame. If the drawing room faced the village, then the village had to go. Goldsmith recoiled at this destruction in *The Deserted Village* (1770), a description of enclosure as a new kind of plague, in which "wealth accumulates, and men decay."

> . . . *a bold peasantry, their country's pride,*
> *When once destroyed, can never be supplied.*
> *A time there was, ere England's griefs began,*
> *When every rood of ground maintained its man;*
> *For him light labour spread her wholesome store,*
> *Just gave what life required, but gave no more . . .*

Seventy years later, Friedrich Engels described paupers adrift on the turnpikes with their emaciated, rickets-enfeebled children, begging at the kitchen doors of country estates, sleeping in churches before being driven into London workhouses for the barest relief, turned out faint and feverish with typhus, then dying on the streets, their bodies "dumped into the earth like infected cattle" atop a pile of rotting corpses fourteen feet deep. Supporters of the new system fastened it to the motions of the stars and asserted that any tampering with market mechanics would result in disaster, yet they ended up in a paradox. They justified human suffering as indispensable to the attainment of human progress.[40]

The new system was supposed to create more wealth and more food. Why then did paupers proliferate when the abundance made possible by enclosure should have put an end to all want? Food did pour out of improved farmland. Between 1600 and 1800, the combined average of all cereal crops (wheat, rye, barley, and oats) in Norfolk increased from twelve to twenty-two bushels per acre, or by almost 100 percent. Between 1801 and 1871, yields for the same crops throughout England rose by 47 percent. Diets diversified, especially for the well-off. Bread and oats gave way to potatoes and green vegetables. But many still starved. Between 1700 and perhaps as late as 1900, writes Robert Fogel, "even prime-aged males had only a meager amount of energy available for work." The English laboring class of 1750 didn't merely fall short of the daily dietary minimum—they missed it by one thousand calories.

The cause of hunger was not technological but social. The working poor could not afford to eat regularly. The average yearly income for a laborer in 1750 (in one region of England) ranged from eight to twelve pounds, but the cost of living for a family of five came to more than fourteen pounds. According to the historian Keith Wrightson, "only a minority of skilled workers could have maintained their families adequately on their own earnings." This is why England needed poor laws even at the peak of its economic and commercial power. Capitalism did produce more of everything but at the cost of overturning a social order that, while based in a rigid hierarchy, also protected people from hunger and homelessness. "Few people living in this world bequeathed to us by the enclosing and improving farmer," writes the historian Joan Thirsk, "are capable of gauging the full significance of a way of life that is now lost." Even Arthur Young had second thoughts, though no one advocated so strenuously for enclosure or did more to boost the productivity of lordly estates. "I had rather that all the commons of England were sunk in the sea, than that the poor should in future be treated on enclosing as they have been hitherto."[41]

No other place replicated conditions in England, its peasantry, aristocracy, or Parliament. But to insist on England's uniqueness would be to misunderstand its importance. Enclosure has never stopped. The same lordly families who seized the common lands invested in plantations on the island of Jamaica and in the Tidewater counties of Virginia. What else were the wars against the Cherokee and the Sioux but acts of accumulation by dispossession? Enclosure continues today in Africa, where corporations lease land from financially fragile governments to produce sugar and rice. The enclosure of West Virginia happened differently. Legally speaking, the commons there was not really common. Much of it already belonged to capitalists. But the people who took from that land for a century regarded it as theirs. It *functioned* as common property.

I will say more about all this in a later chapter. For now, there is one other similarity between seventeenth-century England and every other example of enclosure. The entities that confront each other in these conflicts are incongruous. Capital is a creature of state power, but peasants can get along fine without either. The political scientist Göran Hydén, who studies development in Africa, puts the problem neatly: "History has demonstrated that the development of modern society is inconceivable without the subordination of the peasantry." Though the scale and complexity of this epochal conflict might not always seem apparent to those who live in the United States and Europe today, it lies behind much of the history of western societies during the last four centuries.[42]

⁂

ENCLOSURE ALONE DOES NOT EXPLAIN how capitalism works. For that we need to go back to the gentry and the novel situation they entered when the commons became private property. Lords no longer ruled over resident peasants who provided for them. They now owned real estate, land valued in money and legally alienable, meaning that it could be sold and the money invested in some other venture. All this meant that lordly estates needed to continually justify the value they represented by showing a profit. When land became a commodity, all the things it produced became commodities. But gouty, puffy, land-rich lords were not farmers. They would not be the ones who turned over the earth in order to make it pay.[43]

Enter the tenants. Tenancy had existed for hundreds of years by the sixteenth century. Even under capitalism, tenants and lords followed long-standing customs that controlled things like subletting, cutting timber, and opening probate when a tenant died. Left over from the old feudal tenures and obligations, these customs placed a greater emphasis on community survival and mutual obligation than on profit. As early as the sixteenth century, however, aristocratic proprietors began to favor more flexible arrangements, in order, as Wrightson puts it, "to carve for themselves a bigger share of the income to be derived from the land." A series of pressures and squeezes set off a chain reaction. Population increased during the recovery from the Black Death. Competition among tenants drove higher rents, which placed pressure on tenants to amplify their yields.

What happened next was a kind of Big Bang. After tenants paid rent, any money left over belonged to them. If they used their earned coin to purchase improved tools or rent additional fields, they harvested more, exchanged more, and increased their net profit, allowing them to invest more, and so on. Tenants who deployed their gains to make greater gains entered a circuit. Rather than grow food and exchange some of it for money so they could go on sustaining their households, they began with money in order to turn it into more money. They entered the circuit of *capital*.[44]

Capital is money in motion. It's not a bag of seed or a college education or an idea for a new business or your terrific potential as an artist or the car you drive to work. It's not even the same thing as wealth. If capital is any of these things, then no one knows how long it has existed. If we count a spear or topsoil as capital, then capital has no historical specificity. *Capital is a social relationship connected to the modes of production essential to its continual creation.* It is surplus value in the act of generating surplus value—profit that creates profit. Marx expressed it as $M \rightarrow C(MP+LP) \rightarrow C' \rightarrow M+\Delta M$, in which money (M) is advanced to buy commodities (C). These commodities consist of the means of production (MP) (which includes things like land and factories but also raw material like wool) and labor-power (LP). My labor-power is my capacity to work, and it's the most important purchase, because it's the only factor that creates more value than it costs. Think of it like this: If a manufacturer pays me ten dollars for a day's work, he can turn my strength and stamina into a hundred dollars or a thousand dollars in sweaters or anything else. Production results in these second-order commodities (C'), the finished goods that go to sale for the original money advanced, plus an increment ($M+\Delta M$). Money does not become capital until or unless it is advanced, until it is set into motion to complete another circuit. To paraphrase Forrest Gump, *Capital is as capital does.*[45]

The word *capital* first appeared between the twelfth and thirteenth centuries for the top or head of something (from the Latin *caput*, or "head"), like the capital of a marble column. Between 1400 and 1600, it came to refer to the greatest height or degree of something, like capital crimes and capital cities. At the same time, the word developed the meaning of an important sum of money. Fernand Braudel found this sense in Italian as far back as 1211. Saint Bernardino of Siena wrote in the late fourteenth or early fifteenth century of "that prolific cause of wealth we commonly call capital." But sums of money had not yet become perpetuating funds.

Other English words carried similar meanings. *Cattle* and *chattel* came into English between the thirteenth and fourteenth centuries, not as words for barnyard creatures but for property, goods, and even money itself.[46] Horses, oxen, and bovines became *cattle* (around 1400) because they amounted to significant forms of property; the word did not become specific to bovines until the sixteenth century. *Stock*, another word for accumulated value, denoted something that sprouted and spawned endlessly, like a stem or tree trunk, until about 1380 when it shows up as a word for domesticated animals. It did not describe a growing herd of *livestock* until the sixteenth century. But around that time, *stock* took a turn. It began to take on meanings similar to *capital*. By 1526, it referred to money that could be invested; by 1714, it was in common use as the subscribed capital of a merchant house.

Capital pulled away from these other words. By the time Smith had published *The Wealth of Nations* in 1776, political economists in Britain and France had already given it the meaning it carries today. Smith used the term *capital stock*, suggesting money that reproduced a percentage of itself in a given time. According to Braudel, a Russian consul made the essential distinction, reporting that France under Napoleon Bonaparte fought "with her capital," while the countries that France invaded fought "with their income." For centuries, few institutional pathways existed for employing income in order to earn additional income. *Capital* appeared along with these pathways, as people needed a word to differentiate this new entity from merchant wealth and the dividends represented by lambs and calves.[47]

Braudel offers a useful way of thinking about what made capital different from other forms of value. He identified three parallel economies in fifteenth-century Europe. Most people produced household food and commodities and then exchanged them in towns. Other people lived in towns where they bought and sold in a freewheeling marketplace. These two groups describe a competitive commercial world. But a few merchants derived exceptional profit from trade and manufacturing and then reinvested it, sometimes through international channels. Braudel makes a distinction between a market society (represented by country and town) and the world of capital. Capitalist firms came from the very same messy, chaotic social division of labor—just as Walmart began as a family-owned discount store in rural Arkansas. But while capitalist firms *require* markets, they attempt to *create* monopolies. Their goal is to dominate competitors, something impossible for the nearly undifferentiated fruit sellers in the town square.

What makes someone a capitalist? If the owner of the shoe repair shop near Fordham University on Columbus Avenue in New York City reinvests some of his net profit in leather and new tools, does that make him one? If the owner of the nail salon a few doors down adds some of her income to a retirement account that includes corporate stock, is she just like Warren Buffett? Braudel said no. To argue otherwise blurs categories by equating modest proprietors who consume most of their surplus value in order to maintain themselves and their businesses with corporations that continually expand internationally, innovate technologically, invest in countless other industries, and have no stake in the places where they operate. Is this just a difference of scale? Maybe, but at some level a quantitative increase becomes qualitative. Walmart in 2017 (11,500 stores, $470 billion in sales) and in 1962 (one store, $100,000 in sales) operated in entirely different ways. The nineteenth-century mountain household described in the following pages sometimes paid wages for labor and sometimes used money to buy land. But merely because they needed to survive in a society increasingly organized around money did not make them capitalists.

Capitalism is now so replete in the social order that some see it as having come from the natural order. Since its first century, its advocates have misattributed the motives and aspirations that it instills to universal human propensities. When markets appear to set rents and wages, the effect is to displace the rule-making power of people and institutions to an indifferent and mechanistic universe. When people buy and sell commodities, they appear to be working for their own betterment even if they are really satisfying imperatives set by others. This is how capital shapes our very identities. Our occupations derive from it whether we generate it or not, command it or not, manage it or not. Capital requires every institution to function in its favor and our constant consent, even though it is indifferent to human needs. "The worst error of all," writes Braudel, "is to suppose that capitalism is simply an 'economic system,' whereas in fact it lives off the social order, standing almost on a footing with the state."[48]

"A new way of life spread over the planet," wrote the historian Karl Polanyi, "with a claim to universality unparalleled since the age when Christianity started out on its career." Capitalism makes powerful demands on people and environments. It needs constant inputs of geographical space and dependent labor and justifies this taking by asserting its own necessity and inevitability. But what about all the people who lived in its path but didn't want to become part of it? How did they organize themselves and why does it matter? The conflict we will explore in the southern mountains will not be clear without a sense of the internal logic of makeshift economies. Being an agrarian in England or West Virginia or Mali or anywhere else promised very little in comfort or security from any number of hardships. But it did promise one thing: autonomy from the tyranny of money.[49]

※

MOST OF THE PEOPLE who have ever lived grew their own food. We know them as *settlers*, *peasants*, *campesinos*, *smallholders*, or generally *agrarians*, all words for country people. They have included Natufians in the village of Jericho in 8500 B.C.; Roman peasants on the frontiers of Gaul in A.D. 1000; Scots-Irish ridgetop farmers in West Virginia throughout the nineteenth century; escaped African cassava cultivators in their Caribbean provision grounds circa 1750; Cherokee gardeners in the upland South before their forced removal in the 1830s; Indonesian rice planters and rubber tappers in 2000; and others in countless variations on almost every continent over the last ten thousand years. Some plowed broad-acre fields, but most preferred more intensive practices. "I am not talking here about amber waves of grain," wrote the anthropologist Robert McC. Netting of smallhold-ing, "but about gardens and orchards, about rice paddies, dairy farms, and *chinampas*." Others created forest openings by burning before planting. Some owned land, while others occupied frontiers in advance of private property. Still others squatted on the holdings of absentee owners. Where possible, they supplemented arable farming with foraging, hunting, and fishing. Taken together, agrarians compose the largest class in human history.[50]

Country people usually identify themselves as members of lineages or families or villages, but the most basic unit is the household. It consists of any family group who work together, share the same living space, and eat from the same pot. A household always includes parents and their children. It might also include grandparents. Older sons disappear and sometimes reappear. They might farm their own plots while they take care of elderly parents, then leave to seize opportunities for trade, and perhaps return for security before launching into marriage and their own households. The household is a collective of individuals in which "family solidarity provides the basic framework for mutual aid, control and socialization." It spreads the risk of its ventures, reproduces its skills and traditions, transmits its vast ecological knowledge, and catapults its young into adulthood.

No other human institution does these things. Netting captures the collective function and the protective one. "The household is the scene of economic allocation, arranging collectively for the food, clothing, and shelter of its members, and seeking to provide for these needs over the long term with some measure of security against the uncontrollable disruptions of the climate, the market economy, and the state." But the household is also the scene of domination and control. What happens under the roof is often a struggle for power between fathers and sons and a form of servi-tude for daughters and wives. In the vacuum of authority that prevailed on the western frontiers of North America, the household served as a state unto itself: sometimes a little commonwealth, sometimes a totalitarian regime. The historian Honor Sachs says more: "The very concept of a household constructs a mythology of human relationships that manifests inequality in ways that seem organic and natural . . . Only by understanding inequal-ity within the household can we see how the denial of rights for huge swaths of the population did not constitute a dark exception to democratic aspirations but rather a triumph of original design." The fulfillment of human needs came along with fears and despair.[51]

Finding a word or phrase to describe the flow of material and money through households is surprisingly difficult. *Self-sufficient* is altogether wrong. No household is, was, or could be self-sufficient, and none wanted to be. *Self-provisioning* narrows what is autonomous about agrarians to raising plants and animals for food, but it's a little awkward. *Competency* refers to an adequate supply of something or the land necessary to create that supply. When a young couple attained "a competency," it meant that they had established their household and could raise a family. I prefer *subsistence*.

We tend to define it as the minimum necessary for existence. Such a definition has no historical significance. Agrarians did not live at the margin of life and death. They met their own needs and attempted to live as well as possible, to thrive. Integral to thriving is partaking in a larger division of labor by exchanging. Yet exchange requires people to produce more than what they would require for bare survival. Economists like to call anything traded a *surplus*. It sounds like something left over. But agrarians did not make clear distinctions between what a household raised, gathered, and hunted for their own consumption and what they exchanged for other things. They considered it all equally essential. Human needs never adhere to a minimum. This is the problem with the commonplace conception of subsistence. It describes an imaginary condition, and thinking about it this way eliminates an entire realm of human economy. Another word for what I mean is *makeshift*, meaning to do the best that one can with whatever one has.[52]

It is strange that no precise word exists in English to describe something that billions of people consider obvious. The paucity of language seems like an artifact of capitalism and its tendency to eliminate all competing economic forms. In this way of thinking, the legitimacy of makeshift economy lies in the past. Conceiving of subsistence economy as vestigial and linking it to poverty limits the horizons of human endeavor. It says that those who still live this way await something better. It dismisses their knowledge as irrelevant and their tenacity as naive. "Smallholders may not always live well," Netting tells us, "but they are seasoned survivors. They may moonlight as craftsmen, petty traders, field hands, or factory workers, but they do not keep one foot on the farm out of sentiment or stupidity." None of this should be taken as an excuse for the poverty so many agrarians suffer, for disease, malnutrition, and lack of educational opportunity. But to what extent do we misunderstand the problem? Is it that a smallholder existence is identical to poverty? Has no one ever lived well in a village? Or is it that events have degraded their capacity to thrive? Smallholders depend on specific conditions, without which they become desperately poor. The question is whether development should strive to maintain those conditions. The alternative is to say that agrarians are not made for the world as it is, that the resources they use for subsistence and barter are too valuable. The forest will be turned into lumber; the river will be diverted for irrigating sugarcane. In that case, the demise of agrarian existence is self-fulfilling. I will take up some of these questions in the last chapter.[53]

The single most important thing to know about settlers, peasants, campesinos, and smallholders is that they do not conform to the particular rationality described by capitalist political economy. What they maximize and waste, how they regard money, and how they organize work come from different assumptions and circumstances. "The distinctive economic behavior of the subsistence-oriented peasant family," as James Scott puts it, "results from the fact that, unlike a capitalist enterprise, it is a unit of consumption as well as a unit of production." All such families use their production to enhance their consumption in a circuit, one different from the one that creates capital. This one begins and ends with commodities, not money. Agrarians create useful things, consume some of what they raise, and swap the rest for money or other useful things. They exchange in order to gain the tools and luxuries that they cannot make. Marx expressed the circuit this way, $C \rightarrow M \rightarrow C$, where the two Cs are commodities of various kinds and the M is money. Depicted in its most simple form (though it's never simple), the commodity circuit does not result in accumulation. Its purpose is to sustain and reproduce the household without end.[54]

The circuit begins with production. All agrarian households must manage the tension between available acres, working hands, and wanting bellies. Among the first economists to model peasant economy was a Russian named Alexander Vasilevich Chayanov. Writing during the 1920s, Chayanov found that the peasants he studied did not attempt to maximize profit or minimize labor. Peasants, said Chayanov, will "purchase the increase of the total year's labor product at the price of a fall in income per labor unit." They showed no concern for diminishing returns but kept working for as long as they needed in order to create a necessary stock of food and commodities no matter how long it took them. Exactly what it means to have "enough" is always debatable. But unlike capitalist firms, peasants have an acute sense of "enough" and only exert themselves to attain it. As the anthropologist Enrique Mayer explains it, "Because householding is self-provisioning, the cycle is complete when all that is needed is produced." The true product of the agrarian household is the survival and reproduction of the household itself.[55]

And yet, there is another sense in which peasants can attain great efficiency. They produce more energy (in calories) than the energy they expend. In Mexico, with no draft animals, corn yields nearly 11 units of energy for every 1 unit expended. In the Philippines, with animal labor, it yields 5 to 1. Compare this to the United States, where combines and nitrogen fertilizer recently produced yields of 3 to 1. Cassava production in Nigeria attains an output-to-input ratio of 7 to 1. Wheat in Kenya, using only human power, reaches 3 to 1. Draft animals reduce the ratio because they require food and human attention. Still, Filipino wet-rice planters who use animal traction realize a ratio of around 3 to 1, while mechanized rice production in the United States does no better than 1.5 to 1. Then there is *swidden*, a term for the way people have used fire to burn off vegetation before planting in the rich ashes. It can deliver rice at an amazing 25 to 1, allowing families to provision themselves by working just two hours a day.[56]

There is much more to consider here, like the nuanced relationship between the number of people and the intensity of cultivation. How do wanting bellies change the way working hands cultivate available acres? Historically, how agrarians have lived has varied from extensive hunting and gathering, with little or no farming, to remarkably intensive gardens and rice paddies and little use of the wider landscape. In the first case, households externalize much of their subsistence needs. The forest or savannah gives them lumber and cattle fodder. In the second, most ecological functions must be replicated within domesticated spaces. The open range becomes the hayfield. The difference is very often population. When common lands become crowded, cultivators feel pressured to redouble their labor on the land they have. This amounts to a kind of law that is the perfect inverse of the one first popularized by Thomas Robert Malthus at the end of the eighteenth century. Under the right circumstances, more people do not starve for too little food; they create the additional food they need. And yet, there are exceptions to the pattern. The people of the southern mountains had trouble making this transition. (I will return to this subject in chapter 4.)[57]

English-speaking travelers who visited peasant societies often admired them. Henry Colman, once the commissioner of the Agricultural Survey of Massachusetts, spent the 1840s going village to village throughout Europe. "A more civil, cleanly, industrious, frugal, sober, or better dressed people than the French peasantry . . . I have never known," wrote Colman. He saw two and a half acres in Flanders "give ample support for a man and wife and three children . . . add to it three acres more, which this amount of labour is more than sufficient to cultivate, and you add a considerable surplus for other purposes." John Candler, a British Quaker, toured the West Indies between 1839 and 1841. In Haiti he found a nation of proud smallholders cultivating land that once belonged to the very slaveholders who owned their parents and grandparents. He noted their "few wants . . . common faire, coarse clothing, and enjoyments of a mere animal nature: it is true, they work to live, as without some labour they cannot subsist; but they do not, and they will not[,] work hard to please anybody." Their dwellings were well kept, continued Candler, "their coffee is clean and vigorous, their gardens are flourishing, their fences neat—every thing indicating order, industry, and content[ment]." Agrarians suffered under adverse climate and political turmoil beyond their control, but they did not suffer *because they were agrarians*. Into the twentieth century, those who knew them best noted their resilience, industriousness, and productivity. But I have only suggested what is required for an agrarian household to produce. The next turn in the commodity circuit is exchange.[58]

Raising stuff leads to selling stuff. This might seem obvious. Only in capitalism do people live on money and nothing that they produce themselves, and even most wageworkers the world over grow at least a portion of their food. (This is the subject of chapter 6.) No one has ever willingly lived without exchange. "Market-less households do not exist," writes Mayer. "We therefore commonly say that the household's integration to the market is partial." How much to produce for exchange is a more vexing question. Chayanov concluded that although the Russian peasants he studied sold things for money, they didn't see money as essential. After a certain point, moneymaking became "an excessive burden on the undertaking." The anthropologist Marshall Sahlins elaborates: "If 'surplus' is defined as output above the producers' requirements, the household system is not organized for it. Nothing within the structure of production for use pushes it to transcend itself." An organization drawn together for survival cannot also operate as a profit-making business. Money *supplements* the household but does not *sustain* it. Agrarians go to market to acquire tools and clothing that they cannot make, but the limits of family labor translate into limits on what households have to sell and therefore what they can purchase.

And yet, it would be a mistake to emphasize the commercial limits of an agrarian economy. That thinking leads to one of the worst misconceptions, that such people are too isolated to exchange very much and have little interest in it. Yet political economists often failed to see the rich market engagement of smallholders. James Steuart asserted that those who practiced "a direct method of subsistence" sold nothing because they had nothing to sell. "The articles of food and necessaries are hardly found in commerce . . . because the principal occupation of every body is to procure them for himself." It's a perplexing statement because it contradicts human behavior for centuries in every environment and on every continent. Steuart might have been thinking of the Scottish Highlands, which he considered primitive compared to regions with more money and more complex divisions of labor. Regardless, peasants and smallholders always participate in the wider commercial world. Chayanov said the same, that peasants everywhere had "been drawn into the system of the capitalist commodity market," including "exceedingly complex social interactions with . . . the present-day economy."[59]

Mayer proposes an elegant structure that embraces the core of Chayanov's conception but moves beyond it. The Andean peasants he studies maintain two kinds of cultivated spaces, one for subsistence and the other for cash. They keep these "accounts" strictly separate. What they grow in order to eat never enters the market, and the money they earn by selling commodities enhances their standards of living but does not sustain their households. In other words, they can endure a complete loss on the cash crop with a shrug—nothing gained and just a little labor lost. Such a failure might prevent them from buying certain things but without posing an existential threat. Andean peasants recognize two "transactional realms," one in the village and the other beyond the mountains, one grounded in social relationships within the community and the other purely for profit and therefore impersonal. The village represents certainty and familiarity, where everyone is taken care of. The distant market offers the possibility of gain and the excitement of risk. Trading over the mountains or down the river carries none of the social strictures of kin and household.[60]

The crucial point is that agrarians use markets. They have sold rubber, whiskey, quinoa, coffee, and textiles without becoming dependent on money. If we are to understand settlers, peasants, campesinos, and smallholders, we have to reject the falsehoods that they lived in isolation and that a makeshift economy is a bubble that bursts whenever it comes into contact with the "outside world." We also have to abandon the related fiction that depicts exchange as a stage toward full capitalist social relations. *Peasant entrepreneur* is not a contradiction in terms. Exchange is integral to subsistence economies.

The anthropologist Michael Dove spent years living with Indonesian smallholders in West Kalimantan on the island of Borneo. They plant rice in burned-over mountain openings or swiddens. Spirits and rituals attend the rice and the regeneration of the forest, rendering the final product something more than food. They never sell it. They regard it as a sacred form of sustenance that is identical with the community itself. The same people also tap *Hevea* rubber trees in forest stands. They have no use for rubber. Instead, they sell it worldwide, a practice that began in the early twentieth century "as just one element in a portfolio of economic activities." Rubber tapping emerged from their long-standing custom of gathering and trading forest products. Rubber falls under entirely different rules than rice. No spirits get involved with it, and the profits do not need to be distributed. If a household moves from a longhouse, where a number of households live together, rice land remains with the longhouse to be used in common. But rubber gardens go with the household. The villagers recognize the moral dangers of money and try to control them in a variety of ways. Land where rubber grows they call "dead," in the sense that it does not generate the community.[61]

As long as rubber tapping doesn't compete with rice planting for land or labor, it does not impinge upon the villagers' subsistence, seasonal patterns, or rituals. Most amazing of all, Kalimantan villagers dominate national production. Eighty percent of the raw rubber sold abroad comes from smallholders. The other 20 percent comes from capitalist plantations. The villagers attain this stunning market share through efficiency and low costs, even though successive governments have favored and promoted the plantations. As Dove puts it, "There is a presumption that forest-dwelling smallholders live outside the market and must be assisted into it. This is a remarkable premise, given that the involvement of the region's smallholders in production of commodities for global markets is ancient." Not only does this strange presumption erase two thousand years of history, says Dove, it reverses the real problem smallholders have, "which is not how to get into the market, but how to stay—partly—out of it."

It is important to keep in mind that humans existed for 200,000 years without currency stamped in silver or issued by a bank. They exchanged things for money that they themselves created, money that provided a convenient conduit of value. But seashells and barley were mediums of exchange that could not be centralized or monopolized, at least not like Federal Reserve notes. Most of all, life did not depend on accumulating them. So, the question of a tipping point, a movement toward greater dependency after which money ceases to be an *option* and becomes a *compulsion*, did not exist before recent times. It has to do with financial institutions and international trade (which proliferated currencies), nation-states and colonial governments (which taxed), and loans against land (which created debt). Valuations in money reached peasant producers, who had to decide how to respond. On one hand, money opened possibilities for comfort and novelty that did not exist before. On the other, it brought into question whether they could exist without the exchanges they desired. One researcher argues that anyone who dedicates significant time to creating commodities really works for money. Even if smallholders keep their subsistence and commercial "accounts" separate, in some sense their work is already subsumed by their expectations for consumer goods. "The enigma of production for use," writes the anthropologist Stephen Gudeman, "is not whether a surplus is produced but why the surplus which is produced does not accumulate and transform the system."[62]

Leaving aside Gudeman's enigma, there are two primary ways that money can wreck agrarian systems. The first is debt and its state-sponsored version, taxation. Agrarians have turned themselves into commodity producers in a hurry whenever a creditor or colonial official has given them a choice between paying up in cash or rotting in prison. (I will have more to say about this in chapter 3.) The second is the destruction or enclosure of those common resources that enable production and consumption without money. Remove the ecological base and agrarians have no choice but to sell their labor in order to live. But a rising population can also grind down the viability of shared resources, multiplying users in a limited space. New farms cleared from a dwindling forest will be smaller though they have to support more people. The solution is and has always been for gardeners to exert more effort and innovate, to make two stalks of maize grow where one grew before. The mountaineers of West Virginia struggled to do this. When they felt the limits of the landscape, when their own increase and events out of their control narrowed the commons, they lost the capacity to create commodities. They faced the crisis of replacing the money that the forest no longer provided. Their quandary, to echo Dove, was not how to get into a circuit in which everything, including their labor, could be exchanged for money but how to keep themselves partly out of it.[63]

Here are a few summary points.

Agrarians depend on an ecological base, from which they derive subsistence and commodities. There is no fishing village without a fishery, no culture of hunting and grazing without a functioning forest. Too many people or poor management can erode an ecological base by extracting more from it than it can restore. But a functioning base is primary to agrarian existence. As long as people maintain access to environments unencumbered by private property or its enforcement, they can create commodities on their own terms. They can sell into markets without becoming dependent on markets for everything they need to live.

People who practice the economy of makeshift live within limits imposed by land and labor. Agrarian households have only so many hands, so much land, and so much time, imposing limits on what they can make, sell, and consume. They cannot exceed these limits without turning into full-time commodity producers.

Subsistence production includes the vigorous pursuit of money and exchange. These are not contradictory. Every smallholder lives within social divisions of labor that include neighbors, nearby villages, and distant cities. Money from exchanges becomes new tools and seeds, candy and kettles. A farmer who distills whiskey from his own rye, harvested by his family and neighbors, and uses the money to improve his fences or buy a new rifle is an entrepreneur. (Just for comparison, a planter who grows sugar with funds advanced by London merchants, using enslaved Africans purchased from Dutch traders, is a capitalist.) Exchange is the core of the commodity circuit, the cycle of production that describes most of the people who have ever lived.

It would simplify things if we could leave it at that. But we can't. At some undefined point, money can change in its role from an attribute of a household to its controlling purpose, from freedom to imperative. The question is whether or not a household can reproduce itself independent of its exchanges. The answer often hinges on the size and robustness of the ecological base. In other words, dependency often does not require outright dispossession. The means of production are a package of resources, a lattice of land uses. As we will see, the erosion of the base and the acceptance of wages often occurred at the same time. Mountaineers behaved just like other agrarians in the same situation: they sold their labor for money to make up for the commodities that they could no longer produce themselves.

The American peasantry composed a multifaceted, highly varied set of agrarian cultures. In the U.S. history we all learned, peasants came to these shores and soon embraced commercial farming or sought the cities for greater opportunity, leaving antiquated practices behind. But that view erases who and what they really were and what they wanted. It buries their political struggles as historically irrelevant. A political ethic emerged from the experience of the American peasantry, *agrarianism*, a position that enshrined subsistence production and vigorous exchange in a social identity: the *yeoman*. What follows is a brief attempt to portray agrarian peoples and ideas before we find our way back to the southern mountains.

⁓

"THERE ARE NO PEASANTS IN AMERICA," according to Alexis de Tocqueville. Most Americans would probably agree that the pioneers who rolled with Daniel Boone bowed in deference to no one. The historian Frederick Jackson Turner made the same distinction. English peasants arrived on the Atlantic coast, he said, but American farmers went forward, "becoming more and more American" with every westerly footstep. Social identities only exist in the context of actual relationships, actual environments, where they are continually created and reinforced. In this sense, Turner was right. Rather than a pecked-over island and a labyrinth of private property, refugees from enclosure found wild animals for hunting, spaces for grazing and planting, and trees of such astonishing size and number that North America must have looked to them like a new planet. Rather than the nobility seizing their land, they seized the land of others. Abundance, plus ownership, plus interaction and violence with Indians changed them. "He is become a freeholder, from perhaps a German boor," said J. Hector St. John de Crèvecoeur of the peasant in possession of a deed; "he is now an American."[64]

But *peasant* is a perfectly good word to describe a country person. Settlers, peasants, campesinos, and smallholders are all agrarians in differing political worlds, practicing the economy of makeshift, taking full advantage of their environments and opportunities for exchange. Even if Tocqueville meant that there were no *serfs* in America, he was still wrong. African-American slaves endured similar kinds of control and violence and raised their own food, like Spanish and English medieval serfs. Woodland Indians lived much like free peasants in northern Europe, by gardening and hunting. British North America before about 1790 was a great and vast peasantry, with some living free of any lord and others in chains. What follows is a brief tour of those rural societies, a discussion of what endangered and changed them during the eighteenth century, and a few words about the distinct politics that came out of that time.

The English-speaking peasantry of North America crossed the Atlantic for all sorts of reasons. The Puritans were Protestants who believed that the English Reformation had failed. They included separating and nonseparating factions of the Anglican Church. They fled rather than be prosecuted for speaking out. But their immigration had just as much to do with the bleakness, lack of opportunity, and hopeless deprivation that covered England in the seventeenth century. The minister Thomas Shepard abandoned the country for offering him no calling, "nor way of subsistence in peace and comfort to me and my family." Still, only a few took the risk. It required money to finance the journey and family members who could be extricated from obligations or servitude. Poverty was the push. The pull was the thing that wrapped religious fundamentalism in livelihood—land unencumbered by lineage or rent and in quantities of which Englishmen had only dreamt. The pull was so great that young men signed up for seven years under the whip of a Virginia planter expecting a competency if they survived.[65]

A young man who survived indenture might have become a yeoman. In England, a yeoman owned and operated a farm with no obligations to a lord. Unlike peasants, yeomen could vote in Parliament, a right that placed them just below the lowest gentry. Americans borrowed the English term for its sense of worthy work, free and clear ownership, and political participation. The term did not apply everywhere or to every farmer. A yeoman produced commodities for subsistence and exchange and embraced civic responsibilities, paid taxes to the county, and might have served in local government. Squatters did not qualify. The term escaped its strict meaning at some point. It figured in the American imagination as an aspiration and political identity because it combined liberty, autonomy, and dignity.

Tens of thousands of would-be yeoman families crossed the waters during the seventeenth century. They joined a global settler migration that transformed almost every continent. The cold and scarcity that followed the plague and the onset of the Little Ice Age drove Europeans outward. They went to Tibet and the Nile; Hudson anchored at Manhattan; and La Salle sailed the Mississippi. Colonization and trade outsourced soils, forests, and labor to more fecund regions. Between 1600 and 1800, Britain added 3 million "ghost acres" on other continents to the 17 million acres of arable it had at home.[66] World population increased from 400 million to at least 900 million during the same period, and most of those humans wanted land for planting and hunting. During the seventeenth century, the great powers opened their frontiers to avoid political turmoil. They funneled agrarian frustration into state formation. Ax-wielding invaders entered the Brazilian Atlantic Forest, the Volga River Valley, and Manchuria, where they brought hundreds of millions of acres into production. Nothing about pioneering is unique to British North America. The practices for taking control of territory and opening soil to the plow are as old as agrarian societies themselves.[67]

The agrarian incursion into Massachusetts and Virginia transformed the dispossessed of Britain into dispossessors. English and Scots, replete with cattle, wheat, and an ideology that stressed divine purpose, entered territories occupied by dozens of nations, most of whom practiced a more extensive land use and maintained smaller populations than they did. What followed was a prolonged conflict, the various instances of which are known by many names: the Pequot War (1637–1638), Cleft's War (1643–1645), Metacom's War (1675–1676), the French and Iroquois Wars (seventeenth century), King Philip's War (1675–1676), the Tuscarora War (1711–1715), the Yamane War (1715–1717), the Chickasaw Wars (1720–1760), the Natchez War (1729–1731), the Cherokee War (1759–1761), Pontiac's Rebellion (1763–1764), Little Turtle's War (1790–1795), and the Creek War (1813–1814). A New England militia deported seven thousand French-speaking Acadians from Nova Scotia in 1755. The commanders justified the dispossession in bluntly expansionist terms, calling it "one of the greatest Things that ever the English did in America; for by all Accounts, that Part of the Country they possess, is as good Land as any in the World: In case therefore we could get some good English Farmers in their Room, this Province would abound with all Kinds of Provisions." This was not an offhand observation. By then, good English farmers were running out of good farmland in New England.[68]

Around the time that New Englanders invaded Canada, their households had entered a crisis. By 1771, farmers in Concord, Massachusetts, had plowed every available acre, breaking the town's record for the largest area cultivated in a year. This was not a so-called Malthusian crisis. Plenty of ground could be found in Vermont, New Hampshire, and Maine, and also in New York and Pennsylvania up against Indian country. Some people headed north, but they made a bad bet. That land was not only farther from market, it was rockier and hillier. Land at the margins of profitability would never pay off a mortgage. Many decided to stay where they were, even as generational subdivision left them with smaller fields. They redoubled their labor and managed to feed themselves but with less and less left over for exchange.[69]

We are looking for the market revolution in New England, and we will find it in the way rural families adapted to stagnant returns to labor. Country people had always made things at home, like textiles. Mothers and daughters put more time into piecework, because it paid better than what came from fields. Between the 1790s and the 1820s, the merchants who bought woolens from Massachusetts families requested greater output from these households in order to satisfy larger orders. When mothers and daughters strained to meet this demand, they virtually worked for the merchants in a putting-out system.[70]

Suddenly, rather than money from woolens supplementing the farm, truncated farms increasingly subsidized incomes from home manufacturing. In the meantime, Boston merchants and their mechanics reconfigured the water-powered mill into the first water-powered factories. The price of coarse textiles fell below the price necessary to make the putting-out system viable. In order to hold on to a cash income and save the household, daughters went from piecework at their mothers' looms to standing twelve hours a day at a clanking spinning frame. They became the first industrial workers in the United States.[71]

That's not the end of the story. There is an ecological component that tells us how Concord came to be planted fence post to fence post. Why did its farms become truncated? At the beginning of the eighteenth century, husbandmen managed their fields as part of a larger ecological base. Recall that a base is a renewable resource that provides spaces for fields, fodder, and gathering without requiring investment in money. Concord's ecological base was the Great Meadow, the wetland at the heart of the town. It provided a nutrient infusion conveyed from grasses to animals to manure that ended up in damp furrows. The Great Meadow gave without taking, and everyone in Concord thrived.

The only rule for living on an ecological base is to observe its limits. In the 1770s, the agrarian reformer Jared Eliot noticed a disquieting imbalance. "The necessary stock of the Country hath out-grown the meadows." Writes the historian Brian Donahue, "That single phrase . . . foretold the end of the yeoman era in New England." In order to make money beyond what the meadow would allow, farmers ran too many cattle. The system of mixed husbandry no longer functioned to restore itself from within itself. Fifty years later, the old system of management was gone. Towns all over New England underwent similar changes. Meadows and forests did not disappear, and communities continued to manage common spaces for a century, but they did so as part of a more intensive commercial world. If the ecological base does not provide fertility and space to shift in, then something has to replace what it once provided. That thing is money.[72]

Farms became increasingly oriented toward money, with some families sending daughters and sons to factories in order to earn it. But here is the point and a reason for why money is so important for understanding agrarian economies and how they change. It allows the value of things to be transmitted to others. We assume that the value of our work is represented by a paycheck. But when value passes from employer to employed or when workers use their incomes to buy necessities, someone else can take value from them by paying them too little or by charging too much. After the Revolution, farmers worried about this. They counted up the implications. When workers received a wage, they might not be paid enough to meet their needs. When land had a price, it could be bought up for speculation and locked away from active use by an owner who did not live in the community. Farms that cost money had to make money, especially if the farmer was in debt to a bank. That changed what farmers planted and how much land they cleared. It changed the countryside. And when a farmer owed a debt he could not service for lack of money, or when the price of gold fluctuated, leaving him with worthless paper but his debts undiminished, his land could be taken away, along with his freedom. When farmers protested and criticized money and greed in order to advocate for themselves as a class, they began to shape a political language that came from their experience—agrarian politics.

Thomas Jefferson is often thought of as representing agrarianism. But he said little about it and did even less to further it. In *Notes on the State of Virginia* (1781), Jefferson referred to those who labored in the earth as "the chosen people of God," in whose incorruptible breasts God had deposited "genuine virtue." He wrote vaguely, never specifically, about those virtuous laborers because he was not one of them and did not know them. Though he gazed at the Blue Ridge from the windows of Monticello, he remained aloof from the log-cabin dwellers just a county or two away. More pointedly, Jefferson did not limit the expansion of slavery into the lower Mississippi River Valley, near New Orleans. The region had been a backwater to the slave-and-cotton economy. All sorts of displaced people, including the evicted Acadians, had ended up there with small allotments. He could have protected them. Instead, he said nothing as enslavers moved in and planted sugarcane during the first decades of the nineteenth century. Jefferson's engagement in agrarian politics was more symbolic than substantive. As a planter himself, he represented the very land regime that caused smallholders to flee to the mountains.[73]

One of the greatest examples of American agrarian thought consists of a series of letters written by an aristocratic Frenchman, the son of the count and countess of Crèvecoeur, who became a resident of Goshen, New York. After serving with France in the French and Indian War, he settled down as a farmer, raised a family, and changed his name to J. Hector St. John de Crèvecoeur. In 1779, he learned that his father was ailing and left his farm to make his way back to France. Crossing British lines in New York City, Crèvecoeur was arrested and held as a spy for three months. He published *Letters from an American Farmer* in London in 1782, during the same sojourn. When he arrived home, he found his farm in ashes, learned that his wife had died, and went in search of his scattered children. Later, he returned to France, where he went into hiding to escape the guillotine. He died in 1813 after returning to his family's ancestral estate.

In his letters, Crèvecoeur lends his voice to a fictional farmer who does and does not resemble him. It is an essay on the glory of simple autonomy, in which the author weaves elements of his own life with the generalized condition of any other plain practical farmer of his time and place. Consider this famous reverie from Letter II:

> I owe nothing but a pepper-corn to my country, a small tribute to my king, with loyalty and due respect. I know no other landlord than the lord of all land, to whom I owe the most sincere gratitude. My father left me three hundred and seventy-one acres of land, forty-seven of which are good timothy meadow, an excellent orchard, a good house, and a substantial barn. It is my duty to think how happy I am that he lived to build and to pay for all these improvements. What are the labours which I have to undergo? What are my fatigues when compared to his, who had everything to do, from the first tree he felled to the finishing of his house? . . . My negroes are tolerably faithful and healthy. By a long series of industry and honest dealings, my father left behind him the name of a good man. I have but to tread his paths to be happy and a good man like him.[74]

The farmer says he owes a peppercorn to the colonial government, employing a metaphor that links back to a feudal custom. English peasants who were granted lifelong leases needed to be reminded that the resident of the castle had not given up his right. Lords charged a symbolic annual fee, sometimes an actual peppercorn (later called peppercorn rent), in order to reinforce the social hierarchy. In other words, this is all the farmer owed king and colony—honorific lip service, nothing more.

Next, Crèvecoeur gives thanks to the settler generation. His actual father lived in France and did not give him his farm. Crèvecoeur uses his fictional father to make an important point. Yeomen did not have much money. *Their economy depended on the subordinate role of money.* A mortgage on the farmer's 371 acres would have run him in debt for most or all of his life. Either that, or he would have become the tenant of a rich man. George III might have extracted a peppercorn, but creditors extracted far more. Every would-be yeoman was willing to work a lifetime for a farm free and clear ("He will not be encumbered with debts and mortgages; what he raises will be his own"), even if that was mostly a dream in New

York and New England by Crèvecoeur's time. The farmer's duty is to do well by his father's generosity and pay the equity forward to his own children. The paragraph is a poetic ledger that details how much and to whom the farmer owes: nothing to his king, everything to God and his father. More obliquely, it speaks to the destructiveness of debt, the way it threatens the agrarian idyll.

Slaves might seem entirely out of place among the farmer's possessions. Crèvecoeur attempts a fine distinction. In his ninth letter, he condemns the cruelty of planters with the ferocity of an abolitionist. He cringes at the thought of Africans at auction in Charlestown, "whole families swept away, and brought, through storms and tempests, to this rich metropolis! There, arranged like horses at a fair, they are branded like cattle, and then driven to toil, to starve, and to languish." The farmer says at one point that the contrast between planters and slaves "has often afforded me subjects of the most afflicting meditations ... O Nature, where art thou?—Are not these blacks thy children as well as we?" These are searching words, but the farmer does not say that all of God's children should be free. Planters bidding for black children sicken him but not slavery.[75]

Crèvecoeur could not have imagined that African-Americans longed for the same security that he did. In the American South and the Caribbean, slaves carved out a realm of freedom by raising their own food. Some traded poultry and eggs with their masters for consumer goods. After emancipation, freed people from Georgia to Barbados found feral spaces where they established gardens of their own. Writes one observer of the Caribbean, "After the abolition of slavery, the ex-slaves and their descendants continued to refer to their homegrown food as provision and any piece of land over which they had some control or ownership, whether freehold, leasehold, or as squatters, as their piece of ground." Ground provisions included breadfruit, plantains, yams, eddoes, and dasheen (taro). The fugitive slave William Wells Brown wanted nothing more than "a little farm." Solomon Northup desired "the possession of some humble habitation, with a few surrounding acres." Josiah Henson urged free blacks to make a clearing in the woods and "undertake the task ... of settling upon wild lands which we could call our own; ... where we could secure all the profits of our own labor." Frederick Douglass exhorted his readers in words that could have come from Crèvecoeur, "To be dependent, is to be degraded . . . Go to farming. Be tillers of the soil."[76]

Yet provision grounds hidden in the woods and the fugitive existence of so many black agrarians make this story entirely different from Crèvecoeur's. Former planters wanted to recapture the labor of former slaves. All over the Atlantic World, white landowners and colonizers set out to eliminate the material foundation of black autonomy and force them to work for money. A critic wrote of the black agrarian in 1875, "If he settles on a small tract of land of his own, as so many thousands do now-a-days, he becomes almost a cumberer of the ground [a burden or detractor], caring for nothing save to get a living, and raising only a bale of cotton or so where with to get 'supplies.' For the rest he can fish and hunt." James Steuart said it no more frankly. In other words, in spite of attempts to obstruct them, such farmers succeeded in maintaining themselves in food and money without wages.[77]

White agrarian writers of the 1850s feared the same thing that former slaves did. They believed that slaveholders and industrialists wanted to seize the public lands for themselves, dispossess farmers, and employ them as hirelings. Two writers came to the defense of plain, practical farmers.

"A Nation will be powerful, prosperous, and happy, in proportion to the number of independent cultivators of its soil," lectured Representative George Washington Julian of Indiana. In 1851, he addressed the House to urge the passage of a homestead bill. Julian defined landed prosperity as a right, one "as inalienable, as emphatically *God-given*, as the right to liberty or life." He dwelled on this. "The gift of life, I repeat, is inseparable from the resources by which alone it can be made a blessing." Such a right could not mean a mere right to breathe. "The right to life implies what the law books call a 'right of way' to its enjoyment. It carries necessarily with it the right to the means of living, including not only the elements of light, air, fire, and water, but land also." But for all his eloquence, Julian lacked a universal vision. The inalienable right of the common farmer would be cut from the "unpeopled regions of the great West," Indian country. Of course, no unpeopled regions existed. Julian regarded Indians as expendable, unentitled to their own right of way.

But Julian worried that the smallholders he championed might be as expendable as he supposed Indians to be. The idea that the United States should give away homesteads to antislavery farmers on the Plains came from Julian's fear that slaveholders would try to influence the formation of states there. Three years before the Kansas–Nebraska Act, he saw the possibility that a popular sovereignty provision would throw the northern Plains into dispute. He also worried that great combinations of capital would get hold of the Plains and turn it into a wheat factory. "The freedom of the public lands . . . will weaken the system of chattel slavery, by making war upon its kindred system of wages slavery." Homesteads would advance a virtuous economy against two immoral ones.[78]

The New England naturalist Wilson Flagg echoed Julian's fears in 1859. Flagg trembled at the thought of the steam engine. He made the crucial distinction between the machine and its social relations, between its "*apparent* benefits upon mankind" and the "inevitable tendency of this great invention to concentrate all wealth and power into the hands of capitalists." Joint-stock companies in western New York planned to farm on a new scale. "These corporations, executing almost all their heavy labor by steam power and mammoth implements, would crowd out of the ranks of agriculture all those whose farms were of such small extent, that steam could not be profitably used by them." He calculated. If steam power cut and threshed the same commodity for ten dollars that the small farmer grew for a hundred, then it wouldn't be long before agents arrived at every kitchen door offering to buy. Husbandmen would then sell, for any price.

Flagg imagined a bleak, machine-driven landscape. State legislatures would order the sale of land under laws of eminent domain, just as the railroads had engrossed for private gain by claiming the public good. Agricultural corporations would consolidate a varied countryside into fields of five hundred, even one thousand acres. He envisioned the gentleness and diversity of the landscape—oaks and maples, hills and ponds—uprooted and swept away "by some giant infernal machine" and graded into "one vast level," all to make it possible for engines to do their relentless gauging and skimming. He saw farmers falling into the same hellish maw. Their labor had been hard but sweet. Not for much longer. Flagg reported from the near future. "The farmers, their wives and their children, have all been reduced to servitude in this grand manufactory of corn and vegetables."

Flagg fought the times and offered a rearguard policy. "We should refuse to agriculture any aid which is not beneficial to the agriculturist—for the farmer is of more importance than his crops."

Most of the factors of what would become industrial agriculture existed by the 1850s. Within a decade, growing wheat on the northern Great Plains and in the San Joaquin Valley of California took on a scale unprecedented in North America. Farmers became hirelings in the service of infernal machines, just as Julian and Flagg feared.

There are a few ideas to take away from this brief history of the American peasantry and its fate. It is not a tale of freedom leading to abundance. Every movement of transplanted Europeans resulted in the bereavement of Native Americans. The yeoman farm was never a stable institution. It was impinged upon by debt, taxation, commodity prices, war, and a decline in its ecological base. Agrarians resisted technological change. They saw innovations like steam power as threatening everything they required to reproduce themselves as a class—control over a diverse landscape, the terms of work, and the members of their households. It is easy to see them as fuming and thundering on the wrong side of change, but they held a different vision of what the United States should be. Yet all throughout the eighteenth century and well into the nineteenth, none of the eloquent advocates for the interests and endurance of agrarian economy mentioned another European peasant culture, the people who had climbed into the southern mountains.[79]

DANIEL BOONE'S CULTURAL ANCESTORS, if not actually his genetic ones, were Swedish woodsmen who arrived in the lower Delaware River Valley, north and south of what would become Philadelphia, in 1638. Swedes do not figure much in the following pages, but they brought the tools, houses, and temperament that eventually covered the southern mountains. In other words, the culture of Appalachia began in practices imported from the hardscrabble northern fringe of Europe. The emigration of the first Swedes was really more of an exile. Even by the standards of other forest dwellers, these *kirvesmiehet* were considered volatile. They hated permanent farming, preferring to follow the hunt no matter where it led them. The Swedish government didn't want them roaming around and somehow persuaded them to ship for North America.

For seventeen years, they colonized along the Delaware River. They planted rye in burned-over clearings and built houses of jointed logs. The Dutch took over in 1655 and the English in 1665. Neither could stop the Swedes. Finns of the Savo-Karelian culture arrived at about this time, bringing many of the same skills. By 1681, a culture group had formed, numbering around one thousand people in scattered enclaves up the tributaries into New Jersey. Over the next century, this hybrid continued to hybridize, absorbing emigrants from Wales, France, and Germany. They lived in the territory of the Lenape, who taught them foodways, herbal cures, and warfare. The Ulster-Scots or Scots-Irish were another people from the hardscrabble, another hybrid. They had been thrown together by the British colonization of Northern Ireland before fleeing to North America around 1715. The Scots-Irish rapidly emerged as the majority ethnicity of the woodland settlement culture.[80]

These fire-wielding hunters with their long rifles and log cabins composed one of the most land-extensive and socially explosive agrarian societies the world has ever known. They scattered from their hearth along the Delaware River into Maryland, Pennsylvania, and western Virginia, through the Cumberland Gap and into Kentucky, Tennessee, and the Ohio River Valley. Generations linked to the same core group sought unencumbered land in Illinois, the Great Plains of Kansas and Nebraska, and the Willamette Valley of Oregon, where they finally ran out of continent. In the midst of this feverish movement, they became soldiers in the British wars for North America and in the expansion of the United States. And they engaged in violence with Indians, in innumerable skirmishes and massacres. They disrupted relationships, as well as landscapes, wherever they went.

The earliest cabins appeared in southeastern Pennsylvania in the 1650s. A group of Delaware sachems complained to a Dutch general that the Swedes settled wherever they wanted. "The Swede builds and plants . . . on our lands, without buying them or asking us." The sachems decided to vacate to the Dutch so that when the reckless interlopers "pull down the Dutch houses and drive away the people," the Delaware wouldn't be blamed for it. The sachems explained again and again that the land in question had not been gifted or sold but taken. A Dutch report concerning the same borderland between New Sweden and New Netherland said much worse of the Swedes. They had invaded sovereign territory, "disregarding all our protests." An indignant officer called them arrogant, insolent, and contemptuous.

Over the next century, the same hunters continued to move westerly, without asking anyone's permission. After the Quaker William Penn arrived in 1681, he exercised remarkable control over the woods granted him and his family by the king of England, Charles II. One of the first things Penn did was sign a treaty with the Delaware and allied nations that launched seventy years of negotiated coexistence. But backwoods households often complicated the work of Conestoga and English diplomats. In 1731, a group of Conestoga reminded Penn's descendants that the Indians had "lived in Good Friendship with the Christian Inhabitants" and that Penn himself "had promis'd them they Should Not be Disturbed by any Settlers on the west Side of Sasquehanah." The government of Pennsylvania took these complaints seriously, but found it increasingly impossible to manage the frontier.

Settlers claimed to protect their families from Indians while they employed vigilante violence to seize Indian land. Writes the historian Honor Sachs, "By negating Indian agency . . . backcountry residents embraced a racist ideology of Indian hating that portrayed the enemy as savage, predatory, less than human." Penn saw Pennsylvania as a kind of republican empire, with many peoples each in their homelands. But backwoods settlers saw themselves as a force of racial purification, clearing Indians away in order to replace them with people like themselves.[81]

They had arrived in southwestern Pennsylvania by the 1780s and crossed over into western Virginia at about the same time. Others traveled down the Shenandoah Valley where they followed the Wilderness Road into Kentucky a few years behind Boone. They thought they would be left alone. But if perfect isolation from government administration defines the frontier, it didn't last very long, if it ever existed at all. Surveyors walked the same wilderness, some hired by distant landowners. Virginia divided its mountain territory into counties, each with courthouses and tax collectors. The settlers signed on to fight with George Washington in the Revolutionary War, aligning with a nation-state whose leaders had their own ideas about the backcountry.

A century later, the descendants of these same woodland hunters had lost control of the woods, found themselves politically vulnerable, their agriculture insufficient to protect them against forces that pried them out of the same hills that had once provided them with abundance and autonomy. They endured an American version of enclosure. That process began not with the discovery of coal or the first railroad but when the Federalists came to power in 1789. It did not begin with eviction and disputes over deeds but with a failed attempt to impose an excise tax. One Federalist, in particular, represented the entire complement of North Atlantic universals. Facing west, he acted to extend his conception of capitalism and constitutional authority to every hill and hollow.

3. The Rye Rebellion

WHY ALEXANDER HAMILTON INVADED
THE MOUNTAINS

Civil power . . . is capable of diffusing its force to a very great
extent; and can, in a manner, reproduce itself in every part of
a great empire.

—Alexander Hamilton, *The Federalist*, No. 13 (1787)

THEY COULD BE SEEN on the roads for miles, a force the size of
the Continental Army. The soldiers came from Pennsylvania, Virginia, Maryland, and New Jersey. They met at
Harrisburg to begin their advance through Carlisle. Word that George
Washington led the column jolted the insurgents, but the president took
the militia just halfway before placing Alexander Hamilton in charge. It
was Hamilton's fight anyway. He'd thought it up, mapped every movement, and outfitted thirteen thousand men with shoes, coats, and rifles.
One soldier who watched the secretary of the Treasury striding around in
camp, dressed in his old uniform, called him "the master spirit" of the
operation. Hamilton marched into the mountains to enforce the authority
of federal law. Yet in a larger sense he marched as Political Economy personified, headed for a confrontation with Agrarian Autonomy.[1]

Before the invasion or the tax, the backcountry seethed with rebellion and intrigue. George Washington dreaded the West, which he considered a haven for "banditti who will bid defiance to all authority." That authority seemed everywhere under attack and in decline. Here are just a few of his frontier problems. James Wilkinson, a brigadier general residing in Kentucky, took it upon himself to negotiate an agreement with the Spanish colonial governor in New Orleans to open the Mississippi River to upcountry commerce. To seal the deal, Wilkinson swore allegiance to Spain in 1787. Around the time of the Whiskey Rebellion, Washington learned that British Canadian officials and Pennsylvania rebels had been planning the secession of the western counties of that state.

Indian nations demanded their own independence, like the confederacy led by the Miami chief Little Turtle in the Ohio Territory. Washington did not follow a unified policy to hold the West steady. With one hand, the administration sent waves of violence against Little Turtle. With the other, it signed a treaty that enforced Creek boundaries against the interests of Georgia politicians and speculators. Some blamed the disorderly frontier on the size and complexity of a nation-state too big to govern. Washington's secretary Tobias Lear predicted, "Within fifteen years the inhabitants to the westward of the Alleghany will be a separate, independent people."[2]

The fears and motives of the Federalists, however, get us only so far in understanding the Whiskey Rebellion. The politics of the 1790s create a thick context, overwhelming other kinds of interpretations. The event itself should not be buried as the "frontier epilogue" to the Constitution, with Shays' Rebellion playing the part of prologue. When agrarian protest becomes a phase or stage, a lingering tension between old and new that is inevitably resolved, writes Ed White, "rebellions themselves have no place in the larger history . . . So one of the most stunning manifestations of early American culture is frequently evacuated of meaning." Seeing the Whiskey Rebellion ideologically has its uses, but it might lead us into thinking that only ideology matters. We might fail to see the intricate material world of the rebels and how stress against their household economies provoked them to rise up.[3]

Agrarian protest suffuses the history of British North America. Shift the focus and the Whiskey Rebellion takes its place as one event in an era of agrarian violence: Bacon's Rebellion (1676), Virginia's Plant-Cutter Riots (1681–1683), the Conojocular War (1732–1737), the Jersey Land Riots (1745–1755), the colonial New York anti-rent riots (1753–1766), the Paxton Riots (1763–1764), the North Carolina Regulation (1769–1784), the Vermont insurgency (1770–1775), Shays' Rebellion (1786–1787), and John Fries' Rebellion (1799). They were wars over autonomy and against taxation or the penalties of debt. Others enforced racially defined realms of control. War with Indians (like Little Turtle's War of the 1790s, just to the west of the Pennsylvania border) took place on the same frontier.

These conflicts should be understood as political rebellions in which settlers and Indians asserted their own conceptions of independence. The United States attempted to crush their autonomy in order to achieve legal and economic uniformity. Insurgency shaped the United States itself—its military, land laws, territorial integration, and Constitution. Frontier revolt should also be seen as an Atlantic-wide response to administrative power. For 125 years, the West unleashed a barrage of violence comparable to the 300 years of peasant uprising in Europe that Fernand Braudel called "a latent social war . . . a structural kind of warfare without end."[4]

Hamilton fought this structural war—an attempt to bring administrative control to the unruly people of the West. The Revolutionary leadership had all learned from the ineffectual Proclamation of 1763 that fictitious lines promote fictitious authority. The land ordinances of the 1780s attempted to get around the problem of an imperium ruling over subordinate provinces. The law of 1784 called for the land west of the mountains and north of the Ohio River to be divided into states. The law of 1785 stitched the wilderness with a grid. It created the federal survey system: townships of six square miles divided into thirty-six sections, each of which consisted of 640 acres. This conceptual infrastructure facilitated the transition of wilderness into private property. The acts of 1787 and 1789 created the Northwest Territory as an administrative unit, anticipating the eventual establishment of six new states. Yet like Britain's attempt to enforce the Proclamation Line, declaring a boundary did not produce thoroughly governed space. Borders on a map meant nothing to people living in the folds of the mountains. Hamilton imagined the United States as a legal and economic totality, but he confronted it as a relentless process of integration. State formation, in Jean-Paul Sartre's terms, is an attempt to "make each part an expression of the whole."[5]

The Whiskey Rebellion took place in four western counties of Pennsylvania, which is to say that it took place in northern Appalachia. Though the best-documented series of events draws our attention to the region south of Pittsburgh, we should think more broadly about what happened. Nearly the entire population of Kentucky nullified the tax. In Morgantown, Virginia, a crowd surrounded the home of the excise collector, allowing him to escape only after he resigned. Washington and Hamilton considered sending a punitive expedition against western North Carolina. But more important, the tax and the invasion represented the first attempts since the end of the Revolution to force the backcountry into the Atlantic economy. Hamilton's method of choice was to lever open western households by compelling them to sell more of the things they made. As he had learned from Adam Smith, value comes from labor exerted against environments in making useful things. Money converts this value into a form that can travel far away and accumulate in banks. A nation-state can grab its share by collecting taxes. The Whiskey Tax proposed to do something that Hamilton once called impossible. It reached into the relationship between mountain farmers and their land by requiring that they convert one very important product of their labor into money.

Looking ahead a century or so, we can see that the industrialization of the mountains extended and deepened this very process. But coal and lumber companies did not want to monetize *only a portion* of the value highland folk created. They sought to separate them from land altogether, compelling them to turn all their labor into money. Mountain people became enmeshed in the national economy and the global division of labor. Hamilton did not have this in mind when he marched an army into Fayette County. But like the corporations that followed, he believed that moving people from rye and beans to coins and currency furthered capital, the power of the United States, and historical progress.[6]

One way to understand Hamilton's thinking is by comparison with his rival Jefferson. They did not disagree about whether or not the United States should seize and rule territory but about the concentration of governmental power that should prevail. They worked from different conceptual "maps." In Jefferson's realm, the whole would be present in some of the parts, but not all. He might have had in mind something like William Clark's dead-reckoned pencil sketches of the Missouri River watershed. Jefferson annexed those hundreds of millions of acres in order to dilute centralized power, without diminishing that power where it existed. He wanted places for planters and yeomen to escape into. But Jefferson had his own imaginary nation, one without Indians, whose presence violated his ideal as surely as untaxed Pennsylvanians violated Hamilton's.

Hamilton's map looked more like the peace of 1783, stressing enforceable borders and internal improvements. He wanted one seamless system that governed every acre of the United States. One way of doing this was to tie distant people to the central government by making them pay a tax. The tax, in turn, would demand an infrastructure and instill a national presence. Taxation was so essential to Hamilton because it fused authority and economy. His political economy is more accurately understood as a *governing economy*. The future of the state could not be separated from the commercial evolution of its people. In his optimistic phase, Hamilton saw a virtuous cycle. A thoroughly administered nation fostered a widening division of labor. Money from commerce sustained taxation. And taxation created a robust and powerful state, with institutions and internal improvements. This led to further widening of the division of labor as the state reached into new territories.

But Hamilton's map was inadequate for his task. It told him nothing about the people he confronted. This is part of the context and meaning of the Whiskey Tax. It came out of a search for order. The measurement, quantification, and public identification that it demanded tied western Pennsylvania to the United States by forcing distillers to submit to distant forms of definition and value.[7]

Hamilton knew that taxes provoked anger. He led his own insurgent artillery unit against the British in the battles of White Plains and Trenton, part of the tax rebellion known as the American Revolution. He must have known about the English excise riots of 1733 and the violent resistance to a malt tax in Scotland. In 1725, crowds enraged by the high price of beer attacked collectors in Glasgow and destroyed the homes of members of

Parliament. Adam Smith used the malt tax to recommend caution to rulers in *The Wealth of Nations*. "It must always be remembered . . . that it is the luxurious and not the necessary expense of the inferior ranks of people that ought ever to be taxed." But when revolutionary leaders become a post-revolutionary elite, they often consolidate their political victory by turning to social transformation. Whatever Hamilton thought about debt and taxes in 1777, a decade later he saw them as "national exigency," as tools in the social consolidation of the United States. We can glimpse his thinking at an early stage in his response to another uprising, Shays' Rebellion.[8]

After the Revolution, Europeans merchants hesitated to extend credit to American merchants. They would only be paid in gold. The hard-money policy tumbled down the financial ladder until it hit the bottom rung. Farmers owed local storekeepers, mortgage holders, and landlords. They were overwhelmed by threats of foreclosure and imprisonment. They depended on easy currency to cover their debts. Daniel Shays had just returned from the Continental Army—wounded, never paid, and in arrears. He found his neighbors in the same bind. One of them grieved,

> I have laboured hard all my days and fared hard; I have been
> greatly abused; been obliged to do more than my part in the war;
> been loaded with class-rates, town-rates, continental-rates, and
> all rates, lawsuits, and have been pulled and hauled by sheriffs,
> constables and collectors, and had my cattle sold for less than they
> were worth: I have been obliged to pay and no body will pay me.
> I have lost a great deal by this man, and that man, and t'other
> man; and the great men are going to get all we have; and I think it
> is time for us to rise and put a stop to it, and have no more courts,
> nor sheriffs, nor collectors, nor lawyers; I design to pay no more.

Another said, "The great men pocket up all the money and live easy, and we work hard, and we can't pay it, and we won't pay it." But creditors made no exceptions for difficult circumstances. The plowmen petitioned the state-house. They asked for lower taxes, more paper currency, and security from arrest and trial. Unable to endure their hardship any longer, they did rise and put a stop to it.[9]

On August 29, 1786, an army of 600 led by Shays stormed the Court of Common Pleas at Northampton, shutting it down. Protestors in Great Barrington, Worcester, Taunton, and Concord did the same. Some of them wore their Continental Army uniforms. Governor James Bowdoin had no soldiers to meet the insurgents. No federal army existed. He and General Benjamin Lincoln raised funds for a private militia from 125 merchants. In January 1787, a force of 3,000 invaded Worcester. In the meantime, Shays led 1,500 to take over the federal armory in Springfield, but 1,200 local militia under William Shepard outgunned them, killing four and wounding twenty. In a surprise attack on February 3, Lincoln's army scattered the rebels and made arrests. Eighteen received death sentences for treason. Two were hanged. Governor John Hancock commuted the remaining sentences and released the prisoners, including Shays.

It is often said that Shays' Rebellion moved the Revolutionary leadership to "establish justice and insure domestic tranquility," but it did not move them to address any of the reasons given by farmers for their insurrection. Instead, the framers of the Constitution instilled the chief executive with the power to crush future uprisings by calling up federal soldiers and state militias. As for the most talented political economist in North America, he was not moved to write a treatise on the paradox of rebellion in a democratic republic, nor did he examine the economic condition of the agrarian class. Hamilton didn't blame a credit crisis or an inadequate money supply or the end of the war. No. He dismissed a revolt involving thousands of citizens as one man's personal failing. "If Shays had not been a desperate debtor," sneered Hamilton in *The Federalist*, No. 6, "it is much to be doubted whether Massachusetts would have been plunged into a civil war."[10]

Hamilton elaborated in the months that followed. There could be no exception to the sovereign right to tax, which he propounded in *The Federalist*, No. 12: "As revenue is the essential engine by which the means of answering the national exigencies must be procured . . . the federal government must of necessity be invested with an *unqualified power of taxation*." Unqualified power was exactly what anti-Federalists feared most. Hamilton stared them down with the unrelenting argument that political power did not exist without financial power. Money flowed through any nation-state like blood. Duties on trade were somewhat more popular because they taxed other countries (though they raised domestic prices). But if tariffs ever proved insufficient, only one source remained. "If the principal part be not drawn from commerce, it must fall with oppressive weight upon land." He understood the risks. Farmers, he admitted, would "ill brook the inquisitive and peremptory spirit of excise laws." He called their property "too precarious and invisible a fund" to be attached, meaning that government had no way of identifying assets as mobile as cattle and ephemeral as rye. In 1787, he balanced the forces in play. He sensed and dreaded the consequences of revenue raised the wrong way. Such a tax would not "fail to be productive of glaring inequality and extreme oppression."

Hamilton squared the contradiction between the necessity of taxation and the incapacity of farmers to pay by falling back on the theory of stages. Social evolution would make money appear where it was needed. Time would bring economic development and the mutual dependency that comes from a complex division of labor. "In the usual progress of things," he lectured assuredly in No. 30, "the resources of the community, in their full extent, will be brought into activity for the benefit of the Union." In other words, *the full extent* of the value derived from land and labor would be available to the nation-state, eventually. The state could then impose itself by taking a portion. Hamilton offered a now familiar formula for the changes he expected. "The ability of a country to pay taxes" depended on "the quantity of money in circulation." Since commerce circulates money, it "must of necessity render the payment of taxes easier." The problem of taxation only required people to move from one stage to another, for farmers to grow more for market sale. But in 1791, Hamilton was secretary of the Treasury. By then, he had determined that an excise was necessary and that whiskey would be its source.[11]

A humdrum bill dealing with the importation of alcoholic beverages shifts focus at section fourteen, declaring duties on anything distilled within the United States. For alcohol other than rum, between nine cents and twenty-five cents per gallon would be collected, depending on the proof. The government did not excise the sale or consumption of whiskey but its production, as estimated by the size or volume of stills. But the tax made no distinction between whiskey for profit or for domestic use. Even distillers who drank all they made needed to pay it. Commercial distillers needed to pay in advance of sale.

We can read in the legislation itself the outlines of a comprehensive vision. The Whiskey Tax encouraged exchanges by penalizing those who produced for home use. Similarly, it encouraged the accumulation of money by requiring distillers to pay this month's tax from last month's sales. But if the tax was really an attempt at social engineering, what change did Hamilton hope it would cause? He wanted the people of the backcountry to make more things for money, to live on money (to some degree, at least), and to pay taxes with surplus money. For the Atlantic elite, money separated the value of a thing from its use. It was the sine qua non of the social division of labor and the evolutionary transition from subsistence to commercial social relations. The proliferation of money as a medium of production and exchange encompassed much of Hamilton's conception of the *United* States.

But what distillers found as obnoxious as the tax itself was the government's thuggish way of collecting it. Those who made whiskey needed to paint the words DISTILLER OF SPIRITS on their houses so agents of the state could ride into a village and quickly identify them. They needed to make an "entry in writing" at a central office three days before distilling. No one could remove whiskey from any distillery at night. All stills needed to be inspected with the liquor percolating in situ, not after the fact. Officers needed to brand each cask with a serial number to mark its origin, its quantity, and its proof ("ascertained by actual gauging"), then collect the tax and write a receipt. Only then could a cask travel the roads and rivers to market. Congress piled on the penalties for fugitive stills and noncompliance. Officers who came across unmarked goods on the turnpike had the authority to seize all casks, horses, cattle, carriages, harnesses, tackling, boats, and the full value of the cargo (not just its taxable value) on the spot. The penalty for erasing or changing serial numbers was forfeiture and a fine equal to the highest market price. Other infractions carried a hundred-dollar fine—an impossible sum. Anyone operating a single still under fifty gallons did not have to keep records or mark his house, but he was otherwise subject to the law.

The whole procedure represented a never-imagined reach into the economy of everyday life, surpassing the most inflammatory British policy. Yet neither Washington nor Hamilton anticipated an armed response. Washington wrote on July 20, 1794, during a tour through the South, "From the best information I could get on my journey . . . there remains no doubt but it will be carried into effect, not only without opposition but with very general approbation in those very parts where it was foretold that it would never be submitted to by any one." Most people Washington met told him what he wanted to hear. Hugh Hammond Brackenridge had seen local people calculate their responses to powerful outsiders, appearing "moderate in their transactions," while they suppressed "the most hostile sentiments." He noted of officials, "They could not know, so well as others, the general rage of the country, against the excise law."[12]

In fact, hostility had broken out during Washington's tour. When collectors showed up in Westmoreland, Fayette, Washington, and Allegheny counties, armed men coated them with tar and feathers and whipped them. The insurgents destroyed the stills of any who cooperated. They kidnapped a federal marshal and stopped the courts from operating. On July 16, the regional inspector in charge of collection, John Neville, had just served a writ, accompanied by a local marshal. A band of men on horseback came up behind them. A gun went off. Neville locked eyes with his pursuers and told the marshal to run. Neville rode hard to his home seven miles outside of Pittsburgh. The next morning he awoke to a standoff. No one knows what words the two sides exchanged before Neville opened fire. The rebels pelted the wood-framed house with musket balls, as Neville's slaves met the volume of the attack. One person lay dead and others wounded. The following morning, Neville wrote to his son in Pittsburgh that five hundred insurgents were massing nearby. The younger Neville reached the house hours after an all-out assault, finding it burned to the ground. Hamilton learned of Neville's story in early August and briefed Washington on the "almost universal noncompliance" and acts of violence "presumed to amount to Treason." That's when he vowed that the republic would come down on the rebels with mammoth force.

Hamilton could have taxed other things. He had recommended that the state of New York tax meadows, salt, tobacco, and houses by size. He thought up a tavern tax and a lawyer tax. He could have placed duties on slave sales or absentee land ownership and the proceeds of speculation. Merchant houses were flush with foreign currency. Deriving revenue from malt and brewing enraged the Scots, but it would have been a fairer production to attach because it affected people in every state. He could have squeezed money from citizens who actually had it, in other words, rather than from those whose property sometimes consisted of a cow and a horse. Instead, he taxed something with inestimable value to the people who made it, something deeply rooted in the makeshift economy.[13]

Most of the things raised and manufactured on any homestead moved from production to consumption in very small circles. *But whiskey was different.* Its low perishability translated into stable value. It moved in big circles, entering the second transactional realm of the agrarian world, where things traveled far away and brought back money. Its lengthy transits made it visible to the state. Percolating liquor looked to Hamilton like the ideal taxable commodity. But the people who made it saw it differently. It was the most lucrative form of the rye they harvested from forest clearings. For those who consumed their own whiskey or exchanged it locally, as many did, their stills produced no coin. In the conflict that ensued, agrarians insisted that the secretary of the Treasury had put them in an untenable position. Hamilton didn't listen to them.[14]

THE WOODLAND CULTURE LIT OUT for the Allegheny Front. Emigrants traveled with long rifles and large families. Their adaptive traits stressed versatility over specialization, extensive land use over intensive. A German botanist came upon them in the 1780s. "These hunters or 'backwoodsmen' live very like the Indians and acquire similar ways of thinking. They shun everything which appears to demand of them law and order, dread anything which breaths constraint. They hate the name of a Justice, and yet they are not transgressors . . . An insignificant cabin of un-hewn logs; corn and a little wheat, a few cows and pigs, this is all their riches but they need no more." The unhewn life depended on a great run of woods where settlers could continually re-create an Arcadia of hunting and grazing. But like every Arcadia, this one was in trouble from the beginning.[15]

Settlers emigrated to stay ahead of something they could not abide—the valuation of land. The conversion of wilderness into real estate sent them higher and higher into thousands of narrow valleys. Between 1780 and 1810, nonresident planters and merchants engrossed 4.5 million acres, or 93 percent of the land in western Virginia. The average holding consisted of 5,485 acres. Actual settlers occupied the other 7 percent, or 324,000 acres, in various degrees of possession. In 1794, fourteen individuals bought 2.5 million acres from the Commonwealth of Virginia for 2 cents each. Twenty-one speculators claimed one-quarter of Kentucky.

No one got into the game earlier than George Washington. While a soldier in the French and Indian War, he received an on-the-ground tutorial on the western country. In 1763, as a reward for his military service, the royal governor of Virginia gave Washington a warrant for five thousand acres in the undulating plateau between the rivers Kanawha and Ohio. (He would eventually own thirty thousand acres.) That was the same year that King George III forbade any colonist from putting up a cabin or even setting foot there. Washington and other grantees might have reasoned that the Proclamation Line would not exist for long. After all, what did it mean to own land that one couldn't legally visit? So he broke the law. In 1767, he ordered his personal surveyor, William Crawford, to cross into the highlands "under the guise of hunting game." There, Crawford would identify the most advantageous portions of Washington's warrants. "Ordinary or even middling lands would never answer my purpose," wrote Washington, sounding like any other speculator. "No; a tract to please me must be rich . . . and, if possible, level."[16]

The maps that Crawford drew for Washington in this and subsequent expeditions indicated ground as flat and wide as anyone could hope to find in a region where that kind of space hardly existed. In 1774, he marked off nearly three thousand acres along the Kanawha River, blazing G W on a sycamore, a white oak, and (of all things) a cherry tree. What is important about this survey describing the banks of the Kanawha near its intersection with the Coal River is not what it includes but what it leaves out—everything but the bottomland. The topography rises five hundred feet from the valley floor within a quarter of a mile, but no one would know that by looking at Crawford's map. He left it all blank. In the decades that followed, every acre of

Virginia would be granted and engrossed, sometimes to more than one person. Senator Humphrey Marshall of Kentucky, a Virginia-born Federalist, complained of the "infinitude of conflicting claims." The federal survey system, enacted in the Ordinance of 1785, didn't settle the confusion because it didn't apply to the original states or to the western territories under their jurisdiction. Since the states didn't perform their own surveys for decades, who owned what remained unknown. Such grand omissions cast a cloak of invisibility over oceans of ridges and valleys where dispossessed Indians, escaped slaves, and poor whites found all the resources they needed to live. In fact, we should not think of a single land system as taking shape but two. Official grants and private surveys represented the first. In the other, settlers occupied and later exchanged scraps of landscape with impunity.[17]

Some of these scraps are known as *runs*, *coves*, and *hollows*. From six miles above the earth the country looks like wrinkled paper. Each fold is a tiny watershed with a stream or *branch* that flows into a larger creek or river. Broad and steep at the top, hollows often taper down the middle, where sunshine is limited, opening into marshy glades at the bottom. Floods can rise quickly in a hard rain and can take away topsoil. No one searching for top-quality farmland considered felling trees to plow up a dim and damp hollow. "It seems very strange that any person should have settled there at a time when the whole country was almost vacant," wrote one observer in 1771. But people who placed a high value on game animals saw nothing strange about it. The folds of the mountains allowed them space for hunting, for burning, and for plowing up to plant rye. They settled at high altitudes out of necessity, but they searched and deliberated to find the greatest advantage. They knew what they were doing. The archaeologist Barry Cunliffe describes the first peasants to colonize Western Europe. The ecological niches they chose "suggests an awareness of geography that could only have come from knowledge based on reconnaissance." The same can be said about the first white settlers of Appalachia.[18]

By the end of the eighteenth century, settlers arriving in the southern mountains entered a landscape that often belonged to other people. Households sometimes received grants from the Commonwealth of Virginia, the same kind of grants Washington received. But more typically, they moved onto land regardless of who owned it. One of them recounted years later,

"Many squatted down on lands, not knowing or caring whose they were." While no one was looking, they wrote and recorded their own deeds, surveying by metes and bounds in the hand of anyone literate. A grantee residing in Philadelphia often had no idea that hundreds or thousands of people regularly bought and sold parts of his estate.

The backwoods thrived on this neglect. Ten thousand acres on the far side of the Blue Ridge might have looked like inviolable private property inscribed on filigreed parchment. But from ground level it looked much more chaotic and its ownership less obvious. The owner of the filigreed parchment might have acquired the land before counties existed. But these local bureaucracies recorded sales and collected taxes. During the early nineteenth century, new counties formed from older ones like cells dividing. New counties did not, necessarily, receive all the relevant records. In the meantime, anyone who improved a spate of woods and was in good standing with the county began to accumulate rights, even if it turned out that someone else could claim to own the same land. A patchwork of boundaries soon overlapped one another. Courts attempted to adjudicate, but the landscape became a kind of game of hiding in the blank spaces, of right against right. I will have more to say about all this in the next chapter.[19]

When absentee owners found out about squatters and locally written deeds, they had to act, even if it meant traveling long distances. If they did nothing, they risked challenges by adverse possession. If Party A owns a piece of land but makes no use of it, and if Party B grazes cattle on it and puts up a cabin, then Party B can assert title after a designated period, usually ten years. Absentees could defend themselves in court, but they needed to explain why they had never visited or turned a spade and why the interlopers did not deserve the benefits of their "sweat equity." This happened to George Washington.[20]

In September 1784, Washington "found it indispensably necessary to visit my Landed property west of the Apalacheon [sic] Mountains," in what would become Washington County, Pennsylvania. The general acquired this tract as he had most of the others he owned in the region, as a reward for service during the previous war. But by the time of the Revolution he had neglected it, allowing a community to occupy it. He had a few other errands in the same area, so he took a trip. He visited tenants and collected rent. He dined here and there, chatted with friends and relatives, inspected a mechanical boat, and learned about the navigation of the Cheat River in western Virginia. When he arrived at his 2,800 acres, Washington came face-to-face with a breakaway sect of the Associated Presbyterian Church. They weren't happy to meet him.

At dinner that evening, the violators asked the general to relinquish the entire tract. The Presbyterians wanted the improvements they had made to around four hundred acres of meadow, arable, houses, and barns. They also wanted all the remaining unimproved land. They believed they had a solid case for adverse possession, that no judge would rule against them. Still, they might have hesitated to drag Washington into court. So the Presbyterians offered a compromise. They would buy the land for a little money on easy terms. Wrote Washington, "I told them I had no inclination to sell." When he heard their story of schism and hardship, he softened a little and reconsidered. The general's "last offer" was to sell for twenty-five shillings an acre, in three annual payments, with interest; or they could become his tenants by signing a 999-year lease. This was a common way around adverse possession. By agreeing to pay for the use of land, tenants secured the position of the owner.

Unintimidated by the most powerful politician and military officer in the United States, the squatters countered that they would pay Washington's price but over a longer period and without interest. He said no. The negotiation ended. One of the squatters claimed that Washington stood from his seat, "and holding a red silk handkerchief by one corner, he said, 'Gentlemen, I will have this land just as surely as I now have this handkerchief.'" What is more certain is that Washington asked each of the squatters to stand or sit in a roll-call vote of their individual intentions. He called their names one by one, dramatically and with kingly gravitas, hoping to break their unity. They held firm.[21]

Washington did not travel out west for the trial. His lawyer began the assault by suing the squatter with the strongest claim. He won a jury decision by proving that his client had neglected the property because he was too busy commanding the Continental Army and founding the United States to visit it. The attorney then asked the judge to consolidate the other cases into one. That trial went quickly to the same conclusion. The squatting Presbyterians were evicted. By one estimate, judges in Westmoreland, Washington, and Fayette counties ruled on 654 cases of contested title and ejectment between 1785 and 1795, a number that suggests that squatting was rampant and, often enough, successful.[22]

Settlement by preemption and squatting made agrarian existence possible in the mountains. Settling in advance of towns and dense populations ensured an extensive ecological base, a de facto commons if not de jure, that produced everything for subsistence and commodities for exchange without requiring money. And yet, many people in western Pennsylvania owned no land. Were they *landless*? It all depends on what that means.

If *landlessness* refers to one denied access to woods and waters that they owned or not, then the word did not apply to anyone in the Pennsylvania backwoods or anywhere else in Appalachia during the eighteenth century. Consider that segment of the population who owned animals but no land. In 1783, Uriah Glover of Westmoreland County had fourteen animals but not an acre of meadow to his name. Susanah Robertson owned four horses, three head of cattle, and fifteen sheep but not a run of forest for them to graze in. Did Glover and Robertson lack any way of feeding their livestock? Of course not. The same goes for those who owned no taxable property whatsoever. Some were unmarried adult sons who would soon set up their own households. Others worked as tenants, with gardens and fields that they farmed on shares and forest meadows that they used with or without permission. In total, 51.6 percent of the 492 names on the county tax list owned no farm, but they all had access to the ecological base. In this sense, *landlessness* is a misleading term.[23]

And yet, we should not overestimate access to a functional commons. In some places, tenants and wage laborers faced tighter control and greater dependency. We tend to think of manufacturing as organizing work in eastern cities, not in the backcountry. But that's a false distinction. In the 1780s, a saltworks in Kentucky at Bullitt's Lick employed landless white men, African-American slaves, and children who spent their days boiling the water of a saline pond. Their situation reveals that household autonomy could be elusive. The tensions within the spectrum of access and ownership added an essential stressor that made the Whiskey Tax intolerable. Still, we should keep these categories open and flexible, as highlanders themselves did. Labor for others formed a limb on the tree of the makeshift economy. No matter who owned the woods, if use-rights prevailed in the shadow of absentee neglect, then everyone from titled yeomen to laborers could feed their children on bear meat, let their pigs fend for roots and acorns, and plant rye for whiskey in fugitive clearings.[24]

George Washington had no interest in occupying land but in holding it and turning it over as real estate. The common folk looked at land differently. They shifted their fields and gardens around in it. They roved and hunted over it. They used all the resources they could gather into their households, from the trickling water lapped up by a cow to the mushrooms that grew in spring. To them, the landscape composed a breathing, mossy, muddy lattice. And though they surely speculated when they could and did not always treat the woods in their possession especially well—running too many head or cutting too much timber—their dependence on it made them environmental managers by default.

The homestead consisted of a tripartite ecological structure: wood, tillage, and garden. But it was never a static thing. Agrarian economy in the eighteenth century differed from that of the nineteenth century. The extent of woods, the degree of labor intensity on a given piece of land, the frequency of burning, the area of pasture, the supply of wild game—all these changed in time, forcing adaptation. One thing never changed, however. The agrarian economy of the mountains depended on the forest.

The backwoods culture was not founded on farming, but hunting. This single subsistence activity formed the core of a land-extensive, open-range materialism. Hunting yielded spectacular quantities of food for little exertion. But it also posed a problem. Nothing provided like the hunt, and yet nothing was as fragile. Animals migrated and their numbers fluctuated for ecological and other reasons. Too many hunters in the woods resulted in smaller and fewer creatures. Disruption in the supply of game prompted families to move on. But when moving on was not an option, a scarcity of game compelled households to fall back on farming. As a combined subsistence strategy, hunting, herding, and farming spread risk in the backwoods. But these practices, it should be clear, required an extensive landscape, unencumbered by private property.

The strategy of seeking the high elevations had its pull and push. Hunting pulled; slavery pushed. The members of makeshift households fled in advance of slavery, not because they loathed the idea of it or had any empathy for African-Americans. They escaped the economic pressure exerted by the cotton economy, especially the transformation of land into a commodity. Full-scale tobacco and cotton production spread along with the money invested in human chattel. Another reason might have had to do with diminished opportunity to earn wages. Planters had no reason to hire when they had a captive labor force. "Far more whites moved from slave to free states than from free to slave states," writes Allan Kulikoff. "Because cotton production so thoroughly focused the migration paths of slaves, whites who moved west from the old South often found themselves in virtually free societies."[25]

Like agrarians everywhere, the first backwoods settlers used swidden, burning and planting in spatial rotation through the ecological base. The method is known by many other names, like *forest fallow, burnbeating*, and *shifting cultivation*. Agriculture transfers fertile nutrients from soils to plants to people. There is a constant limiting factor of production, whether nitrogen or phosphorus, below which production is inefficient or plants won't grow. The purpose of forest fallow is to use forest dynamics to replace nutrients by allowing trees to regenerate before again releasing their stored-up elements with fire. The American practice might have come from Delaware Indians. But the anthropologists Terry Jordan and Matti Kaups believe that Finns and Swedes brought their burnbeating method and that American swiddens (clearings) probably looked like those of northern Europe. Settlers burned in two stages: first the understory and small trees, then the larger ones after they fell. After planting for a number of years, they cleared another area while the old one grew up in bramble and young trees.[26]

The author of a popular handbook for settlement described turning trees into grass. The farmer begins by removing brush under the size of an arm—the laurel, sumac, and sassafras—and then throws hay on the ground in the fall and winter so the cattle will scatter the hayseed. "In early spring all the timber not wanted for fencing and other purposes, is cut down for browse, and permitted to lie as it falls for a few years, until the limbs are rotten or tramped down by the grazing stock, when fire is set to the trunks in seasons of leisure, and the last snag is reduced to ashes." Another method was to girdle the trees by cutting a band around the trunk. After the canopies died, the trees could be burned or planting could begin amid the standing skeletons, as long as sunlight reached the forest floor. Forest and farm formed a whole, a revolving, shifting landscape of uses. Remove the forest from the seasonal cycle and the agrarian economy no longer makes sense. It turns into something else.[27]

By the time John Lorain encountered mountain farmers, around 1820, he saw them removing deadened branches and logs and burning them in a pile. This method kept the fire under control, so it was better adapted to closer neighbors and snake-rail fences. Lorain saw them shifting, too. Right after they had finished clearing one stand, they girdled and cut the next. He saw their land overworked and hard-run, "so much exhausted that cockle, cheat, and other weeds form by far the principal part of his crops." But Lorain wrote thirty years after the Whiskey Rebellion. Swidden had already become a questionable strategy where a larger population made land to shift in more scarce.[28]

Burning created spaces for planting. We know little about how much land households claimed as their own or used in extensive and intensive systems. A range of two to four hundred acres seems to have been common on the border bracing western Pennsylvania and western Virginia, in the Monongahela Valley. Joseph Doddridge, whose family lived in that region, recalled that no one could claim more than four hundred acres. "Many of our first settlers seemed to regard this amount of the surface of the earth as the allotment of divine providence for one family, and believed that any attempt to get more would be sinful." This begins to point to the agroecological problem at the core of the Whiskey Tax.[29]

The largest and most labor-intensive spaces in the tripartite system were clearings for fields. A mountain farm did not consist mainly of fields. Someone who used, claimed, or owned an area of two hundred acres usually improved no more than around twenty. About half of all landowners maintained between one and ten cleared acres at any given time. And because the classification of improved land included pasture, the number of acres dedicated to corn and rye would have been substantially lower. Ninety percent of a typical farm in Springhill Township, Westmoreland County, remained in forest in 1783. But here is the crux of the numbers and the agroecological window they open. The extent of tillage a household could maintain was "expensive" in terms of the labor and time it demanded. We can only guess at how they organized the work of fields, but evidence from other places suggests that a group of five to seven people could have sown, weeded, and harvested eight to ten acres of grain. In other words, whatever they planted represented a significant investment, resulting in a commodity they would have prized and protected.[30]

Corn was the preeminent crop of the backcountry. The food it generates for the labor it demands is unlike that of any other plant. But highlanders also planted another domesticated grass, one known for its hardiness and versatility. They loved rye. Archaeological evidence for a domesticated cultivar of *Secale cereale* links it to Anatolia and Iran, where its wild relatives can still be found. By the Bronze Age, it had arrived in what is now Poland and the Czech Republic. It showed up on the frontiers of the Roman Empire, along the Rhine and the Danube, but rye was never given much respect. It seems to have been more of a tolerated weed than a major food crop. To the untutored rambler, it looks like wheat. Rye is the only other bread grain, though it does not work up to the same light texture as its close cousin. Settlers in hardscrabble places embraced it for the way it thrives in environments too cold, dry, acidic, sandy, or worn out for wheat. It can be planted later in the season and at higher altitudes. As a winter cover crop, it returns nitrogen to the soil when it is folded under in the spring. It requires less time and attention than wheat or corn and doesn't attract the same plethora of diseases. Rye survives in the crevices of the agrarian world, which made it ideal for the southern mountains.[31]

Highlanders in Pennsylvania did more than plant rye. They conducted it. They put it down for pasture, threw it to pigs as feed, and ate it themselves as porridge. Some planted a mixture of rye and wheat, producing flour known as *meslin*, which makes a heavy, dark bread. Others used it as a rough form of coffee. And just about everyone turned it into something else entirely. "All the back country of America is very favourable to the growth of rye," wrote the English traveler William Strickland. "This grain is entirely consumed in the distillation of whiskey, chiefly for the consumption of the Irish frontier-man." Converted into spirits, rye became nonperishable, densely valuable, and transportable.

Whiskey accelerated trade and exchange. A horse carried three or four bushels of grain, but it carried the equivalent of twenty bushels converted into liquor. In a world where most production fulfilled subsistence needs, whiskey connected agrarians to that second transactional realm, where distant commerce offered profit as the reward for entrepreneurial risk. Locally, it could be used to acquire every item of necessity and luxury. It paid the wages of workers and bought consumer goods. Anything that siphoned off its value threatened the entire economy of the backwoods. In effect, Washington, Hamilton, and Congress did not attach a duty to whiskey but to the ecological base. It was a hard enough policy that they attempted to remove some of the scarce value that came from the nexus of labor and the land. Even worse, they insisted that this scarce value take the form of something else that was scarce in the backcountry: money.[32]

NATION-STATES EXACT TAXES in the form of money, either coin or paper currency. Anything can serve as money as long as users agree that it makes the value of different commodities commensurable. Americans favored notes issued against gold or silver reserves, or they used metal itself. Yet little of either circulated in the southern mountains. "The situation in this Country at present is very alarming for the want of Money," complained a Pittsburgh merchant. "Very few in this Town can procure Money to go to market. And as to pay . . . a Debt it is out of the question." In 1798, a Kentucky congressman estimated the total circulating currency in the state at less than ten thousand dollars. The distance from banks was one reason, but another was that money wasn't necessary for most transactions. Regardless of the supply of money, however, the Whiskey Tax demanded that distillers lay their hands on it. The bluntness of this requirement is central to any materialist interpretation of the rebellion. It ignored the way people bought and sold things. Placing additional stress on money-earning commodities brought their production into question. The tax reverberated through stills and into the landscape.

Out of necessity, western people had an all-embracing view of money. A Pittsburgh storekeeper in 1786 accepted flour, whiskey, beef, pork, bacon, wheat, rye, oats, corn, ashes, candlewick, and tallow. Others traded for ginseng, snakeroot, skins and furs, and homespun linen. Everyone accepted gold and silver whenever it came around, regardless of whose head was stamped on it. By one estimate, fifty currencies circulated in and around Pittsburgh, including Spanish, French, English, and American. But notes issued against gold or silver reserves posed a problem. Every transaction began as a negotiation over their value. They traded at a higher discount the farther they traveled from the issuing institution. Did the South Carolina bank that printed its own bills have any gold?[33]

But just because money was scarce or absent did not mean that it played no part in exchanges. People held it in mind. We tend to misunderstand exchange in kind, also called *barter*. The monetary version of the theory of stages says that people barter before they adopt a representation of value. After money comes credit, followed by collateralized securities divided into thirty-year amortized bonds. But no anthropologist has yet found evidence for this supposed evolution. They have searched the world and the most ancient cultures but have never discovered "the land of barter." Writes the British anthropologist Caroline Humphrey, "No example of a barter economy, pure and simple, has ever been described, let alone the emergence from it of money; all available ethnography suggests that there never has been such a thing."[34]

To understand why, consider this definition from an English work of arithmetic published in 1789: "*Barter*, adjusts the *exchange* of one Commodity for another, so as neither Parties shall sustain Loss. *To know how much of one Quantity must be given for another*; find how much the given *Quantity* is *Worth*; and then, find what Quantity of the other, *this Sum* will purchase." A barter exchange does not result in profit because nothing is left over. Each quantity is adjusted to match the value of the other. This is the commodity circuit condensed into a single transaction (C→M→C), in which both parties end up with equal value in commodity form. But the second sentence is the one that matters. In order to barter, each party must first determine *the money value* of their goods. They come to the table with this worth in mind. Barter is an exchange of things measured in some currency without currency present.[35]

The reason that no one bartered "pure and simple" is that it isn't easy to do. My desire for your whiskey is likely far greater than your desire for my woolen sweaters. How much of one equals the other? We could go ahead and make the trade, but one of us is going to walk away feeling ripped off (you). People get angry when that happens, which is why that kind of trading is dangerous. But if each of us first converts our commodities into pounds or crowns or dollars, then we're not trading incommensurate things. We're trading the value of our labor as expressed in things and calculated in money.

The myth of barter assumes that people traded for use-value, but that makes no sense at all. The "double coincidence" so often hauled out to make barter seem stupid says that people meeting to trade must happen to need what each happens to have. This so-called problem runs close to depictions of the Savage State, in which isolated individuals roam around a foggy landscape bumping into each other accidentally. It denies the existence of communities of producers and divisions of labor. Most of all, the "double coincidence" says that no one in the murky past had the brains to buy stuff in order to resell it. In reality, anyone who buys one hundred pounds of anything has no personal use for it. He knows of a buyer in the next town. But if a barter exchange is not a comparison of use-values, then it has to be a comparison of exchange-values.

This is exactly what we find in the documents. Nimrod Warden kept an account book for a merchant house and farm in Hardy County, Virginia, in 1806. That January he bought 12 tuns of claret wine. (A tun is an English cask, a unit of liquid volume, not weight, that holds anywhere between 200 and 250 gallons. A hogshead [Hhd] is one-quarter of a tun.) Warden wrote, "Bartered with a north-county merchant 6 Hhds claret at £10 per Hhd for 40 pieces of linen cloth at 30s per piece." He recorded his cost as sixty pounds, the same sum that the north-county merchant paid him. The north-county merchant *did not swap cloth for wine*. He paid sixty pounds' worth of cloth for sixty pounds' worth of wine. If one quantity had a higher agreed-upon value than the other, a scratch in the account book rectified the credit or debit to be settled another time or folded into another transaction where the discrepancy would be absorbed. Parties to such an exchange walked away with a profit by tinkering with the ratio of value to quantity. But each had to accept the other's ratio in order for the trade to be completed.[36]

The "land of barter" doesn't exist, but economists won't let go of it for lack of evidence. By erasing money from exchanges where it has always existed virtually, the myth presents money as a yet-to-be-achieved evolutionary stage. By extension, it posits that people who use little money make fewer exchanges, the sign of an undeveloped division of labor. But the backcountry *churned with exchanges*. Western communities sponsored expeditions to carry furs, whiskey, and ginseng by flat-bottom boat to Philadelphia, to the Ohio River, to the Mississippi River Valley, and as far south as New Orleans. The sale of these goods purchased others, like iron, glass, salt, and spices. Settlers had tastes and preferences; they valued variety and novelty. A French observer in Kentucky around 1800 saw peddlers canoeing on the Ohio River with haberdashery on board. Merchants imported pewter and porcelain, delicate glassware and books. One woman bought cups and saucers, a pinch box, and a butter boat from a merchant in the Virginia backcountry.[37]

And yet, to political economists, if exchanges did not circulate money, they hadn't happened at all. Recall that money travels, it holds and transmits value far and wide. This is why political economists considered barter primitive. Hamilton had read James Steuart on the subject. (I found *Inquiry into the Principles of Political Oeconomy* in a list of the books in Hamilton's library.) Steuart was among the first to call barter a stage in the development of trade. Barter satisfied needs, he said; money satisfied wants. It proliferated production and consumption. "Before a guinea can travel from London to York, it may be the means of consuming a thousand times its value, and as much more, before it can return to London again. Every stop the guinea makes in its course, marks a want of desire to consume." A free-floating conduit of value could buy anything anywhere. It could also be acquired and stockpiled. It could also pay a tax.[38]

Hamilton could not have separated households from land, regardless of what he thought about enclosure. If he was going to liberate the value of commodities from the tight grip of backcountry households, he would have to do it another way. He knew that while most things people made stayed close to home, whiskey traveled and money returned. If the United States could skim off some of that money, it would skim off some of the value created by labor and land in the western counties. Doing that might force people to conduct other exchanges with money, and that would make more and more value accessible. This multiplication of trade would unify the United States into a national economy and fill the treasury.[39]

The Pittsburgh merchant who complained about the paucity of currency said something else: "a Debt it is out of the question." He meant that there wasn't enough currency flying around for people to pay debts with it. After all, debt has no limit. People can owe more money at a given time than all the money that will ever pass through their hands. For debt to be paid in currency, there needs to be a great deal of currency in circulation. A tax is a debt that must be paid in gold or banknotes. Anything that siphoned away what little money existed would have been deeply threatening. To demand it from people who didn't have it was unreasonable. To demand it from the production and exchange of the preeminent commodity in the backcountry was infuriating.

Hamilton argued that the tax would cost distillers a trivial sum—$1.50 a year for a family of six. Whatever the burden, he believed it could be passed on to consumers as part of the price. But he derived the annual cost by distributing whiskey consumption over the 4 million citizens of the United States. That assumed Pennsylvania whiskey was available everywhere and that all 4 million people (presumably including children and those held in slavery) could have bought it if they wanted it. None of this prevented him from asserting that the tax could not possibly lay a burden. Whiskey prices tell us otherwise. The tax made distilled spirits more expensive in Philadelphia, and that almost certainly affected demand.[40]

The cost of the tax, however, does not explain the rage over it. We will never know how smallholders felt about the power of local elites and whether or not *they* should have been taxed instead. But we do know the extent of the disparity. The richest people in Fayette County owned

50 percent of the wealth, while the poorest owned less than 1 percent. Visitors noticed the class system in the woods. One wrote in the 1790s, "Pennsylvania lands are now so rapidly rising in price, that within the last two years they have increased almost one-third." A Methodist missionary writing about western Virginia in 1788 said, "The people are, many of them, of the boldest cast of adventurers, and with some the decencies of civilized society are scarcely regarded," but he worried, "the great landholders who are industrious will soon show the effects of the aristocracy of wealth, by lording it over their poorer neighbours, and by securing to themselves all the offices of profit or honour." County leadership correlated almost perfectly with wealth.[41]

If the farmers, graziers, and distillers of the Pennsylvania backwoods in the 1790s had only Hamilton's tax to pay, they might not have risen up. One thing poorly understood about the Whiskey Rebellion is that property owners already paid local taxes. During the 1780s, 62 percent of the population owned property, either livestock, land, or both. Of these, 60 percent owned land and 40 percent owned horses, cattle, and sheep. (The other 38 percent of the total population owned no taxable property whatsoever—not even a horse. One man died with an estate consisting of little more than two coats, a hat, a pair of shoes, and a blanket.) Around 7,500 individuals paid county taxes. These same people recoiled at an unprecedented additional tax on a commodity that they relied on to furnish them with money.

Credit and debt added another stressor. Those who could afford to buy land often did not buy it outright. They borrowed from speculators and merchants. But with money always scarce and credit fluctuating and tightening, some households found themselves with obligations they could not meet. The political volatility of western Pennsylvania in the 1780s and 1790s came, at least in part, from a fear of foreclosure. From 1782 to 1792, 270 debtors faced imprisonment by the sheriff of Westmoreland County and 980 lost their property to repossession. Settlers or their children had come to a region known for its land abundance, only to end up as tenants or laborers with little if any property. Some owed rent to landlords. Others gave shares of their crops for the use of land. This is the entry into frontier poverty. Some households did not achieve sufficiency. This might not have described those who distilled whiskey, but it suggests that while the tax itself might not have been onerous as a dollar amount, it represented an incursion into intimate territory.[42]

Citizens in Westmoreland wrote their grievances before they strapped collectors to timber and coated them in tar. They petitioned against the bill in 1790, arguing that it took aim at a foundational practice. "In this new country, labourers are exceedingly scarce, and their hire excessively high and we find that liquor proves a necessary means of engaging their service." In other words, where people have universal access to land, no one is available or much willing to work for anyone else. Households exchanged work, of course, but in cases where someone had to be paid, whiskey was as good as gold. "For these reasons," they continued, "we have found it absolutely necessary to introduce a number of small distilleries into our settlements, and in every circle of twenty or thirty neighbours, one of these are generally erected . . . without any commercial views whatever. The proprietor thereof receives the grain (rye only) from the people, and returns the stipulated quantity of liquor." If making whiskey was like minting money, this currency appeared and disappeared; it was created and soon destroyed. It did not float around for very long, transmitting the value of labor. By defending themselves with these arguments, the people did not persuade Hamilton not to tax them. They convinced him that he was right all along.

The petitioners also reflected on rye in its different consumable forms. Stills turned it into whiskey like mills turned it into flour. "Why we should be made subject to a duty for drinking our grain more than eating it, seems a matter of astonishment to every reflecting mind." It's a nice turn of phrase. They meant to make the tax look arbitrary. Yet everyone knew that the government chose whiskey because it was not at all like flour. It was not a dietary necessity, lasted much longer in storage, and had a much higher exchange-value.[43]

Another delegation meeting at Pittsburgh on September 7, 1791, felt a deep foreboding that something had gone wrong in the young republic. "Having considered the laws of the late Congress, it is our opinion that in a very short time hasty strides have been made to all that is unjust and oppressive." They especially feared great fortunes that could influence power and "evade the Constitution." They had all sorts of worries, conspiracy theories, and complaints of corruption—all signs that they already felt disaffected from the Revolution. Coming to the point, the petitioners attacked the tax as "obnoxious to the feelings and interests of the people in general," as a fine on "a domestic manufacture," and as "insulting."

Then they said this: "*Resolved*, That there appears to be no substantial difference between a duty on what is manufactured from the produce of a country and the produce in its natural state . . . The excise on home-made spirituous liquors, affects particularly, the raising of grain, especially rye and there can be no solid reason for taxing it more than any other article of the growth of the United States." The way the Pennsylvanians looked at it, skimming part of the value from the finished product diminished the value of the raw material. Push the logic back another step, and the tax placed a duty on the field cut from the forest—the ecological base itself. All agrarians need land and labor to cost little or nothing and yet generate commodities that could be turned into money.

The importance of the two "accounts" comes clear here. If they did not depend on money, if they consumed here and bartered there, then not everything needed to be profitable in money terms. Stephen Gudeman explains it like this: "A house can use extra-marginal land to sustain itself and produce for the market because its expenditures are not accounted in the trading calculation: the home crop, raised with few monetary costs, is sold at a competitive price, because it receives a subsidy from the base." This was the magic of it, the beauty and genius of it. The things not accounted for allowed the commodity to be sold for a competitive price. But what if the base and all that came from it *were* accounted for? What if every input had a price? Agrarian products might not be profitable enough to justify making them. To monetize any part of the production of whiskey brought it into doubt.[44]

An early historian wrote of the sense of violation. It was "as if flour and bacon were to become agents in replenishing an exhausted treasury." This is why highlanders railed against the tax, declared it dead, and then resisted it with violence. This is why they blockaded the roads, digging craters in the turnpike so deep and so wide that nothing moved past them for weeks. Hamilton knew their limitations, but maybe he didn't know what he was doing. Or maybe he did.[45]

※

THE CONSTITUTION CREATED A GOVERNMENT, but the tax on distilled spirits attempted to forge a territorial republic. This brings us back to Hamilton's "map" of the United States. In a single sentence in *The Federalist*, No. 13, he asserted a stunning conception: "Civil power, properly organized and exerted, is capable of diffusing its force to a very great extent; and can, in a manner, reproduce itself in every part of a great empire by a judicious arrangement of subordinate institutions." With that he predicted the postal service, national parks, military bases, and the Federal Bureau of Investigation. The sentence is remarkable because with the exception of frontier forts no such institutions existed. "State sovereignty is fully, flatly, and evenly operative over each square centimetre of a legally demarcated territory," writes Benedict Anderson, and this also describes Hamilton's imagined community. What James Scott writes about another place and time applies just as well to the secretary of the Treasury. He sought nothing less than "a fully governed, fiscally fertile zone . . . the complete elimination of non-state spaces."[46]

A writer can reveal much more than he intends in a word. Hamilton did that with *empire*. It comes from the Latin *imperium*, or "all-encompassing territorial power." Any Atlantic elite would have had in mind the British Empire, the Roman Empire, and Napoleon Bonaparte's empire. But in a more quotidian sense, the word described a group of states or peoples united and ruled by a sovereign government. Hamilton used the word in the very first paragraph of the first article in *The Federalist* to argue that an American empire divided into states without a powerful central administration wouldn't be an empire at all. It would be vulnerable to domestic conflict and foreign attack.

For Hamilton, the Constitution had been anointed absolute ruler over an assortment of preexisting political entities, like New England towns, the Iroquois Confederacy (and perhaps fifty other indigenous territorial groups), the thirteen states, the Northwest Territory, and the residents of settlements in the mountains and on the lands claimed by Virginia and Georgia that extended into the West. Each had its own claims to autonomy from the full authority of the empire. He considered them all subject to the same law, although only certain people could vote, others were nonvoting citizens, and the rest had no political representation. Roads would connect them; a bank would mint their currency; and an army would patrol the frontier and enlist them as soldiers. Perhaps most of all, the secretary envisioned a liberal empire that bound citizens in a single division of labor, in which they would yield up a portion of the value they created in the form of taxes.[47]

It is easy to assume that every white male holder of property from Cape Hatteras to the Ohio River had the same idea of what independence meant. In a sense, backwoods settlers fought a different revolution than Hamilton did, a difference masked by a shared rhetoric and a common enemy. Hamilton assumed that the Revolution had secured the independence of the United States, but he confronted backcountry citizens who believed that they had fought for *their own independence*. Every revolution is based on a working misunderstanding. Just so, the Revolution turned inward under the Federalists, attacking political dissent in the cities and the autonomy of the backcountry. In Peter Onuf's words, "American revolutionaries were thus compelled to develop a counterrevolutionary argument against the independence of frontier regions." As far as Hamilton was concerned, citizens might be sovereign in the sense that they owned their persons and property within natural rights that no lawful government could deny them, but they were not independent. Those who argued otherwise he called "dangerous to the very being of government."[48]

For their part, highlanders privileged survival and reproduction over conformity to abstractions like the national exigency. Every household in the mountains, yeoman or squatter, came into its subsistence and commodities at great cost in exertion and hardship. They expected institutions to acknowledge this fact, not coerce them into exceeding their natural limits. And where speculators took up vast tracts of land, whiskey making was a rational response to diminishing opportunities for a freehold. Agrarians often increase their manufacturing of craft and trade goods as available land declines. In this sense, the Whiskey Rebellion was the response of those who held to this moral economy against the claims of the liberal empire.[49]

Whatever sympathy Hamilton once expressed for those who used money whenever it happened to fall into their hands had vanished by 1792. By then, he had flipped the position he outlined in *The Federalist*. He would no longer wait for farmers and distillers to evolve into money-using, tax-paying, fully commercial citizens. Writing to Washington, he clenched his teeth. "Moderation enough has been shown; it is time to assume a different tone." He would wield the excise as a spur to compel the backcountry into getting money. *By insisting on the tax, Hamilton insisted on the means of paying it.*[50]

Hamilton saw the West as backward; it needed a heave into the next stage. He would have agreed with Benjamin Rush of Philadelphia. Not only did the unruly settler of the western counties refuse to "surrender up a single natural right for all the benefits of government," he "by no means extracts all from the earth, which it is capable of giving." Extracting all the earth could give signified production for wealth rather than subsistence. It is inconceivable that Hamilton thought differently, but he made just one comment. In a report to Washington, he attributed backcountry resistance to an "indisposition, too general in that quarter, to share in the common burthens of the community." For Hamilton, the burden of the community was always financial, so he likely meant that highlanders resisted turning their product into money, with which they would contribute their share of the national revenue. One way or another, he said further, "the resources of the community, in their full extent, will be brought into activity for the benefit of the Union."[51]

We find another clue that Hamilton saw westerners as backward in his thinking about agriculture. He used the language of capital. When the protestors complained that a tax on anything made from the product of land was a tax on land itself, Hamilton threw their argument back at them. Obviously! "Taxes are laid upon *land* as the *fund* out of which the *income* of the proprietor is drawn; or, in other words, *on account of its produce*." But no one who broadcast rye in stumpy swiddens thought in terms of capital and interest. They consumed all or most of the value they created and spent all the money that came to them. But Hamilton assumed money, not subsistence, as the true product of land. It follows that he considered agriculture an investment like any other. As he concluded in his *Report on Manufactures* (1791), "The rent of the landlord and the profit of the farmer are therefore nothing more than the *ordinary profits of two* capitals belonging to *two* different persons, and united in the cultivation of a farm." Here is the dissonance between economic cultures, the essence of the rebellion. In Hamilton's world, the evolution of society meant that the ecological base would cease to sustain households with the food it generated. Instead, it would generate money. It would be cleared and cultivated for full-time commodity production.[52]

Taxation transmits power. It makes people behave in specific ways. It's not merely a source of revenue. After all, if a government wants gold for equipping armies or building roads, it can mine it, hoard it, and store it. Why strike metal or print notes, circulate them, and then demand them back? Like centralized money itself, with its images of patriots and its symbols of prosperity, taxes combine State and Market. The combination seems to say that when we use these symbols to represent the value we create and when we pay taxes out of our fund of labor, *we become citizens.*

A century later and an ocean away, French colonizers imposed a head tax on every household in Madagascar. They actually called it an "education tax," because it instructed the uninitiated in the civilizing process of earning money. Malagasy farmers learned that the colonial state would torment them if they did not pay up. So they sold rice to come up with the needed cash. But the glut of rice that resulted drove prices downward, forcing them to sell too much, leaving them with too little to eat. That compelled them to buy rice on credit. Debt, in turn, compelled them to plant market crops like coffee and pineapple. To make up for their shortfalls, they sent their children to earn wages on plantations. Some of the money paid for consumer goods and luxuries, creating a circuit of debt, wages, and consumption that fundamentally changed Malagasy culture. The colonizers declared their lesson a success.

Most of all, from the vantage of the colonizers, by resulting in commodities shipped to France, the education tax tied the Malagasy people to the Empire. Frederick Lugard, first governor general of the Colony and

Protectorate of Nigeria, expounded on the method: "In a country so fertile as this, direct taxation is a moral benefit to the people by stimulating industry and production." The implication being that Nigerians produced all the food they needed from their own reserves without working for "industry and production," which the colonizers measured in money. Lugard completed the circuit by demanding back the currency that Nigerians earned. The tax "must be collected in cash wherever possible . . . The tax thus promotes the circulation of currency with its attendant benefits to trade." But this kind of debt can never be repaid. We service it without ever diminishing the principal. We are bound in this relationship and default at great personal risk. Taxation does not merely fund the state. It creates its territorial and financial power.[53]

Hamilton did not behave just like a colonial governor of a century later. I do not contend that his *only* purpose was to coerce the backcountry into increasingly monetized circuits of production and exchange. But think of the Whiskey Tax as an education tax and it makes more sense. There is at least one bit of evidence that Hamilton thought about it in exactly this way. It's in a letter he wrote to the financier and speculator Robert Morris, which he might have titled "In Praise of Debt." It's well known that Hamilton favored a national debt (which he described to Morris as "a national blessing") because he expected that the credit earned by paying it off would attract investment and advance the good name of the United States. He also wrote that a national debt served a social purpose by creating the necessity of taxation, calling this a "powerful cement of our union," a "spur to industry." All citizens needed to work, their individual debts forming slices of the great national debt that united their efforts. "We labour less now than any civilized nation of Europe, and a habit of labour in the people is as essential to the health and vigor of their minds and bodies as it is conducive to the welfare of the State." No political economist or colonial governor would have disagreed. They all believed that nations form when citizens assume a collective debt and work together like bees in a hive to pay it down.[54]

But the compulsion of taxation was not Hamilton's only tool. In the middle of the controversy, the secretary's protégé came up with an audacious development project. Tench Coxe had been a merchant during the

Revolution and an advocate of industrial policy. As assistant secretary of the Treasury, he invented a commercial town from out of nothing. It would be propitiously located between two rivers, the West Branch and the Lower Susquehanna, a watershed comprising about one-third of the state of Pennsylvania. Pittsburgh already functioned as a market for the western counties. Commodities entering Coxe's hub would flow south by southeast, entering the Atlantic trade. In his published plan, he strolled down his imaginary Main Street, deciding what should go where: tanning yard, gristmill, bake house, steel furnace, soap and tallow shop, brewery, bleach yard, wheelwright, potash works. This eighteenth-century version of Brasilia would be as *the bottom of a great bag or sack, into the upper parts of which natural and agricultural produce is poured.* The implications for the subsequent history of Appalachia are worth considering. Hamilton and Coxe realized that the monetary dependency they sought could be created by other means. Markets do create opportunities for making money. They do encourage people to sell more of the product of their labor. Coxe predicted the Appalachian Regional Commission of the 1960s by suggesting that infrastructure and social engineering promised to end what he saw as the savage isolation of the mountains.[55]

And yet, Hamilton had another option, one that he must have known about all along. The United States could use the army to distribute money in the backcountry. When soldiers spent their pay, they infused the economy with new currency. Hamilton claimed, "More money has in the course of the last year been sent into the western country from the Treasury, in specie & Bank bills . . . than the whole amount of the tax in the four western counties of Pennsylvania and the district of Kentucky is likely to equal in four or five years . . . Hence the government itself furnishes and in all probability will continue to furnish the means of paying its own demands." In other words, the secretary printed notes, circulated them, and then wanted them back. The irony is that a military invasion intended to enforce the tax made all debts easier to pay, even though the United States never tried to collect the tax again. Hamilton did not live to see the more frequent exchanges in money that he desired or the wayward mountains become fiscally productive governable space. But in the 1790s, he expected that bank bills would stitch up a far-flung republic, instilling the whole in each of its parts.[56]

※

WORD OF THE ARMY'S ARRIVAL caused the insurgents to dissipate like road dust. Hamilton found no one to fight. It isn't known who killed an innkeeper and a small boy, but these outrages added murder to the highlanders' grievances against the government. During the night of November 13, troops seized men from their beds and marched them barefoot through the cold to Pittsburgh. Soldiers penned the suspects without food or heat for two days while Hamilton interrogated them. One of the detainees died. None provided information. Yet the secretary came up with a short list of offenders, leading to ten arrests. Even when juries in Philadelphia found that the defendants had assaulted government officials, they did not convict on grounds of treason or any other crime, except in two cases. Washington pardoned them both.[57]

Looked at one way, victory belonged to the highlanders. The tax not only turned the backcountry against the Federalists, it contributed to the "revolution" that brought Thomas Jefferson and the Republicans to power in 1800. Jefferson oversaw the repeal of the Whiskey Tax, an action that appeared to nullify the entire idea of an excise on domestic production. From the end of the Rebellion through the end of the Civil War, the federal government made no attempt to impose an internal tax.[58]

But victory did not protect the backcountry folk from all the things that pressed against their household economies like snow piled heavy on a roof. No trend broke their way. Absentee ownership continued to reduce the area available for makeshift economy. Fleeing debt, tenancy, and diminished opportunity, many of the first settlers moved on to avoid these troubles, but they ran up against a barrier. At the very moment that the Rebellion flared, the United States escalated its war with the Miami, Shawnee, and Delaware in the Ohio Valley. Little Turtle's confederacy of northwestern nations skirmished with settlers and destroyed two armies, one in 1790 and the other in 1791. In the second battle, a militia under Arthur St. Clair lost 623 soldiers out of a force of 1,400, or 44 percent. (A retreating soldier carved a tree with the words "This is the road to hell.") In response, the United States assembled a force of 5,000 commanded by Anthony Wayne to destroy the Indian army. The battle took place at Fallen Timbers in 1794, the year of the Rebellion. The point is that during the entire period of conflict over the Whiskey Tax, the Ohio Valley boiled in violence, contributing to a sense of crisis. Those wanting to escape Hamilton's excise might have felt hemmed in.

For all these reasons, the Rebellion was a threshold response. Things piled up. They had to endure tenancy and debt to a western landed elite; a lack of currency and various demands on what little money households accumulated; population pressure that eroded the possibility of small-holder competency; and Indian wars to the west. To these the United States added an excise tax. The agrarians of western Pennsylvania clung to whiskey as the stronghold of their households, an irreplaceable source of stable value, a currency they freely minted. Whiskey held up both sides of their economic existence—autonomy and engagement, subsistence and consumption, community and market. They resisted the tax to preserve its function.

We should not look for simple conclusions in Hamilton's loss. No one in the 1790s would have seen the outcome of the Rebellion as a momentary pause in the inexorable victory of capital and the state over agrarian sufficiency. The dominion of landowners over the backwoods might seem formidable. Many of them were politically powerful. But even when they confronted squatters, few succeeded in ejecting them like Washington did. When households wrote their own deeds and hunted freely, they made a mockery of the absentees. The tax and its uncompromising enforcer joined a continuum of earlier colonial policy that attempted to bring the mountains into the fold of centralized administration. Capturing some of the value created by rye meant getting in between backcountry people and their forest clearings. But Hamilton had few tools for doing this, and he certainly had no interest in and no thought of cleaving them away from the environments they occupied. The industrialists who came after him by a century did just that. They sought to extract value from both, not by compelling people to sell homegrown commodities but by enclosing the landscape and inducing them to sell their labor. During the coming decades, a more potent form of legal and political power expanded from its Atlantic core into the mountain periphery and turned the pioneers into paupers.

4. Mountaineers Are Always Free

ON LOSING LAND AND LIVELIHOOD

> When the pressure of a system is great and is increasing, it matters
> to find a breathing-space, a fortunate distance, from the immediate
> and visible controls. What was drastically reduced, by enclosures,
> was just such a breathing-space, a marginal day-to-day independence,
> for many thousands of people . . . The many miles of new fences and
> walls, the new paper rights, were the formal declaration of where
> the power now lay.
>
> —Raymond Williams, *The Country and the City* (1973)

MOUNTAINS FEND OFF CENTRALIZED AUTHORITY. Roads exist seasonally, washed out by rivers and creeks. Nothing moves in a straight line. Time slows down. Twenty years before Alexander Hamilton's climb into the western counties of Pennsylvania, the English scholar and critic Samuel Johnson took a trip to the Hebrides, the western islands of Scotland. There he posited that elevation determined a people's loyalty to their monarch. He said that highlanders lived in savage freedom, "ignorantly proud and habitually violent," high and away from civilizing influences, where "every new ridge is a new fortress." These states within states were "so remote from the seat of government, and so difficult of access, that they are very little under the influence of the sovereign." Johnson measured mountain wars not in years but generations.

"As mountains are long before they are conquered, they are likewise long before they are civilized."[1]

Representatives of the same sovereign dreaded the American highlands. In 1756, Major Andrew Lewis took a force up the Big Sandy River to attack Shawnee positions along the Ohio River. He found no good path to follow and no animals to hunt. The soldiers starved and threatened mutiny before deserting. One described an interminable labyrinth of sharp inclines "which closed in on both sides," offering no place to ride or camp. But Major Lewis was just passing through; he had no intention of invading any portion of western Virginia. Though a number of battles and limited expeditions pierced northern Appalachia in the eighteenth century, no army attempted anything like an occupation until the Civil War. No campaign previous to that compared in its complexity or lasting effects.[2]

The Civil War in the mountains differed from nineteenth-century warfare as we usually think of it. Famous generals did not often meet on battlefields commanding ranks of uniformed soldiers. Instead, guerrilla forces along the border between Unionist Kentucky and Confederate Tennessee engaged in violence hideous for its intimacy. Each side raided and ambushed the other in familiar forest, exchanging murder, arson, and rape. The Union high command pursued more than one tactical objective in the battles of Harpers Ferry, Cheat Mountain, Chattanooga, Fort Sanders, and Blountville. But without question they wanted control of the Shenandoah Valley, source of the Confederacy's food supply. General Ulysses S. Grant ordered General Philip Sheridan to seize it and torch it. "Do all the damage to railroads and crops you can," Grant wrote to Sheridan. "Carry off stock of all descriptions, and negroes, so as to prevent further planting. If the war is to last another year, we want the Shenandoah Valley to remain a barren waste." During the Valley Campaign of 1864, Sheridan's army burned thousands of barns and mills. This is where he learned subsistence warfare, a method he used again a decade later when he recommended the slaughter of bison during the rebellion of the Plains Sioux.[3]

Sheridan's Army of the Shenandoah didn't conquer the mountains, and some said that was impossible. A Kentucky reverend predicted that a victorious Confederacy would never govern such an empire. "It is a region of 300,000 square miles, trenching upon eight or nine slave States . . . trenching upon at least five cotton States." Ruling over so varied a region seemed preposterous. And yet, we can mark the beginning of the industrial takeover of Appalachia to the Civil War. The damage Sheridan inflicted on the Shenandoah lingered for decades, contributing to a weakened economy that made the entire region more vulnerable to a different kind of invasion in the decades that followed. And that invasion didn't really begin with the industrialists themselves or with their lawyers or even with the absentee landowners. It began with the gathering of geographical and geological information before and especially during the war.[4]

The mineral form of fossilized carbon attracted little attention before the war. Residents of New England were more likely to burn a hydrocarbon rendered from whale blubber than anything that came out of the ground. The first factories in the United States didn't burn anything. At Lowell, Massachusetts, giant mills operated thousands of spindles, turning out tons of cotton cloth, powered by the Merrimack River. As a fuel for steam engines, coal radiated more energy than wood. But in 1838, only 1,850 stationary steam engines and 350 locomotives operated in the United States, and most of them burned wood. Petroleum looked to be more promising than coal. First discovered in western Pennsylvania in 1859, oil could be turned into kerosene, its first distilled form, used for lighting.[5]

Coal gained traction along with knowledge of its abundance. The geologist Richard Cowling Taylor published a work whose title indicates its breadth, *Statistics of Coal, The Geographical and Geological Distribution of Mineral Combustibles or Fossil Fuel, Including, also, Notices and Localities of the Various Mineral Bituminous Substances, Employed in Arts and Manufactures . . . From Official Reports of the Great Coal-Producing Countries, The Respective Amounts of Their Production, Consumption and Commercial Distribution in All Parts of the World, Together With Their Prices, Tariffs, Duties and International Regulations* (1848). Taylor acted more like a booster than a scientist. He helped his readers visualize the new energy frontier by depicting as much statistical information in cartographic form as was possible at the time. What the *Title Map of the Coal Field of the Great Kanawha Valley West Virginia* was to geography, Taylor's *Statistics of Coal* was to geology. It translated the earth into a commercial language, not for people who lived in the mountains but for those who didn't. It took a rich and varied landscape and simplified it to a single purpose.

Another turning point came when a Confederate cartographer noticed an outcropping along the eastern base of Flat Top Mountain in southwestern West Virginia. Jedediah Hotchkiss was born in New York and moved to the Shenandoah Valley during the 1840s, where he opened a school. He served the Confederacy by drawing maps for Stonewall Jackson and Robert E. Lee, including the battle plans for Antietam, Fredericksburg, and Gettysburg. Hotchkiss saw extraordinary deposits of coal close to the surface. He thought the location too rugged for a railroad, but he returned home convinced that Flat Top was one of the richest seams ever discovered.[6]

Many other people also noticed hydrocarbons all over the place. Just weeks after Lee's surrender, with snow still melting on the roads in the spring of 1865, an agent for the Department of Agriculture witnessed "an eager crowd of strangers, on horseback and on foot," treading their way through the narrow valleys, "watching for oil bubbles to rise to the surface on the margins of streams." Geological reports came one after another. Their conclusions sounded like this one: "The amount of coal in the Kanawha and its tributaries, Elk and Coal Rivers, is incredible. There is nothing equal to it anywhere." Their authors marveled at the abundance. Said another report, "The coal-beds *increase* in thickness and number *east* of the Big Sandy." One joint-stock company set the tone for the coming decades, declaring of West Virginia, "Her hills and valleys are full of wealth which only needs development to attract capitalists like a magnet." Full of wealth, they said, and empty; nothing but a vast, neglected "squatter's farm." During the decade following the war, Hotchkiss promoted Flat Top Mountain to anyone who would listen, including a group of Philadelphia capitalists who finally hired him to conduct a formal survey in 1873. Ten years later, they formed the Flat Top Coal Company. But this company and the state in which it operated were not extraordinary. Instead, they exemplify changes going on throughout the southern mountains in the nineteenth century.[7]

All of this is prologue to the scramble for Appalachia. An army could invade but never dominate the mountains. Capital moved differently. It acted through individuals and institutions. It employed impersonal laws and the language of progress. Mountain people knew how to soldier and hunt, to track an animal or an enemy through the woods. But few of them could organize against an act of the legislature or to stop a clear-cut. The scramble built upon these vulnerabilities, but it did not happen all at once. The first thing it required was a conversion in the ownership and uses of land. The vast holdings of the generation that acquired mountain real estate by grant and early purchase did not turn out to be profitable. Speculation offered one of the only ways of turning money into more money, but it contained a contradiction. Passive investment inhibits the kind of production that gives land greater value. The scramble brought the end of the era of the backwoods monopolist. This amounted to a new kind of invasion, one that mountain people could not easily resist.[8]

Another way of saying this is that Alexander Hamilton and the monopolists performed Act One in the drama of extracting value from the mountains: taxation and speculation. A new generation of capitalists performed Act Two: full-scale industrialization. The timeline worked this way: Land purchases to gain hold of resources began as early as the 1840s and intensified after 1865. The state of West Virginia was founded in 1863. Its governors, legislators, and members of Congress all acted to attract industry. Railroad lines extended across the state between the 1850s and 1870s, the Baltimore and Ohio in the north and the Chesapeake and Ohio in the south. By 1880, close to 56,500 stationary steam engines operated in the United States, all of them needing coal.

But mining was not the only or even the primary form of extraction. Felling the forest affected a much larger area. A great many counties had no coal. All of them had trees. Commercial logging began in the 1870s, but the two industries functioned simultaneously, often undertaken by the same companies, dependent on the same railroad infrastructure, and employing the same workers. For as profoundly transformative as coal mining proved to be, it would have left most households in place. Clear-cutting the woods changed everything.[9]

And yet, mountaineer makeshift was fading for its own reasons. The arrival of corporations with designs on the minerals underlying fields of rye and glades of glistening spring ramps coincided with a faltering agrarian economy. Even before the onslaught began, a rising population pinched the extent and robustness of the commons. Everything happened at once. Declining returns from subsistence and exchange made them vulnerable at the same time that capital shifted its modus operandi from passive speculation to active extraction. Coal companies moved to evict the plain folk at the same time that railroads created a mechanical conduit for dismantling the ecological base. But something else happened first, something that formed the political and legal framework necessary to everything that followed: the founding of West Virginia.

⁕

THE VIRGINIA ABOVE ONE THOUSAND FEET declared its independence from the Virginia below. In his inaugural address, Arthur I. Boreman, the first governor, gave a lecture in political ecology. "West Virginia should long since have had a separate State existence. The East has always looked upon that portion of the State west of the mountains, as a sort of outside appendage—a territory in a state of pupilage." He explained, "The rivers rise in the mountains and run towards the Northwest," resulting in two peoples with "little intercourse between them, either social or commercial." He was right. The parallel watersheds of the Blue Ridge and the Shenandoah Valley separate west from east, and the rivers of the Plateau point trade and communication toward Ohio. The two provinces developed different forms of agriculture and were settled by different families.

Slavery also differed on either side of the Blue Ridge. In the oft-told tale about West Virginia's founding, slaveholding and plantations had no foothold. Freedom-loving mountaineers hated the practice, and this gave them different interests from the cotton planters down country. The topography made great plantations impossible anyway. In order to escape the dominance of planters, their influence bloated by the Constitution's "three-fifths" clause, the mountaineers broke away in 1863. They expressed their audaciousness in a motto, *Montani semper liberi*.[10]

What is true about the oft-told tale is exaggerated. Eighteen percent of Appalachian households owned slaves the year the Civil War began, compared to about 30 percent for the entire South. The Virginia counties that eventually composed the state of West Virginia included the fewest number of African-Americans in the region. Around 6 percent of households in these counties owned at least one person in 1860. But the major slave owners were also major landowners and significant capitalists. They financed the salt and iron mines and other early examples of extractive industry. Some of them moved into commercial cattle production. William Dickerson, the richest planter in West Virginia, owned one hundred slaves. He harvested 2,500 bushels of corn a year and ran 117 head of livestock on his plantation in Kanawha County. It's true that the majority of households in the mountain counties owned no slaves, but that fact explains almost nothing about the origins of West Virginia.[11]

The friction between Virginia's western counties and its planter class had more to do with speculation in land than with slavery. Recall that wilderness grantees owned almost all the arable land west of the Blue Ridge. But speculation is a subtle sport. On one hand, the grantees awaited an increase in value that would make all that inert real estate pay off. On the other hand, they conspired with their allies in the General Assembly to keep mountain counties politically disorganized and underdeveloped. They prevented any public money from flowing uphill as improvements because although roads and schools would have increased the value of land, they would have also caused higher property taxes. This behavior might seem self-defeating. But speculators understood that modest improvements would not have resulted in the boom they dreamed of. So even as population surged on the Plateau, Virginia's patrician class continued to regard the mountains as their private tax shelter.[12]

The commercial and political class of the western counties mostly lived in Wheeling. Its location in the panhandle wedged between Ohio and Pennsylvania gave its merchants closer ties to Pittsburgh than any place south or east of Morgantown. Cotton planters must have felt far distant to the people of Wheeling, and yet planters controlled the Commonwealth of Virginia, with designs on the industrial development of the western counties. Since the 1820s, planters had established foundries, forges, and ironworks, some operated by hundreds of slaves. Slaves mined salt and iron. In 1837, Virginia's General Assembly established a joint-stock company capitalized at $500,000 to explore 100,000 acres embracing the upland counties of Nicholas, Kanawha, and Braxton. The planters gazed upon unimaginable wealth in timber and coal. At some point, Wheeling's merchants decided that they wanted this frontier for themselves. They wanted authority over courts, tax collection, and the formation of joint-stock companies. Securing all that meant taking administrative control from the planter-dominated General Assembly. They had no hope of winning an electoral victory or of outnumbering the planters. They needed their own state.[13]

Virginia seceded from the United States in May 1861. Of the nearly fifty-four thousand residents of the western counties, 64 percent voted in a statewide referendum to remain in the Union. Their unwilling part in bringing on the Civil War and the important role Virginia played in the Confederate States of America (Richmond was its capital) drove them to launch a secession movement of their own. The founders of West Virginia included a miller, an industrialist, the owner of a coal mine and brickyard, several general merchants, a cattle dealer, lawyers, and a minister. They did not unanimously agree about the Confederacy or the role of West Virginia in the Civil War, but the northern tilt of their interests resulted in an application to Congress, which admitted the new state to the Union.

Yet the founding was more of a conspiracy than a mass movement. The panhandle voted in favor of the issue by 70 percent. But the middle tier voted it down by 70 percent. And the southernmost tier, consisting of one-third of the new state, including the counties with the richest coal deposits, didn't vote for it at all. The Wheeling merchants might have written off the plain folk as politically irrelevant. Or they might have known that many of them—perhaps a majority—would have voted to fight the Union rather than join it. (One correspondent, writing from Wheeling, said, "The whole country south and east of us is abandoned to the southern Confederacy.") It wasn't that mountaineers had no interest in politics, but the avenue of influence they most pursued led to the courthouse, not the statehouse. Even if word traveled to them through hundreds of valleys, residents of the southern counties tended to pay more attention to the welfare of those related to them, on whom they most relied.[14]

Subsistence societies have strong bonds within and between groups of related people. By themselves, households cannot endure all sorts of stressors and threats. In famine or violence—when lords, enemy tribes, or central governments threatened—survival required alliances, escape, and retrenchment. In the southern mountains of the nineteenth century, a kin group or clan consisted of linked households. These sprawling hierarchies included unrelated people united by proximity, common political interests, and financial dependency. Where few institutions existed for individual expression, family membership facilitated social and political life. That inspired loyalty and insularity. A patronage system emerged, in which one's influence in the county depended on one's well-placed relatives and allies. Certain offices bounced around among the members of certain groups. Two researchers explain it this way: "Personal ties and connections became the foundation on which public politics was transacted and antagonisms from economic life easily spilled over into public policies and governance." This also meant that if one clan endured humiliation or diminished influence due to the actions of another, a larger conflict might ensue.[15]

Feuding cannot be reduced to the political wounds of patronage. It erupted from disputes internal to communities. It had something to do with a culture of male honor within a vacuum of police authority. But it mostly had to do with the environmental and social changes going on in the mountains, the subject of this chapter. No matter the immediate or circumstantial reasons that they fought each other, families did so against a backdrop of declining opportunities for profit and the looming imperative of wage work. I will have more to say about feuding, including the one between the Hatfields and McCoys. For now, the point is that these conflicts should no longer be maligned as bloody acts of revenge over archaic bonds of kinship. They emerged from the changes taking place in the mountains, changes connected to the scramble for Appalachia and the founding of West Virginia. Yet it is also true that kin groups and households tended not to engage in state or national politics, and that left them vulnerable to be acted upon at a crucial moment.[16]

The founders of West Virginia had no interest in the democratic engagement of citizens. They wanted to wield without opposition all the power vested in governing institutions and offices. Liquidating the forests and mineral deposits depended on legally constituted authority. Governments claim dominion over economic activity within their borders. They decide what is permissible on private property. They can charter corporations, thus granting these organizations legal permission to do certain things in certain places. The legislature chartered 150 corporations in 1866 alone, including the Sand Hill and Mud Lick Oil Company, the Marrowbone Oil and Mining Company, the Great Kanawha Petroleum Coal and Lumber Company, and the Hartford Oil and Mining Company. Here we link back to where this book began, with the contradiction between capitalists drawing up maps of their anticipated domains and the occupants of that land. The *Title Map of the Coal Field of the Great Kanawha Valley* depicts this conflict in cartographic form, and it raises an extraordinary question: What made politicians and investors think that they could do whatever they wanted wherever they wanted?

The divide between the merchant-founders and the farmer-hunters resembles that between peasants and the political elite of developing countries today. Malian peasants, for example, don't need the nation-state in order to live, but then the government might proceed with its plans without regard to their interests. Officials perceive peasants as politically irrelevant because the latter more often act through village councils than bureaucratic ministries. (We will look more closely at a story from Mali in the last chapter.) In much the same way, the political leadership of West Virginia in the 1860s employed its power to charter corporations in order to sell off its resources, enriching the merchant elite with little communication with the people most affected by these deals. Had the leadership spoken honestly about it and on the record, they might have said that West Virginia would never join the industrializing world if it allowed its peasantry to stand in the way.

What if investors bought stock in a coal mine, amounting to millions of dollars, only to have it shut down or its gains taxed by a county or town? This is why corporations sought legal protection from local statutes. They also wanted to limit the number of their political clients, thus freeing them from the perplexing and unseemly task of placating every notable citizen. An obscure piece of jurisprudence allowed state legislatures to sanction corporate activities without gaining the consent of anyone whose life might be interrupted. It was called Dillon's Rule.[17]

The rule came from John Forrest Dillon. In 1868, as justice of the Iowa

Supreme Court, Dillon promulgated a diminished conception of local sovereignty: "Municipal corporations owe their origin to, and derive their powers and rights wholly from, the legislature. It breathes into them the breath of life, without which they cannot exist. As it creates, so may it destroy." The idea that a state could close down one of the towns within its borders sounds perfectly crazy, but Dillon said that municipalities existed as "the mere *tenants at will* of the legislature," regardless of the fact that towns in some parts of the country existed for a century before states formed around them. Dillon made these comments in a decision about whether a railroad had the right to lay tracks down a city street. The city objected. Judge Dillon averred that only a state could stop a railroad. The Supreme Court of the United States upheld Dillon's Rule in 1891.[18]

One effect of Dillon's Rule was to streamline access to natural resources. A corporation only needed to sway a governor or a fistful of legislators in order to condemn land, restructure tax laws, defeat striking workers, and otherwise extract where they pleased. Critics spoke up at the time, especially J. Allen Smith of the University of Washington. "The corporate interests engaged in the exploitation of municipal franchises are securely entrenched behind a series of constitutional and legal checks on the majority," Smith wrote in 1907. By shifting power over local environments from towns and counties to state governments, Dillon's Rule contributed to a new kind of powerlessness, one essential to the scramble for Appalachia.[19]

But industrialists didn't really need Dillon's Rule. A revised constitution seemed to clear the way for their greater influence. West Virginia Democrats never accepted Republican influence over the founding of the state. In 1872, they held a second convention to make an instrument of government more to their liking. The new version magnified the power of county judges, elevating them from legal adjudicators with significant authority to government administrators who performed almost every role. They superintended the police and approved all matters of county finance, including roads, bridges, and mills. The effect narrowed the number of influential officials and enhanced their power. To the extent that judges could be bought off or swayed toward corporate interests, the new constitution fed the scramble. The same document loosened laws of title, making purchases easier for investors.[20]

The scramble also required allies in Congress. One of the principal characters here was Johnson Camden. He was born in western Virginia and started his own oil company during the 1860s. When Standard Oil absorbed the Camden Consolidated Oil Company in 1875, Camden instantly became a major stockholder and John D. Rockefeller's representative in the Ohio Valley. Camden made sure that all the oil produced in West Virginia ended up in Standard's Baltimore refineries. He did even more for Rockefeller after 1881 when he was elected to the United States Senate. Senator Camden assembled a consortium of investors who funded a railroad along the Ohio River from Wheeling to Huntington that circumvented the sluggish barges that carried the oil of Standard's rivals. It only overstates things a little to say that Camden didn't represent West Virginia at all. He answered to just one constituent: John D. Rockefeller.[21]

Camden's friend and partner was Henry Davis, whose own empire consisted of the Potomac and Piedmont Coal and Railway Company and the Davis Coal and Coke Company, which he operated with his son-in-law, Stephen Elkins. Davis was elected to the United States Senate in 1871. For two years of his two terms, he and Camden composed West Virginia's senatorial delegation. They embodied astounding conflicts of interest, acting as lobbyists for their own companies while occupying positions that allowed them to direct law and policy. Elkins's career of graft and corruption began in New Mexico. There he was implicated in a scheme to evict settlers from the Maxwell Land Grant and transfer ownership to himself and other members of the Santa Fe Ring. Later, he served as secretary of war in the Benjamin Harrison administration. After that, he took his turn as U.S. senator from West Virginia. None of the three came to their positions in order to legislate for farmers or miners or any other citizens. Their careers remind us that it was not always outsiders who exploited the mountains but that corporations needed accomplices among a mountain-born elite.[22]

From all this, we might assume that the courts, too, acted for corporations in every instance. But they didn't, at least not before about 1890. West Virginia's second constitution bore a strong resemblance to Virginia's, and Virginia privileged its landholding classes. Planters wanted most political power to reside in the counties, and they wanted laws that protected their land in disputes with creditors. West Virginia inherited these principles, and the plain folk benefited. For about thirty years, judges often upheld mountain deeds. But this changed in a single year. In 1890, a judicial revolution brought a new generation of judges to the state supreme court. They reoriented the judiciary toward the interests of industry. For example, where Virginia judges routinely held railroads liable for the fires they caused and the cattle they killed, West Virginia judges forced plaintiffs to prove negligence. It was another step toward eliminating local control.[23]

One politician did his part to further this process. William MacCorkle did not own a coal company or work for one. He had roots in western Virginia and came up through the ranks of the Democratic Party. He was elected governor in 1892. The encroaching influence of industry at all levels of government must have disturbed him because he said this in his inaugural address:

> The State is rapidly passing under the control of large foreign and non-resident landowners. We welcome into our State the immigrant who comes to us with the idea of home seeking and home building with all its profits to the State, with its family ties, with its clearing of the forests, its building of churches and school houses . . . But the men who to-day are purchasing the immense areas of the most valuable lands in the State, are not citizens and have only purchased in order that they may carry to their distant homes in the North, the usufruct, of the lands of West Virginia, thus depleting the State of its wealth to build grandeur and splendor in other States. In a few years at the present rate of progress, we will occupy the same position of vassalage to the North and East that Ireland does to England, and to some extent, for the same reasons.

In the same speech, MacCorkle declared, "I am for the people and in favor of all legislation which will curb and restrain corporate influences from interfering with the right of the people." Long before terms like *internal colony* and *capitalist periphery*, the governor knew something about world-system theory. He knew workers and environments created capital in West

Virginia, though it accumulated in other places. And he clearly knew his words would appeal to members of the Farmers' Alliance, which had organizations in all but thirteen of fifty-four counties. Farmers feared falling prices, rising tenancy, and the high cost of short railroad hauls. They complained of poor roads and schools. So it's remarkable that during his four years as governor, William MacCorkle never mentioned home seekers or church builders or the usufruct of the land of West Virginia in any public statement ever again.[24]

Looking back from the 1920s, the aged MacCorkle distilled his term in office. "My administration was directed almost solely to this essential proposition," the "advertisement of the state to the great national constructive interests . . . advertisement and exploitation." Without irony or trepidation, he defined West Virginia's reason for being as providing capitalists with the cheapest resources, by the cheapest transportation, and (he might have added) with the cheapest labor. Perhaps no political leadership anywhere in the United States or the Atlantic World ever exposed its own people and environment to the same unbridled destruction and abuse.[25]

The confluence of money, private property, and political power accomplished what no invading army could have. It delivered an ax to the neck of the peasant economy within half a century. Demographic changes within mountain society, in motion years before the scramble began, also weakened the viability of makeshift. Dependency has more than one cause. Yet by 1900, if not before, the hunting, gathering, tilling, and herding households of West Virginia had lost the floorboards beneath their social existence. The same thing happened in western Pennsylvania, eastern Tennessee, and eastern Kentucky. But what exactly did they lose? The struggle broke up a lattice of ecological spaces that began and ended with the homeplace.[26]

THEIR MOUNTAIN FORTRESS did not protect the plain folk from the onslaught of extractive industry, but for a time their households did. A domestic mode of production can and often does thrive within a highly commercialized economy. By the early nineteenth century, mountain Appalachia had settled into a pattern of gardens, maize, and woods pasture.

The homeplace was, first of all, a house. Horizontal log construction traveled with the backwoods settlement culture from its hearth in the Delaware River Valley. While botanizing in the 1770s, William Bartram saw low-slung buildings made of tree trunks, "stripped of their bark, notched at their ends, fixed one upon another, and afterwards plastered well, both inside and out, with clay." A long sloping roofline allowed the addition of a covered porch for eating, drying laundry and meat, churning butter, hanging tools, relaxing, and playing. Grass and earth plugged the gaps between the logs, and chestnut bark made the roof. Many cabins consisted of just one room, with a plank floor and maybe a detached kitchen. A woman born and raised in such a house recalled "one big room . . . the kitchen and the living room and everything together." Two cabins placed side by side with a chimney on each end was a "double pen." An open passage between the two structures created a "dogtrot." Enclosing the passage around a central chimney made it a "saddlebag." Into the house and yard flowed all the products from garden, forest, and field.[27]

The most intimate clearing was the garden. Every homeplace had its own provision ground, a space as large as two acres given over to vegetables and fruits. Beans formed the mainstay: greasy cut shorts, half-runners, Kentucky wonders, Logan giants, and peanut beans, prepared by boiling for hours with cured pork. Mountain bean pods came in an assortment of shapes and sizes—mottled, spotted, shriveled at the ends, and fat seeded.[28] The people also harvested cushaw, a smooth winter squash that can grow to thirty inches and twenty pounds, using it as a starchy staple to make soups and breads. They bought and sold lots of things, but they kept the garden for themselves. For one thing, everyone grew the same plants. For another, paths to market were too distended and unreliable for transporting perishable foods. Residents in twenty-four West Virginia counties reported no annual income from their gardens in 1860, and only ten counties reported totals of $1,000 or more. Wyoming County's figure of $2,140 averages to $5.50 per farm. Statewide, household gardens earned households 56 cents each. Yet the garden, by itself, did not produce a livelihood.

Vine-strewn gardens anchored properties that stretched out over extensive areas. Cleared spaces—yards, gardens, and fields—often made up a small portion of the total. In 1860, almost half of all the households in Clay County, Kentucky, cultivated fewer than thirty acres as part of homesteads (in whatever legal status) of up to ten times that size, nearly the same proportion found in western Pennsylvania seventy years earlier. The key metric for understanding the agroecology of the mountains is the ratio of unimproved to improved land. In Upshur County, West Virginia, forested acres outnumbered cultivated two to one. Upshur was thoroughly cultivated compared to Webster County, bordering Upshur to the south, where the ratio stood at twenty to one. In Nicholas County, just south of Webster, it was forty to one.

We might think of a farm as consisting of fields of grain, with a couple of cows and a spate of woods in the background. But that's a particular kind of farm, one that takes its renewed soil fertility from manufactured fertilizers. That farm is geared entirely for commodity production. No farmer before the late nineteenth century thought of a farm as a house surrounded by fields. Every form of agriculture requires a subsidy from the ecological base. The subsidy takes the form of rainwater rich with silt flowing down the coastal plain to rice paddies on the Georgia coast, or it is salt grass in a tidal marsh that feeds cattle in Connecticut, or it is all the things that come from forests. Agrarians without much money but who wanted to buy things with money needed uncultivated spaces to carry much of the burden of commodity production.[29]

The garden's closest relation was not the cornfield but the woods. It might seem odd to compare the most and least intensively cultivated spaces, but both provided fresh green vegetables. With winter stores of dried beans and fruit preserves diminished and the first squashes months away, people bought what they could in town and exchanged with neighbors. The forest made up every shortfall. Households foraged for *uganost*, a Cherokee word for wild greens. They brought home *toothworth* (a horseradish-like root), corn salad (a sweet flower), and especially ramps.

Ramps have been known by more than one name. Bear onion, wild leek, and ramson all refer to either *Allium tricoccum* or *Allium ursinum*, known in both Europe and North America. Highlanders ate them in salads, in soups, and with eggs. (Cut into one-inch pieces and parboil. Fry bacon in a large iron skillet to just before it becomes crisp. Drain the ramps and place them in the hot bacon fat. Season with salt and pepper and fry. Serve with a sliced hard-boiled egg.) The common name derives from Old English, but it might (or might not) be related to the German *rampen* for a platform that connects two uneven surfaces. That would make sense. Ramps provided a subsistence bridge between spring and summer. They represented the role of the forest in providing direct subsistence in addition to commodities. They offered security by spreading risk. But it would be a mistake to think of foraged foods as meager provisions, eaten in desperation. They were a delicacy, a seasonal event, a cherished custom.[30]

The forest offered so much more than greens; it held a diversity of species comparable to Amazonia. Great Smoky Mountains National Park, in the Blue Ridge of North Carolina and Tennessee, might include 100,000 species. In 2009, researchers found 240 birds, 75 fishes, 65 mammals, 40 amphibians, and 40 reptiles. There are 2,700 species of fungus and 1,600 vascular plants. "A single Blue Ridge cove may rival all of Europe in the number of tree species it sustains . . . Acre for acre," writes one historian, "no other temperate region on earth can surpass the southern Blue Ridge in biological wealth." The Appalachian Plateau might not be quite as rich, but it fulfilled the same purpose. The forest did not serve as an attribute of the farm, as just a woodlot, but functioned as its very core.[31]

Between garden and forest came fields, usually planted in maize. As a summer crop, it could be sown after rye. Like rye, it could be used as cattle and hog feed and could be turned into mash for whiskey. But corn made up a larger part of the diet than rye. Mixed with wheat flour, it made bread. Fried in lard, it provided the essential starch at just about every meal. Combined with beans, it formed a complete protein. No other harvested commodity added value to wedding dowries. Most of all, it yielded about twenty bushels per acre, or one thousand pounds. That would have been unimpressive to any farmer in Nebraska at the time, but it was still two to three times the yield of wheat and rye and for only sixteen labor-days a year.[32]

These subsistence practices created an abundance of food. When Frederick Law Olmsted traveled through the highlands during the 1850s, he chatted up everyone he met, a good strategy for getting invited to supper.

Olmsted concluded what many others did: "Extreme poverty is rare in the mountains, but a smaller proportion of the people live in a style corresponding to that customary among what are called in New England 'forehanded folks,' than in any other part of the civilized world." By *forehanded* he meant prudently frugal, not impoverished. In 1882, even a visitor as unsympathetic as the anonymous author of "Poor White Trash" described plenty of food during a two-month stay in eastern Kentucky. "Every mile or so, a little log-cabin sits in a varied growth of beans, potatoes, maize, and tobacco." He saw squashes and melons, pawpaws and apple trees. The author joined a Sunday dinner, sitting elbow to elbow at a table wedged tightly between the front door and the bed. The meal began with a dozen watermelons before moving on to chicken, bacon, green maize, beans, potatoes, sweet potatoes, apple pudding, biscuits, and cake. People with control over a robust landscape work hard, but they don't go hungry.[33]

Makeshift economies also thrive on commodities for exchange. Trading this for that, with money or without, engages people in the wider world and brings novel things to the homeplace. For mountaineers, grains and vegetables usually did not serve as exchange commodities. Of the 7.8 million bushels of corn grown in West Virginia in 1860, little of it left the state or even the cabins where it originated. Something so bulky and commonplace didn't pay for transport. Instead, the most essential products south of Pennsylvania and west of the Blue Ridge were not plants but animals. Since the eighteenth century, visitors traversing winding roads witnessed the visible wealth of the mountains mooing and snorting their way to Lynchburg, Pittsburgh, Harrisburg, and other regional cattle markets. Herders moved in every direction that promised a sale. They migrated northwest to Ohio and west into the Bluegrass of Kentucky. In one account, recorded just after the Civil War, a visitor noted that "the people sell only those things which 'walk away'—meaning cattle, horses, swine, etc. In midsummer the farmers begin to gather their cattle for the drovers, who start usually about the first of September on their way to the Eastern markets."

According to the Census of 1870, livestock (including horses) accounted for 73 percent of all the exchange-value from agriculture in West Virginia. Animals slaughtered on the homeplace or sold for slaughter accounted for 20 percent of all the money farmers earned. But while livestock made up a larger portion of *relative* farm value than in nearly any other state, its *absolute* value was among the lowest. Annual profits from cattle averaged just $432 per farm, placing West Virginia twenty-ninth out of the thirty-seven states. If cattle were money on the hoof, the most valuable product, then why did farmers sell so few of them? Why did they rarely house them in barns or raise hay for them to eat?[34]

The answer circles us back to the patterns of peasant economies. International aid organizations and development agencies often cite low cash incomes as the measure of poverty around the world. (How many times have we heard that farmers here or there live on less than a dollar a day?) But money can be misleading. People who practice subsistence and exchange do not organize themselves for profit. They want money, but they cannot exceed their familial or ecological limits. So although they might have all the resources they need, if a cash income is the standard, they will fail the test of financial adequacy. Mountaineers loved money, not because they lived on it but because it bought them things that made life better, like dishes, dresses, candy, guns, toys, and tools. They didn't need it in order to eat, but without it they existed narrowly. One of the best proofs of this thinking is the near indifference they displayed toward the survival of their livestock.

In the mountains, cattle lived in the woods. Frederick Law Olmsted never saw a cow under shelter. Even in the heart of winter, "they are only fed occasionally, hay or corn being served out upon the ground, but this is not done daily, or as a regular thing, even by the better class of farmers." It was just as common for Olmsted to meet people who never fed their cattle at all, though they might find the animals dead in heaps from starvation or freezing when the snow melted. One author familiar with the practice confirmed that cattle "seldom have any sheds to run to, but are accustomed to 'rough it' under the lee of hills, or timber, as best they may." These hard-bitten animals not only had to survive the cold but also wolves and bears. Olmsted listened as neighbors in one North Carolina county tallied the pigs they had lost to predators during the previous two months. "It amounted to three hundred." By what logic did they allow their livestock to die of neglect? By the logic of the ecological base.[35]

Like other commodities that came from the base, free-range livestock sold for money without costing money. Domesticated animals lived from the general fund of matter available in the forest without making financial demands. But cattle-raising households lost nothing by allowing predators to feed at will. Farmers hedged against the uncertainty of money and markets. Keeping bears in business, so to speak, kept them on the menu just in case it ever became necessary to roast one on a spit. The base gave cattle or it gave bears. All that mattered was that it gave. As long as woods pasture provided something above a total loss, it raised enough animals to be converted into enough money to suit household needs. Paying scant attention brought forth commodities with little labor and nothing spent.[36]

If cattle raised on winter forage gave graziers something for nothing, they got what they paid for. The gaunt creatures that crept out of the icy woods sold for ten or fifteen dollars a head to feeding operations. The beasts needed to be fattened for weeks before final sale. Certain farmers in certain locations wanted a finer product and larger returns. They intensified the practices of feeding livestock, eventually becoming a highland entrepreneurial class.

As early as the 1780s, some farmers over the Blue Ridge began feeding corn to cattle. They invented the feedlot. The method originated in the region known as South Branch, in Hardy County, in what is now the northeastern portion of West Virginia. Young cattle spent the summer in woods pasture before being corralled into cornfields during the fall and winter. They ate the ears right off the stalk. A middling rancher might have run between twenty and thirty head. But making the transition from casual grazier to cattle merchant required specific advantages. A rancher needed land with secure title in order to remain in control of woods, deep river bottom for a steady supply of corn and hay, and close proximity to coal camps and market towns. Completing a circuit of capital, in which cattle could be turned into more land and more cattle, assumed that the price of beef followed the expansion of the industrial economy. Ranchers succeeded when they entered an escalator of demand, capturing a small but ever-greater share of the value generated by logging and mining.[37]

Lowland tourists had trouble recognizing the rich mountaineer. A writer and painter named Charles Lanman visited Tesnatee Gap in northern Georgia in 1848. He went looking for a famous hunter from those parts named Adam Vandever. Lanman found a small man about sixty years old with a "weasel face," gray eyes, and a long white beard, riding a mule named the Devil and Tom Walker. The writer treated the mountaineer with contempt. "I told him that the first portion of the mule's name was more applicable to himself than to the dumb beast." Vandever grinned a rack of broken teeth. Lanman liked to collect colorful hunting adventures, like one in which Vandever killed a bear with a knife in order to save his dogs. The writer walked away sure that the homely hunter owned little more than his horse and a gun. "He tills, with his own hand, the few acres of land which constitute his domain. His livestock consists of a mule and some half dozen of goats, together with a number of dogs."

Not according to the census. Either Lanman failed to notice a greater stock of wealth or chose not to mention it. A census enumerator visiting the Vandever place in 1849 recorded herds of livestock along with a diversity of products, including wheat, oats, rye, corn, peas, tobacco, honey, milk, butter, and fruit. By 1870, the same Adam P. Vandever owned eight hundred acres valued at seven hundred dollars, with combined taxable assets valued at twice that amount. Other visitors wrote with amazement about grizzled men living in smoky cabins, their half-naked children rolling around with the pigs, with estates larger than those of British lords. One known only as Uncle Billy held a deed to twelve hundred acres. He raised top-quality cattle and let out small parcels on shares. The author of *The Virginia Tourist* described Uncle Billy's farm as "a beautiful domain on a broad tableland, probably three thousand feet above the sea level." The author also noted that rich mountaineers lived in the same cabins as those of lesser means.[38]

William Zinn recalled growing up on a mountain farm during the Civil War where the family produced most everything they needed, roasting wheat for a coffee substitute, spinning flax for their own clothing. His father earned $650 a year on three hundred acres—not much but not bad either. Yet Zinn became more prosperous. He became an advocate of agricultural improvement, including keeping cattle in pens during winter and hauling their manure to meadows. During the 1920s, the family made $3,000 a year from potatoes alone—on one-third of the land his father cultivated. And yet, like Adam Vandever, Zinn's success did not change his family's desire for self-sufficiency. "I attribute largely what financial success we have had in life to the fact that we have produced on the farm almost our entire living." They still made their own brooms. They were unusual in another way as well: all the women in their household went to school and contributed to the management of the farm business.[39]

Adam Vandever, Uncle Billy, William Zinn, and also "Devil Anse" Hatfield (of whom more later) represented a highland entrepreneurial class. We get a larger view of them from the census. In 1870, West Virginia had 285 farms larger than five hundred acres, accounting for less than 1 percent of the nearly 40,000 farms in the state. Counties in the Shenandoah Valley included the highest number and the highest value of livestock. Harrison County, with 21 large farms, recorded $400,000 in cattle value. On the other side, the poorest 50 percent of counties included only 10 farms larger than five hundred acres. Of these, only five counties reported a livestock value greater than $100,000. McDowell County produced just $10,000 worth of cattle, hogs, and horses.[40]

Most households did not have the choice to intensify. They entered capitalist social relations as workers, not entrepreneurs. Mountaineers had long been part of the capitalist world by selling commodities into it, like whiskey, lumber, and cattle, without becoming subject to wages. "As a rule," writes the historian Robert Brenner, "the transition from pre-capitalist to capitalist property relations cannot occur as the intended result of the rationally self-interested actions of *individual* pre-capitalist economic actors, even given the appearance of new opportunities for exchange or new technologies or new demographic trends." Instead, for the majority of these families, the transition came about under four linked conditions: population pressure, the loss of the homeplace itself, ecological destruction, and the dwindling value of mountain commodities. Subsistence regimes die by a thousand cuts, and the wounds proliferated after 1860.[41]

The first cut came from within mountain society itself. The plain folk increased at a terrific rate, an indication that their practices and strategies succeeded. But subsistence economies are sensitive to population. More people require more cleared spaces for fields and gardens, more cattle browsing for forage, more ramps and mushrooms gathered in springtime. In the decade leading up to the Whiskey Rebellion, residents of western Pennsylvania shot up 61 percent in seven years, to 63,500 by 1790. The thickness of humans across the region, at about 19 per square mile, might not seem very impressive, but it likely rid the woods of large game animals. And since so much land was already in the hands of financiers, proliferating households competed for land to set down on. Those who decided not to risk an ejectment suit or who had lost one accepted tenancy.

Jump ahead about a century to 1880. Population on the Appalachian Plateau (including western Pennsylvania and most of West Virginia) had risen by 156 percent in the previous thirty years. The area that became West Virginia counted just 56,000 people in 1790, or 2.3 per square mile. There were 300,000 mountaineers in 1850 and 960,000 in 1900, or 40 per square mile. Though an increasing number of men went to work as miners and loggers, most households continued to live on a dwindling and crowded ecological base. Between 1870 and 1900, West Virginia added almost 115,770 farms, a 100 percent gain. In the same period, the total number of acres in farms expanded by 24 percent, while improved acres (gardens, fields, and cultivated meadows) gained almost 90 percent, or 3 million acres. All of this points to the fate of the average farm in West Virginia (including wooded and cultivated land), which shrank from 214 acres in 1870 to 103 in 1910, or by 52 percent. Behind all these changes was the rise in population, which forced downward the number of cleared acres per person from 34 to 21. These statistics, by themselves, do not establish that the landscape could not support the fecundity of the people. But in order for agrarians to thrive in such a situation, they have to change the way they do things.[42]

In the 1920s, a seventy-year-old man told a journalist of the changes he had seen since his father's time. "The farm I inherited was 225 acres, of which forty-five were in cultivation. Now it is occupied by ten families and 150 acres are in cultivation." That meant that each family ate from 15 acres, with only 75 remaining in forest. The journalist commented, "Year by year the axe clears the steeper slopes and the plow tears them open . . . Up a two mile 'branch' you may find twenty to thirty farms, becoming more Lilliputian as you mount to the head of the 'branch' where the valley has narrowed into a ravine." More and smaller farms, some on marginal land, along with the loss of a common range for grazing and hunting, posed unprecedented challenges. The absolute number of cleared acres fell along with the relative area available to support each person. But why should this have caused a crisis? Coal and lumber production caused the rise of towns and cities. Charleston went from 1,000 residents in 1850 to 11,000 in 1900. Ten years later it had doubled to 22,000. Townspeople should have provided a market for local farmers. There should have been more money around and greater demand.[43]

Agrarian people have a long history of adapting to population pressure, but for some reason adaptation didn't often happen in Appalachia. The relevant thinker here is Ester Boserup, a Danish economist who while working for the United Nations in Asia after the Second World War found conventional models inadequate to explain smallholder agriculture. Boserup rejected the conventional wisdom. She rejected technology and fossil fuels as the only possible pathways for increasing returns. Most of all, she rejected Thomas Robert Malthus and his unsubstantiated assertion that increasing numbers of people will always outstrip increases in food. Boserup revealed that whenever smallholders feel the stress of mouths against supplies, they spend more time in their gardens, apply more manure to their fields, and generally redouble their labor. "The reaction normally to be expected would be an increase of the average number of hours worked per year so as to offset the decline in return per man-hour."

Though Boserup didn't know of West Virginia in the nineteenth century, she explained what people there faced. Rapid population growth in an agrarian economy presents hard choices, she said. "The cultivators must be able to adapt themselves quickly to methods which are new to them, although they may have been used for millennia in other parts of the world, and—perhaps even more difficult—they must get accustomed, within a relatively short period, to regular, hard work instead of a more leisurely life with long periods of seasonal idleness." No Arcadia here. Adding to working hours yields more food but less time for leisure. It interrupts chatting with neighbors by imposing tasks like building terraces and hoeing into evening.[44]

But modest increases from longer hours should have been easy in Appalachia. What if a family had cleared fifteen acres, as in the above example? Let's take this farm out of West Virginia for a moment. Let's put a large garden and an orchard on five acres, with a small field of corn and space for chickens and pigs on another five. Then, we'll use the last five for meadow and wood. Assuming a neighborhood and town, and perhaps some off-farm income, fifteen could be enough for a family of five or six and within their capacity. Safe subsistence can be achieved on a third as much land—even less. Cash would come from berries, apples, and eggs, along with occasional wages and home industries. So why didn't this farm appear all over West Virginia after the Civil War? Why didn't this intensification take place? Why, instead, did Appalachia experience poverty and dependency?[45]

Mountaineers needed to think differently about how they did things as their condition rapidly worsened. But they approached the landscape with long-standing assumptions that they could not (or would not) adjust or abandon. It was not that they failed to understand what it meant to harvest more food from a limited space. Everyone who has ever kept a garden knows how. But extending an intensive system over their fields as well required a kind of knowledge they did not have at hand. Instead of continually clearing for new fields, they needed to restore the soil in those already planted. Doing that would have required them to build new structures and plant fodder crops. An intensive system called for them to internalize some of the functions that the forest had always provided, to reduce the subsidy they received from the wider landscape. While lowland farmers were busy modifying breeds and seeds over the previous half century, improving the biological component of farming at the same time that they experimented with new ways of restoring fertility, mountain people strove to keep on living as they always had.

There were exceptions. Some highlanders did change their ways of doing things and succeeded. Those who became ranchers made the transition from the come-and-go-easy method of raising cattle to one designed to produce profit. But not every grazier could become a rancher. It required good flat land. That fifteen-acre farm that I dreamed up would have been difficult to replicate in McDowell County. Sloping fields could not be intensified. They lost topsoil immediately, accelerating the need for shifting, even as farmers ran out of forest to clear. This meant their labor would not be recompensed with an adequate harvest, that they would work harder and harder just to stay in place.

The mountains seemed to close in on them. In 1916, the geographer

J. Russell Smith asked a man plowing in a hollow what he did when his corn showed signs of infertile soil.

> "I kin turn the field into grass a couple o' years."
> "Then will you put in corn again?"
> "Law, no; by that time hit will be so pore 'twouldn't raise a cuss-fight."
> "Then you must begin all over again with a new one?"
> "That's what we ben a-doin.'"

But where would he begin again? No higher altitudes awaited. Some might have left for the Plains to become small-scale commodity producers on arid quarter sections, but perhaps not many. Emigrating cost money and entailed risk. Men owed a debt here and a favor there or awaited the inheritance of land. The perceived lack of options further limited their view. Increasingly trapped in place by a web of private property and the disadvantages of topography, mountaineers had no way to make up their losses. Smith said that what might have been an agricultural Eden had become "a slum with a high death rate."[46]

J. Russell Smith was the Ester Boserup of his time. In spite of what he had seen, he believed that nothing made the demise of the mountain farm inevitable. The people simply needed new ways of doing things and credit that would allow them to make investments. But scientific institutions did not address their problems and credit remained almost nonexistent.[47] Smith responded to those who condemned the mountaineer as a savage. "He is doing the best he can . . . He should be taught better, and that is the task of the schools and of the great organizations that we have built up for the dissemination of agricultural knowledge. We have a Federal Department of Agriculture, many State departments, State colleges, State experiment stations . . . Can they not among them develop and teach a mountain agriculture that will make the mountaineer prosperous and leave him his mountain?" No one else asked that question.[48]

And yet, it is difficult to imagine a scenario in which the Appalachian Plateau could have thrived in the late nineteenth century. Between 1840 and 1880, almost every commodity raised there—corn, potatoes, cattle, and pigs—deteriorated in quantity and value. As the mountains diminished, the flatlands bounded. Ohio, Indiana, Illinois, Michigan, and Wisconsin had matched or surpassed the Plateau in every one of these products. During the 1880s, West Virginia farmers hauled in twenty-three bushels of corn per acre. Wisconsin farmers hauled in thirty. The prairie and Great Plains attained tremendous economies of scale compared to the mountains because their large, square, flat, and unobstructed fields were ideal for machinery.[49]

But it wasn't just the shape of the land that contributed to the rise of the Corn Belt. As Smith said, an unprecedented complex of institutions emerged to accelerate commodity production. Merchants and later banks offered credit, and though easy credit sometimes led to chronic indebtedness, agriculture is not possible without it. Farmers borrowed to expand the land they tilled, to buy a tool or machine, to start a cattle herd, and to build a house or barn. Merchants did offer credit to mountain farmers, often in the form of store accounts and promissory notes. But the potential of the borrower to make good on the loan was as thin as the soil running up the side of a hollow. The institutions that defined emergent industrial agriculture were not designed to function in a world of subsistence and barter.[50]

It might seem that agriculture in the southern mountains never had a chance. An agronomist might argue that no one ever should have plowed up the Plateau. Yet agrarians have flourished in all kinds of places. They've created durable cultures, lasting thousands of years, in the mountains of South America and around the Mediterranean Sea. The makeshift world of the southern mountains faded for its own internal reasons and because of the enormous aggression it faced. The struggles of mountaineers against narrowing options cannot be separated from their weakening hold on the homeplace. One set of families faced all these hardships. Before mining engineers and timber mills arrived, the Belchers and the Tottens began to lose control of their land, hollow by hollow, without an armed invasion or a shot fired.

⁂

FIFTY-THREE OF WEST VIRGINIA'S FIFTY-FIVE COUNTIES lie within the Appalachian coal-bearing region. But to say that the mineral exists in a certain location is not to say that it can be profitably mined. In 1902, only sixteen counties turned out at least 200,000 tons. Before a stock-issuing scheme could make the transition from a chartered pool of capital to an organization capable of blasting tunnels into the sweltering depths of the earth, it needed to acquire great stretches of the countryside in one of the advantageous counties. After that, it needed to remove anyone living there. Like British lords and their allies in Parliament, the managers of newly capitalized ventures deployed various tactics intended to pry agrarians out. And like the history of British enclosure circa 1680, the dispossession of the Appalachian peasantry circa 1880 is no simple story. It begins with how mountain folk held mountain land because that begins to explain how they lost it.[51]

In 1889, Thomas K. Totten wrote a deed in the form of a will. Totten wanted to ensure that his wife and five children would inherit his land and take from it "a good and peaceable life maintenance." He meant it literally. His will transmitted useful things, like kitchen furniture, two horses, two cows, two calves, eight hogs, and assorted blacksmith's tools. But while Totten wanted his family to remain on the homeplace, he stipulated that this land could be sold, "if the family ever became needy of anything." The same document revealed that Totten claimed more than thirteen hundred acres that he admitted he did not own. He anticipated that he or his family would gain title to it somehow, and he brazenly assumed that its eventual sale would pay his outstanding debts. The deed in the form of a will reveals the economic realms Totten attempted to hold together. He tended to his household with an agrarian's sense of makeshift practicality while making a gambit for gain elsewhere.[52]

Humans have organized the use of land many ways. Mostly, they have created regions for collective hunting, gathering, and cultivation and limited access to a band, tribe, village, or town. They justified their appropriation by their active use. Private property is different. It carries an exclusive right regardless of use. Governments that create private property often eliminate collective rights because the two are usually incommensurate. Mountain households in the nineteenth century tended to see land as fulfilling both roles. Some of it they held close, as homeplace, where they farmed and gardened. Other pieces they exchanged within families, to launch a young couple or to provide for an elderly relative. When they established ownership, they sometimes sold to speculators and corporations. But operating across the two transactional realms generated a contradiction. Subsistence livelihood cannot endure the widespread commodification of land. When every knob and hollow carries a price, young couples can't start out. Household reproduction can no longer continue outside of wage dependency. And when highlanders attempted to profit from the rising value of coal and timber by selling their land, they often ended up with too little in cash to buy a farm somewhere else.[53]

The mere act of selling land took on different meaning in western Virginia. Imagine a game with hundreds of rules but all sorts of exceptions. Every squatter making a bid for ownership and every absentee with a colonial deed navigated the most fraudulent, dysfunctional, and maddeningly complicated property regime in the United States. Virginia had no clear entry procedure and no standardized method of survey, leading to shingled boundaries and multiple grants of the same land to different people. Agrarians thrived when the legal crevices they could exploit were as deep and rich as the geographical ones they inhabited.[54]

The reason that so many of them lived with impunity on private land was that much of that land belonged to a handful of people, none of whom did anything with it. Whether settlers knew it or not, they had likely trespassed on one of the largest estates in the history of North America. Its first owner was Wilson Cary Nicholas, a Virginia Federalist who served as U.S. senator and governor of Virginia. Like George Washington, Nicholas didn't buy this domain. Virginia gave it to him. He likely owned 1 million acres by 1795, including almost the entire drainage of the Guyandotte River in what became McDowell County and the Flat Top Coalfield. A year later, he sold it to Robert Morris, the financier and signer of the Declaration of Independence. Morris already owned 500,000 acres in Virginia. His grants and purchases throughout the southern mountains likely summed to more than 8 million acres. Why did the legislators and governors of Virginia give all that land away?

They knew it had no value. Little of it could be planted in cotton or any other commodity crop. Granting made sense for more than one reason. The original thirteen states owned nothing but land, but they found no buyers. From the point of view of politicians and boosters, leaving it alone would have forfeited it to the Shawnee. It would have defined millions of acres as a dead asset, a wilderness liability. Turning all those hollows into profit-making space first required turning them into real estate. Legal property required owners to pay property taxes, ensuring at least some revenue. A tax burden, it was hoped, would encourage the grantees to kick-start the transformation of quiet woods into profit-making space. Virginia's leadership anticipated some form of development at some time in the future, even if they didn't know what that would be. But without a doubt, the tangle of watersheds would earn nothing if it remained the property of the state.

Yet while all that land made financiers important, it did not make them rich. Morris found out the hard way that they call it speculation for a reason: using land to store value is risky. Other capitalists invested in trade. New England merchants opened up communication with China at around the same time, accumulating the capital they would advance into manufacturing after 1815. But Morris, the would-be baron of the wilderness, couldn't squeeze enough money out of his fiefdom to pay his debts. He declared bankruptcy in 1798 and spent the next two and a half years in Philadelphia's Prune Street Jail. He died broke in 1806. Albert Gallatin, Thomas Jefferson's secretary of the Treasury, understood better than Morris that speculation kept land locked away from the only people who actually increased its worth—settlers. Gallatin also knew that the people he and Jefferson championed did not wait for legislators to act before they went where they pleased and took what they wanted.[55]

Morris lost a kingdom that he had never ruled. The swidden-and-cabin folk hunted deer, gathered ramps, and planted corn and beans as though the forest belonged to them. A variety of use-right customs continued under the awareness and without the knowledge of absentee owners. For about a century, households came and went in hollows that they used without paying anyone. Use without ownership triumphed over ownership without use. Squatter households eventually claimed to own land they had improved, establishing boundaries with neighbors as best they could. They wrote their own deeds or asked a literate relative to do it for them. Often they filed these deeds at the county courthouse, but not always. Sometimes they paid taxes on land owned by absentees as a way to establish a claim to it, but not always. All deeds were written in the language of geographical features, by the English practice of describing land by metes (or terminal points) and bounds (like rivers). Deeds give us a sense of how people understood the capillary landscape. One farm embraced an area from the white oaks by the bend in the creek, west to the smooth rock, fifty rods north to the three chestnut trees, then east as far as the dogwood on the top of the spur, southeast to a walnut stump, and back to the oaks.

Sometime around 1820, William "Billy" Floyd Belcher and Sarah Elizabeth Kingery Belcher moved with their four children from Tazewell, Virginia, through Peeled Chestnut Gap to enter the Appalachian Plateau. They settled at a place known today as Big Four, taking up the north side of Elkhorn Creek, part of a vast tributary system. They built a cabin on a riverbank once owned by Robert Morris. Did they know about Morris's bankruptcy and death? They might have. Perhaps they moved when they did with the expectation that land locked up for decades no longer had an owner. They had reason to think this. After Morris died, his creditors seem to have concluded that his only asset was worthless. They wrote off their losses, allowing the entire estate to be forfeited to the Commonwealth of Virginia for nonpayment of taxes. Between 1815 and 1832, the whole thing sat in a fund for schools. But then the state changed course. In 1832, Virginia released all of Morris's delinquent land. Anyone willing to pay the back taxes, plus interest, could buy whatever they wanted. Land not redeemed (meaning its taxes were paid) by 1838 would be exposed to sale without qualification. This might have been what the Belchers had been waiting for.[56]

The Belchers proliferated. They moved along Elkhorn Creek, spreading out over an area of about two hundred square miles. Billy Belcher might never have owned an acre of land in his life, but his son did. Between 1850 and 1857, William Belcher, Jr., received full title to 326 acres, all located on the ridge separating Tug Fork from Elkhorn Creek. Some mountaineers became landowners, but most continued to trade their own deeds for land with disputed or overlapping titles. They might have believed that after the breakup of the Nicholas and Morris estates, ownership had reverted to them. They were wrong.[57]

The game of squatting in the crevices worked only as long as absentee landowners remained remote and unwitting. This is what began to change.

First, landowners asked legislatures to secure their titles, whether or not they visited their land or did anything with it. In 1826, lawmakers in Kentucky wrote one of the first laws intended to fortify the rights of absentees: "It is of great concern to the quiet and happiness of society . . . that the tenure of landed estates in this Commonwealth should be fixed and stable." Kentucky, they promised, would act to "confirm existing interests." Second, new investors moved into West Virginia after 1832. They paid the back taxes on old grants and organized some of the first companies for cutting lumber and mining iron. Few of them actually extracted anything, but what is important is that they operated with a new model, not speculation but direct extraction. The Belchers and Tottens were also on the move. Their children needed farms of their own, as would their children after them. But the deeds they wrote and traded conflicted with the ones written in law offices in Wheeling, Charleston, and Richmond. As the two classes—agrarian and capitalist—ran into each other with increasing frequency, they ended up in court. By the 1840s, the Commonwealth of Virginia confronted the problem of whose deeds—indeed, which species of deed—would prevail.[58]

All rights to property come from governments, which modify these rights to serve their most powerful constituents. English common law recognizes the *jus* and the *seisina*, the title that comes from law and the one derived after years of illegal but flagrant occupancy, called adverse possession. The Commonwealth of Virginia acknowledged that people high in the hills who had never paid for their farms made legitimate claims to land that had been neglected by absentees. At this point, the General Assembly could have strengthened the principle of adverse possession. They could have granted title to anyone who demonstrated that a distant owner had failed to put up a fence or turn a spade in ten or fifteen years. But politicians, many of whom were owners themselves, were not about to transfer millions of acres to the Belchers and Tottens. They were not about to reinforce the rights of households over those of capitalists at the moment when extraction looked to be technologically feasible. The political leadership needed a legal device that acknowledged certain rights without delivering outright ownership.

Judges throughout the southern mountains began to promulgate an inferior right of occupancy, a kind of squatter's title. In the 1820s and 1830s, courts in Kentucky, Alabama, and North Carolina used the phrase "color of title," meaning the appearance or façade of ownership. Said one judge, "Color of title is a legal fiction . . . a device whereby to secure to the settler that which strongly appealed to their inherent sense of fairness." The Commonwealth of Virginia passed a law to this effect in 1849. This and other laws began to define officially deeded and recorded real estate as having a senior patent. Anyone who lived in a hollow that belonged to someone else could regard that land as property in practice but not in fact. This was called a junior patent, really just a use-right that extended only to areas plowed and planted, only to the homeplace. Residents with color of title did not own the land they tilled, but they could "buy" and "sell" their use-rights nonetheless. In other words, color of title created a second-class market that actually reinforced the first-class status of the one dominated by elites. The system bought time for absentees, allowing them to form their companies and cut their deals without having to worry about who actually owned a piece of land. None of this meant that a household couldn't challenge an absentee, but it made success less likely.[59]

Color of title handed them an incalculable tool in the structural war. But dispossession in the southern mountains, like in England and Ireland a century earlier, followed more than one script: freely agreed-upon purchase, trickery and bamboozlement, judicial process, environmental destruction, and handcuffs.

One of the most important methods involved fracturing the meaning of land itself. William H. Edwards acquired more than eighty thousand acres in the upper Kanawha Valley. With other investors located in New York, Philadelphia, and England, he incorporated the Paint Creek Coal and Iron Mining and Manufacturing Company in 1849. Nine years later, Edwards prepared suits to remove the residents. But he had a problem. Challenges to deeds and ejectments jammed the county courts. Edwards might have won every dispute, but each required its hearing and trial, committing him to years of litigation. His attorneys might have advised him to find another way. As the first of his ejectment cases was about to begin, he made an offer to the defendants. He would not contest their deeds if they gave him rights to the minerals beneath their fields and woodlots. Likely bewildered and misled into thinking that they had prevailed, many of the residents compromised their already compromised titles.

Edwards did not invent this practice, though he might have been the first to use it in the southern mountains. (There is reference to "spirited adventurers" in Cornwall, England, in 1811 who bought rights to search for silver.) At first, mountaineers probably didn't know what it would mean for Edwards to exercise his right. Excavating coal requires access to the surface. It requires roads cut through hollows, dams spanned across creeks, and hillsides blown to gravel. What they actually owned, in effect, amounted to little or nothing as a consequence of what they traded away. The same thing happened all over western Virginia and elsewhere in Appalachia during the 1840s and 1850s. In some places, major disputes over who owned what had been resolved by the time full-throttle industrialization began. More than a century later, Cody Dickens of Raleigh County, West Virginia, remembered how the Rowland Land Company arrived while his father was hoeing corn. "They went on top that mountain, where he was hoeing corn . . . and they said well . . . make a deal with you . . . You make us a deed to the mineral rights, and we'll make you a clear deed to the surface. That's the way the Rowland Land Company got it all. The old people didn't know what they was doing."[60]

But the old people had their reasons. They sold their subterranean real estate to relieve the stress of debt, environmental depletion, and vanishing outlets for the sale of their diminishing yields. They liquidated this asset for the same reasons they worked for wages—to replace the hard money that no longer flowed through their hands. As the historian Robert Weise explains, "They did so with an eye toward shoring up the fleeting independence and elusive security that defined the household economy. For them, mineral sales meant a new way to deal with the continuing problem of debt." Weise makes the point that many compromised their titles as a way of saving their farms.[61]

Then came the Civil War, and the explorations of the Confederate cartographer Jed Hotchkiss. When the Philadelphia capitalists asked Hotchkiss to conduct a formal survey of Flat Top Mountain, he hired a former Confederate captain and civil engineer named Isaiah Welch to do the groundwork. Sniffing around McDowell County, Welch documented a seam thirteen feet thick at Laurel Creek. Flat Top Coal organized and made its first delivery in 1883. Then the company pivoted. It renamed itself the Flat Top Land Trust and set out to acquire surface and mineral rights, which it then leased to coal operators. It established offices at Pocahontas, Virginia, but immediately set out to acquire property on the other side of the state line, in McDowell County, West Virginia, especially along the Tug Fork River and Elkhorn Creek, homeplace of the Tottens and the Belchers.[62]

Agents performed surveys and examined deeds against country records. They set out to catch every error and missed step that would make a given tract vulnerable. But they found local practices perplexing, if not maddening. Wrote one investigator, "It would seem that all the lands of James M. Totten [father of T. K. Totten] were forfeited [by failure to pay taxes] because none of them appear to have been consecutively on the books. While the lands entered year to year are so entirely different in quantity as to puzzle one how they came there." One tract changed hands in one configuration one year, then as two smaller tracts the next year within the same family. Then it was deeded to other family members who were not named. Then it disappeared from the books for a year before reappearing. A farm might be described in a deed as having one owner, then appear in county records under a different name. "How could land certified by the [tax] auditor as having been forfeited and *not* redeemed be alternatively redeemed?" Perhaps someone with local influence had let his taxes lapse and asked the help of an aspiring officeholder or his cousin or someone who owed him a favor. The company's complaints suggest the kinship ties and procedural informality of local government.[63]

A deed might seem like an impersonal legal instrument, but local deeds told stories and traced the transfer of land between and within families. Between 1875 and 1895, members of the Belcher family made at least one hundred exchanges, with approximately seventy-five of those between individuals named Belcher. One farm went from Tobias to Andrew in 1871 and to another relative in 1875. Owen deeded to Tobias, who turned it over to Henry, who turned it over to John T., who turned it over to Andrew. Belchers also traded land with Lamberts and Tottens. Since the families were intertwined by marriage, cabins and their adjoining fields and woods ping-ponged inside the same group. These documents sometimes mentioned money but not often, because they recorded transfers, which were not necessarily the same thing as sales. The notion that mountain people did everything on a handshake and never wrote things down isn't true. They seemed to have written deeds obsessively even if some of these documents remained within the family, never entering into county records.[64]

The Belchers and the Tottens also sold land to mining companies. A series of letters reveal direct dealings between highlanders and the Flat Top Land Trust, sometimes through speculators. In one instance, John C. Belcher wrote to the trust after the sale of his father-in-law's farm. He asked permission for the elderly man to live out his life there. Belcher had spoken to a manager the year before, in 1882, at the courthouse in McDowell County. "You told me that I could have the benefit of the orchard and the grazing of the place[.] he wants to cultivate some ground[,] if you have no objection[.] [he will] take care of the fencing as well as he can[.] write to me as soon as possible[.] yours truly[,] John C. Belcher." The letter illustrates a common arrangement in the process of dispossession: use-rights separated from ownership as an intermediate step to removing people.[65]

A second letter is more complicated but reveals all sorts of relationships often invisible to historians. A member of the Belcher family wrote on behalf of a family member or a neighbor. The recipient was James W. Davis, a land speculator and attorney who represented Flat Top: "Enclosed you will find leases of Hill H. Cecil. Cecil is on your land in a House he built some time ago and left it and another man had taken possession and sold his improvements to a Mr Edwards. Mr Edwards wants Cecil to give him possession[.] you will have to decide between them . . . Truly yours[,] G. W. Belcher."

Cecil had rented out land owned by Davis, who appears not to have known that Cecil lived there. Cecil then sold or abandoned it to another man, who sold it to Edwards. (He could have been the same William H. Edwards who was buying up land in the same region at the time.) Edwards did some due diligence and found that the last recorded deed belonged to Cecil. Three weeks later, Belcher again wrote to Davis, telling him that Edwards had "taken out a warrant from a justice in McDowell and has dispossessed Cecil." In other words, Edwards convinced a judge to uphold his deed.[66]

The land belonged to Davis, but that didn't stop three people from exchanging deeds for it. And yet, something else was going on. Someone in the Belcher family decided to tell Davis the whole story. Did they want to stop Edwards? Or did they take pleasure in grinding the whole mess in Davis's face? There is no way of knowing. The point is that speculators and financiers didn't have control over their property. If Edwards believed he had title, then he and Davis would have had to fight it out in court. In the meantime, the next person to move into the cabin probably hunted at will and planted a garden.[67]

That strategy would soon fail. The Flat Top Land Trust likely owned all the easy-to-acquire patents by 1888. After that, the company doubled down to get hold of the parcels they still needed to form a contiguous estate. The pile of notes and lists that I read at the small archive in Bluefield, West Virginia, could only have been written by someone traveling by horse from creek to branch in order to see who lived where. Someone knocked on cabin doors, seized a vacated farm in one hollow, and wrote a check in the next. This work required a fixer who knew the topography and represented the company. The fixer was Isaiah Welch.

In one instance, managers sent Welch to protect them from adverse possession. "In regard to the 3225 acre tract 2/3 of which is owned by the trust . . . [you are] advised to put someone on the property at once and take possession, as without this is done there is no title. I want you to attend to this as soon as possible. If there is no house on the tract, you had better select someone and have a cabin put up at once and the Company will pay for it." Another fixer watched a piece of land for twenty years, keeping track of who used it and how often. When the Totten family failed to pay taxes for five years, the company got hold of it.[68]

The Tottens might have sold it anyway, even the homeplace. When Belcher met Davis they talked about land. Such meetings must have been common. The declining output and rising subsistence adversity that plagued mountain residents lay just under the surface of every communication they had with mining and timber companies. This helps explain why Thomas K. Totten released his heirs to sell the homeplace itself "if the family ever became needy of anything." Neediness swirled around them in a way it hadn't a generation before. To put this differently, mineral and timber rights amounted to the only equity in land, since no one would buy a farm intending to farm it where everyone knew coal companies would soon operate. So when mineral buyers came around, any ridge with an outcropping of coal, any river bottom that was not part of the homeplace, must have looked like a stack of cash.

Nothing about the sale of land to coal companies took place on an equal footing, even if both parties entered into a contract without overt coercion. Flat Top brought in attorneys who knew the entire history of title and intimidated residents into selling, telling them that they would never get a better deal. One farmer turned over 740 acres for $3.58 each, maybe a big sum to him but a trifle to the company. The companies knew things their targets didn't. They knew the depth of coal seams and their value. They knew the future routes that railroads would take and where towns would be located. "Capt. Welch has just returned from his trip to Tug," wrote a manager to the president of the Flat Top Land Trust. "The Hunt option is very short and must be decided soon. It is a very valuable tract and we ought to own it in view of the R.R. extension West."[69]

The Belchers and the Tottens entered into a contradiction. The purpose of speculative profit was to ensure household autonomy, when it actually did the opposite. Men sought to maintain their social positions, their role as providers, and their power over wives and children. The problem was, land no longer could do for them what they needed it to. Holding on to it meant squeezing it dry for a paltry livelihood. But selling it to replace income lost from a degraded environment and to pay debts traded the only thing of any value for an ephemeral substance. Even when the money was good, a pile of cash hardly guaranteed a household's security. People with limited financial knowledge could not invest it to earn an income. Once they burned through it, they had nothing. They knew that they were dealing with a new order of power, but they might not have sensed until late what that power wanted from them.

In 1889, the Trust made a triumphant announcement. Flat Top Land now owned "a vast unbroken . . . coal bed traversing an area of over 200,000 acres, undisturbed by a single break or fault and until recently comparatively unknown to the commercial world." The money was about to pour in. "Within two or three years a large revenue will be derived from this part of the large territory controlled by your Association." They owned rights from the surface to the center of the earth, just what they needed to begin large-scale mining. That same year, miners in McDowell County dug and shipped 586,529 tons of bituminous coal. Thirteen years later, they sent 5,459,655 tons down the tracks, most of it from the vast unbroken Flat Top Coalfield.[70]

For a century, highlanders played a game of trespassing, squatting, and sometimes asserting rights to ownership. They depended on using the forested landscape at will. Deeming all private property common property made their lives possible. After the Civil War, the rules began to change and the game ended. A new generation of capitalists extracted commodities directly from land rather than wait for real estate to increase in value. Mountaineers tried to maintain their old practices, but they found it increasingly difficult. When the new owners took active control, they diced up the functional commons. Mining operations closed off old hunting and gathering grounds. Most destructive of all, lumber companies ripped out the forest and hauled it away.

Cutting down trees frequently preceded digging coal. Often, the same companies did both. Mining receives more attention because it eventually defined the region's role in the capitalist world. But felling the woods affected a larger area and many more people. It removed the ecological base, the foundation of makeshift livelihood. It turned the mountains into an alien landscape. We need to retrace the same decades since the Civil War in a story that runs parallel to the direct dispossession of land and the coming of coal. At the same time that the Belchers and Tottens wrangled with the Flat Top Land Trust, the Great Appalachian Forest had come under assault.

IT LOOKS LIKE A LOCOMOTIVE with a ship's mast. It clanks and spits, chugs steam, and sweats grease from its wheels and pistons. The power from the coal is released by the engine and transmitted to long cables that extend from the mast every which way. Workers attach them to fallen trees, pulling or skidding the logs hundreds of feet to a railroad flatbed. During the 1880s, the high-pitched whistle of the steam skidder echoed in the coves. The men worked in crews, cutting everything, leaving the slopes barren but for the stumps, branches, and bark that burned whenever a spark from a railroad wheel or glowing ash from a tinderbox fell on the detritus. Dorie Woodruff Cope, who grew up in the Great Smoky Mountains and moved to a logging camp with her family as a child, recalled the fires that burned through cutover hills, the eerie orange skies, the pine needles that shot like darts, and "the hissing sound of sap boiling."[71]

Mountain people had always cut trees and sold them. In winter and spring, when nothing else went for sale and money ran low, they felled a giant yellow poplar or a black walnut. They would build a dam across a creek to hold back its flow, then roll their logs into the pool that formed against the earthworks. Opening one of these dams let go a torrent that heaved logs, rocks, and tons of debris down the hollow, into the river. They lashed the logs into rafts and steered them west toward the Bluegrass or Cincinnati. John Fox, Jr., traveled down the Kentucky River during a spring flood. "Sweeping around the bend I saw a raft two hundred feet long at the mouth of the creek—tugging at its anchor—and a young giant of a moun-taineer pushing the bow-oar to and fro." Rafting logs only worked in one direction. To reach the seaboard they assembled yokes of oxen to haul the trunks overland to sawmills. This was the cottage phase of logging. Households directed it, managed it, and took the profits.[72]

And yet, like every other aspect of land and livelihood in the moun-tains, cottage logging shuddered before the earthquake struck. The sense of looming change generated fear, competitiveness, and suspicion between those loyal to different families. It caused clashes over who controlled what fragment of forest in anticipation of scarcity and hard times. County courts settled most disputes. But smoldering animosity sometimes escalated into violence. The most famous feud in the history of Appalachia took place along the banks and tributaries of the Tug Fork River. It began in 1878 when one of the Hatfields of West Virginia and one of the McCoys of Kentucky found no way to settle a disagreement over the earmarks on a free-ranging pig. But the ambiguous ownership of a small mammal did not set off more than a decade of violence, in which twelve people died. The

Hatfields and the McCoys confronted each other across a rising current of economic and ecological deterioration that reduced the viability of mountain makeshift.

The central figure in the conflict was William Anderson "Devil Anse" Hatfield, an aggressive logging entrepreneur. His litigiousness—not any act of violence—earned him his nickname. Devil Anse did not represent backward-looking traditionalism or a refusal to adapt. His financial success and cussed tenacity stirred resentment in others, most of all in Randolph McCoy. McCoy's own attempts in the same business had not gone as well. Yet it is entirely likely that no feud would have erupted had there been sufficient forest for cutting and grazing. Hatfield and McCoy attempted to turn the landscape into money because subsistence practices were failing. Their coteries murdered each other at the very moment that the state of West Virginia allowed corporations to seize the Tug River Valley.

The most revealing aspect of the feud is also the thing most misunderstood about it. Kinship does not explain it. Members of both families crossed sides. Fewer than half of Hatfield supporters were related to Devil Anse. And of those who took his side, 85 percent worked in his logging crew, including three men named McCoy. Financial dependence on wages and anxiety over how they would provide for their own households created new loyalties among young men. When it ended in 1890, writes the historian Altina Waller, "the conflict was no longer rooted in the internal dynamics of the community; instead, the feudists were now enmeshed in a raw struggle for economic and political power."[73]

The Norfolk and Western Railway acted as an unnamed instigator of the bloodshed. Everyone involved knew that it would change social life and the landscape, spreading fear. The first major trunk line to cross Appalachia was the Baltimore and Ohio. By 1853, it had set down track beyond Harpers Ferry, across northern Virginia and into the western counties. Other railroad corporations appeared and disappeared; they splintered and reorganized and consolidated. Some of them were called Chesapeake and Ohio; Winchester and Potomac; Wheeling, Pittsburg and Baltimore; Huntington and Big Sandy; Ripley and Mill Creek Valley. The railroad eventually known as Norfolk and Western started out from Chesapeake Bay in the 1830s, moving westward across Virginia to the lower Shenandoah

Valley, arriving at the Flat Top Coalfield in 1883. It carried the first shipment of coal from southern West Virginia. Then, in 1890, the Norfolk and Western initiated an extension that would take the line along the Tug River through McDowell County and from there to Ohio.

The feudists might have known something else. The Norfolk and Western Railway was no longer just a railroad. It had swallowed the Flat Top Land Trust in 1885, creating a giant amalgamation of capital, a liquidation machine whose vortex drew in the entire landscape, from treetops to minerals a mile deep. The company reported a capital stock of $32 million in 1889, a sum equal to about $800 million in the early twenty-first century. The railroad not only connected major towns and cities, it ran steel into almost every hollow. Mills, tanneries, steam skidders, and labor camps spread out behind its locomotives like the wakes that follow ships. With this kind of scale and scope, it was difficult to find a breathing space, any distance from the new source of power. The Hatfields, McCoys, Belchers, Tottens, and thousands like them entered a new mode of production.[74]

Cottage logging and industrial logging had only trees and saws in common. The former provided households with money from the ecological base. The latter funneled profit to shareholders, resulting in a transformation so devastating that it marked the end of an epoch in the history of the southern mountains. The clear-cutting of the Appalachian woods did not happen all at once but in different locations and altitudes at different times. Yet along with the direct loss of homes and hollows through sale, ejectment, and the separation of mineral rights from surface rights, the removal of the forest brought about the enclosure of the functional commons. It uprooted highland society, setting off the transfer of tens of thousands from a subsistence economy to wage earning. They tumbled and splintered down the creeks into camps. Combining logs and workers in sawmills resulted in lumber, the sale of which accumulated money. Their labor had always turned trees into boards. Now it confronted them in alien form, as a commodity owned and sold by someone else.[75]

Professional conservationists urged on the rush for hardwoods in Appalachia as the best use of a neglected region. Bernard Fernow, third chief forester of the United States, directed eastern investors away from the diminished groves of Maine and toward the Blue Ridge. In 1888, he beheld a nation-sized vault of photosynthesizing wealth: 10 million acres of ash, aspen, beeches, and cottonwood; black oak, black walnut, and black locust; red maple, red oak, and red pines; along with chestnut, birches, buckeye, cedar, cherry, and hickory. "The greatest body of uncut hard wood timber of the eastern United States," Fernow announced. He told of stands of poplar, each thirty inches around with a volume of 400 board feet, 16,640 board feet to the acre.[76]

The industrial class in Charleston and Wheeling also cheered the conversion of the blanketing woods into money. They justified the human and ecological fallout of the takeover as the necessary violence in the achievement of something greater—civilization, historical progress, social order. "Already, the peaceful seclusion of those hills and vales is a thing of the past. The timber-hunters, the oil-explorers, the coal-buyers, the projectors of new railroads, the seekers after cheap lands for homes or for investment, are everywhere." This revolution that "put capital and commerce into domination" carried extraordinary costs, this writer admitted. "One sees these beautiful hills and valleys stripped of nature's adornment; the hills denuded of their forests, the valleys lighted by the flames of coke-ovens and smelting furnaces; their vegetation seared and blackened . . . and one could wish that such an Arcadia might have been spared such ravishment. But the needs of the race are insatiable and unceasing."[77]

"Tremendous onslaught has been made upon the forests . . . New sawmills are building every day, new territory being opened, and it is safe to say that now the total cut of all the mills is no less than 500,000,000 [board] feet a year," marveled one newspaper editor. At that rate, the total destruction of the forest took about fifty years. Of the 10 million acres that had never been cut in 1870, only 1.5 million stood in 1910. In that year, mills in a single county turned out 1 million board feet each day. From 1907 to 1914, one thousand mills produced between 1 billion and 1.5 billion board feet each year. By 1920, the Appalachian forest had yielded 30.4 billion board feet. The largest trees went first; then the smaller ones, for telegraph poles and railroad ties. "The forests are being rapidly destroyed," said the editor. A northern lumberman explained his company's plan as rip and run: "All we want here is to get the most we can out of this country, as quick as we can, and then get out."[78]

The liquidation happened so fast and with such efficiency that nineteen years after Fernow had advertised Appalachia to industry, another chief forester predicted doom. After inspecting five thousand square miles of eastern woodland, Gifford Pinchot concluded that the United States would enter a "timber famine" within twenty years unless it adopted a policy of conservation. The Weeks Act of 1911 followed, creating the Monongahela National Forest, a new role for the governing economy, in which the raw material of industry would be guarded and managed for future consumption. But mountaineers had no place in this landscape. They had no way of living on denuded hillsides and no rights to dwell in national forests or parks. Both private and public planning ruled them out.[79]

The system of forest and farm staggered. For a while, graziers borrowed woods pasture in neighboring counties to make up for losses closer to home. They gained the habit "of sending their stock to be summered in the woods, in distant and less improved sections, under the care of some settler of the locality." But the relentless cut finally reached even the highest elevations. Alonza Beecher Brooks watched and recorded the effects of deforestation. Born in Upshur County, he taught himself surveying and attended West Virginia University, among the first of its students to study forestry. In 1910, Brooks published a map of the remaining forest in the state. It showed only 12 percent of the original woods uncut. He described a subsistence economy in shambles. Once-common practices took on a menacing quality when so little forest remained. "The cutting of poles and trees for all manner of domestic purposes is generally indiscriminate; fires are permitted to burn through small areas at frequent intervals in many places; and cattle and other domestic animals are permitted to browse the leaves and tender twigs of valuable seedling trees which are the only promise of a future supply of timber." Yet gathering, swidden, and woods pasture are basic subsistence strategies. The work of living in the forest did not change when the forest disappeared. The people had been cornered, their homesteads made into islands, their economies hollowed out. "The woodlot," said Brooks clinically, "must be made to yield the product which has heretofore been drawn from the larger adjacent forests."[80]

At the same time it disappeared into barren clear-cuts, the forest lost one of its most essential species. In 1904, a fungus accidentally introduced from Japan killed American chestnut trees in New York City. The blight spread west, destroying billions of trees over the next few decades. Before the blight, chestnut represented 15 to 20 percent of all trees in parts of Appalachia and up to 60 percent in others. It can attain a height of two hundred feet. Its rot-resistant wood made furniture and tools. Its bark tanned leather and could be sold for cash. And its nuts provided forage for pigs and a sweet and substantial fall meal, adding to the complement of foods mountain dwellers took from the landscape. By itself, the loss of the American chestnut would have been wounding. Combined with industrial deforestation, it was devastating.[81]

One lifelong resident of the border between Virginia and West Virginia depicted these losses in homely fiction, constructed from a lifetime of hunting and fishing. "The Last Camp Fire" (1940), by G. D. McNeill, dramatizes the displacement and bereavement many felt. Zeke Miller owns a prosperous farm in Kansas, with a ten-room house and one thousand acres, but he feels out of place on the Great Plains. Depressed and recently separated from his wife, Zeke decides to return to Big Black, the mountain where he was born. He will meet up with two childhood friends, Dock and Tone, for a fishing trip.

Entering his home ground on the train, Zeke counts seventy boxcars go by, their open doors revealing stacks of short spruce logs from the Cheat River, one hundred miles away. Pulpwood, a man informs him. "Zeke thought of asking whether there was any lumbering about the Gauley or Big Black, but he dared not make the inquiry." The pulpwood, it turns out, is like a trickle of blood from an unseen wound. Before long he passes the home of old family friends. "The dwelling and the neatly built rail fences were gone. The railroad ran squarely through what Zeke reckoned to be the site of the McClune garden." The farm has become a lumberyard. A band saw consumes a giant white oak at the moment Zeke passes by. The railroad through the garden emphasizes the totality of the violation, the utter destruction of house and home. "He had loved the mountains and the woods," writes McNeill of Zeke. "The trees were personal friends of his, and it made him angry to see them cruelly used by these aliens who, for the sake of dollars, were come to destroy the mountain country."

The three friends pack up food and tackle and walk the trails of their youth. But nothing is as it was. They cannot escape the constant apprehension of what they will see over the next knob. In one scene, they confront a vanished grove. "The spruces were gone!" In their place they find scrub and briar and skid roads where trees as wide as kitchen tables had been dragged away. But nothing prepares them for the ascent that gives them a view of Big Black.

"Boys, boys!" says Dock, at last. "What a shame! What a shame!"
Where, in the other days, the boys had seen blue waves of spruce and hemlock, stretching away mile upon mile, the men now beheld desolation—bare hills, ribbed with shale, from which fire and erosion had swept every vestige of soil; long mountain ranges without a tree . . . a monotonous panorama of destruction, as far as the eye could run.
"Well, fellers," said Zeke, "I knowed it wuz bad; but if I'd dreamed it wuz like this, I'd never a asked ye tu come up here. I'm sorry I seen it."

There is powerlessness in Dock's cry and defeat in Zeke's apology. Though something of inestimable value has been taken from them, they don't express anger. The few voices in the story that belong to lumbermen are anonymous, almost disembodied. It's as though no one is reponsible and no public sphere or political process exists in which the aggrieved men might assert their interests against those of the companies. They have only their memories and each other.[82]

Mountaineers subverted logging companies wherever possible, but companies developed a strategy to neutralize them. The lingering custom of the commons protected subsistence hunting and firewood gathering. The managers of the Elk River Coal and Lumber Company documented their attempts to gain control over trespassing and "undesirable parties," though they knew that no county court would award them damages for browsing cattle, "nor can hunting on the property be stopped." Companies also worried about adverse possession. Elk River Coal needed to prevent flagrant occupancy on tens of thousands of acres it might not log or mine for a

APPALACHIA AS DRAWN BY THE APPALACHIAN REGIONAL COMMISSION, 1967. The ARC offered the widest possible geographical definition of Appalachia, but few historians consider all of western Pennsylvania and any part of New York to be included. There are no generally accepted criteria for what constitutes Appalachia. The region is best understood historically, not geographically or geologically.

ENCLOSING THE COMMONS IN OXFORDSHIRE, 1801. Between the sixteenth and nineteenth centuries, enclosure undermined the system of common lands and community governance practiced throughout England, Scotland, and Ireland. But enclosure was more than a change in the landscape. It brought into existence a new legal category: private property. Owning land gave lords greater flexibility to innovate, but it also created two groups that did not exist before the sixteenth century: paupers with no source of income or support and wageworkers who depended entirely on money.

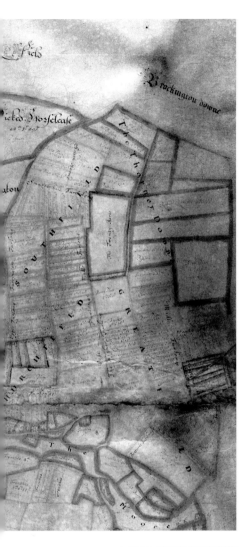

DANIEL BOON,

From a picture by J. W. Berry Painted for James Hall Esq.

DANIEL BOONE, MOUNTAINEER, C. 1832. When a lithographer reproduced a painting of the Great Pathfinder twelve years after his death, Boone's reputation was surging. The actual settlers of the southern mountains benefited from his popularity. Politicians praised them in the same language they used for him, as civilizers of wilderness and emissaries of empire. But while Boone remains a hero, the settlers would become objects of pity and ridicule.

(Image LC-DIG-ppmsca-39572, Library of Congress)

RURAL WHITES RACIALIZED, 1891. A popular illustrator contributed this facial study of "Georgia crackers" for an article about cotton-mill workers in *The Century Magazine.* "They have land but no gardens, pasturage but no stock. Wasting their earnings on gewgaws, drink, and indigestible food. Despite a favorable climate . . . the mortality rate among the poor whites is shockingly high." Few writers asked how poor people became that way. Instead, they assumed that deprivation passed from generation to generation through "some hereditary channel."

(Graffenried, "The Georgia Cracker in the Cotton Mills." Image LC-USZ62-84854, Library of Congress)

Gøbuluc
Eylandt

Dod koff

MINQUAS
kil

S W A N E N

G Ø D Y N S

B A Y

D A E L

Cabo May

Cabo Hinlopen

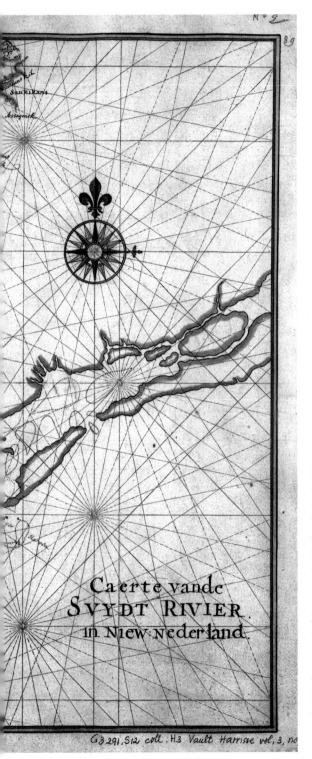

Caerte vande
SVYDT RIVIER
in Niew Nederland.

NEW SWEDEN, 1639. Swedish and Finnish settlements and fortifications moved up the Delaware River into southern Pennsylvania and from there into the southern mountains by the middle of the eighteenth century. Scots-Irish immigrants would join them and become the dominant ethnic group. Note the longhouses to the east of the river. Members of this woodland culture lived close to Indians, not often peacefully.

(Joan Vinckeboons, *Caert vande Svydt River in Niew Nederland* (1639). Image G3291.S12 coll .H3. Library of Congress)

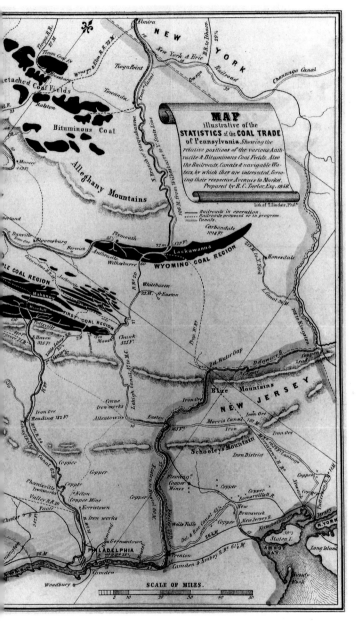

MAPPING COAL, 1848.
This might be the first map of coal deposits in what became West Virginia, part of a "Great Allegheny Bituminous Coal Field" that braced Pennsylvania, Maryland, and Virginia. Maps like this one made a region thought to be remote and inaccessible more attractive to investment.

(Richard Cowling Taylor, *Map Illustrative of the Statistics of the Coal Trade*, from *Statistics of Coal* [1848])

OLD-GROWTH SPRUCE FOREST. Woods formed the ecological base of Appalachian society. The forest gave foods and commodities without demanding more than labor. This functional commons made mountaineer autonomy possible.

(Image 14258, West Virginia and Regional History Collection, West Virginia University Libraries)

HOUSEHOLD NEAR THE TUG RIVER. This family posed for a photographer around the time that the railroad first came through the valley. They were typical of those who attempted to sustain themselves in the hills even as the prices of their commodities collapsed and their common forest was narrowed and enclosed.

(Image 039260, West Virginia and Regional History Collection, West Virginia University Libraries)

RAMPS. Wild onions fed families in the spring, after winter stores were eaten and before their gardens produced. Ramps were one of many foods that came directly from the forest.

LOGGING CREW, 1903. When mountaineers lost their forested land, they lost the resources they exchanged for money. At first, men sought industrial work as a way of replacing the mountain meadow (for cattle) and the foraged foods (like ramps) that the forest once provided their households. As loggers, they participated in the very deforestation that resulted in their dependence on wages.

(Image 10387, West Virginia and Regional History Collection, West Virginia University Libraries)

SKIDDER AT FULL STEAM, 1910. This image from Blackwater Canyon, Tucker County, West Virginia, depicts the scale and rapidity of deforestation.

(Image 050624, West Virginia and Regional History Collection, West Virginia University Libraries)

ALIEN LANDSCAPE. The subject of this photograph could be Nevada. It's West Virginia in the 1930s. A paper mill stands in the midst of cutover hills.

(Photograph by John Vachon. Image LC-USF33-001388-M5, Library of Congress)

COAL MINERS DIGGING WITH A LOW CEILING, WEST VIRGINIA, 1908. Men who became coal miners often maintained ties with family in the mountains, and some planned to return to their own farms when they made enough money. Managers sought to undermine their ability to walk away from work whenever it suited them by importing immigrants from Europe and African-Americans from other southern states. (Photograph by Lewis Wickes Hine. Image LC-DIG-nclc-01060, Library of Congress)

COAL CAMP AT HOLDEN, WEST VIRGINIA. This is a typical coal camp, made up of small houses lining a hollow with a creek down the center. Coal companies owned these houses and threatened eviction for unionizing or any other infraction. The mine itself was less than a mile away.

(Image 004695, West Virginia and Regional History Collection, West Virginia University Libraries)

TWO VERSIONS OF THE CAPTURED GARDEN. The family shown above posed for a government photographer with their garden behind them. Gardens eased the dreariness of the camps and gave high-quality food, but they allowed employers to pay their workers less, increasing exploitation. The backyard of the home shown below was typical throughout Appalachia. The same home had a chicken coop.

(Top photograph by Russell Lee. Records of the Solid Fuels Administration for War, Photographs of the Medical Survey of the Bituminous Coal Industry, 1946–1947. National Archive Number 540313. Bottom photograph by Marion Post Wolcott. Image LC-USF34-050066-E, Library of Congress.)

COAL MINER'S WIFE AND CHILDREN, SCOTTS RUN, 1938. Only a few families qualified to move to the "experimental community" of Arthurdale. Most remained in Scotts Run and other abandoned mining sites. The poorest miners, anyone injured, and African-Americans had nowhere else to go. (Photograph by Marion Post Wolcott. Image LC-DIG-fsa-8c29859, Library of Congress)

STRIKING MINERS IN A TENT CAMP, LICK CREEK, 1922. The greatest challenge for striking miners was finding food. They were highly vulnerable to starvation, since the companies forced them to leave the gardens growing beside their company-owned houses. Some miners kept gardens in the hills or had families still capable of supporting them. (Photograph by Herbert A. French. Image LC-DIG-npcc-30258, Library of Congress)

HOMESTEAD STUDY FOR ARTHURDALE. This sketch of a homestead has the same style and design as the actually constructed homes. Notice the open space to the right for alternating the location of the garden. The planners intended highly intensive household food production to offset the cost of the factory at the center of the community.

(Image 005004, West Virginia and Regional History Collection, West Virginia University Libraries)

Winslow Homer, *Veteran in a New Field* (1865).
(Bequest of Miss Adelaide Milton de Groot, 1967, Metropolitan Museum of Art, New York City)

Thomas Hovenden, *Breaking Home Ties* (1890).
(Gift of Ellen Harrison McMichael in memory of C. Emory McMichael, Philadelphia Museum of Art)

George Inness, *Short Cut, Watchung Station, New Jersey* (1883).

(Purchased with the W. P. Wilstach Fund, 1895, W1895-1-5, Philadelphia Museum of Art)

decade. The solution companies favored was to lease land back to households. As tenants, mountaineers established occupancy for the companies. An internal report defined the practice: "We have about 100 tenants living through the mountains who pay but a small rental and are chiefly of value to us for holding possession of our land." The tenants lived a vestigial existence. "In some cases the lease includes a house and cultivated land; in others it merely covers an old field or unimproved strip . . . None of the land covered by these leases can bring the tenant enough money when cultivated to pay any considerable amount." Elk River Coal had about one hundred tenants in 1908, sixty in 1910. After 1912, the company didn't mention them again.[83]

Displaced people often moved to company-owned camps. Dorie Cope told of the move her family made to a high-altitude lumber camp in 1912. "My childhood was over," said Cope. "Never again would I have the freedom I had enjoyed here in this world of rounded hills and orchards." The accretion of farmers into industrial workers took literary form in Hubert Skidmore's novels. Skidmore was born in Webster County, West Virginia, in 1909. He grew up after the peak of the logging boom, among barren slopes. His novel *I Will Lift Up Mine Eyes* (1936) opens in the 1890s during a year of drought. Nat and Maw Cutlip realize that they will harvest and store less food for the winter than ever before. Maw remembers when the farm was new—the soil that turned out fat corn, the honey in the hives. Two years before, Nat "had found it imperative to clear out more land, to cut deeper into the woods at the top of the field." But the work was hard, and Nat lacks the energy and optimism to do it again.

Nat decides to look for work in order to buy the supplies that would make up for the dry and failing soil. After neighbors decline to take him on as a hired hand, he turns to the mill at the bottom of the valley. He follows the logic forced upon him. He sells his labor. The money opens another world to the family, and they feel happy and secure for the first time in years. Nat brings home fabulous things for Christmas. A golden-haired doll for the youngest daughter replaces the one made of rags. One son receives a pocketknife. There are calico dresses and candy canes. Maw gasps as she opens a box of shoes manufactured somewhere far away, Massachusetts or Philadelphia. But Nat doesn't see the feedback loop he has entered.

As more men like Nat asked for work, owners lowered the wages they offered. Once mill and mine replaced garden and forest as means of subsistence, the flush of abundance diminished.

Dependency looked like a shack on a rocky shelf overlooking the Gauley River. Skidmore describes the shelter that the Cutlips called home as little more than a henhouse. "Maw walked slowly about the room, looking at the thin, wrapped walls and rafters, and feeling the floor give beneath her weight." Aunt Binney had been in camp for a while already and told Maw that the houses weren't meant to last. Once they all moved to a new camp, these would "rot an fall to the airth." Maw disregards the house, at first. She tells a neighbor that she intends to return to the Knob. "Thet is the way with us all at furst!" says the neighbor, "hit's bin six years come cold weather an we're worser off then ever as fer as money is countable." The promise of consumption and a dignified working-class standard of living eluded those on the industrial periphery. "The lumber companies had opened the door to the outside world," wrote Dorie Cope. "We became aware of 'things'—things that money could buy, things that made life easier (or harder), things to see, things to do. Our isolation had ended. They had opened a door—a door we were forced to use as an exit from our ancestral homes. Then, after the exit, the door was closed to us. We were given visitors' rights to the land—to come and look, but not to stay."[84]

The end of the open woods brought an end to the old subsistence. Their forests and fields had always provided them with money, whether as whiskey, ginseng, cattle, or lumber. The makeshift world collapsed when it was no longer possible to create exchangeable value from the ecological base. As with any other enclosure, the assault against the Appalachian commons threw people into wage work. Alonza Brooks mourned: "During a comparatively few years nearly the whole population which originally earned its living from the ground has been pushed out from places of seclusion into a whirl of modern industry."[85] Through all these changes, even as they descended into that terrifying tomb-like deafening darkness, the homeplace remained a dimming possibility and an ideal. Those who hung on in the hills had their misfortunes thrown back at them. The basis of their autonomy gutted or sold, they pecked and scrimped. The words of the engineer who condemned them in 1904 echo here: "forlorn and miserable . . . never having known anything better than the wretched surroundings of their everyday life." Though they often insisted that they could make a living on remnants of the old commons, they had become poor. They had become the horrifying hillbillies that lowlanders had always assumed them to be.[86]

5. Interlude: Agrarian Twilight

THE ART OF DISPOSSESSION

The farmer sows in faith, he toils in hope, but reaps in
disappointment and despair.
—Leonidas Polk, *Agricultural Depression. Its Causes—
the Remedy* (1890)

THE HARVESTER SWINGS A SCYTHE through a forest of grain
almost as tall as he is. He has set aside his Union coat and
canteen to bring in his first crop. We cannot see his face, a
point of view that renders him no particular veteran but rather *every* veteran. He is the people as a whole. He gathers into himself all those who
yearn for the security of peace and the sufficiency of a quarter section.
Winslow Homer's transporting *Veteran in a New Field* (1865) relies on a
common Union image, emblazoned on envelopes during the war, of wheat
in abundance. As Abraham Lincoln said, "Out of eight bushels of wheat,
seven are raised by those men who labor for themselves, aided by their
boys growing to manhood, neither being hired nor hiring, but literally laboring upon their own hook, asking no favor of capital, of hired laborer, or
of the slave."

Twenty-five years later, Thomas Hovenden painted another young man and another farm in *Breaking Home Ties* (1890). He stands in a drab dining room with his coat on, hat in his hand, bags packed. He looks west with mystical stoicism. The ceiling is dirty. The carpet is worn. The china cabinet is empty. His pale mother stands before him, trying to gain his attention, but his mind is already far away. The family has just finished breakfast when the coach arrives. His sisters wilt, nearly in tears. Grandmother sits motionless, as the young man's father carries his carpetbag out the door. The two men stand with their backs to each other, facing opposite directions.

Sons always went their own way. This is what it meant for the household to reproduce itself. But this young man is not leaving for marriage and his own farm in the next county. He is leaving because nothing his father has is worth owning. We can imagine the young man on a train to San Francisco or Chicago. In the next scene he enters a boardinghouse for working men. He apprentices as a department-store clerk or assembles reapers in the McCormick factory or keeps timetables for the Union Pacific Railroad. He struggles for working-class respectability, like the protagonist in any story by Horatio Alger, Jr. His parents sell to the owner of a neighboring farm and move to town. One sister becomes a teacher and marries a more prosperous farmer. The other marries a mechanic.

The two paintings bracket an era of unrelenting ejectment, seizure, bankruptcy, and loss. They tell a story bigger than Appalachia, about other peoples and places in the United States, so that we might see the southern mountains as connected to other events. And yet, ejectment and loss seem averse to the predominant fact of this period. Between 1870 and 1900, the number of acres in farms more than doubled. Farmers cleared as much land in those thirty years as they had in the previous two hundred. But if we look a little deeper, another trend emerges. Farms of fewer than three acres fell 37 percent between 1870 and 1880, 47 percent by 1910. Yet farms of one hundred to five hundred acres increased almost 550 percent. Those over a thousand acres increased by over 1,000 percent. The fate of farmers also differed by region. California entered a flush of growth, while South Dakota and Nebraska lost small and midsized farms and gained giant ones. Agriculture did not falter. Wheat, corn, and cattle boomed. But those households with little money strained under drought and debt, finally yielding to repossession by banks and the sale of their land to corporations. Those tillers neither hired nor hiring but literally laboring upon their own hook often gave up. They became the hired, working for wages on industrial farms or in factories.

The losses I consider in this chapter include agrarians whose suffering and defeat the government did not quantify. The golden quarter section harvested by Winslow Homer's veteran had been the hunting grounds of the Lakota, Cheyenne, Comanche, Crow, Apache, Pawnee, or Shoshone. Possession and dispossession were locked together, impossible to extricate from each other. Former slaves with tenuous provision grounds found themselves manipulated into sharecropping. They were farmers by occupation, but as indebted tenants they owned nothing, often earned nothing, and existed more like serfs than smallholders. Henry David Thoreau and Ralph Waldo Emerson tried to come to terms with the cultural irrelevance of Yankee farmers, many of whom no longer lived within their means or the limitations of their environments and yet, as farmers, no longer reflected the commercial impulse of the United States in 1850. What follows is an exploration of painting and writing that depicted this moment of change.[1]

THE ENCLOSURE OF THE BUFFALO COMMONS did not unfold like the seizure of village fields in England. It came about in a manner similar to what happened in colonial ventures: by warfare. The Civil War should be understood as a conflict with two Union fronts, one in the South and the other in the West. The Plains nations had their own confederacy. Like the other one, the Sioux and Cheyenne did not want to be part of the United States. The defeat of the Confederate States of America closed one front but not the other. Ulysses S. Grant ordered Phil Sheridan to the Department of the Missouri in 1867. There, along with William Tecumseh Sherman, Sheridan applied all he had learned in the Shenandoah Valley about subsistence warfare to defeat a different enemy.[2] Warfare ended ten years later, when Crazy Horse and Red Cloud surrendered, but the United States had not won a military victory. Add up the bodies dropped on both sides, and the Indians destroyed the invaders by nearly two to one.[3]

Sheridan fought the Plains nations with subsistence adversity. He declared war on the bison. Speaking to Congress in 1875, he said of professional bison hunters, "Let them kill, skin, and sell until the buffaloes are exterminated," calling this the way to a lasting peace. Three years later, the Plains nations were famished. When agents of the Bureau of Indian Affairs arrived at the Colorado River Reservation in 1878, they saw hunters returning "completely demoralized with fear." The agents dispatched an emergency request for beef and flour, "to alleviate the sufferings of those starving creatures . . . for their bodies were so emaciated from want that they proved an easy prey to disease." Those sturdy enough found plenty of work "cutting and hauling wood for funeral pyres to burn the bodies of those deceased."[4]

Dispossession did not end with military violence. Over the next fifty years, Congress created reservations and then picked away at them, finally attempting to compel Indians to undertake commercial agriculture. By the 1880s, self-appointed reformers argued that reservations encouraged collective rather than individual behavior, embodied by what they considered the archaic office of the chief. Allotment emerged as a vehicle for assimilation. Not only would people born to the chase enter the socializing relations of agriculture, they would become property owners. "Where everything is held in common," wrote the commissioner of Indian Affairs in 1873, "thrift and enterprise have no stimulus of reward . . . The starting-point of individualism for an Indian is the personal possession of his portion of the reservation."[5]

The General Allotment Act of 1887 (known as the Dawes Act) extended surveyors' lines across reservations. The law granted 160 acres to every head of household, 80 acres to anyone over the age of eighteen, and 40 acres to each child. Any adult male who worked his allotment into a farm qualified for citizenship. But most of the land Indians received was ill-suited for agriculture, making their task even more arduous, if not impossible. Even worse, the turn from homeland to real estate opened every targeted reservation to a Trojan horse. Any land not allotted went up for sale, allowing whites to infiltrate and speculate. Senator Henry Teller of Colorado orated against the bill in 1881, condemning it as a legalized scheme "to despoil the Indians of their lands and to make them vagabonds on the face of the earth." The Dawes Act appealed to reformers as a mechanism for moving Indians to a further stage of social evolution, but Teller proclaimed its true purpose. "The provisions for the apparent benefit of the Indians are but the pretext to get at his lands and occupy them . . . If this were done in the name of Greed, it would be bad enough; but to do it in the name of Humanity . . . is infinitely worse."[6]

By the 1890s, the Plains nations were in despair. But their resistance did not cease. They continued to argue for their sovereignty even as the United States denied them citizenship and declared their religious practices illegal. The Indian Citizen Act of 1924 finally recognized their rights after thousands served in the armed forces during the First World War. A new generation of reformers and Indian leaders secured passage of the Indian Reorganization Act (1934), which restored unallotted land to tribal ownership. Throughout the twentieth century, various nations launched legal challenges on the basis of violated and neglected treaties. The struggle of first nations against false narratives of progress continues.

This is how the veteran in Winslow Homer's painting ended up swinging a scythe on the Great Plains. By the time the bison population collapsed and the Dawes Act threw reservations open, farmers like the veteran had been moving into Kansas, Nebraska, and Dakota Territory for nearly twenty years. The Homestead Act of 1862 transferred 100 million acres from the hunting grounds of the Plains nations to the public domain. Thousands of farmers, many of them immigrants from Scandinavia, Poland, Bohemia, and Hungary, arrived in the 1870s to raise wheat—not for their own food but for greenbacks. Many of them endured a different process of dispossession from that of the Plains nations. The small-scale commodity producers who acquired that droughty land did not hold on to it for very long. Within little more than two decades, a confluence of factors removed thousands of them and consolidated their homesteads into giant agricultural holdings.

As they crossed the 100th meridian, farmers entered a dangerous environment for wheat—a different planet, in a sense, from the humid longitudes. Emigrants who arrived during the 1880s had no idea that they had stepped onto a roulette wheel of climate risk. Between 1871 and 1873, annual precipitation on the northern Plains averaged just eight inches. It did not reach twenty inches—the threshold for planting wheat with some security—during the next three years. A writer for *The Atlantic Monthly* visited Kansas in 1879. He found dwellings forlorn. The few gardens he saw "appear generally to have ended in partial or total failure." Homesteaders had a cow and a few chickens or no livestock at all. The writer met people "fleeing from the country." One couple had paid the entry fee for land and all expenses, including buildings, fences, and dairy cattle. But the first year left them nearly broke. With their animals dying and no wage work available, they sold for less than they had spent and moved to the state of Washington. They told the writer that everyone they knew would leave the Plains if only they had the means.[7]

Then the rains returned. In 1882, homesteaders in Dakota planted 720,000 acres of wheat. "They plowed up the rich buffalo grass and planted grain in its stead," wrote one historian. Two years later, they had plowed up an additional 1.5 million acres, followed by another 2.6 million two years after that. They put out money for tools and machinery at a frantic rate, betting on good weather and high prices. Wheat became a fever, and the fever drove farmers into debt. They lived in shelters built from the brick-like sod they turned over with their steel plows, little more than dugouts that clung to any rise in the landscape for protection against the unceasing wind. The earthen floors turned to mud whenever it rained. They endured this and zero degrees in winter because fifteen bushels per acre promised them something unheard of among the agrarians of previous generations: a cash income they could live on.[8]

After 1887, everything turned for the worse. The hazards that descended upon them form the lore of the Plains: prairie fire without warning, tornados that carried off barns, locusts by the billions that devoured the labor of months. A drought set in by 1888 that destroyed most of what households had built over the previous decade. One editor described "climate changes or planetary influences . . . that have roasted our fields, decreased our crops, and killed our meadows." The winter of 1889–1890 plunged South Dakota into subsistence crisis. In Miner County, when harvests fell to under three bushels an acre, twenty-five hundred people nearly starved to death. The geopolitics of food also killed the boom. Australia, Russia, and Canada sent wheat into world markets. Prices collapsed. The average grade of spring wheat lost forty cents a bushel between 1882 and 1887, regaining twenty cents by 1891. Rural editors urged farmers to diversify, to go into dairy cattle, to plant a garden. Some did. Yet the Great Plains frontier was not where households went to live on their gardens but where they went to make money.[9]

"We live in the nineteenth century," wrote the Minnesota commissioner of labor. "We must reckon with its forces and tendencies." He tried to come to terms with the losses he had seen. But as wheat became integrated into world markets, the array of forces that determined its price became so varied, so obscure, that almost no one could reckon them. Together, these forces almost guaranteed failure for anyone with a quarter section. Tariffs imposed by France and Germany made exports less profitable, causing gluts. A new milling process increased the supply of flour and lowered the price of wheat. Homesteaders confronted rising railroad rates, which sometimes wiped out their profits. Speculators cornered the market, or tried to. Banks charged interest as high as 10 percent on short-term chattel mortgages. When creditors came calling during the Panic of 1893, they sometimes demanded the immediate payment in full after a single monthly default. In 1870, a farmer who owed $1,000 on a mortgage needed to raise 600 bushels to pay it off. Twenty years later, if he still owed half of it, the remaining $500 required almost the same number of bushels (590). "In other words," lectured the agrarian writer Leonidas L. Polk, "the farmer must pay his debts with the products of his labor, and he must work twice as hard, and give twice as much cotton, corn, or wheat to-day as was required in 1870 to pay the same debt."[10]

The point is simple, though it played out in complicated ways. Whenever farmers with a few hundred acres fastened their fate to the price of any global commodity (wheat, corn, or cotton)—whenever they entered into debt and depended on money—their failure was almost certain. Still, believers in the never-ending bonanza demanded more land. The only piece of Dakota Territory yet unplanted was the Sioux Reservation, of which 22 million acres was exposed to sale under the terms of the Dawes Act. In one grotesque spectacle of seizure, legislators engineered a free-for-all and gathered at Pierre to watch it. On February 11, 1890, hundreds of land seekers lined up on the border. A cannon went off as a crush of horses and coaches rolled across the frozen Missouri River into the Sioux homeland and the land seekers took whatever they wanted.[11]

The arid phase of an arid climate that caused so many to abandon the Plains turns out to have been the North American visitation of a global drought and recession. A series of El Niño oscillations shifted the location of the monsoons from the western to the eastern Pacific. The redistribution of heat and moisture affected the entire Northern Hemisphere. The droughts of the 1870s and 1880s caused human misery from the Deccan in the peninsular interior of India to the Sertão in northeastern Brazil. But the vanished monsoons account for only part of the cause. As Mike Davis argues, tens of millions died of starvation across the tropical world from their recent incorporation into commodity markets. "They died in the golden age of Liberal Capitalism," not because they were isolated from the emerging world-system "but in the very process of being forcibly incorporated into its economic and political structures." (Frank Norris gives these words to a grain dealer in *The Pit* [1903]: "Think of it, the food of hundreds and hundreds of thousands of people just at the mercy of a few men down there on the Board of Trade. They make the price. They say just how much the peasant shall pay for his loaf of bread. If he can't pay the price he simply starves.") Under British colonial rule, Indian peasants lost long-standing methods of compensating for climate risk, as the British continued to extract from them in a downward spiral of dependency and hunger.[12]

Farmers on the Great Plains did not starve to death. But their experiences followed a general pattern of adversity tied to smallholder integration into commodities markets. In response to these and other stressors, a social movement among Plains farmers arose during these decades. The members of the Farmers' Alliance attempted to recapture a modicum of control. Throughout the 1880s, speakers traveled around giving lectures, holding tent meetings, gathering the people into an organized protest against finance capital and commodity exchanges. Alliance economists thought imaginatively about money and credit. Their plan for a series of subtreasuries would have replaced the predatory loans offered by furnishing merchants with a government-backed system of crop storage. They called for land reform to prevent dispossession by bankruptcy. In the words of Luna Kellie, the thousands of farmers who had lost their homes demanded "that *occupancy and use shall be the sole title of land*." This insistence on sweat equity amounted to a producer's political economy, in which wealth flowed to all those who labored. The People's Party ran candidates for president in 1892 and 1896. Populists were elected to city boards, state legislatures, and Congress.[13]

This challenge from the hinterland, this democratic uprising rooted in agrarian moral economy, carried enormous implications. For even though eastern politicians dismissed the radicals, they responded with nothing less than a new version of the state. The political agenda of agrarian radicalism touched all affairs, foreign and domestic. It included trade policy, income taxes, the public control of banking and currency, antitrust law, and the government regulation of railroads. Populists attempted combinations with industrial labor unions and deeply influenced the metropolitan reform movement, known as progressivism. These events shaped the way working people thought about themselves and the United States into the middle of the twentieth century.[14]

Though pieces of their legislative agenda reverberated for decades, the People's Party died when they merged with the Democrats during the election of 1896. Economists stepped over the body. David Wells, perhaps the most influential advocate of the gold standard, yielded nothing to populism. He defined agriculture as a sector of the economy, not a form of social life. Wells narrowed the conditions for its existence to a singularity. "The only possible future for agriculture," he wrote in *Recent Economic Changes* (1899), "is to be found in large farms, worked with ample capital, especially in the form of machinery, and with labor organized somewhat after the factory system." At one moment, the families who took possession of the Plains represented progress and the possibility of modest accumulation. At another, they appeared unfit for that task. In the estimation of economists, they were as obsolete as the mountaineers of West Virginia.[15]

When the New England naturalist Wilson Flagg imagined a nightmare of steam power in 1859, he fairly described the first vast mechanized grain-growing operations on the Plains. A bonanza farm of ten thousand acres consumed enough binding twine in one season to encircle the coastline of England, Ireland, and Scotland. But binding wasn't necessary with machines that cut, threshed, cleaned, and sacked the grain without human hands. In 1775, it required two and a half hours of labor-time to harvest and thresh one bushel. In 1896, the same operation required five and a half minutes. A journalist for *Harper's Magazine* saw twenty thousand acres under cultivation, part of a fiefdom consisting of seventy-five thousand. Each tract of five thousand acres had its own superintendent, foremen, and harvesters. The journalist called it "the army system applied to agriculture." A general "marshals his men, arrays his instruments of war, and . . . moves forward to conquer and extract." He observed, darkly, "It absorbs great tracts of land, and keeps out smaller farmers. It employs tramps, who vanish when the harvest is over."

Twenty years later, a social scientist trekking through western Kansas found "no farming in the usual sense of the word . . . Not even home life is found here, for the year around the bulk of the work is done by transient laborers." The author followed hundreds of migrating men, part of an estimated 28,000 farmers without farms, perhaps some of them refugees from the enclosure of Appalachia. Managers promised them wages, beds, and food but sometimes locked them up at night to prevent them from leaving before the end of the harvest. The smallholder's Arcadia died in the very field where Winslow Homer saw it born.[16]

IN 1865, FARMERS HAD REASON for optimism, especially African-Americans. A number of them came to the Plains, having migrated from Mississippi and Louisiana to Kansas. Some of them were former Union soldiers, veterans in their own new fields. But if Homer had looked around for an African-American farmer to depict, he might have chosen one from another recently emancipated community, located on one of the Sea Islands off the coast of South Carolina.

On November 7, 1861, seven months into the Confederate rebellion, the Union Navy sailed into Port Royal Sound. Their cannon assault crushed the town's modest defenses. The next day, planters set fire to their cotton and packed their valuables into boats just hours ahead of the invading soldiers. The first regiments to reach Beaufort witnessed ten thousand free people dismantling the mansions. Commanders had no idea what to do. In January,

William Tecumseh Sherman called on Christian missionaries to offer help and advice. They arrived in March and put into place an innovative policy. The Port Royal Experiment, as it came to be known, carved up the plantations, giving former slaves acres of their own on which to grow food and cotton. They traded within and between communities, some acquiring enough money to buy additional land. In January 1865, Sherman was in Savannah, having just torched crucial pieces of the Confederate infrastructure. Thousands of freedmen followed on foot behind the Military Division of the Mississippi, needing food and asking to serve. Sherman thought back to the black smallholders on the Sea Islands and decided to formalize the Port Royal Experiment into military policy.

In one of the most remarkable gestures of authority in the history of the United States, Sherman issued Special Field Order, No. 15. On Cane Island, Hilton Head, Saint Helena, and at least ten other islands, Sherman seized 195 plantations to create enclaves of autonomy from vengeful whites. He declared, "The sole and exclusive management of affairs will be left to the freed people themselves." He offered each household "a plot of not more than (40) forty acres of tillable ground." A detachment of the military would protect the settlers until Congress approved their titles. Sherman waved his hand over the mainland like a monarch. The region from Charleston to the Saint Johns River in Florida and thirty miles back from the ocean would be "set apart for the settlement of the negroes." But in another sense, the Port Royal Experiment was no experiment at all. African-Americans were already skilled farmers, already believed that the land they had cleared and cultivated as slaves belonged to them by usufruct rights, already had a developed sense of the connections between property and citizenship.[17]

Winslow Homer did not paint African-American farmers, but his contemporary Thomas Anshutz did. In *The Way They Live* (1879), a mother scrapes the weeds between cabbage heads somewhere in the southern mountains. The corn is high. Her daughter brings her a pitcher of water. The family built a home of planks, with a stone chimney. The proud mother is another veteran in another field. That same year, Anshutz painted *The Farmer and His Son at Harvesting* (1879), in which a white father sharpens a scythe as his son drinks from a pail. They stand on a hillside, about to cut grass for hay. Their cabin is at the bottom of the hollow.

The two images fit together, forming a simultaneous moment. The houses and mountains in each are identical. Anshutz mixed the same greens and blues, depicted the figures at the same distance and scale, and gave them the same kinds of tasks. The mother and father each concentrate on the use of a tool. The son and daughter each have water. And when the paintings are placed side by side they match up. The mountain in one connects seamlessly to the mountain in the other, as though Anshutz meant them to be viewed together. The effect presents the families as equals, each doing the best they can, not starving or desperate but sufficient.[18]

As for the Port Royal Experiment, Sherman's order did not stand. President Andrew Johnson returned much of the confiscated property to its former owners. Congress never moved to grant title to the black farmers. Johnson wouldn't have signed the bill into law if they had. When the Freedmen's Bureau Act came up for renewal in 1866, Johnson vetoed it. He stood shoulder to shoulder with planters who wanted to reconstitute the former labor system to the greatest extent possible. A commonplace conspiracy appeared all over the South. In North Carolina, "It was recommended that no lands be rented to negroes, but that they be hired at good wages," according to the minutes of the Duplin County Agricultural Society. In South Carolina, "In the upper part of Charleston District the planters are quietly holding meetings at which they pass resolutions not to sell land to negroes . . . In Beaufort District they not only refuse to sell land to negroes, but also refuse to rent it to them." White landowners threatened aspiring black farmers with execution if they signed a lease "and undertook to work for themselves."[19]

One of the most effective tools of coercion was enclosure. During Reconstruction and well into the 1880s, counties all over Georgia passed statutes requiring that domesticated animals be fenced from grazing in the open woods. Landowners asserted rights over land they rarely visited, not to make use of it but to prevent it from functioning as a commons. A statute for fencing livestock might not seem very manipulative, but it trapped black forest squatters in a double bind. They could neither afford the cost of building fences nor the impoundment of their cattle. In Steven Hahn's words, planters moved "to circumscribe the freedmen's mobility and access to the means of production and subsistence. The legal and extralegal actions taken by the planting elite to prevent blacks from owning land ... were products of such an offensive." The same legal and extralegal enclosure drove English peasants into wage work and West Virginia smallholders into mills and mines.

Georgia's General Assembly voted to restrict open-range grazing in Taylor County in 1888, declaring that heretofore, "it shall not be lawful for any horse, mule, cow, or hog, or any other domestic animal used, or fit for either labor or food, to run at large." The landless saw the trick. "The law would benefit the extensive land owners," lamented one resident of Gwinnett County, calling it "the greatest curse for the poor laboring men that ever befell them." Said another, "The stock law will divide the people ... into classes similar to the patricians and plebeians of ancient Rome." White yeomen in North Carolina, in addition to local elites, often resisted stock laws because they, too, let their cattle roam free. But the laws gained in county after county by the end of the century.[20]

Landowners invented other legal tools for coercing blacks and whites into peonage. Among the most effective were vagrancy laws that criminalized poverty and unemployment. The idea that the poor are redeemed from immorality and sloth through value-creating labor goes back to early capitalism. Just as English lords of the seventeenth century believed that taking land away from peasants improved society, white southern landowners of the nineteenth century said that taking freedom from former slaves did the same. It might seem like an injustice impossible to rectify with American rights and principles, but the Constitution said nothing about the practice until the passage of the Thirteenth Amendment in 1865, which prohibited servitude "except as a punishment for crime." Prisons leased their inmates to plantations for harvesting, to state governments for road construction, and to corporations for iron and coal mining. In 1886, there were 64,349 convict laborers in the United States, most of them in the South, all of them once slaves or agrarians. Every one of them had been denied landed autonomy and endured incarceration for a condition forced upon them yet obscured behind the veil of law and civility. After they lost their freedom, many lost their lives. Of the 285 convicts who pounded spikes for the South Carolina Greenwood and Augusta Railroad, 44 percent died.[21]

Yet farmers of modest means gained in the South and West following the Civil War, including black farmers. Though many African-Americans ended up shackled to crop liens owned by landlords and furnishing merchants, others abandoned the South at nearly the moment Union soldiers withdrew after the negotiated end to Reconstruction in 1877. These emigrants recalled that whites in Colorado and Kansas had favored abolition before the Civil War, and they knew that the Homestead Act offered favorable terms. One group founded the town of Nicodemus, Kansas. Brick buildings and a newspaper suggested a thriving community before the drought of the 1880s destroyed harvest after harvest. When three major railroads bypassed Nicodemus, almost everyone moved away.[22]

ROMANTIC ESSAYISTS MIGHT NOT SEEM like the obvious commentators to turn to at this point. But they expressed a commitment to agriculture through their larger commitment to Nature. Even before the number of farms in New England began their decline, Henry David Thoreau and Ralph Waldo Emerson speculated darkly. Each predicted that Yankee makeshift would be eclipsed.

The most famous American agrarian of the nineteenth century was not a farmer. In 1845, Emerson invited Thoreau to live on a woodlot he owned about a mile from the center of Concord, Massachusetts, on the edge of Walden Pond. Thoreau built a small cabin and planted beans a few steps away. The journal he kept during the next two years, two months, and two days—published as *Walden* (1854)—established him as an important writer. He was a contrarian philosopher who advocated asceticism amid rising consumption, an exemplar of the waning virtue of thrift, a holdout against the capitalist logic on display at Lowell, twenty miles from his cabin door.

Thoreau did not engage in a caricature of makeshift economy, growing all his food and buying nothing. He planted a considerable bean field, far larger than he required. If the rows of his two and a half acres could have been placed end to end, they would have spanned seven miles. From this he harvested twelve bushels (or ninety-six gallons, an exceptionally low yield), reserving three for himself and selling nine. The profit from his market crops, including potatoes and hay, came to $8.71. Not an impressive sum. Add in the rice, molasses, and rye meal he bought, in addition to the $28.12 he spent to build his tiny house, and the venture lost money.

But money was never Thoreau's goal. Like anyone else with a garden, a pond for fishing, and a stretch of woods where he gathered and hunted, a monetary loss didn't hurt him. Thoreau's negative financial result actually confirmed his peasant existence. He sought money without depending on it for survival.

> I learned . . . that if one would live simply and eat only the crop which he raised, and raise no more than he ate, and not exchange it for an insufficient quantity of more luxurious and expensive things, he would need to cultivate only a few rods of ground, and that it would be cheaper to spade up that than to use oxen to plow it, and to select a fresh spot from time to time than to manure the old, and he could do all his necessary farm work as it were with his left hand at odd hours in the summer; and thus he would not be tied to an ox, or horse, or cow, or pig, as at present . . . I was more independent than any farmer in Concord.

This is the true yield of Thoreau's political economy. Like Crèvecoeur or any other agrarian advocate, he believed that material independence translated into freedom of thought and being. Like any peasant, he worked only to meet his needs, refusing to take on additional land or domesticated animals. His good-enough yields rewarded him with time each day to swim, write in his journal, and observe ants at war. When he said that property seemed to own its owners, he sounded like the socialist Albert Brisbane. He also sounded a little like Karl Marx.

They were born one year apart. Marx was twenty-six in 1844 when he first wrote on political economy. Thoreau was twenty-eight in 1845 when he moved to Walden Pond. Both sought to experience the fullness of human expression, leading them to reject moneymaking for its own sake. Thoreau pitied the owners of hundred-acre farms, calling them "serfs of the soil" who spend their days "laying up treasures which moth and rust will corrupt." Marx noticed that those who dedicated themselves to wealth often renounced basic pleasures. "The less you eat, drink and buy books; the less you go to the theater, the dance hall, the public house; the less you think, love, theorize, sing, paint, fence, etc., the more you save—the greater becomes your treasure which neither moths nor rust will devour—your capital. The less you are, the less you express your own life, the more you have, i.e., the greater is your alienated life, the greater is the store of your estranged being." Thoreau didn't dance or carouse in the public house like Marx did, but he would have agreed that money makes everyone its servant. And what else did he resist at Walden than alienated life and estranged being?[23]

The estranged beings Thoreau knew best were the improving farmers of Concord. The improvers advanced a kind of prosperity gospel, in which the rewards of the market flowed from land well tilled. They experimented in manures, cover crops, and animal fodder in order to increase the productivity of land and thus its returns. Restoring worn or otherwise infertile soil and making it pay became the highest virtue, the sign of grace. But one thing plagued Thoreau about his commercializing neighbors. Their greater output changed the landscape in ways that he loathed and feared. Railroad links to Boston and experiments with cattle breeds enabled them to produce more milk. A bigger business called for larger spaces cleared from the woods.

Thoreau responded with barely restrained rage, calling them mad with greed. "Farmers are respectable and interesting to me in proportion as they are poor,—poor farmers. A model farm! where the house stands like a fungus in a muck-heap . . . A great grease-spot, redolent of manures and buttermilk! Under a high state of cultivation, being manured with the hearts and brains of men! As if you were to raise your potatoes in the church-yard!" The historian Robert Gross thinks that Thoreau preferred to poke fun at the improvers rather than condemn them. Gross imagines Thoreau's bean field as a philosophical prank. "By contrast, Thoreau claimed to have done just the opposite. He started with exhausted, barren land, did nothing to improve it, obtained little from it, and announced himself quite content."[24]

Thoreau was anything but content. His experiment in subsistence was not intended merely to satisfy him or prove to the world that he could farm. Nor should we think of it as a romantic retreat into an untouched Nature, a communing with wildness, when Thoreau knew well that the people of Concord made constant use of Walden Pond and the woods that surround it. The key lies in his anger and the suggestion that greedy farmers exceeded their limits and sacrificed society to their narrow ends. Seen from these passages, *Walden* looks like the jeremiad of an ascetic intellectual in the midst of change he could not control. Thoreau set out to embarrass his neighbors by creating a viable subsistence on a strip of marginal ground, some of the worst soil in Concord. His denunciation and the alternative he constructed came from his anxiety about the pursuit of wealth and the commodification of the landscape.

Thoreau offers a complicated legacy that I cannot assess here. I sometimes think that his puritanism and psychological introversion explain more about him than anything else. And like other critics, I cannot help but see his contradictions. He overstated the purity of his economy by neglecting to mention that he paid nothing for his few rods of ground and lived there rent-free with the permission of the landlord. Thoreau said more about private property in *Civil Disobedience*. Owning land required one to pay taxes, which required one to make money. His solution was a fugitive existence, without community or continuity. "You must hire or squat somewhere, and raise but a small crop, and eat that soon. You must live within yourself, and depend upon yourself always tucked up and ready for a start, and not have many affairs." It tells us something unflattering about him that rather than write letters to the newspapers and form a coalition against speculation in land, he recommended dissolving all social bonds and leading a life on the run.

The most significant American intellectual also struggled with autonomy and freedom as they related to rural life. Emerson's two abysmal essays on the subject are known today as "Farming" and "Wealth." The first began as "The Man with the Hoe," an oration delivered at a cattle show in 1858. It would be unfair to compare it to the hundreds of similar addresses published in New England between the 1820s and the Civil War. Almost every one of them is superior in conception and content to Emerson's catalog of platitudes.

Emerson's essay opens with this flourish: "He stands close to Nature;

he obtains from the earth the bread and the meat. The food[,] which was not, he causes to be. The first farmer was the first man, and all historic nobility rests on possession and use of land." Emerson moves on to compare farmers to the managers of a faultless machine. "In English factories, the boy that watches the loom, to tie the thread when the wheel stops to indicate that a thread is broken, is called a minder. And in this great factory of our Copernican globe, shifting its slides, rotating its constellations, times and tides, bringing now the day of planting, then of watering, then of weeding, then of reaping, then of curing and storing,—the farmer is the minder." Soils, plants, the weather itself, he said, were as tools in the hand of the husbandman. It is impossible to imagine Wilson Flagg saying anything like this. No farmer would have spoken with such confidence when hail or drought or the Hessian fly could wreck a season's labor in a day. Emerson's philosophy is so devoid of reality, his language so insipid, that he could have been describing Virgil's Arcadia but certainly no earthly location in 1858.[25]

In "Wealth" (1860, revised 1876), Emerson mulled over a tougher problem. How did the ascent of a money-dominated economy change the meaning of self-reliance? He once fretted over the deepening division of labor in New England and the fracturing of the human totality it appeared to represent. "There is one man," he insisted in "The American Scholar" (1837). "Man is not a farmer, or a professor, or an engineer, but he is all." But the onset of "the *divided* or social state" sorted people into professions, to the point that "this original unit, this fountain of power . . . has been so minutely subdivided and peddled out, that it is spilled into drops, and cannot be gathered. The state of society is one in which the members have suffered amputation from the trunk, and strut about so many walking monsters,—a good finger, a neck, a stomach, an elbow, but never a man." Emerson further condemned the times in "Self-Reliance" (1841). He rejected progress as a metaphysical force in history. "Society never advances . . . It undergoes continual changes; it is barbarous, it is civilized, it is Christianized, it is rich, it is scientific; but this change is not amelioration." The New Englanders of the nineteenth century compared badly to the savage foil Emerson created, "the naked New Zealander." Riding in a coach made them too weak to walk. Wearing a Swiss watch made them forget how to tell time by the sun. Writing in notebooks ruins memory! Not even Rousseau was so hostile to the simplest innovations.[26]

But two decades later, Emerson strained to find a coherent way forward that would salvage some of the old creed. "Every man is a consumer, and ought to be a producer," he tells us, and his definition of wealth sounds like good old Yankee wisdom. Wealth begins "in a tight roof that keeps the rain and wind out; in a good pump that yields you plenty of sweet water; in two suits of clothes, . . . in dry sticks to burn; in a good double-wick lamp." Affirmed the great individualist, "Each man should feed himself." Then he swerves. The farm that provided everything, that "begins and ends with itself," existed in the past. It's gone, he says. "When men now alive were born, the farm yielded everything that was consumed on it. The farm yielded no money, and the farmer got on without. If he fell sick, his neighbors came in to his aid . . . Now, the farmer buys almost all he consumes,— tin-ware, cloth, sugar, tea, coffee, fish, coal, railroad-tickets, and newspapers." Emerson created a farm that never existed and then justified the money economy against it. There was nothing new or shocking about farmers buying sugar and newspapers. This is the false distinction between autonomy and exchange. No farm ever "yielded everything that was consumed on it." Emerson's Yankee farmer is the same caricature as Adam Smith's savage.

In "Wealth," Emerson tells us that the farm can no longer provide the central metaphor of the age. He saw agrarians as narrow and pinched, their tight roofs dripping, their suits looking frumpy and worn. He asked and answered a new question. "Will a man content himself with a hut and a handful of dried peas? He is born to be rich. He is . . . tempted out by his appetites and fancies to the conquest of this and that piece of nature, until he finds his well-being in the use of his planet, and of more planets than his own." Hopelessly tied to Earth, farmers failed Emerson's test of universality. But buying and selling seemed to harness the forces of the cosmic order. The merchant's laws "are laws of the Universe." Like any of the mediocre political economists churning out pamphlets at the same time, he blandly naturalized capitalist motion as heat and light. "The Merchant has one rule: absorb and invest: he is to be capitalist: the scraps and filings must be gathered back into the crucible; the gas and smoke must be burned, and earnings must not go to increase expense, but to capital again." This is where Emerson leaves it, with phony physics and the Protestant austerity that Thoreau and Marx ridiculed.[27]

"Farming" and "Wealth" are not about dispossession but the demise of New England makeshift as a cultural virtue. The first partakes of that faint praise for agriculture that lasted well into the twentieth century. The second says goodbye to the farmer as the exemplar of social and national progress. Emerson never seems to have understood that businessmen and bankers are entirely reliant on everyone else's labor. They consume without producing. But like many others, he had moved beyond self-reliance. When oysters collected from Long Island Sound could be served ten days later in Buffalo, what did it mean to live within oneself or a small community? What did it mean to refrain from consuming in all the new ways? Other intellectuals struggled with similar questions, including the ownership of the landscape itself. Among them was George Inness.

THE FIGURE HOBBLES ON A CANE across a footbridge spanning a dry and shadowy creek. The creek runs down the center of a meadow, where other figures stand or sit in the middle ground, as a locomotive slices across the horizon in the opposite direction of the walker. The gloom and uncertainty of the ravine heaves in the foreground, all the more threatening because the footbridge is rickety and rotted, suggesting the demise of the walker and the world of the meadow. This is the action in George Inness's *Short Cut, Watchung Station, New Jersey* (1883), a painting that depicts the end of one rural land regime and the ascent of another.[28]

Short Cut is interesting for reasons other than the tension it expresses between Nature and Culture, the most common way scholars have approached depictions of the American countryside since the publication of Leo Marx's *Machine in the Garden* (1964). The locomotive in *Short Cut*, however, is not merely set against the meadow, like the whale against the ship in *Moby-Dick*. Let's not talk about the sound of the whistle from the woods. We know how the railroad "gave rise to a symbolic motion away from centers of civilization toward their opposite, nature, away from sophistication toward simplicity." Yet the *Machine in the Garden* says nothing about the social and environmental dislocation inflicted on people. It ignores those represented in the painting who practiced some version of agrarian household economy—growing a portion of their own food, hunting where and when they could, and exchanging vigorously for all the things they did not make.[29]

Imagining engine smoke as harmonizing with clouds elides the totalizing claims of industrial technology to replace certain people and practices with others. It misses dispossession as the dominant social fact of the countryside in the nineteenth century. In *Short Cut*, Inness chose not to look away from the rural poor of New Jersey, who increasingly lost or sold their land to join the urban working class. In a series of paintings quite different from others in his catalog, Inness depicted relationships and individuals on the cusp of change.

Short Cut evokes a much more famous Inness painting, *The Lacka-wanna Valley* (1855). Both depict a locomotive crossing a cultivated plain with a figure in the foreground, but where the earlier work is grandly sphinxlike in its refusal to resolve its ambivalence about progress, the latter one is more pointed as social commentary. *Lackawanna Valley* presents a country path meeting steel tracks at the edge of a third space, a stump-covered hillside. But that hillside could belong to either the agrarian or the industrial economy, and the tracks themselves curve, as though asking a question or offering a proposition. *Short Cut* is more blunt. As the locomotive rushes onward, the peasant world is poised (literally) to topple over.[30]

A shortcut saves time or distance between two points, but only someone who knows how the parts of a place fit together knows where to veer off into bushes or through a backyard. In this sense, the man with the cane knows how to get across the creek without having to go all the way to the road, where there might be a stone overpass. But what moves through time faster than a locomotive? It always travels the shortest distance between two points. And what could be more tedious and circuitous than the path the walker takes? *Short Cut* might be interpreted as presenting local knowledge as a viable alternative to the worldly industrialism, but for the decrepit bridge barely spanning the ominous creek. Together, these visual elements present the bent-over walker on a shortcut to nowhere. If we assume a northern orientation, the train heads west while the walker crosses east—against the direction of time. The tension in the painting cannot be reduced to Nature versus Culture. It is not nostalgic. Inness does not give the viewer a past to return to, an alternative to the railroad, or an idyll to dwell in.

Seen this way, the walker's posture and the futility of his journey mark him as degenerate. Metropolitans increasingly saw the persistence of agrarians as a social disease. A varied literature of rural degeneracy claimed that such people lived in social isolation from communication and commerce, resulting in a low order of intelligence and a higher incidence of criminality. "The claim that rural places were rearguard," writes the scholar Maria Farland, "found its counterpart in the view that the habits of mind found in the cities were more forward-looking and avantgarde."[31]

Degeneracy is an aspersion, a projection from those supposedly forward to those supposedly backward. On the Wilderness Road near the Cumberland Gap, the novelist James Lane Allen watched a wagon approach, "faded and old, with its dirty ragged canvas hanging motionless, and drawn by a yoke of mountain oxen which seemed to be moving in their sleep." A boy drove the wagon, "a faded, pinched, and meager mountain boy." Allen doesn't speak to the boy. In the moment it takes for the wagon to pass him, he sees an expression of "mental excitement" on the face of the driver and notices that "in one dirty claw-like hand he grasped a small paper bag, into the mouth of which he had thrust the other hand, as a miser might thrust his into a bag of gold." The boy eats something and enjoys it. Allen spins the scene into a Tarzan-like story. "He had just bought, with a few cents he had perhaps saved no one knows how long, some sweetmeal of civilization which he was about for the first time to taste." Allen watches as boy and oxen roll toward the gap, passing behind steam from a sawmill. "Hidden in that steam, they disappeared. It was the last of the mountaineers passing away before the breath of civilization."[32]

Allen entirely invented the grotesqueness of this scene. Where did the boy's pennies really come from? He had just come from town. He probably spent the small change he received after buying something on an errand. There is no reason to believe that pie or candy would have been so very extraordinary to him. This is why boys liked to go to town. Instead, Allen eliminated consumption and money from mountain life, rendering the boy a stranger on his own road, a foreigner in his own county. The sawmill did represent the seizure of the forest and its conversion into commodities that produced capital, but Allen wrongly identified it with town and set both against the boy's home in the hills, which he assumed to be a pocket of irredeemable degeneracy.[33]

Degeneracy also carried a sense of moral danger. As Farland shows, the image of the deviant farmer saturated social science and fiction at the turn of the century, in books like Henry Goddard's *The Kallikak Family: A Study of the Heredity of Feeble-mindedness* (1912), Charles Davenport's *The Hill Folk: Report on a Rural Community of Hereditary Defectives* (1912), and more obliquely in Liberty Hyde Bailey's report for the Commission on Country Life (1908), Edith Wharton's *Ethan Frome* (1911), and Robert Frost's "The Mending Wall," in which the narrator describes his neighbor as "an old-stone savage." The genre's sociological watershed might have been Robert L. Dugdale's *The Jukes: A Study in Crime, Pauperism, Disease, and Heredity* (1877), in which Dugdale attributed the criminality of the anonymous Juke family to their "ancestral breeding spot . . . along the forest covered margin of five lakes so rocky as to be at some parts inaccessible." Thomas Cole, Frederick Church, and Asher B. Durand—foremost among the painters who cherished the countryside of upstate New York— would have been surprised to read Dugdale describe a wooded lakeshore in Ulster County as "one of the crime cradles of the State of New York" and a seething nest of convicts.[34]

The book promotes the libel of rural depravity. The shiftless ancestor of the clan was a single Dutch settler about whom Dugdale knew nothing except that "he lived much as the backwoodsmen upon our frontiers now do," drinking often, fishing and hunting rather than farming, and hating hard work. The old Dutchman committed the Jukes' original sin. He owned no land and all who followed him lived as "squatters upon the soil," in "log or stone houses similar to slave-hovels, all ages, sexes, relations and strangers 'bunking' indiscriminately." This last bit gives *The Jukes* its prurient quality. Somehow, illegitimate occupancy made him think of sexual impropriety. During the winter the family slept fanned out on the floor, feet toward the hearth. For hundreds of thousands of years, no one had a better idea for how to pass a frigid night. Dugdale, however, saw something creepy about it (which makes him seem creepy). That kind of "proximity, where not producing illicit relations, must often have evolved an atmosphere of suggestiveness fatal to habits of chastity." Incest, in other words, followed directly from sleeping in a heap. Inbreeding, however, was little more than a libel against outliers whose distance from the urban core exiled them from civil society, just as unmarried women who lived a little too far from church in seventeenth-century Salem were more likely to be accused of witchcraft.[35]

George Inness did not have to look far for a model of degeneracy. New Jersey had its own Appalachia. Just twenty miles northwest of Watchung Station (and a mere six hundred feet higher in elevation) lived a community of Scots-Irish and African-American ancestry who maintained a subsistence economy. *Appleton's Journal* wrote of the supposedly reclusive residents of the Ramapo Mountains: "They buried themselves deep in the fastness and gorges of the mountains, and reared children, wilder and more savage than themselves." But their real transgression was to live outside of the expanding capitalist economy, or as *Appleton's* put it, "Their desire is simply to live. That they must live for something never occurred to them." The proximity of the Ramapo Mountains and the popular characterization of the people there is at least suggestive of the figures in *Short Cut*.[36]

Whomever Inness saw in and around that meadow, he seems to have looked upon their dispossession as an injustice. We know that he embraced Henry George's single-tax reform movement. George believed that profits from the ownership of land, including rents, should be redistributed to all the members of society. The steam engine was supposed to set people free so they could philosophize, he wrote; instead, it enslaved and pauperized them. Wherever machines and capital spread, George saw insufficiency replace sufficiency. "Go to a new community where the race of progress is just beginning," he wrote in *Progress and Poverty* (1879), meaning before the transformation to a capitalist economy took place. "No one makes an easy living, or even a very good one—yet everyone can make a living. While you won't find wealth and all its effects, neither will you find beggars." He was talking about the household mode of production.[37]

Viewed through *Progress and Poverty*, *Short Cut* doesn't depict degeneracy but dignity. The walker becomes the universal peasant, who belongs to land that does not belong to him. The footbridge becomes the perfect inverse of the railroad, an authentic means of getting around, made by the hands of the people who used it. *Short Cut* could be interpreted as the critique of a public policy that failed to protect or compensate the rural poor for the land they were quickly losing to suburbanization and capitalist agriculture.

The same could be said for Inness's other canvases from his Montclair series of the 1880s. Many of these stand out in his catalog because they don't depict tiny figures at the edges of immense landscapes. They show people up close and doing things: gathering (*In the Orchard, Milton [New Jersey]*, 1881); herding lambs (*End of Day, Montclair*, 1885); collecting firewood (*The Old Barn*, 1888 and *Winter Morning, Montclair*, 1882); bringing in a stray cow (*Homeward*, 1881); and chatting during the workday (*Gossip*, 1884). In another departure, he left the studio and used live models, perhaps in an attempt to meet local residents. One painting that illuminates some of the themes is *The Old Veteran* (1881). An infirm man walks on crutches made of branches. Climbing beans weave through a broken enclosure behind him. The image feels journalistic, even voyeuristic, like a domestic moment we're not supposed to see. (The contrast with Winslow Homer's veteran couldn't be sharper.) It's the same man, or nearly, whom Inness painted two years later inching his way over a waterless creek.[38]

The Old Veteran and *Short Cut* both convey loss. Framed in terms of Henry George's political thought, Inness's paintings imply that the old veteran is owed a public debt for serving the Union and an income from the rents collected by wealthy landowners. Such policies would ease the old veteran's agedness and help him care for his grandchildren. As Inness lectured before a gathering in honor of George, "At present we can not help seeing [that poverty] arises out of false social conditions." By false conditions he meant property relations that undermine basic human needs. Individuals deserve to profit from what they create, he believed, but "that which he [the individual] does not create belongs to the community, and that is land."

Inness moved to Montclair in 1885, joining the middle-class strivers who commuted to work on the railroad. At some point during the 1880s, according to a local historian, as many as six thousand people traveled to work every day. Land changed hands furiously in the decades between

1870 and 1890, part of the transformation of Montclair into a suburb of New York City. The population of Essex County, including the Township of Montclair, increased by 32 percent between 1870 and 1880 and another 34 percent during the next decade, driving up real estate prices and property taxes. The irony of these changes and Inness's participation in them was that they displaced the herders and gardeners he painted. A number of self-sufficient agricultural colonies, founded by Italian and Jewish immigrants, failed during the 1880s. Inness witnessed the transformation of New Jersey from farm to suburb.

All of which hints at a final possibility for the meaning of the painting. The limping walker is himself a new commuter. He wears a white shirt and vest appropriate for a clerk. He crosses from agrarian subsistence to wage work, using the footbridge to save a few minutes before the next train. In a world in which the single tax did not become law, the only escape for the figures in *Short Cut* was to sell their labor. For them, survival meant finding the fastest way to Watchung Station, thereby traveling in a straight line between past and future.[39]

FEW PEOPLE AT THE TIME ever viewed one of Inness's paintings. If they had, many in New York City or Chicago would have recognized themselves or their parents or their grandparents in the figures he drew and would have felt something of the pathos he expressed for gardeners and herders. They read another kind of description in newspaper accounts of feuds and shootouts in mountains not far away. These stories recast the society and sufficiency of Appalachia as the cause of pathological behavior. The stories made an implicit argument. If isolation was the cause of violence and degeneracy, then extractive industry was the solution.

City newspapers began to carry articles about depraved people living high and away. When *The New York Times* learned of an ongoing conflict between families named Hatfield and McCoy, editors used it to comment on the barbarity of the region and its people.

> This is a queer story to be told of a civilized country . . . The McCoys and Hatfields and other "well-known families" of the

mountain region will doubtless go on bequeathing freedom's battle from bleeding sire to son until either they are all killed or the region they inhabit is brought into the pale of civilization. The discovery of metals and minerals in paying quantities would have the latter effect, but so long as a difficult agriculture is the only employment that can be followed in the mountains, their population will be small and scattered.

Industrial discipline, not legally constituted democratic authority, the equality of women, or education, would bring an end to such conflict. "Just as the feud was blamed on some inherent moral failing in the mountaineers," writes Altina Waller, "social disruption caused by economic transformation was blamed on their inferior culture." The disruption itself contributed to, if it did not cause, the feud, but metropolitans blamed mountain people for their hardship either way. And plain people had no way of countering the stories told about them. Yet those stories exercised real power. They justified people's dispossession as progress.[40]

Consider the example of John Fox, Jr., a Kentucky-born social climber with ties to the coal industry. He was born near Lexington, in the Bluegrass, and brought up the son of a schoolteacher. He didn't fit in at Harvard—not into the culture of affluence or the social display of masculinity. Fox attempted a career as a playwright and moved to New York City. Needing an income, he agreed to raise funds for his brother's coal-mining venture. ("It takes monumental cheek to . . . talk to a man about investing $10,000 when you have but $10 in your pocket. It makes me feel like a fraud," he wrote in a letter.) Fox finally moved back to Kentucky, where he joined the swindle that deprived mountain people of land. He learned how to bust unions by hiring convicts as scabs and by calling in state troopers. He bragged about his membership in a "guard," a racist death squad made up of college graduates who lynched a black railroad worker near Big Stone Gap, Virginia. For our purposes, Fox referred to coal companies as "missionaries in the cause of culture" who offered to save the souls of Anglo-Saxon primitives. Fiction was his way of promoting these ends.[41]

On a tour of the mountains near the Cumberland Gap, Fox's brother

James and the writer James Lane Allen saw a young woman riding an ox. They declared her an Appalachian version of the mythical Europa, the Phoenician woman who rides a bull that turns out to be Zeus in disguise. This became the premise for Fox's first novel, *A Mountain Europa*, begun in 1888 and published in 1892.

Clayton has just returned to Jersey City from a German university after a financial panic makes it impossible for his family to support his studies. His father abruptly sends him to Kentucky to make something out of the "mineral lands" the family had bought in the 1860s. Six months later, Clayton takes in the scene of the coal camp he founded and manages—miners stripped to their waists "bathing their blackened faces and bodies," while their dirty children play and their wives cook. But Clayton has no connection to his workers or much interest in coal. He prefers to spend his time walking in the woods with his dog. One day, he sees a young woman riding a bull. Clayton wants her instantly, "her supple figure swaying with every movement of the beast." He especially notices the way she carries herself, with confidence and strength, "so different from the timid mountain women who shrank with averted faces." The golden-haired woman who meets his gaze and tells him to call off his dog is Easter Hicks. Her volatile father has recently disappeared after being implicated in a murder over moonshine. She lives with her mother, and Clayton starts hanging around the cabin.

Easter is defiant and unwilling to compromise, but she yields to Clayton. Fox has no sense of them as a couple and continually degrades Easter's ability to do anything other than hunt. Clayton is a scholar and businessman, the Atlantic elite personified. He knows the past and owns the future. But Easter exists only in the present. Fox describes her as some kind of wild nymph with no capacity for thought. Seeing her looking out into the distance, Clayton wants to know her thoughts. "Probably she could not tell them, should he ask her, so unconscious was she of her mental life, whatever that might be. Indeed, she seemed scarcely to know of her own existence."

Then Clayton goes home to Jersey City for a visit. Seeing old friends and familiar places makes him rethink what he's doing in Kentucky. His father tells him that he is "fast making up his losses," meaning that Clayton might not need to remain in the hills much longer but could get a job in his father's firm. Should he cut ties with Easter and leave her to the mountain boy who loves her? Clayton loves her, too, but not very convincingly. Worse, he thinks he's saved her, "lifted her above her own life" and "taught her to love him."

Returning to the Cumberlands, Clayton sees everything differently. "Were these hovels, he asked himself in wonder, the cabins he once thought so poetic, so picturesque? . . . The novelty and ethnological zeal that had blinded him to the disagreeable phases of mountain life were gone; so was the pedestal from which he had descended to make a closer study of the people. For he felt now that he had gone among them with an unconscious condescension." The romantic veil was somehow lifted, but Clayton's unconsciousness persists. He no longer sees the people as noble savages, but he has no awareness that his own work and the movement of capital that he represents in any way contributes to their poverty.

With the local color draining from his picturesque fantasy, Clayton decides to marry Easter in order to take her away. He would end his industrial sojourn and live the metropolitan life promised him. She would be redeemed from ignorance and backwardness to realize her noble nature. That's when Easter's father returns. Bill Hicks hates all "furriners" and demonstrates his potency when he hands a flask to the soft-handed college boy. "Clayton took a swallow of the liquid, which burned him like fire." But Hicks unexpectedly endorses the marriage. At the wedding, the moonshiner is drunk and disruptive. Suddenly he aims a gun at Clayton, who had just spent his first moment alone with his bride. As the gun goes off, Easter leaps forward and takes the bullet. She dies moments later and is buried on the mountain.

Easter's death parallels the death of the animate environment—full of life, defiant, wild, unconscious, and being ripped apart. Her marriage to Clayton, however, seems even more dismal. It carries no hope for either society, and its bloody ending leaves everything as before. The novel's controlling myth also contains Fox's purpose. Zeus turns himself into a white bull to get closer to Europa by mixing in with her father's herd. At first she wants nothing to do with this bull, though he is alluring. When she finally climbs onto his back, he carries her off to Crete, where the two become lovers. In Fox's parallel, Clayton comes from a world of gods and tries to mix into the social world of eastern Kentucky. But that's impossible.

A Mountain Europa tells readers that historical change comes from the roar of the industrial gods. Clayton has a reverie: "It was soon plain to him, too, that a change was being wrought at last—the change of destruction. The older mountaineers, whose bewildered eyes watched the noisy signs of an unintelligible civilization, were passing away." Fox believes in the redemptive power of ecological and social destruction, resulting in a new order. Yet the destruction only affects the mountains and their residents, never the mine or its owners. Clayton embodies this unilateral historical agency. After Easter falls dead, he walks away unharmed and unchanged.

Fox did not publish in obscurity. He educated the eastern elite, shaping their conception of an aggressive and inscrutable white mountaineer at a time when labor violence exploded in the West Virginia coalfields. Theodore Roosevelt wrote to Fox in 1894: "What you said in your letter . . . was so interesting that last night I read it to Cabot Lodge and Henry Adams." Fox interpreted Appalachia to the painters Frederick Remington and George Luks, the writers Owen Wister and Richard Harding Davis, and influential publishers, including Charles Scribner and William Dean Howells. Fox went on to write *The Cumberland Vendetta and Other Stories* (1895), *Hell-fer-Sartain and Other Stories* (1897), *The Kentuckians* (1898), *Crittenden* (1900), *Blue-grass and Rhododendron* (1901), *The Little Shepherd of Kingdom Come* (1903), *A Knight of the Cumberland* (1906), *The Trail of the Lonesome Pine* (1908), and *The Heart of the Hills* (1913), among other novels and articles.[42]

The most revealing moment in all of Fox's literary production might be a scene in *The Kentuckians*. A geologist named Reynolds responds to a journalist who says what many others must have believed—that the poor whites descended from Scots-Irish castoffs. In other words, one degenerate people came from another. Reynolds shoots back, "That is a foolish theory . . . Until a man has lived a year at a time in the mountains he doesn't know what a thin veneer civilization is. It goes on and off like a glove, especially off." Take any well-schooled, well-churched family from the Bluegrass, continues Reynolds, and put them in their own hollow. A century later, they'll be stupid and lawless, too. Fox offered his own sociological theory: the hillbilly could become white again by removing him from the hollows. The character of Boone Stallard in the same novel is just such a redeemed savage, having attended a state university. The stories give literary force to the controlling narrative of the times. Like Richard Henry Pratt, founder of the Carlisle Indian Industrial School, Fox thought that the metropolitan invasion would "kill" the mountaineer but save the man.[43]

By 1913, however, Fox appears to have regretted his insulting and degrading depictions of mountaineers. Bitter and destitute, he wrote *The Heart of the Hills*, one of his last novels. A child named Jason befriends a geologist pecking around Kentucky for coal seams. The geologist tells Jason what removing coal from the hills will mean to him and his family. Later, Jason quotes the geologist in a confrontation with Colonel Pendleton, a wellborn gentleman and investor from the Bluegrass:

> He said as how you folks from the big settlemints was a-comin'
> down here to buy up our wild lands fer nothin' because we all was
> a lot o' fools an' didn't know how much they was worth, an' that
> ever'body'd have to move out o' here an' you'd get rich diggin' our
> coal an' cuttin' our timber an' raisin' hell generally . . . He said that
> our trees caught the rain an' our gullies gethered it together an'
> troughed it down the mountains an' made the river which would
> water all yo' lands. That you was a lot o' damn fools cuttin' down
> yo' trees an' a-plantin' terbaccer an' a-spittin' out yo' birthright
> in terbaccer-juice, an' that by an' by you'd come up here an' cut
> down our trees so that there wouldn't be nothin' left to ketch the
> rain when it fell, so that yo' rivers would git to be cricks an' yo'
> cricks branches an' yo' land would die o' thirst an' the same thing
> 'ud happen here. Co'se we'd all be gone when all this tuk place,
> but he said as how I'd live to see the day when you furriners would
> be damaged by wash-outs down thar in the settlements an' would be
> a-pilin' up stacks an' stacks o' gold out o' the lands you robbed
> me an' my kinfolks out of.

Jason calls everyone involved a fool. Mountaineers sell their birthright for nothing, he says, while the people from the Bluegrass (the "big settlements") undermine themselves by tearing out the trees. The boy knows that trees hold soil, which holds water, preventing erosion. When only stones and roots remain, says Jason, folks like him will be gone. Everyone ends up with nothing. It's a stunning rebuke. For reasons we might never know, Fox renounced everything he had accomplished during his entire career.

⁂

WINSLOW HOMER'S *VETERAN IN A NEW FIELD* and Thomas Hovenden's *Breaking Home Ties* brace a quarter century better characterized by land lost than land gained. The number of farms in the United States increased between 1850 and 1900, driven by the shift of wheat planting on the Great Plains, irrigated fruit growing in California, and cattle ranching in Texas. Some of these were family farms, but during each decade more and more were profit-generating experiments in industrial agriculture. After 1910, the number of farms held steady at about 6 million, peaking at 6.8 million in 1935. The crisis of ownership that would cause the family farm nearly to disappear began during the Great Depression. By the 1970s, the number of farms had fallen to 2 million. And while thousands of families across the Midwest lost their fields of corn and soybeans during the 1980s, total acreage changed little after 1935, indicating that small farms were absorbed into larger ones.[44]

Inness and Hovenden did not predict this decline. Like other artists and writers, they portrayed a more general agrarian twilight. John Ise, Laura Ingalls Wilder, Willa Cather, Hamlin Garland, and Ole Rölvaag fictionalized the settler generation as worthy but troubled and finally as part of the past. Some of these writers presented rural life through the eyes of children or adults gazing back on childhood. They told stories of torment and failure. Garland dedicated *Main-Travelled Roads* (1891) to his parents, whose half century of farming had rewarded them with "only toil and deprivation," while acknowledging their "silent heroism." These authors moved beyond depictions of everyday privation to speculate about the fragility and possible extinction of the agrarian household.

Rölvaag's *Giants in the Earth* (1927) tells the story of Norwegians in Dakota Territory during the 1870s. Per Hansa, the male head of household, catches only glimpses of the smallholder's dream. "The suffering was great that winter. Famine came; supplies of all kinds gave out; for no one had thought, when the first snowfall began, that winter had come . . . Some had to leave their potatoes in the ground; others could not thresh the grain; fuel, if not provided beforehand, was scarcely to be had at all." The environment pressed relentlessly against the peasant universe. In shock after a tornado shreds her sod house, Per Hansa's wife, Beret, whispers, "Out here nobody pays attention to our tears . . . it's too open and wild." The story is haunted by madness. Per Hansa walks off into a snowstorm on a hopeless mission, an echo of the settlement itself. Children find his frostbitten body the following spring, eyes wide open, "set toward the west."[45]

Other stories stress fallen virtues. *Little House in the Big Woods* (1932) depicts the Ingalls family as content with little and confidently self-sufficient. "Pa and Uncle Henry traded work. When the grain got ripe in the fields, Uncle Henry came to work with Pa, and Aunt Polly and all the cousins came to spend the day. Then Pa went to help Uncle Henry cut his grain." Young readers have been riveted by the crises and triumphs of the characters, but the novel is wrapped in nostalgia. It's set in the narrator's memory. It speaks to bonds of kinship that vanished along with the Big Woods of Wisconsin. This and other stories suggest no clear place for agrarians in the present.[46]

Farms operated by households did not disappear just then, however. They changed into something else. They became the *family farm*, an attempt to conduct husbandry as a wage-paying, commodity-producing, technologically competitive enterprise. This is not to say that these small businesses did not produce any of their own food, nor does it say that family members and hired hands took no pleasure in agriculture. The university experiment stations (founded by the Hatch Act of 1887) and the United States Department of Agriculture (founded in 1862) urged them to keep financial records, study business, replace harvest labor with machinery, buy bird guano or bonemeal to fertilize their soils, and look upon their work as managerial. The family farm first appeared in New York and Massachusetts, represented by improved farms that made a leap into profit-making from subsistence during the era of the Erie Canal. In the decades following the Civil War, smallholders like Winslow Homer's veteran took up arid quarter sections to grow wheat for flour milling, with all the insecurities and false assumptions built into that model. The family farm reinvested its surplus value, paid its taxes, and strove for a middle-class standard of living.

Playing by the rules, however, often meant losing the farm. Industrialization transformed the relationship of families to their land and themselves. The more they specialized in the best-paying crop, the more alienated they became from what they produced, to the point that they became servants of their mortgaged fields. In *Now in November* (1934), Josephine Johnson's novel about a Missouri family struggling through the 1930s, the narrator offers this lament: "We never seemed able to make much over. All that we saved above what it cost to live . . . all went into the mortgage-debt. It would have taken so little to make us happy. A little more rest, a little more money—it was the nearness that tormented." They carried the mortgage like a bushel of rocks. "There was a bitterness in sowing and reaping, no matter how good the crop might be . . . And there was the need, the awful longing, for some sort of permanence and surety; to feel that the land you ploughed and sowed and lurched over was your own and not gone out from under your feet by a cipher scratch." The family farm replaced the possibility of subsistence adversity with financial adversity, but whereas the old household could maneuver within most bad situations, the new one owed its existence to creditors.[47]

Farm subsidies would seem to have offered the solution to the discordance between the homestead of a few hundred acres and the perplexing forces of the global economy. During the Great Depression, Congress paid farmers not to produce, in order to maintain higher commodity prices. The purpose of the Agricultural Adjustment Administration was to preserve the number of farms and farmers and to ensure them a dignified standard of living. This thinking changed during the presidency of Richard Nixon. Secretary of Agriculture Earl Butz reengineered the subsidy. Henceforth, the government encouraged the largest harvests with the maximum efficiency possible, resulting in the greatest quantity of corn for the lowest prices ever seen. Congress used public money to shore up the difference between low prices and the cost of production. "Get big or get out" described the new policy and the end of any pretense to promoting a way of life.

This shift followed the changing landscape of agricultural politics. As the number of family farms declined, consolidated land came under the ownership and management of corporations. Monsanto, Cargill, and Archer Daniels Midland can exist in an atmosphere of low prices. They make money on small margins and titanic volume, most of it sold on world markets. Subsidies allow corporations to make a profit even when the prices resulting from supply and demand run below their costs. In other words, the policy insures them against the depressed values that they cause. The effect is to undercut smallholders in other countries by making it impossible for their crops to compete. This is how the United States has set off a race to the bottom that feeds global dispossession. Nation-states with few resources other than farmland, seeking to boost GDP, act rationally when they propose to replace smallholders with corporations. Only corporations can pay long-term leases and turn out commodity crops on an industrial scale. The use of public money, once a mechanism for keeping family farmers in business, now drives them out all over the world.[48]

The American family farm was a hybrid species that didn't survive. During the century between Reconstruction and the 1980s, public policy depopulated the American countryside one cipher scratch at a time. Patented seeds and ammonia fertilizer flooded markets with cheap food, leaving families vulnerable to the slightest market fluctuations. Since farmers of undifferentiated commodities like wheat, corn, or soybeans cannot set their own prices to compensate for their costs, they must increase yields any way they can, often by taking on debt to buy out neighbors or to purchase larger machines. Yet this chain of reasoning ushered them into bankruptcy. The boom years of the 1970s were followed by their perfect reversal. Under high interest rates and falling commodity prices, thousands of farms went out of business.

On December 9, 1985, a third-generation farmer named Dale Burr entered the Hills Bank & Trust Company in Johnson County, Iowa, with a shotgun. He discharged it into the head of his banker. He had already killed his wife, Emily. Later that day, he killed another farmer before killing himself. His brother-in-law said that Burr was $1 million in debt. He reportedly told Emily, "I'm sixty-four years old and for the first time in my life I don't have money for groceries." On August 19, 1986, an Oklahoma farmer named Bill Stalder killed his wife, his son, and his daughter with a shotgun. He burned his farmhouse to the ground before shooting himself. The police found his diary in the barn. On the last page, he wrote "responsible" over and over again. A woman facing foreclosure committed suicide; so did a banker who could not stand the burden he had placed on others.[49]

Dispossession has immense social consequences. It should be understood as a government policy, not as the inexorable work of historical forces set in motion with the Big Bang. If the United States had wanted family farmers, it would have done more to sustain and encourage them. Yet the commonplace narrative creates the illusion of unavoidable tragedy and historical necessity. Any Scots-Irish, Cherokee, or African-American with a cabin and garden knew that dispossession served someone else's purpose. It was an instrument of control, not a sign of progress.

6. The Captured Garden

SUBSISTENCE UNDER INDUSTRIAL CAPITALISM

I want to propose a more radical notion of displacement, one that,
instead of referring solely to the movement of people from their
places of belonging, refers to the loss of the land and resources
beneath them, a loss that leaves communities stranded in a place
stripped of the very characteristics that made it habitable.

—Rob Nixon, *Slow Violence and the Environmentalism of the Poor* (2011)

IN MARCH 1907, AN ITINERANT MINISTER arrived among the shanties owned by the Pocahontas Coal Company. In a sermon given where he stood, the preacher declared that the miners deserved more than the company paid them. A manager approached the visitor and invited him to dinner at his home that evening. As soon as the door closed, a squad of armed bookkeepers and clerks surrounded the preacher, clubbed his head and face, broke his ribs, and dragged him to the church, leaving him to bleed through the night on the floor. The miners threatened war when they learned about the attack. One vowed in a letter to the company president that if any of his thugs walked the streets of Davy, West Virginia, they would be "wiped off the face of the earth."

Everything about coal mining instigated class warfare. Whenever miners attempted to improve their lives within their constitutional rights to assemble and organize themselves, coal operators responded with violence. The camps operated like small police states, unincorporated private municipalities where company rules functioned as martial law. But while militant strikes, fought with bats, bullets, and poisonous gas dropped from military airplanes, made newspaper headlines across the country, slow violence cut across the underbelly of mining families. Their dependency on company housing and company money spent for food in company-owned stores amounted to a constant threat of eviction and starvation. Coal operators wielded subsistence as a weapon. Miners tried to take it away from them.[1]

When mountain households entered the coal camps, the trapdoor of dependency slammed behind them. James Watt Raine, a professor of English at Berea College in Kentucky, had seen them seeping out of the hollows for twenty years. Raine traveled around talking to people and recording what he saw. In *The Land of Saddle-Bags* (1924), he wrote of their peril. The mountain man who became a miner "moves his family and a few household goods from the picturesque cabin in the cove or on the ridge to a desolate shack in the sordid village that has sprung up around the mine. He had not realized that he would have to buy all his food . . . He has to pay even for water to drink." Rent on their uninsulated board-and-batten shanties ran against these families all the time, even when the mines were closed, a policy meant to "bind them as tenants by compulsion . . . under leases by which they can be turned out with their wives and children on the mountainside in midwinter if they strike." Raine saw every autonomous path to money and exchange blocked, leaving them not just deprived of goods but ground down, impoverished, and subject to the "unspeakable danger . . . of a ferocious and devouring social system."[2]

Raine also noticed the gardens. Mining households didn't really buy all their food, except perhaps in winter. They continued to grow it just as they had before. In fact, though most of the remaining communities of subsistence hunters and farmers in North America lost the wherewithal to provide for themselves during the last decades of the nineteenth century, self-provisioning continued on the industrial periphery. When the location of a garden changed from the hillside to the camp, its beneficiaries changed along with its economic purpose. Mining companies encouraged household gardens, and even required them, when they recognized that these gardens served their interests.[3]

Political economists only complained about subsistence food production when it enabled smallholders to avoid market compulsion. Adam Smith knew that the same gardens that seemed like a holdover from a savage past could also further the circulation of capital. Smith described a class of "out-servants of the landlords," who "receive from their masters . . . a house, a small garden for pot herbs, as much grass as will feed a cow, and, perhaps, an acre or two of bad arable land." British capitalists did not eliminate self-provisioning when they enclosed the commons but absorbed it—in a sense, captured it—reassigning the garden and livestock from their long-standing role as pillars of household autonomy to their new function of subsidizing the wages of laborers.[4]

The captured garden took two forms—private accumulation and public relief. The former appeared much more often, with many more examples, than the latter. Both appeared in West Virginia between the 1880s and the 1930s. The same gardens that once produced beans and squashes as part of the spectrum of mountain land use arrived in colliery villages after corporations gained title to hollows. Later, the United States resettled unemployed miners in industrial villages, as part of the Division of Subsistence Homesteads. The story of dispossession in West Virginia and capitalism in the Atlantic World includes the political ecology of the household garden at the moment it moved from the commons to the company, from the clearing next to the cabin to the yard beside the shanty. Yet the captured garden also provoked resistance to its logic. All over the Atlantic World, provision grounds became contested grounds between the poor and the powerful over who controlled food and the terms of labor.

⁂

COAL COMPANIES DID NOT INVENT the captured garden; the British aristocracy did. Landlords realized that they could ensure adequate nutrition for their workers and reduce the wages they paid by shifting the burden of survival onto laboring households. Political economists tended to ignore collective arrangement, preferring a simplified social physics based on the behavior of individuals. But lords knew that the drive to survive among workers was a collective undertaking. When wives, sisters, young sons, and grandparents pulled weeds and thinned potato stems, they made up the difference between an inadequate wage and their bodily requirements. In effect, by expending their own labor to support the male earner, they became co-earners. Employers accumulated additional capital as though by magic—without raising wages, extending the working day, or purchasing additional tools. In this way, gardens increased exploitation. They allowed employers to pay below the market price for work.[5]

The earliest example of the captured garden was the cottar: one who paid rent on a small house. The agricultural improver John Sinclair represented the interests of enclosing lords when he suggested that the cottar "raise, by his own labour, some of the most material articles of subsistence for himself and his family." Cottar households could even sell their extra in local markets, but not enough to make them independent. Instead, they would continue to "assist the neighboring farmers, at all seasons, almost equally as well *as if they had no land in their occupation.*" Sinclair figured that hired hands needed only three acres and 80 days a year to raise all or most of their food. The work would take up "bye hours" and Sundays, leaving 285 days for "ordinary hand labour." One source from 1808 refers to cottages as a form of "bondage."[6]

But nowhere did the cottar achieve greater popularity among British capitalists than in Ireland. In the 1840s, dislodged Irish peasants composed an indigent labor force, obtainable, wrote Sir Robert Kane, "on lower terms than almost any other in Europe." There was only one problem. Starving people couldn't work. "Supplied only with the lowest descriptions of food," in Kane's icy assessment, "they have not the physical ability." Landowners allowed them to feed themselves, substituting cheap soil nutrients for money. Irish cottars improved their diets and gained a sense of proprietorship that dissuaded them from rising up (as they did time and again during the nineteenth century). In one example, households received ten roods of land each, or about one and a half acres. Lords allowed them to grow only potatoes, which they could cultivate "without interfering with any regular daily employment he may have, and thus without diminishing his regular weekly earnings." Add a pig and the garden became a tiny farm. The pig could be fed from peelings and kitchen waste. Its dung returned nutrients to the soil. Once fattened, it wound up on the table.[7]

Other versions of the cottar appeared in North America. The biggest difference between them was that most of the arable land in England belonged to lords in the seventeenth century, but no one owned Virginia and Massachusetts. Land purchased or otherwise acquired from Indians posed a problem for Virginia tobacco planters because no immigrant had any reason to stoop for someone else. For a time, men fleeing enclosure indentured themselves with the promise of a freehold at the end of their term. But planters realized that only permanent bondage would assure them a constant workforce. Captured Africans could not write home to warn others not to make the mistake of indenture. This is one reason why planters preferred them by the eighteenth century. Chattel slavery amounted to an enclosure of labor-power. To put this more generally, capitalist ventures need to assemble land and labor. Where labor is abundant, enclosing land brings the two together; where land is abundant, labor must be captured.

Various coercive labor systems arose in response to the abundance of unencumbered land. The Homestead Act of 1862 made farms on the Great Plains available for next to nothing. It actually installed the principle of sweat equity—use as the basis of ownership—into law. This is part of what impelled landowners in the South to find a way of binding black and white households to cotton-growing. They needed workers who would turn out the commodity year after year as though all that free land didn't exist. The agrarian household was itself a coercive institution. Whether in Puritan New England or the Appalachian backcountry, fathers imposed labor discipline and limits to freedom in what must have felt like indenture. Teenage children owed their families a certain term of labor before gaining the right to strike out for themselves.[8]

In England in the nineteenth century, the captured garden also appeared in a benevolent form. Rather than feed households in the midst of a wage, it fed them in unemployment. Here reformers took the lead and introduced various schemes meant to defeat the malevolent Thomas Robert Malthus. Malthus argued that new machinery made certain humans redundant, useless. In his mind, their pointless existence burdened almshouses, churches, and the state. He never bothered to consider the social causes of poverty. Instead, he took industrial capitalism as a stage of social evolution and regarded all those displaced by it as the drag and dregs of society and better off dead. Socialists hated Malthus (none more than Karl Marx) and came up with every imaginable workaround to his horrifying math. In the 1840s, the social reformer Robert Owen published one of the first plans to employ paupers. They would plant their own gardens.[9]

Owen called his method "spade husbandry," to distinguish it from horse husbandry. The spade would replace the plow in most fieldwork, freeing land from supporting animals and making it available for the support of humans. Eight people could live on the area needed to feed one horse, Owen calculated, resulting in a nearly one-to-one ratio of 60 million British poor to 60 million British acres. The redundant would escape Malthusian oblivion by becoming the very beasts of burden that the rich always assumed them to be. But Owen refused that comparison. When his critics claimed that "to exchange the plough for the spade, would be to turn back in the road of improvement," he countered that intensive gardening resulted in finer crops and a richer countryside. "Little do they imagine that . . . the change from the plough to the spade will prove to be a far more extensive and beneficial innovation than that which the invention of the spinning-machine has occasioned." He announced it as "an advance in civilization": progress, not backwardness; improvement, not stagnation.

But anyone who thought that Owen's benevolence placed a burden on the rich or in any way offered a socialist alternative to capitalism misunderstood it. Whether he realized it or not, the unemployed's growing of their own food maintained them as a healthy and available supply of labor for industry. As another reformer put it, child paupers would be trained "in habits of subordination and industry." No less an advocate for lordly interests than Arthur Young recommended internal colonies. He imagined 16 million people supporting themselves well enough to pay £2 million in taxes annually, "a much greater addition to our wealth, income, population, and strength, than we now receive from our brilliant oriental dominations of Bengal, Bahar, and Orixa." Parliament would have collected this

money like rent, an arrangement that would have aided lords by externalizing the cost of maintaining refugees from enclosure.[10]

***

EXTRACTIVE CORPORATIONS MADE COTTARS of their employees. But the relationship between subsistence and wages did not begin once families moved
to coal camps. It began while they still lived in the hills. Families maintained plots as security against seasonal unemployment and for retrenchment during strikes. In *River of Earth* (1940), James Still tells the story of
the Baldridge family. Poised between their cabin on the cutover and the
shanty in the squalid camp next to the Blackjack mine, the family clung
to "the scrap of land our house stood upon, a garden patch, and the
black birch that was the only tree on all the barren slope." Picking wild
hay after a rain, Mother tells Father that she dreams of having livestock
again. The conversation escalates into a debate over the family's fate:

> "If we had us a cow her udders would be tick-tight," Mother said.
> "It would be a sight the milk and butter we'd get."
>
> "Won't have use for a cow at Blackjack," Father said. "I hear
> the mines are going to open for shore. They're stocking the
> storehouse . . ."
>
> "I had a notion of staying on here," Mother said, her voice small
> and tight. "I'm again raising chaps in a coal camp. Allus getting
> lice and scratching the itch . . . Can't move a garden, and growing
> victuals."
>
> "They'll grow without watching. We'll keep them picked
> and dug."
>
> "I allus had a mind to live on a hill, not sunk in a holler where
> the fog and dust is damping and blacking. I was raised to like a
> lonesome place . . ."
>
> "Notions don't fill your belly nor kiver your back."
>
> Mother was on the rag edge of crying. "Forever moving yon and
> back, setting down nowhere for good and all, searching for God
> knows what," she said . . . "Forever I've wanted to set us down in a

lone spot, a place certain and enduring, with room to swing arm and elbow, a garden-piece for fresh victuals."

Mother wants constancy and continuity. She had followed her husband from coal camp to coal camp before. This time, she wanted to hold the family on the very edge of Blackjack without allowing them to fall in. Father argues that he's better at mining than farming, and all that matters is what he brings home. "It's bread I'm hunting, regular bread with a mite of grease on it. To make and provide, it's the only trade I know." Yet Father also knows that growing victuals beyond the reach of company managers insures the family against arbitrary unemployment, that betting everything on Blackjack would lead to misery.[11]

The drama unfolds in tiny spaces, with the reader standing in the room as someone sleeps or food is prepared. In the smokehouse one evening, Father digs a plow blade into the salt box to count the rinds of pork within. The possibility of hunger hangs like a ghost. Two cousins come live with them at great cost. "'It's all we can do to keep bread in the children's mouths,' Mother told Father. 'Even if they are your blood kin, we can't feed them much longer.'" She knows that the beans stored from last fall aren't enough to hold them over until the garden yields. Father becomes grim and determined. He tells Mother that he'll go to the store. But Mother knows they won't give him credit. "'We've got to live small,'" she says. "'We've got to start over again, hand to mouth, the way we began.'"[12]

Mother's contribution to the existential decisions of the household would have been out of the ordinary. Men dominated families to such an extent that many women felt imprisoned. One Kentucky woman referred to her husband as "a very bad & dangerous man" after she rebuffed his demand for land she inherited from her father. In her testimony before the circuit court, she described her husband and his brothers standing over her as she signed the deed. "She cried and begged and . . . says that this was her own land that she did not intend to sell." Perhaps no woman from the mountains expressed the day-to-day oppression like Emma Bell Miles. She was born in 1879 and grew up in Red Bank, Tennessee. In "The Common Lot" (1908), Miles tells the story of a young woman who must decide whether or not to marry a local boy. The story is set against the backdrop of her mother's drudgery and sadness. "Life had resolved itself, for her, into conditions of greater or lesser weariness . . . Her day was always long, her night was short; she had no time to think of the sunshine and roses in her own dooryard." In the end, with no other options, the young woman accepts two cows and a cabin and hopes for the best. "Before them," writes Miles of the new couple, "lay the vision of their probable future—the crude, hard beginning, the suffering and toil that must come."[13]

Men and women faced the failing ecological base and the decision to move to coal camps together, though they experienced these hardships differently. Like the Baldridge family, households did not move right away, and those that did often kept fugitive plantings somewhere high and distant or ate beans cultivated by family members who remained in the hollows. They held on to the simulacra of autonomy amid an industrialized landscape in which survival increasingly required dependency on wages. When garden and forest reinforced each other, subsistence did not subsidize wages but the other way around. We know how well this arrangement worked. Workers with a functioning commons and a secure source of food carried themselves like free people and vexed labor managers.

This is why Justus Collins hated local-born miners. Collins served as vice president of the Louisville Coal and Coke Company, operating at Flat Top Mountain. In 1905, he introduced larger coal cars in an attempt to trick workers into more work for the same pay. The men refused. They slowed their shovels or dropped them altogether, disappearing for days at a time. They could walk away because their kinship networks could still sustain them. Some managers turned away anyone with an alternative means of support or who admitted to using wages to regain household autonomy. Bert Wright of the Pocahontas Coal Company made this entry in his journal in August 1898: "Attempted contract with B.P. Good[,] called off. His intentions are to make enough cash to pay for some stock and land." Wright complained every day of workers who showed up only when they had no other option.[14]

By around 1900, if not before, managers attempted to create dependent populations of miners by importing them from other states and countries. Workers with no kin in the hills and no idea where they were composed a more pliable labor army. Managers used emigrants to overwhelm the situational advantages of mountain-born miners. Justus Collins referred to imported workers as "Hungarians," regardless of where they came from, as in, "I would suggest that we get a carload of Hungarians . . . The miners we have, as you know, will not work but three or four hours a day." Testimony given to Congress in 1888 revealed how companies succeeded in keeping "thousands of surplus laborers on hand to underbid each other for employment," how they held these workers "purposely ignorant when the mines are to be worked and when closed, so that they cannot seek employment elsewhere." The journalist Henry Lloyd gave testimony to the Interstate Anti-Trust Conference in 1893. He described a laborer who was "virtually a chattel of the operator," constantly robbed of his wages by the company store, subject to rents he must pay in every season (whether working or not), and under the arbitrary authority of private security guards, "armed as the corporations see fit with army revolvers, or Winchester rifles, or both . . . provoking the people to riot and then shooting them legally."[15]

This is how families identical to the Baldridges ended up in settlements identical to Blackjack. Once Hungarian or Irish or African-American workers arrived in the coalfields, they became artillery for breaking the defiant highlanders. Two days after the miners at Louisville Coal and Coke refused to fill the larger cars, Collins evicted those who lived in the camp. A week later, the first train of "Hungarians" arrived. A sociologist who knew the game called the immigrant inflow "a godsend" to employers: "Foreign labor was introduced into an industry not from lack of hands but in order to replace the too-demanding natives." The strategy of retreating to the hollows would never work the same way again. All of a sudden, survival required local men to adhere to industrial discipline. For a time, Mother and Father held on to their garden and cabin overlooking the mine. But with the possibility of autonomy falling away with the forest, when a money income required submission to company control, they felt compelled to give them up.[16]

In the coal camps, subsistence became a source of corporate power. This happened because companies often took over state-like services wherever they operated, especially where counties exercised little or no authority. They built roads, hired their own police departments, and even established governing bodies. In one example, Fairmont Coal imposed a nonunion collective bargaining process. It established a system of "industrial representation," composed of powerless committees. The company dictated every "agreement" and determined the breadth of "representation." The anthropologist David Graeber explains that corporations copied the bureaucratic techniques of government, "techniques that were thought to be necessities when operating on a large scale." For our purposes, the most important of these state-like services allowed companies to avoid paying wages. They minted their own money.[17]

Coal companies issued coins or coupons, called scrip, redeemable in stores owned by the companies themselves or allied merchants. The system obscured the dollar value of work by paying and charging miners in unconvertible units. It also kept miners in hock to the companies. Owners paid out less than miners and their families needed to live, subtracting rent, medical services, and even funeral expenses. Whatever scrip miners had left, they handed right back to management for food. If their scrip fell short of their household needs, they ended up in debt, their flour and bacon charged against future labor, with interest. A hard-won raise bought workers nothing. Companies simply recollected it by jacking up prices at the store. But scrip did not lower the fixed costs of coal mining. Sustaining a workforce required owners to spend limited cash reserves to import food from outside the region.[18]

This is why owners encouraged families to plant gardens. A patch of vegetables and a flock of chickens reproduced the household with household labor during household hours. Time in the garden never competed with wage earning. The entire family became deputized workers, contributing their labor without compensation to subsidize the male wage. Not only that, but the companies profited from the greater health and capacity of workers; they improved productivity without buying new machinery or extending the working day. Companies either made gardens compulsory or encouraged them by providing seed and fertilizer and by offering prizes—like two or three months' rent or a gold coin for the most beautiful plot.

To allies of the industry, gardens looked progressive, like a rejection of radicalism. In their eyes, gardening miners made the best of their situation, working with companies by beautifying the camps. The American

Constitutional Association was founded by businessmen to foster "reverence for law" and Americanization among foreign-born miners. It used patriotism to dissuade immigrants from joining the United Mine Workers of America. The businessmen commissioned a survey of forty-one mining camps. "In no instance was a company found other than glad to have the people of the community utilize any available ground for gardens. Absolutely no rent is charged for a foot of garden space. In the majority of cases the company supplies a mule and plow free." The report found that, on average, 53 percent of miners in the forty-one camps planted gardens. Agronomists estimated that the average annual value of an average yield was a hundred dollars.[19]

European workers brought the same skills as the mountain-born. They had almost all been agrarians themselves, most of them recently uprooted by enclosure and penury. The industry magazine *Coal Age* gave dispossession a cheerful spin. "The few Americans in a colliery village have been drawn from the farming population, and should naturally take readily to garden culture. The people from England, Scotland and Wales are known for their delight in all kinds of seeding and planting, and the miners who hail from Central Europe are like our own people, mostly farmers in origin, and should naturally till the soil." The same could have been said of African-Americans, whether former slaves or those fleeing tenancy. No matter where they came from, miners must have taken pleasure in corn tassels and squash flowers. Some gardeners used climbing beans running up wire to create shaded porches that gave relief from the smoke and heat of the railroad just feet away and the barrenness of the hills.[20]

But the pleasures of colliery gardens did not change their exploitative purpose. An extraordinary conversation explains why. A former secretary of the United Mine Workers visited West Virginia in 1896 and reported what he saw. He noticed gardens all along the Kanawha River and commented to his tour guide that the miners were very industrious. "They are," responded the guide, "a darn'd sight too industrious; they are so industrious that they can dig coal for almost nothing." The secretary thought about it. "If the land in West Virginia was used as an adjunct to the pluck store in the production of coal, how were our miners in other parts of the country to meet this kind of competition?" By sustaining themselves, mining households lowered their own wages. Managers in other parts of the country copied the method.[21]

Yet this is only one side of the political ecology. Provision grounds became battlegrounds over the control of life and work, with companies restricting access to food during labor actions. One journalist called it "persuasion by starvation," and pointed out that if a miner held an owner's family hostage to starve them, "you would be unable to express your horror." But "the mine owner who starves the miner's wife by refusing credit acts within the limit of the law." Mining companies could mask the violence they inflicted by depicting unions and strikers as acting illegally and indecently. They could be sure to have law enforcement on their side, lending legitimacy to their position. And by linking food and shelter to compliance, they made it look as though miners violated the terms of their employment and caused their own suffering. "Power exercised in one part of the system could evoke a response in another," writes John Gaventa, "disobedience of a single rule could mean eviction from the game all together."[22]

The key example is the Paint Creek Strike of 1912. The strike began in April. The activist Mary Harris "Mother" Jones had been organizing from time to time in southern West Virginia since 1901. The week she returned to Kanawha County in 1912, miners attacked facilities at Mucklow, burning coal tipples. The governor escalated the situation by declaring martial law, commandeering company guards, and subjecting all the accused to military courts. In July, management sent out notices of eviction after gardens had been planted. The miners appealed to the courts, but a circuit judge upheld the evictions. A labor organizer explained that the judge likened the relationship between miner and employer to that of master and servant. Miners rented their homes from the company but held no leases. They could claim no rights as tenants. Fired for any reason, they had to leave, regardless of whether they had paid for the month. The striking miners became refugees, setting up a tent city at the mouth of Paint Creek.[23]

When strikers attempted to return to their gardens, company guards prevented them. By August, the miners had begun to starve. Guards caught one attempting to cross battle lines. They ordered him to turn around "or they would kill him." Driven by hunger, the man managed to outmaneuver his pursuers and got away with his cow in tow. Guards sent all the household goods of another miner floating down the river, then threatened to kill him if he tried one more time to remove his livestock. A week later, a reporter described the inhabitants of Paint Creek as having "lapsed into a state of primitive savagery, spurred on by the depredations of the private guards . . . The miners are desperate, and their attack centered on the company's stores." In the eighteenth century, James Steuart and Alexander Hamilton insisted that anyone who converted but little of the value he created into money did not contribute to society. Peasants and settlers, they both believed, were not fully part of the state. Coal miners did exactly what Steuart and Hamilton would have wanted them to do. Everything they produced took the form of a commodity. Even the beans and corn they grew contributed, indirectly, to the same end. But in what meaningful sense were they citizens? In what sense did coal mining forge a place for mountaineers in modern society?[24]

Yet beans and corn could not be entirely captured. Other miners during other strikes grew them in the folds of the mountains, beyond company reach, where they aided resistance and rebellion. One wrote to John L. Lewis, president of the United Mine Workers, in the midst of the 1919 walkout in Coral, Pennsylvania, "We're not worrying about strike benefits . . . because we are killing hogs and gathering corn and other crops and squirrel hunting." Two men interviewed by the Library of Congress in the 1990s recalled the sufficiency of an earlier generation. Kenny Lively said, "Because they had all those gardens, and they canned so much, and they killed that hog, they could go on strike. They could go out for two months; they were stocked and ready." This is how small-scale domesticated food production became central to the structural war between workers and owners in the mountains.[25]

Regardless of the coercion and control they offered managers and the desperate objective they became for miners during strikes, industrial gardens looked benevolent to reformers of the 1930s. With the onset of the Great Depression, West Virginia miners truly became pauperized—lacking income or access to land. That's when reformers discovered the other version of the captured garden, the one Robert Owen advocated a century earlier.

It offered the United States a way of keeping the unemployed from starving while burdening them with the entire cost of their relief.

⁂

IN 1933, ELEANOR ROOSEVELT VISITED Scotts Run, a long hollow near Morgantown, West Virginia, that had become among the most destitute places in the United States. If Eleanor took a walk up Ramp Hollow, she would have seen how companies put up houses along the steep sides and tributaries of Scotts Run, like the one I saw abandoned and overgrown seventy-eight years later. She might have met families recently removed from cabins like the one I visited on Hoard Road just a few miles away. Coal production had always fluctuated with prices. Companies shut down when it didn't pay to operate and started up again when it did. The industry expanded almost without pause from the 1880s into the 1920s. West Virginia miners numbered 78,400 in 1909. Twenty years later, the state ranked second in the nation behind Pennsylvania. One hundred thousand miners worked 830 mines, sending coal down the tracks that earned the companies $217 million in sales. But when capital vanished after the stock market crash, the mines closed, leaving thousands of people stranded. Only a paycheck distinguishes a working-class enclave from a slum, and Scotts Run had become an influenza-ridden slum. Families starved within sight of stuck and silent coal tipples, rusting in the damp atmosphere. One journalist found a family of thirteen huddled over a gasping fire, "with the children packed like sacks on the floor and one wakeful adult prodding the coals alive in order that they all might not freeze to death."[26]

The only people capable of helping were the Quakers. They had invented a travel-ready humanitarian aid organization at the outbreak of the First World War. Pacifist church members could join the American Friends Service Committee as an alternative to military service. It worked so well that in 1918 President Herbert Hoover appointed the Quakers to feed and clothe German orphans and refugees. Fifteen years later, they came to Scotts Run to do the same thing. When the Quakers moved some of the unemployed to small farms where they could plant gardens and tend small livestock, Eleanor heard about it. She invited executive secretary Clarence

Picket to Hyde Park for a briefing. Once in office, Franklin Roosevelt wrote the details of the Quaker resettlement program into the National Industrial Recovery Act, establishing an agency within the Department of the Interior with a budget of $25 million. They called it the Division of Subsistence Homesteads. Its most visible project was the community of Arthurdale, West Virginia, located fifteen miles southeast of Scotts Run.[27]

As he cooperated with industry using his right hand, Franklin Roosevelt organized plan B alternatives with his left. The fact that 30 percent of working-age Americans were eating in soup kitchens and sleeping in public parks emboldened critics who argued that capitalism had failed to deliver the most basic human needs. The Division of Subsistence Homesteads attracted antimodern social engineers, some of the same people who had supported back-to-the-land experiments for years and endorsed the Indian Reorganization Act of 1934, which freed American Indians from government coercion and promoted tribal authority and self-governing communities. Small-scale self-sufficiency was riding high in the highest offices of government. Stated one report by the division, "In the pinch of distress, we lose faith in the bright new world . . . we seek to escape our ills by a return to the land, to 'nature,' or to an older tradition." A typescript report prepared for a small circle around the president announced, "A Partial Pattern for the New American Way of Life . . . from which dozens of similar communities may be founded." For a moment, the president of the United States contemplated the garden as a viable mode of production.[28]

The Division of Subsistence Homesteads was among the most controversial relief programs of the New Deal. Gardens for the poor did not exactly give industrial capitalism a resounding endorsement. Would homesteads liberate settlers from wages and taxes? Did subsistence gardens represent a rejection of the division of labor and the economic citizenship that Alexander Hamilton tried to impose in the 1790s? Would gardening sustain the poor by itself, or would it be linked to factory wages? Would homesteaders escape exploitation under the largesse of the nation-state? The Roosevelts and a coterie of social engineers debated these questions.

They arrived at an awkward hybrid, a policy that attempted to fuse the two versions of the captured garden. In a sense, the government version looked nearly identical to that advocated by Owen and other reformers who rejected Malthusian malevolence. There is something of a response to Malthus in section 208 of the National Industrial Recovery Act, which allocated the initial funds, "to provide for aiding the redistribution of the overbalance of population in industrial centers," toward the humanitarian resettlement of stranded workers. The project's chief economist, Milburn Wilson, confronted the same criticism Owen did a century before—that Arthurdale represented "a retreat from the age of machinery," a regression to an earlier stage. Wilson flipped the criticism just as Owen did. He called homesteads for the poor the essence of "a new high standard of living."[29]

But the plan included another component. There would be no experiment in agrarian autonomy. The garden would be wedded to the factory. The residents of Arthurdale would grow their own food when they weren't assembling vacuum cleaners for General Electric. Some planners objected. One insisted, "Private profit will endure just as long as that which produces profit contributes to social progress." The planners must have felt pressured to monetize the labor of homesteaders, to keep them connected to the urban industrial world. Eleanor endorsed the factory. She had committed herself to Arthurdale. She visited often, picked appliances for the homes, and promoted the plan. "The idea is that families engaged in subsistence farming consume their own garden products . . . [and] shall be situated near enough to an industry for one member of the family to be employed." She believed that wages would ensure that residents had money to buy "the things which the families must have and cannot produce for themselves." Whether the model represented dependency or benevolence is not an easy judgment. What does seem clear is that accommodating General Electric undermined Arthurdale from the start.[30]

Arthurdale opened in 1934. It took shape hurriedly. Fifty prefabricated cottages arrived, but the houses didn't fit the foundations prepared for them. The planners didn't consult the people who would live and labor in the community about what they wanted to plant. Instead, crews spent days installing grapevines, weaving the tendrils over trellises to create a lived-in look for photographers. "Planning was done for, rather than with, prospective homesteaders," wrote a journalist. "Perfection rather than reality became the goal." But the bargain with General Electric caused more lasting damage. The company had no desire to enter into a social experiment and made sure that it would profit no matter what happened to Arthurdale. The deal GE worked out with the government had them paying forty homesteaders (at a time) 35 cents an hour, 36 hours a week, for 36 weeks a year to work in their newly built factory. The annual income came out to $450. But these wages did not fall into the homesteaders' pockets free and clear. Each household returned $180 of their earnings to pay for the factory.

In other words, they started out in debt. Two socialists, Harold Ware and Webster Powell, pilloried the plan in the pages of *Harper's Magazine*. "The subsistence worker has to help pay for the factory in which he works to get a subsistence wage." That was troubling enough, but it contributed to an overall arithmetic that never worked in favor of the homesteaders. Subtracting the originating debt from income left each household $270 for dishes, clothing, tools, shoes, transportation—everything but food for a year. Any family that couldn't cover its costs had to send someone away from Arthurdale in search of work. Even stranger, the factory only employed homesteaders on a revolving basis, meaning that households earned no wages at all for part of the year. This is why the designers placed such emphasis on food production. It had to underwrite everything—the survival of the residents, the participation of the corporation, and the cost of the factory. The planners put the residents in debt and then asked them to get out from under it with part-time work at 35 cents an hour.[31]

Arthurdale ran into every species of trouble. General Electric pulled out. The residents briefly made faucets. Then the government proposed that they make equipment for the Postal Service. But Congress killed the idea, some members calling it "socialistic." The term of the original funding under the National Industrial Recovery Act expired, after which the president funded it by executive order. Residents expected too much over and above what a garden and a cow could provide. The USDA concluded in 1942 that homesteaders wanted "the security of employment and the adequacy of income which a properly functioning economy could offer them, but which the subsistence homesteads alone could not." Residents in other settlements complained of "broken promises," but some of their frustration came from unrealistic expectations.[32]

Pressure against the Division of Subsistence Homesteads mounted under intense controversy from both the left and the right of the political spectrum. Harold Ware and Webster Powell condemned the model as a dictatorial attempt to isolate potentially rebellious workers and harness them to factories. The authors compared Arthurdale to similar settlements maintained by Adolf Hitler and Emperor Hirohito. Hitler seems to have inherited a preexisting project of the German state to settle the unemployed in cottages. Ware and Powell reported that "Hitler hopes to increase his food supply, reduce unemployment, and keep satisfied (and ready for war) what otherwise might become a restless part of the population." They pinned this same "transmutation of discontent" on the Roosevelts. They further accused the administration of "planning for permanent poverty," or in other words, of collecting the unemployed in "self-liquidating" communities, in which the indigent provided their own relief while suppressing wages for other workers.[33]

Business advocates responded with revulsion. To their ears, the Division of Subsistence Homesteads sounded like the Division of Decline into Primitivism. The Austrian-born business consultant Peter F. Drucker condemned self-provisioning in 1939. "Subsistence farming represents by definition a regression from market economy and from the division of labor on which the economic achievements of our society are based." Drucker considered it a necessary but "temporary remedy to tide the displaced farmers over until a permanent solution has been found." Growing one's own food, he went on, "would amount to social disenfranchisement, as the subsistence farmer is practically cut off from the main stream of social life and pushed into an isolated position outside of modern society." And yet, Drucker and many others like him somehow overlooked the cause of the social calamity going on before them, as though capitalism itself had not caused an unprecedented regression from the market economy.[34]

Critics from the right also ignored the prevalence of the capitalist form of the captured garden. Its popularity extended far beyond Appalachian mining camps. Henry Ford loved the idea. In 1931, Ford made vegetable gardens compulsory for all employees at Iron Mountain, Michigan, where workers assembled the wooden portions of Ford automobiles. He threatened to fire any head of household who failed or refused to plant an area "of sufficient size to supply his family with at least part of its winter vegetables." One journalist derided Ford's "shotgun gardens." The fusion of farm and factory appealed to industrialists for the many ways it capitalized uncompensated labor. Henry I. Harriman, president of the United States Chamber of Commerce, chirped, "The majority of these industrial workers live where they have enough ground to raise a large portion of their food supply for the summer and to put by a certain amount for winter consumption." Ware and Powell made little distinction between Roosevelt's Arthurdale and Ford's Iron Mountain. "The most hard-boiled of business men need not look upon subsistence homesteading as merely another experimental effusion of impractical theorists. The experimental stage is over."[35]

In both American versions of the captured garden, residents received wages only to pay them back. The designers of both set out to ensure industrial dependency, not agrarian autonomy. The Division of Subsistence Homesteads imploded from the confusion and anxiety within and outside government over what it meant for Americans to grow their own food. For unlike victory gardens, in which homegrown vegetables patriotically (and temporarily) offset the dietary needs of soldiers overseas, subsistence gardens suggested backsliding into primitivism. Arthurdale faltered under its debilitating contradictions and fading support. The garden as a form of public relief vanished with it.

✺

AFRICAN-AMERICANS KNEW THE CAPTURED GARDEN WELL. As slaves, they produced their own food. Many took pleasure in this and used gardening to create a realm of freedom. After emancipation, they faced a defiant planter class, dedicated to re-creating the conditions of slavery.

The majority of freed African-Americans and their children, and their children's children, spent their lives working land that belonged to white landowners, often the descendants of planters. Those who could not find a way to own their own farms or squat on the unvisited land of absentees worked for wages. But they often found themselves in debt to landowners and their allied merchants. In order to service their debts, they entered into an arrangement closer to slavery than freedom. The historian Pete Daniel has spent decades studying the social and environmental history of the

South. He compares the evolving coercion of black farmers "to an unfinished patchwork quilt; year by year the design would change—a contract law added here, a lien law there, while lynchings, beatings, vagrancy laws, and illiteracy eventually pieced it out." One of the first patches appeared during Reconstruction, a form of tenancy stitched in with the violence required to hold the suffocating quilt together.[36]

The number of nonwhite farm owners throughout the United States increased with rising cotton prices, peaking in 1920 at 175,000. They were tremendously skilled at provisioning themselves in response to declining cash incomes. When the boll weevil ripped through Georgia cotton fields in 1915, black farmers doubled their garden production. They planted okra, beans, peas, potatoes, and field corn for animal feed. They also milked cows and churned butter. One woman recalled, "We didn't have to buy anything. Only thing . . . was sugar, maybe coffee. Raised our own chickens, had ham, fatback. We canned in jars . . . We had everything we needed." Only black farmers who owned their land could make this adjustment. But black farmers faced a cascade of trouble during the twenty years that followed the peak of ownership. Fields flooded or desiccated. Insect pests proliferated. Prices plummeted. Between 1927 and 1934, the annual income of black farmers in one Georgia county fell by half, from $500 to under $240. Those who fell out of smallholding often signed sharecropping contracts.[37]

Landowners dictated the terms. Tenants grew cotton and gave half the crop to the landowner as rent. They could sell the other half. But they always needed provisions on credit before they could plow and plant. A merchant (sometimes the landowner himself) provided seed, tools, food, and other necessary things to keep the family alive and working. These necessaries were advanced against the tenant's half, but they almost always added up to more than the value of the cotton. The merchants wrote down the difference to collect it the following year, and the same thing happened. In sharecropping, the appearance of the agrarian household in a voluntary contractual arrangement concealed a form of bondage. Tenancy increased from 25 percent of all farmers in 1880 to 42 percent in 1935, mostly concentrated in the Cotton Belt. In that year, tenants operated more than 700,000 farms in the United States, or 10 percent. Two-thirds of all tenant farmers in the South were white in 1935 and one-third were black. African-

Americans operated 42 percent of Alabama farms in 1900, and their rate of tenancy was around 85 percent.[38]

Sharecropping substituted the slow violence of debt for the shackles of slavery. Debt can only exist between people with the legal standing to enter into contracts. Landowners took advantage of this narrow attribute of social equality in order to trap African-Americans in arrangements that really enforced their social inequality. Debt, in another sense, is an incomplete exchange. It's what happens when two parties initiate a transaction but cannot complete it. It binds them together. Neither can walk away. But that was the point. Landowners did not want sharecroppers to complete the transaction because its purpose was to subordinate debtor to creditor. Add to this the humiliation of being controlled and living under threat, the shame and guilt of failing to pull one's loved ones out of poverty, and the feeling of inadequacy that comes from the impossibility of remitting what one owes. Regardless of its inefficiencies and poor yields, the system lasted into the 1950s because it gave racist landowners dominance. But though sharecroppers might have looked something like serfs bound to lords, they were an entirely industrial labor force that turned out the raw material of textile manufacturing.[39]

The debt essential to sharecropping worked much the same way as scrip in coal mining. Though households worked entirely within capitalist assumptions, little cash money ever changed hands. The transactions that paid them often produced no currency, just an entry in an account book. To a greater extent than the families who lived in colliery towns, sharecroppers labored as households. They worked for their collective reproduction even though their most intimate garden work really served the landowner. Because they divided any cash and everything advanced to sustain every household member, the compensation per person was egregiously low. And like coal mining, sharecropping needed local police power to hold it in place. The county sheriff stood watch to make sure tenants didn't make a run for it and along with merchants and landowners removed every other option for employment, leaving only the contract. Landowners opposed public works projects for the threat they posed to the bubble-like exploitation in many counties, unless convicts tarred the roads or laid the tracks in chained gangs.

Ned Cobb resisted the racial and economic strictures of tenant farming in Alabama, in part by growing as much of his own food as he could. Cobb spoke to Theodore Rosengarten, a historian who met Cobb in 1969 and recorded a series of their conversations. The astonishing memoir that Cobb dictated (in which he is known as Nate Shaw) blends his father's tormented striving for autonomy, as a slave and then a sharecropper, into his own. Cobb put into words the assertion of racial power that he had heard from white landowners time and again during his lifetime: "'Nigger, just go out there and do what I tell you to do, and if I see fit to take all you got, I'll take it and get away with it.'" He says at another point, "If I could have made a livin raisin vegetables and corn crops, watermelons and such as that, I'd a let cotton alone. But I just couldn't realize it." Cobb once arrived in town to find that no one would buy from him. Another time, whites forced him to sell for prices they dictated, prices not high enough to justify the trip to market.[40]

But Cobb endured and realized a great degree of autonomy, becoming among the most successful and independent tenant farmers in the South. He and his family ate well from their garden: okra, collards, tomatoes, cabbages, squash, beans, turnips, potatoes, onions, radishes, cucumbers, apples, peaches, plums, watermelons, cantaloupes, and muskmelons. He had pigs of such size that white neighbors seemed threatened. Said Cobb, "They didn't like to see a nigger with too much; they didn't like it one bit. They also didn't like his rising political activism. Cobb helped establish the Sharecroppers' Union in 1931. *All God's Dangers* (1974) belongs on the shelf next to the greatest of agrarian autobiography and description, including J. Hector St. John de Crèvecoeur's *Letters from an American Farmer* (1782) and Wendell Berry's *The Unsettling of America* (1977)."[41]

Coal miners and sharecroppers experienced the end of agrarian autonomy differently, but both engaged in a struggle against power that played out as a struggle over subsistence. The notion that capitalism eliminates household production along its frontiers is false. It spreads by absorbing the garden, the rice paddy, and the survival strategies of the village. "It is only a minority—even today, even in the core zones," says Immanuel Wallerstein, "which come close to the 'classical' image of the proletariat." The uncompensated labor of wives, sisters, sons, aunts, and uncles is essential for reproducing working-class bodies and capital itself. The captured garden is not an anachronism within the global manufacturing economy; instead, it's essential to its functioning.[42]

ANOTHER KIND OF INVASION attended the industrial takeover. Experts arrived, often employed by government agencies. They came; they saw; they wrote reports. Some of them gathered data reliably, and their conclusions could have shaped a progressive and empathetic public policy. Others relied on false assumptions rather than their own eyes and ears. They misread the people and the landscape. Tourists came, too, not to visit beside the fire as a Sunday guest but to imagine themselves in uninhabited forest.

Among the most influential studies was *The Southern Highlander and His Homeland* (1921) by John C. Campbell. Born in Wisconsin and educated in Massachusetts, Campbell became president of Piedmont College in northern Georgia in 1904, where he dedicated his career to folklore and reform. Campbell concluded that mountaineers didn't understand the income they could derive from resources close at hand. He visited a woman who cooked her supper over embers of black walnut. Campbell pointed out that she was burning a valuable wood. "She replied that it was 'a right smart of trouble to haul timber down the branch,' and that there were 'several walnut trees' (a goodly number) about there, and moreover, they 'didn't need the money nohow.' The needlessness of this waste was the more apparent as one saw on all sides cheap timber suitable for firewood." The woman knew what the wood was worth and had her reasons for burning it. When Campbell declared her use a waste, he spoke the language of the expert class in general and conservationists in particular.

For conservationists, the opposite of waste was efficiency. The gospel of efficiency said that rivers shall not run to the sea without irrigating something or generating electricity. Fire shall not consume forests. Wolves shall not eat cattle or wild game, and valuable timber shall not be used as cooking fuel. Foresters sought the "optimum" relationship between agriculture and woodland, which usually meant that government acquired an area and then sent experts to decide what to do with it. In some cases, land needed to be utterly destroyed for the public good. The ultimate example of efficiency through sacrifice was the Tennessee Valley Authority, the largest regional plan ever conceived of or executed in the United States. Planned in the 1920s but built in the 1930s, the TVA integrated electricity generation, flood control, fertilizer manufacturing, and economic development. Its nine main dams and many tributary dams flooded thousands of hollows, affecting over forty thousand square miles. Conservationists interpreted modernization as the careful use of scarce resources. Once in control of government, they eliminated managed commons with some of the same arguments that capitalists used to privatize these landscapes. In this view, folk practices wasted a forest like wildfire. Both needed to be stamped out for the benefit of all.[43]

Conservationists had trouble comprehending the forest as a cultural landscape. Apparently baffled by swidden agriculture, the United States Forest Service sent a psychologist to figure out why people in the Blue Ridge Mountains set fires. The psychologist worked up a patient profile. The person who set these fires lived in poverty, had a third-grade education, and consumed less-than-adequate food. Like so many other experts, the government psychologist took mountaineer poverty as a sign of moral failure, as though he had no idea what had happened to them. Further displaying his lack of wisdom, he measured them with standards they could not meet. "We saw no evidence of painting, draftsmanship or sculpture," he reported, as though he expected to visit a school of design. Getting to the point, he declared their agriculture "outmoded" and captive to "the tradition of their forefathers who believed in woods-burning."

According to the psychologist, the people of upland Virginia burned for two reasons: for revenge against the incursions of outsiders and because their ancestors did it. The first motive made up the lesser part of "the fire problem." The second motive he called vestigial, "a survival of the pioneer agrarian culture." That's all that the psychologist said about fire as a tool for getting things done in a landscape, because he knew nothing about it. But that did not prevent him from proposing social engineering to convince every "pappy" to stop, hoping for the practice to vanish.

One other thing about this patient profile is worth mentioning. The psychologist interviewed scores of people, yet only a few of their statements appear in the report. One informant explained the purpose of fire with perfect clarity. "Fires do a heap of good . . . Kill th' boll weevil, snakes, tick an' bean beetles. Greens up the grass. Keeps us healthy by killing fever germs." Asked if more timber would improve his life, another answered that timber holds water, preventing floods, but to cease burning would "make living harder and we'd see more rattlesnakes." The Forest Service seems to have decided beforehand that swidden indicated a stupid folk ritual or pathological self-destructiveness. Their chosen investigator told them what they wanted to hear.

But something else operated in the report. The Forest Service increasingly privileged the desires of vacationers who complained that smoldering stumps ruined the woods and the view. "Outsiders visiting or motoring in the South during burning season . . . are shocked and appalled by the miles of fire running free in the woodlands and the palls of smoke that dull the sun and often make motoring hazardous." Weekenders in their motorcars increasingly set the terms of use for millions of acres acquired by the United States. Some of it would be cut for lumber and leased for coal, but large portions would be set aside for scenery.[44]

In one of the largest appropriations of mountain land in the twentieth century, the Blue Ridge became a recreational reserve. In 1931, Horace Albright, director of the National Park Service, went riding through the Blue Ridge with President Herbert Hoover. Hoover stopped to gaze into the distance and said, "You know, Albright, this mountain top is just made by God Almighty for a highway." Albright's plan for Shenandoah National Park included Skyline Drive. The plan also required that mountain farmers be removed from the valley. Some were employed in the building of the road. Many others served meals and made beds at new hotels. The park, the highway, and the conservationist vision contained an irony. The Park Service seized a landscape that had been shaped for centuries by Monacan hunters and Scots-Irish farmers and refurbished it as wilderness. Albright himself advanced this act of forgetting. "Here in the Blue Ridge of Virginia, in the very heart of civilized America, lies preserved for our use a bit of nature that is identical with the virgin territory found by Captain John Smith and his heroic followers."[45]

Residents knew that Shenandoah National Park had erased their presence, and they tried to reinsert themselves into the narrative. In a letter to Hoover urging him to abandon the project, the farmer Lewis Willis described the region as a working landscape: "Part of it has been cleared, plowed, and pastured; and well nigh all of it has been logged at some time or another." Willis also made an acute economic argument, that the government's purchases would not compensate mountaineers for their losses. "Many of us who are now self-supporting cannot support ourselves by investing the sale value of our lands somewhere else." They would not come away with enough money to purchase anywhere near the extent of land previously available to them. Another resident refused to leave. Melanchton Cliser accused the Commonwealth of Virginia of acting in the interest of a resort entrepreneur and a cabal of landowners who stood to benefit from the development of the area. When he turned down the state's offer to buy his store and filling station, officers arrived with handcuffs. A photograph shows Cliser digging his shoes into the dust as three government men haul him away.[46]

In *Machine Age in the Hills* (1933), a Quaker journalist named Malcolm Ross wrote, "When West Virginia was young and hopeful it chose as its motto: 'Montani semper liberi.' This was living truth to men who found shelter in the hills from grasping lowlanders. Today it is merely an epitaph cut in the marble façades of Charleston's public buildings. The mountaineers of West Virginia have not even the freedom to earn bread for their bellies." The General Assembly kept that motto even as they preferred another one more suitable for tourists: "the Switzerland of America." The slogan had appeared as early as the 1880s in guides for visitors and in geography textbooks. But calling the state "the Switzerland of America" took away its identity by describing it as an imitation. Besides, it's difficult to imagine that anyone would have mistaken toxic rivers, violence on the scale of warfare, and desolate clear-cut hills for the relatively thriving agrarian landscapes of the Alps. The members of the General Assembly must have expected that no one would actually compare them.[47]

Some mountaineers still lived in the mountains. One of the most significant documents produced by the United States on life in Appalachia was a miscellaneous report by the Department of Agriculture. Its lead author was Lewis Cecil Gray, an economist and historian of the South. The researchers found that household subsistence endured as the most common form of livelihood in the upland counties of Maryland, Virginia, West Virginia, Kentucky, North Carolina, South Carolina, Tennessee, Georgia, and Alabama. There were 150,659 "self-sufficing" households in the survey area in 1930, or between 50 and 70 percent of the total. The most typical farm consisted of sixty-seven acres: thirteen in crops, eleven in plowed pasture, five in hillside pasture, and the rest in woodlot, bare ground, or eroded gullies. Most such families owned one or two cows and the same number of pigs. But self-sufficing went beyond food. Between 60 and 100 percent of households in two Kentucky counties were found to have churned butter, canned fruits and vegetables, butchered hogs, and made soap. These farms produced food and other commodities valued at $450 annually, of which they consumed $320, leaving an excess value of $130.[48]

Self-sufficing people know how to survive in the crevices. No one told them that doing so meant that they were poor. John C. Campbell quoted a woman who argued to him, "'What more does a body need?' . . . pointing to her little corn field and garden. 'Yonder is a right smart chance of corn and a heap of cushaws, and the shoats will be big enough to kill for meat after the mast [nuts and acorns] is gone.'" Another writer said of the Blue Ridge in the 1930s, "While the local economy was focused overwhelmingly on subsistence agriculture—and barter and exchange labor were far more important than cash in the local economy—most families didn't regard themselves as poor or deprived." A brushy second growth appeared where giant spruce once shaded, providing grazing spaces and limited forest products. About 70 to 80 percent of children attended school, and illiteracy had fallen to around 2 percent in most of West Virginia.[49]

Still, no one argued that mountain people were thriving. Planted area declined between 1900 and 1930 from 16.5 percent to 14.1 percent of the upland landscape. The average farmer cultivated between five and ten acres, depending on location. Five acres is surely enough to feed a family, but how much food it gives depends on the diversity of products and the quality of its soil. As for the decline in the area planted, Gray speculated that erosion had caused "compulsory abandonment." A body might have needed more in calories and nutrients than cushaws and shoats. Some of the first dietetic research began in the 1920s, leading census takers to ask about milk consumption as they traveled from cabin to cabin in 1929. "On more than 65,000 farms no cows were milked in 1929, indicating that many of the families may not have had an adequate supply of milk for family use." Milk alone does not make an adequate diet, nor is it necessary for one, but it isn't irrelevant either.[50]

Foresters, economists, and New Dealers had a word for these farms: *submarginal*. Any farm that presented barriers to full-scale commercial production (like steep topography inhospitable to machinery) was submarginal. When they converted the product of mountain homesteads into dollars and cents, they declared the people poor. But the economy of makeshift continually denies that measure. The experts talked about resettlement, moving people who apparently knew no better to richer valleys or out of farming altogether. Marginal people would be redeemed from marginal land by working at the new hotels on the Blue Ridge. They could build dams on the Tennessee River and manufacture nitrogen fertilizer at Muscle Shoals. Rotting cabins in steep and stony hollows looked to conservationists like rural versions of the same slums being demolished in the cities under pressure from reformers. The solution was eviction and clearance.

And yet, the lead author of the USDA's study didn't see the self-sufficing farm this way. "By every normal criterion a large proportion of the farms in the Southern Highlands are submarginal . . . Yet, I am inclined to believe that we should go very slowly in undertaking a program of elimination." Gray's reading of the census data convinced him that highlanders did not always suffer in privation and that life in a hollow could be better than life in a coal camp. He moved beyond the language of backwardness. "The mountain farmer can gradually be taught to improve greatly his standard of living without the intervention of that uncertain and unreliable medium called money."

Gray looked to wages with such dread because money, by itself, never seemed to deliver stability. Many families abandoned the hollows to move closer to the mines, only to find the worst imaginable ground for planting. "Back when I had liberty on the farm," explained a resident of Whitaker, Kentucky, speaking to an interviewer about the 1920s, "I could have my garden where I thought it would produce, I could put out anything I wanted to. Lots of times in the coal camps if the company allotted that miner a little garden spot [it was] halfway to the top of a hill." Imposing an inferior space for planting on one side and a poverty wage on the other locked them into a standing wave. Gray called this kind of partial employment "uncertain, impermanent, or exploitative."[51]

He acknowledged that gardens and fields were mostly unprofitable, but planners could reach out to farmers. Gray advocated "farm-forest communities," a commons much like what mountain people maintained by themselves. He recommended local control over woods for cottage logging, combined with subsistence cultivation and off-farm wages. This model would have maintained autonomy, rejuvenated the ecological base, and provided cash. It endorsed the commodity circuit and suggested a stable place within the United States and American society for agrarians. Gray asserted this report as the basis of an Appalachian policy, concluding, "It is along these lines that I should like to see the 'new deal' . . . come to the Southern Highlands."

Appalachia during the 1930s presented some hard questions for reformers. Did the people who endured in compromised hollows represent a distinct southern tradition worth preserving? Were they practicing a legitimate form of economy that should be encouraged, or were they the abject poor, underserved and neglected? Did they need a relief program to help them get through hard times, or should they be moved to lowland towns and cities with running water and dependable roads? Yet instead of clearsighted programs meant to address the causes of poverty, studies that followed tended to depict Appalachia in all the old ways, as eternally poor and seized by static cultural beliefs.[52]

The authors of *Hollow Folk* (1933) saw them at their nadir—crowded together in hollows that could not possibly sustain them, deficient in cattle or much else for exchange, lacking anything to hunt but rodents, and dependent on tourists and industry for the money that connected them to the rest of the world. But whereas *Hollow Folk* might have addressed the social and political roots of poverty, instead it falls back on the old tropes.

"Social evolution" presumably still goes on but so slowly do groups go forward under their own power that no movement can be discerned through generations,—or so rapidly do more highly evolved people change that all the intermediate stages are lost. It may be only a short way, on a scale of evolution, from the medicine man's antelope skin stretched across a hollow log to the radio, but left to themselves, it would take a very long time indeed for a jungle tribe to begin attaching aerial wires to the tree-tops.[53]

It is the language of degeneracy and cultures of poverty. Slow-moving groups stagger and backslide. Yet those "highly evolved" skip stages, which raises the question of whether stages actually exist. (After all, how can something be universal if it doesn't universally apply?) The authors also universalize one particular technology against which the backsliders continually demonstrate their failure. But the hollow where the authors conducted their fieldwork was not strange or static or primitive, but poor. It was cut off from its previous sources of food and commodities, not left behind by history. The book offers a kind of Appalachian gothic rather than empathic social science.

Appalachia became a place where metropolitans experienced a vanishing American authenticity, where rocking chairs and baskets could be procured from people who could trace their artisanship back to the vanishing point. Depth of time and primitive skills gave folk objects a strangely modern virtue. They seemed to emerge from outside the flow of events that produced the present. But they embodied a contradiction. They increased in cultural value as industrial capitalism undermined their environmental and social basis. According to one critic, they gained allure from the destruction of the culture that created them. Tourists driving the Blue Ridge Parkway went looking to buy handcrafts. Each of these transactions was a little performance, with the artist acting as a representative of the world gone by. The circumstance of any exchange shapes the commodity itself. Visitors to Appalachia, like visitors to Indian reservations, deceived themselves into thinking that they bought something used by the maker, rather than something mass-produced for them.[54]

Tourists seeking handcrafts continued to arrive as Appalachians continued to flee. By the 1920s, outmigration from Appalachia was nothing new. It had been running parallel to the crisis in mountain farming. At first no one noticed it. The surge in the number of industrial jobs during the interwar period combined with a high birthrate compensated for the people leaving. It masked what would otherwise have been a downward trend. Thousands took off down the Hillbilly Highway, the name for any road leading anywhere out of the region. West Virginians and Kentuckians traveled Route 23 into Ohio. They stamped out tires in Akron and steel for Armco at Middletown. They made paper, rolled cigarettes, and assembled cars in cities like Cincinnati, Greensboro, Flint, and Detroit. They became Appalachians or just southern whites when they arrived in these cities, having lost their local identities.

The flow reversed course during the 1930s. When the factories shut down, some of the same people (or their children) returned to grow their own food, hunt whatever they could, and reconnect with family. The number of new farms increased by 51 percent between 1929 and 1934 but without an increase in the area cultivated. Families subdivided their already unproductive farms into smaller, even less viable fields and gathering grounds. Government relief, in the form of direct cash payments from a variety of agencies, sustained those who continued to subsist as other opportunities for earning cash disappeared.

After the Depression, the outmigration began again. The increasing mechanization of coal production resulted in layoffs and retirements. Destitute men sought work in nearby counties rather than emigrate—anything to keep their households and family networks intact. But the region lost at least 700,000 people down the Hillbilly Highway during the 1940s. For those who remained, a granular poverty set in that government did not address until the 1960s.[55]

7. Negotiated Settlements

THE FATE OF THE COMMONS AND THE COMMONERS

> If there is any hope for the world at all . . . it lives low down on the
> ground, with its arms around the people who go to battle every
> day to protect their forests, their mountains and their rivers
> because they know that the forests, the mountains and the rivers
> protect them.
>
> —Arundhati Roy, *Walking with the Comrades* (2010)

PEASANTS RULED DEVELOPMENT THOUGHT during the twentieth century. Eighty-five percent of the population of Africa lived in the countryside in 1950, slightly higher than the ratio of peasants to city dwellers in China, India, and all of East Asia. Americans grappled with what it meant that so much of humanity existed in social forms they considered primitive. W. W. Rostow borrowed from Lord Kames and Adam Smith to write *The Stages of Economic Growth* (1960), among the most influential works of development theory of the century. Along with most other economists, Rostow assumed that peasants had always struggled to feed themselves, that their suffering was endemic. His confidence stood upon the Allied victory in World War II and the belief, written into the Atlantic Charter, that growth would eliminate poverty and backwardness, that affluence through trade came along with self-determination—toward "a world free of want and fear." Behind it all, economists imagined the peasant working interminably with nothing to show for it, neither producer nor consumer, left behind, outside the borders of civil society.

Backwardness demanded a program of *modernization*. That was the watchword of the age, the self-justifying consummation of stage theory, an amalgam of institutions and individualism predicated on technological and social change. Seven hundred and thirty delegates from forty-four nations met at Bretton Woods, New Hampshire, in 1944 for a United Nations conference intended to reconfigure the world's monetary policy toward a new economic order. The delegates created the International Monetary Fund and the International Bank for Reconstruction and Development, known as the World Bank. The year before, a United Nations conference on food and agriculture dedicated the postwar world to connecting farmers to sources of credit. With their institutions in place, the representatives of modernity undertook an unprecedented project to end poverty by re-creating global peasantry in their own image.[1]

Yet even before the Great Depression, an antimodernizing counter-movement had spread among intellectuals. The small town, the aboriginal nation, the self-sufficing farm—forms of social organization and modes of production once confidently slated for oblivion became inspirations. The National Folk Festival began in 1934. Appalachian handcrafts surged in popularity, displayed in museums and purchased by vacationers. Among the coterie of intellectuals who sought out American authenticity, the notion that every society moved through the same stages (or failed to) met resistance. The sociologist Carle C. Zimmerman saw a trend contrary to the course of progress—population flowing toward the countryside. "The cities have passed into a stage of rapidly diminishing returns . . . The magical system of beliefs which surround the individual and make his economic system work has lost much of its force." Even an industrialist argued for the recovery of agrarian values. The soap manufacturer Samuel Fels worried that the political order had become "detached from the soil from which it sprang." People needed to declare their independence anew, to "again exert a self-reliant mastery over our scheme of subsistence or we may lapse into a new peonage—this time to the machineries we have set up."[2]

Millions of Americans knew how to grow some or most of their own food. Keeping a robust garden was hardly a fringe activity. Of the 30 million households in the United States, around one-third grew some, most, or all of their food. Weary industrial workers looking for a way out of breadlines found a shelf of books published between 1900 and 1940. *Three Acres and Liberty* (1907) and *Five Acres and Independence* (1935) became popular guides, but *Flight from the City* (1933) by Ralph Borsodi demonstrated greater authorial voice and narrative force than the others.[3]

Borsodi declared a new American independence. He wanted to "release men and women from their present thralldom to the factory and make them masters of machines instead of servants to them," in order to "free them for the conquest of comfort, beauty and understanding." He told a story about himself. "In 1920 the Borsodi family . . . lived in a rented home. We bought our food and clothing and furnishings from retail stores. We were dependent entirely upon my income from a none too certain white-collar job." Evicted when the landlord sold the house, their crisis led them to a farm just outside of New York City. There, Borsodi had his revelation. "We began to enjoy the feeling of plenty which the city-dweller never experiences. We cut our hay; gathered our fruit; made gallons and gallons of cider . . . We ended the year with plenty not only for our own needs but for a generous hospitality to our friends." Borsodi looked forward to a reverse migration toward a desired agrarianism that afforded a dignified (if not a middle-class) standard of living.[4]

The new agrarianism took many forms. In 1928, Robert Winslow Gordon (and later John A. Lomax) assembled field chants and folk ballads into the Archive of American Folk Song at the Library of Congress. John Collier became commissioner of the Bureau of Indian Affairs in 1933 and immediately reversed a century of policy that outlawed religious practice and ritual observance. Collier upheld the Navajo as an exemplary community who had "preserved intact their religion, their ancient morality, their social forms and their appreciation of beauty," like "an island of aboriginal culture in a monotonous sea of machine civilization."

In 1930, a group of writers who called themselves Twelve Southerners (also known as the Agrarians) published *I'll Take My Stand*. They condemned northern industrialism and leftist collectivism as brutalizing concentrations of power and redefined the Confederacy as a radical experiment in "moral, social, and economic autonomy." But the Agrarians constructed a racial fantasy. For example, Allan Tate's "Notes on Liberty and Property" is a study in denial. Tate makes no attempt to reconcile his genteel defense of agrarian values with the legalized suppression of black sharecroppers, whose own liberty, property, and agrarianism he never acknowledges. By conflating rural antimodernism with the Confederacy, the Twelve Southerners entombed their thought in white supremacy.[5]

The most famous advocates for subsistence economy were a couple of communists. In 1932, Scott Nearing and Helen Knothe Nearing established a farm in Vermont as an experiment in living. Scott Nearing was born in Morris Run, Pennsylvania, and grew up in a house on a hill overlooking the Morris Run Coal Company. As the son of its owner, he stood to inherit it. Instead, he declared himself a Marxist and denounced private property. Nearing taught economics at the University of Pennsylvania's Wharton School of Business during the First World War but was refused reappointment in 1915. A career in politics followed, in which he opposed the war as a pacifist, visited the Soviet Union to write about its educational policy, and joined the Communist Party of the United States. Innumerable writings and lectures had not brought about revolution by 1930, so he and Helen bought a farm in order to recover the only source of autonomy available to them amid an economy they considered hopelessly corrupt. They relocated to the coast of Maine in 1952, founding Forest Farm.

The Nearings published *The Good Life* in 1954. The book made them celebrities among readers looking for alternatives to industrialized food, suburban sprawl, and a society increasingly dominated by corporate power. They described their farm as a "subsistence homestead" (without any apparent reference to the New Deal) and "a semi-self-contained household unit, based largely on a use economy and, as far as possible, independent of the price-profit economy which surrounds us." They advocated the concept of dual transactional realms decades before it entered anthropology. Aside from maple syrup, they declared, "we will not sell anything else from the place. Any garden or other surpluses will be shared with neighbors and friends in terms of their needs." The Nearings became peasants by choice, linking an old New England makeshift with an antimodernist agrarianism.[6]

The United States itself advocated self-sufficiency as part of a nationalist campaign to send food grown commercially to soldiers overseas during two world wars. In 1917, a timber-industry millionaire named Charles Lathrop Pack organized the United States National War Garden Commission. "Food gardens for defense" rallied citizens to "sow the seeds of victory" by planting their own vegetables. And in 1943, the USDA estimated that 20 million households had harvested 40 percent of the fresh fruits and vegetables they consumed that year.

Nation-states, however, are complex bureaucracies that often pursue contradictory policies. That same year, a different branch of government promulgated a contrary position on self-provisioning when the Supreme Court decided the case *Wickard v. Filburn*. Roscoe Filburn owned a farm in Ohio where he planted wheat. Under the authority of the 1938 Agricultural Adjustment Act (or AAA), the United States limited the area planted in wheat and other crops to prop up prices and ensure farmers a basic standard of living. Filburn believed that he followed the law when in 1940 he seeded the eleven acres allotted to him, plus an additional twelve acres for his own use. Someone complained, and the government levied a fine of 49 cents on each of Filburn's 239 "illegal" bushels. Filburn argued that his own bread made from his own wheat had no effect on the national price, so it didn't fall under the law. When a federal district court ruled in his favor, the United States appealed, naming as plaintiff Secretary of Agriculture Claude Wickard.

The Court rejected Filburn's argument. Justice Robert H. Jackson wrote the unanimous opinion. The purpose of the AAA was to maintain a high price for wheat, and that required the government to limit the volume in the market. Jackson averred that homegrown wheat influenced the market by its absence. Farming that "supplies a need" eliminates purchases, affecting the price of wheat in commerce. Filburn did not do anything as radical as declare his farm an autonomous commune. He merely wanted to monetize half of his crop but not the other, to live between transactional realms by playing community and market off each other. He did what farmers had always done—eat this and exchange that. But the Court advanced a capitalist metaphysics. For farmers who planted key commodities, the market was not an option. It enveloped them.[7]

Some of the same controversy followed the United States into its first decades of purposeful international economic development. The reformers, folklorists, and avant-garde farmers did not make that policy, but it borrowed something from their desire to see peasant agriculture succeed. The New Deal's administrative legacy of social planning and environmental engineering, coupled with the compulsion to remake the world during the Cold War, prepared the soil for a scientific project that eventually proposed the transformation of peasant societies. But not everyone involved understood the project the same way or agreed about it. American anthropologists and economists pursued research into how peasant farmers did things, how hard they worked, and what they yielded. American technocrats entered Mexico, the Philippines, and India and discovered unincorporated peasants growing unhybridized crops—like history standing still.

⁂

THE GREEN REVOLUTION WAS SUPPOSED to modernize the great heathendom. After the Second World War, the Ford and Rockefeller foundations proposed to export American agricultural science to the developing world. They would give peasant farmers improved plants and other tools in order to boost their harvests, ending hunger and poverty. The Green Revolution provoked new interest in peasant food systems and household economies among anthropologists, economists, and others interested in theories of development. At the center of this extraordinary debate was the question of what peasants accomplished with their labor. Some experts believed that agrarians produced little more than what they needed to meet their most basic needs.

William Arthur Lewis offered a model that gained enormous influence when he published it during the early 1950s. Lewis argued that nonindustrial rural societies include lots of people with little or nothing to do. Though he offered no evidence, he maintained that labor was so ineffective and yields so low that the contribution of each additional person could be calculated at close to zero. When industrial production begins in these regions, said Lewis, the differential in wages attracts underemployed villagers. Wages don't need to be much higher than the value of food grown on the homeplace. New mill and mine workers would seem to offer a market for household farmers to sell their surpluses, if any, but Lewis said that peasants just can't win. Growing more food causes prices to drop, leaving them no better than before. Lewis came up with an elegant model of a so-called dual economy, in which subsistence and capital exist together until the latter devours the former.

But there are problems with the model. For one thing, the historical relationship between the two modes of production more often finds subsistence surviving by being incorporated into the circuit of capital. This was part of the argument of the last chapter. In this sense, there is no dual economy but a single economy, in which the household mode of production is co-opted. And while Lewis was right that those lacking money but wanting it migrated to wage-paying work, he had no sense of the historical reasons behind that transition. An enclosed or degraded ecological base has its own story, one apparently beyond economic analysis. The condition and ownership of the landscape forms no part of the model, making it look like the decision to work for wages comes from rational economic calculation, not desperation. It's no great insight to say that people waste their labor whenever they plow up gullied soil or that a vanished forest leaves nothing to hunt or gather. Most of all, how did Lewis know that agrarian labor produces zero value? He didn't.[8]

Other economists repeated the same statement as fact. The assertion came from almost every development economist working in the 1950s and 1960s. Paul N. Rosenstein-Rodan advised the World Bank, "All the agrarian economists of the world agree that if those people were removed from the land agricultural output, far from falling, would increase." Labor productivity shimmers as the ultimate standard of economic viability, yet, by that measure, peasants appeared to waste the land they occupied. Every development economist of the era owes something to James Steuart. They tended to depict the peasants of the world like Steuart's vinedresser: primitive and obsolete, their labor futile, their product invisible and useless to the state.[9]

Anthropologists did not suffer from the same failure of imagination. They might have had much less influence than economists and administrators over the direction of the World Bank, but they had one thing that these others lacked: evidence from fieldwork. In a sense, economics and anthro-

pology both traced their origins to the speculations of Enlightenment philosophers about the origins of modern times. What passed for the study of
cultures in the nineteenth century was "human geography," a delusional set
of racial theories derived from environmental determinism. After 1900,
with the ascent of Franz Boas and his students Alfred Kroeber, Ruth Benedict, and Margaret Mead, anthropology emerged as a powerful empirical
study. But it took decades for attitudes to change. In 1952, Carl Sauer still
rebuked the old orthodoxy in an address to fellow geographers: "There is
no general law of progress that all mankind follows; there are no general
successions of learning, no stages of culture, through which all people tend
to pass." One researcher exemplified the new empiricism. He transcended
the prejudices of his time and championed a despised form of land use, revealing its internal coherence and ecological logic. His name was Harold C.
Conklin.[10]

In 1957, the United Nations Food and Agriculture Organization published Conklin's dissertation on the upland burning and rice planting of
Hanunóo farmers on Mindoro, one of the largest islands of the Philippines. The subject might sound hopelessly obscure. It isn't. The remarkable
thing about *Hanunóo Agriculture* is that it provides a detailed rationale for a
kind of farming no economist thought about, not for one second. Reformers regarded "slash and burn" as a nuisance at best; at worst, thoughtless
destruction. Burning appeared to lay waste to valuable timber. Among people
accustomed to constant cropping—who could not recall a time when fire
played a part in shaping the world's landscapes, who measured other systems against their own reliance on industrial fertilizers—the shifting cultivators of the tropics were savages.[11]

Conklin helped to promote the word *swidden* and explained it in spectacular detail. The Hanunóo burn the forest and plant rice among the
smoldering branches and stumps, cultivating the same clearings over a
series of years before abandoning them. The trees gradually return, and
around twenty years later the slope is burned again. Until Conklin, no
anthropologist had asked how swidden systems function, how villages
organize themselves around forest practices, and what kinds and quantities of food they harvest. He revealed shifting cultivation to be subtle,
restorative, productive, and deeply connected to the lives of the Hanunóo.

Forging knives, felling trees, cutting brush, and setting fire to the mountain itself—all demand divisions of labor according to age and gender and rites for satisfying controlling spirits. The rice that comes off the mountain occupies a central place in offerings and feasts. The book amounts to something more than a report but a case for swidden as one of the world's essential social ecologies.[12]

Conklin might have anticipated the massive development project then simmering during the years of his fieldwork. Rice yields in the Philippines had not increased since 1918. That and a rising population forced the government to import 65,000 tons of rice a year by the 1950s. The Ford and Rockefeller foundations decided that science could turn the trend around. But their solution indicated that they had abandoned much of the original humanitarian project. Instead, they favored high-technology plants that needed other high-technology inputs, like harvesting machines, pesticides, and fertilizers. In particular, they embraced a program of seed invention. One historian has called it "a Manhattan Project for food." The foundations combined to establish the International Rice Research Institute at Los Baños in 1960. Over the following decade, researchers set out to transform rice. Its stalk would be shorter (to minimize the energy expended to grow it), its color darker (to absorb more sunlight), and its head more rigid (the better for machines to harvest it). Six years later, the IRRI announced the first harvest of IR-8, an artifact of the Cold War, a plant that did not come from any specific environment or agrarian culture but that would create such abundance that it would lift the tropics out of poverty all by itself.

If the purpose of the Green Revolution was to produce more food in the same space in order to increase exports, then IR-8 advanced that mission. It doubled rice exports from the Philippines. But it left behind the people it was first intended to help. The reason had to do with the plant itself. Adopting it meant accepting its extraordinary limitations and blind spots. It could not be grown on mountain clearings. The machines needed to harvest it only worked on the flat lowlands. It required more fertilizer than traditional varieties, so it cost more to grow. In other words, it could not be cultivated by peasants. But when farmers met IR-8's considerable demands, it rewarded them. By the 1980s, Filipino rice yielded an average of 2.3 tons per hectare, up from 1.2 tons in the early 1960s.

Writing in 1957, Harold Conklin offered a different solution to the rice shortfall. He suggested that the government of the Philippines encourage shifting cultivation. Smoky forest openings yielded as much rice per hectare as the national average (1.3 tons per hectare), with a labor efficiency of 4 liters harvested for every labor-hour expended. And while this was not nearly the yield of IR-8, the same clearings turned out much more than rice, which accounted for about 20 percent of the Hanunóo diet. Villagers planted maize, millet, sorghum, sweet potatoes, various yams, manioc, taro, bananas, various peas and beans, peanuts, cacao, citrus, mangoes, papayas, onions, eggplants, chili peppers, tomatoes, garlic, various squashes and melons, and cotton. This is not a complete list. Said Conklin, understating his position, "Both technologists and conservationists could profit from a closer look at the varied actual forms of land usage practiced in Philippine forested areas."[13]

Conklin argued a point that those committed to industrial monoculture must have found absurd, that swidden offered an effective means of employing forested land. If it could be brought out of the mountains to other locations and conducted by commercial farmers, he believed, it would feed the hungry and contribute to the betterment of all Filipinos. He gave a contrary vision to that of the high-modernist inventors of IR-8. The Hanunóo didn't need the Green Revolution—the Philippines needed Hanunóo agriculture. Most of all, Conklin upheld agrarian practices as viable and stable, a source of ecologically benign food production, not a problem to be overcome.[14]

Economists became interested in peasant economy at around the same time, influenced by William Arthur Lewis but also by the work of anthropologists like Conklin. With the Green Revolution at full throttle, questions flew as to whether agrarians should be replaced. The economist Theodore Schultz published *Transforming Traditional Agriculture* (1964) to defeat a single often-repeated statistic of the "zero-value" theory—that at any given time, 25 percent of any agrarian population had nothing to do. Not only did this number make no sense to Schultz, it seemed to come from out of nowhere.

No economy has full employment, said Schultz, and farming did not demand eight or ten hours of work a day. He called out development experts who seemed to travel the world looking for rural inefficiencies and decrying them as affronts to the gospel of modernity. Schultz said that they observed people at leisure, not people with nothing to do. The year after *Transforming Traditional Agriculture* appeared, Ester Boserup published *The Conditions of Agricultural Growth* (1965), demonstrating that farmers worked harder and longer whenever they needed to increase yields. Lacking Boserup's insights, Schultz relied on what seems in retrospect a discomfiting and even insulting natural experiment. He asked whether India's influenza epidemic of 1918, resulting in the deaths of 20 million people, or 6 percent of the population, reduced the area sown to crops. It did. This proved, in other words, that not only did all agrarians work, they worked at productive tasks, using their resources to the best advantage. One sentence sent doubt rippling through the development agencies: "There are comparatively few significant inefficiencies in the allocation of the factors of production in traditional agriculture."[15]

None of this should be taken to mean that Schultz considered traditional agriculture worth saving. His goal was its transformation. He simply had a different notion for how that should be done. He helped launch the "human capital" argument. Rather than invest in machines that peasants couldn't use, he said, development banks and foundations should invest in education. Looked at one way, such a policy might have prevented the massive migration to slums that followed from the industrialization of agriculture in Mexico and other countries or might have held it off a little longer. But Schultz ends up in the same place as the technocrats who invented IR-8. The goal of teaching peasants was to adapt them to high-modernist technology. He held fast to the economist's creed that everyone thinks like Adam Smith. Yet if that were true, then why did villagers decline more powerful tools, more fecund animals, and every new advantage offered to them? He was amazed at a report from Guatemala, where farmers insisted on using hoes and machetes though the region where they lived was "not an isolated subsistence economy, but is closely integrated into a larger market economy." He never understood the household mode of production and transactional realms, so he could make no sense of peasant economy.[16]

Around this time, anthropologists began to question the idea that peasant economies needed transformation at all. They applied to agrarian decision making the same assumption of functionality and internal coherence that Conklin applied to swidden. In 1952, Melville Herskovits described his own abandonment of smug triumphalism. "Ten years ago, the word 'primitive' came easily to the lips. It is only with . . . the growing integration of peoples of the most diverse cultures into the world scene, that the essentially pejorative and tendentious character of this designation, like others such as 'savage,' 'backward,' or 'early,' when applied to any functioning way of life, became apparent." The scholar who most fully embraced this revisionism was Marshall Sahlins. He didn't merely write against a decade of development thought and centuries of political economy; he dethroned modernity itself.

In *Stone Age Economics* (1974), Sahlins contended that hunter-gatherers enjoyed greater plenty and leisure than those who struggled to subsist under capitalism. His chapter "The Original Affluent Society" riffed on the title of one of the most popular books written by an economist, John Kenneth Galbraith's *The Affluent Society* (1958). Sahlins based his conclusions on fieldwork he conducted in Fiji and Hawaii. His project was to turn the entire notion of affluence on its head.

> One-third to one-half of humanity are said to go to bed hungry
> every night. In the Old Stone Age the fraction must have been
> much smaller. *This* is the era of hunger unprecedented. Now,
> in the time of the greatest technical power, is starvation an
> institution. Reverse another venerable formula: the amount of
> hunger increases relatively and absolutely with the evolution of
> culture . . . This paradox is my whole point. Hunters and gatherers
> have by force of circumstances an objectively low standard of
> living. But taken as their *objective*, and given their adequate
> means of production, all the people's material wants usually can
> be easily satisfied. The evolution of economy has known, then,
> two contradictory movements: enriching but at the same time
> impoverishing, appropriating in relation to nature but expropriating
> in relation to man . . . The world's most primitive people have
> few possessions, *but they are not poor.* Poverty is not a certain
> small amount of goods, nor is it just a relation between means and

ends; above all it is a relation between people. Poverty is a social status. As such it is the invention of civilization. It has grown with civilization, at once as an invidious distinction between classes and more importantly as a tributary relation—that can render agrarian peasants more susceptible to natural catastrophes than any winter camp of Alaskan Eskimo.

He overstated his point. Stone Age hunter-gatherers lived in every imaginable climatic condition. They sometimes died of cold and starvation, punctuated by periods of warmth and abundance. There is no simple moral we can draw from a period of 3 million years. But in Sahlins's litany we hear the voices of Jean-Jacques Rousseau, Thomas Paine (in *Agrarian Justice*), Karl Polanyi, Karl Marx, and A. V. Chayanov. We see the argument made by back-to-the-land advocates like Helen and Scott Nearing. And we find the essence of what would emerge as the study of economic anthropology and political ecology. One of the basic insights of political ecology is that poverty is not the lack of things that people had never known but a social relation in which people are deprived of the means of subsistence.[17]

A more subtle indictment appeared in 1971, one that comes closer to the problems embedded in economic development. Its author was James P. Grant, who had just finished a term as assistant administrator of the United States Agency for International Development, or USAID. Writing in *Foreign Affairs*, Grant warned of "a new phenomenon in the developing world . . . marginal men," or people with no clear pathway to employment as they reached adulthood. The number of unemployed in Latin America had doubled from 1950 to 1956 to 11.1 percent, with up to 20 percent "increasingly common" elsewhere in the world. An apparent surge in population terrified policymakers and inspired books like Paul Ehrlich's *Population Bomb*, published in 1968.

Grant worried. The rich in the poor countries benefited at the expense of the poor. The foreign luxury goods they bought sent currency to the rich countries. Nothing seemed to work to employ the rising masses at steady wages. Even attempts at manufacturing backfired. Grant saw textiles and shoes from struggling nations arriving in the United States, where they competed with domestic products. The 1970s now seems like a distant epoch, before American corporations moved their factories to China and Mexico. Back then, domestic manufacturers responded to less expensive imports by pressing on American workers to accept lower wages. Unions demanded tariffs that would make the foreign products more expensive, limit consumption, and protect their jobs. Both trends resulted in diminished exports from the poor countries and more unemployment.[18]

Grant wondered if smallholders could exist side by side with industrial agriculture, in enclaves where peasants would plant Green Revolution seeds: "The same economic forces active in industry in such countries as Mexico, India and Pakistan are subsidizing tractors and combines which are displacing the agricultural laborer. As an alternative to the rapid mechanization of agriculture, several countries have developed a system of agriculture centered on small-holders able to use the new seed varieties, small machinery and fertilizer, demonstrating that it can be profitable and create more jobs." This was once the stated goal of the foundations that initiated the Green Revolution. Grant suggested that they return to policy objectives that they had left behind. Unlike Grant, however, the scientists and administrators behind IR-8 understood the technological and economic demands of the seeds themselves. They fully believed that new seeds called for new farmers. Finally, Grant referred to Green Revolution varieties as *labor* intensive, meaning that they would employ more people. He was right, in a sense, but the technological "package" in which the seeds found their way into the ground included tractors and combines. Miracle wheat and rice turned out to be *energy* intensive. They used more petroleum fuel and less human muscle than any plants before in human history.[19]

Grant's essay suggests something that seems to have been commonplace among well-meaning experts of his time. He looked for a way that would have allowed smallholders to function within or alongside high-modernist farming. His overall solution to the problem of employment and poverty consisted of foreign investment, leading to wage-earning industries and exports, leading to higher standards of living, even though he knew that contradictions within the global economy made that outcome unlikely. Not every development policy has reflected the assumptions of capitalism. But the dominant view of the World Bank and other international lenders holds that poverty comes from economic isolation and that development brings peasants into a mutually beneficial relationship with the larger world through commodity production. But poverty has also come from the forced inclusion of smallholders in the global economy, from colonial extraction, structured indebtedness, and dispossession. Nonetheless, most development thought insists that the poor and hungry of the world—people who once took care of most of their own needs by farming and trading in once robust environments—will be saved by somewhat different versions of the same thinking that made them poor in the first place.

〰〰

AMERICAN DEVELOPMENT THEORY turned from matters abroad to those of the southern mountains in the 1960s. Here it confronted the same problem of using the assumptions of capitalism to solve problems created by capitalism. Extractive industry caused the diminution of its own basis. Labor demanded a greater share of the profit from the looting. Both sides were equally dependent on a single economically volatile and environmentally destructive commodity. By 1910, fewer than twenty years after William MacCorkle invited the coal and lumber companies to take what they wanted, West Virginia fell into a recession that predicted the Great Depression. Coal from Indiana, Southern Illinois, and Nova Scotia, regions with proximity to heavy industry or coastal cities, increasingly competed with the West Virginia product. Locomotives that burned diesel fuel reduced demand; so did more efficient boilers. Railroad expansion slowed down. Lower prices might have increased demand for coal, but that didn't happen. When profits fell, companies cut wages and closed mines.

People who had been pulled out of the hollows ten or twenty or thirty years before found themselves scrounging around for something to eat and dry wood to burn in their tar paper shacks. The rush of industry had created some infrastructure, but bridges and houses thrown up hastily in the 1880s began to rot just when wages disappeared. Boom times returned briefly during the First World War, but it now looks like a reprieve before the slide into the unemployment and poverty that Eleanor Roosevelt saw when she visited Scotts Run a decade later. A few miners found homes in

New Deal projects like Arthurdale, but many others left.[20] The activist and journalist Anna Rochester described the ones who remained. "On such farms," she wrote in 1940, "poor soils, poor livestock, poor seed, poor tools combine to hold down the productivity of the family's labour . . . Extreme poverty, comparable to that of the poorest sharecropper, is all that the 'self-sufficing' farm can provide."[21]

Even the black market in whiskey came under attack. The Eighteenth Amendment to the Constitution made alcohol production illegal and brought federal agents to Appalachia. In December 1922, a posse of officers entered what *The New York Times* called the "rocky fastness" of Menifee County, Kentucky. They carried automatic rifles, pistols, and shotguns and had the goal of arresting the person or persons who had shot an agent ten times the day before, killing him. The moonshiners had shotguns of their own, loaded with nails and screws. They lived in caves and underground caverns where the evidence of their distilleries could not be detected. They were engaged in a kind of civil war in the hills between centralized and decentralized order, a never-ending Whiskey Rebellion that had at its core one of the last forms of household production available to many. In this particular battle, moonshiners and officers of the law fired two hundred rounds. When an agent died after being shot in the neck, the government men retreated. The Twenty-First Amendment ended Prohibition in 1933, but the people of the mountains were no better for it.[22]

Industrial work returned after the Second World War, but mining camps had not improved much since 1900. Many shanties had no running water. Only 45 percent of homes in central Appalachia had indoor plumbing in 1960. Seventy percent were heated with wood or coal. By the end of the decade, even with legislation related to the War on Poverty in effect, 17.8 percent of households throughout Appalachia lived without enough food and in substandard housing. The gap between the mountains and the lowlands had never seemed wider, and it inspired writers to explain it.[23]

One of the most important works published after the Depression drew attention to the persistence of human suffering in Appalachia and gave context to a region apparently neglected by the United States. In *Night Comes to the Cumberlands* (1962), the journalist Harry Caudill relied on the old language of strangeness in isolation, calling mountain people "as cynical, hardened and bitter a lot as can be imagined outside prison walls . . . illiterate, uncouth and hard-drinking." He dwelled on their superstitions and familiarity with the devil, all suggesting that they existed outside Christian civilization. The historian John Alexander Williams argues that Caudill's view worked against his better intentions. Stereotypical grotesqueness "gave readers permission to blame the mountain people themselves for their circumstances."

I think more highly of *Night Comes to the Cumberlands*. Caudill captured the allure of the first mining camps ("Alabaster Cities") and the people's hopes for a higher standard of living. He followed the story into the immiseration of industrial life through the Depression and into the 1950s, condemning the "iron clutch of absentee corporations" and the arbitrary exercise of their power. After the book's publication, Caudill kept Appalachia before the public, informing those with no sense of the hardship of seasonal employment, "This is what happens to a great industrial population when you abandon it, give it just enough food to keep it alive and tell it to go to hell." He also gave one of the first descriptions of the environmental devastation of strip mining. "Masses of shattered stone, shale, slate and dirt are cast pell-mell down the hillside. The first to go are the thin remaining layer of fertile topsoil and such trees as still find sustenance in it. The uprooted trees are flung down the slopes by the first cut."[24]

Night Comes to the Cumberlands and other reporting in newspapers and magazines spurred politicians to back reform. In November 1963, *The New York Times* announced, "U.S. Reveals Plan to Fight Appalachian Poverty." Appalachia became the basis for a domestic development project, an infusion of money and attention into the southern mountains. Its bureaucratic title was the Appalachian Regional Commission. ARC strengthened the power of the people who operated it. Its top-down ethos stressed development on the largest scale with the conceit, popular among planners, that highway construction, commercial forestry, hydroelectric dams, and incentives for cattle ranchers would be good for everyone who lived in the mountains. Some of what ARC brought *was* good for them. It brought badly needed jobs. And it created an army of young volunteers from within the mountains that served as a regional peace corps. But ARC left unanswered the larger question of what happens to a region when its major industry sputters and disappears, only to reappear again when conditions favor it.[25]

The Commission's first report announced stagnation and helplessness rather than offering a historical account of dispossession and immiseration, as Caudill did. "Graphs and tables can hardly relate the acutely personal story of a child in a remote valley, his horizons of opportunity limited to the enclosing hills; nor the despair of his father, who, idled by forces beyond his control and seeing no prospect of future employment, must live month in and month out with the vision of that child repeating his own history." The Commission did not interpret Appalachia as a countryside like others in the United States, where people also struggled, but as an almost incomprehensible exception. "For in much of Appalachia, 'rural' comes with a difference; the rural scene is in fact unique. Rural in Appalachia does not mean a checkerboard of rich farms; instead, dense but narrow ribbons of bleak habitation wind along the valley roads and up the tributary hollows." The report conceived of Appalachia as degenerate and left behind, and although the people had fallen into penury under extractive industry, it seemed that nothing but extractive industry could save them.[26]

John Gaventa countered this view with scholarly eloquence and political fearlessness, speaking directly to the Appalachian Regional Commission. After attending Vanderbilt University and completing a Rhodes scholarship at Oxford University, he joined the Highlander Research and Educational Center in New Market, Tennessee, in 1976. Highlander was founded during the Depression to teach social justice and civil rights. It educated a generation of activists, including Rosa Parks and Martin Luther King, Jr. For four years, Gaventa and Bill Horton (with a team of more than sixty researchers) compiled a report on the concentration of land in eighty counties, covering 20 million acres, spanning six states. They revealed that coal-company capital brought stagnation, not human betterment. They revealed a correlation between corporate control and inadequate housing. Banks in coal counties couldn't invest in home construction or other local improvements because the greater share of their deposits belonged to the companies. No sooner did that capital flow in than it flowed out, depriving banks of funds stable enough for community lending. As for the land, absentee individuals and corporations owned 75 percent of the survey area and 80 percent of the mineral acreage. Fifty private owners and ten government agencies owned 41 percent of the 20 million acres covered by the study.[27]

Citizens might have elected county and state officials to represent their interests. They might have imposed a referendum system to bypass a legislature in hock to the coal companies, as citizens did in California to circumvent the influence of the Southern Pacific Railroad. But that's not what happened. Like the three stunned men in the story by G. D. McNeill who had grown up on Big Black, only to confront the obliteration of their childhood landscape, the people of Appalachia often lacked the institutional pathways for real redress and true representation.

In *Power and Powerlessness: Quiescence and Rebellion in an Appalachian Valley* (1982), Gaventa argued that the Appalachian Regional Commission, the agency created to further the region's "development," furthered the powerlessness of its people. One tactic involved offering a non-choice between candidates who offered a non-challenge to the existing order. In the Clear Fork Valley of northern Tennessee, ARC claimed to take on the problem of poverty and underdevelopment. But as Gaventa writes, "When confronted as to why the development district for sixteen east Tennessee counties had not dealt with problems caused by the corporate coal owners, its director replied, 'The local election is coming up. That's where you ought to be working to get your concerns represented.'" In fact, ARC officials insisted on this stillborn process even though everyone involved knew that nothing would come of it. They knew that the declining authority of county boards meant that local government lacked the ways and means to improve local conditions.[28]

ARC did put people to work. It did reduce poverty throughout the region. Poverty fell by 4.2 percent between 1960 and 2000 relative to counties that did not receive federal money. It fell by 10 percent relative to a baseline set in 1960. Per capita income increased 4 percent faster in counties receiving aid than in those that did not. As recently as 2009, the World Bank praised ARC's first report. More households acquired telephone service and plumbing. Fewer of them heated with coal and wood. But these gains were modest and uneven. Unemployment in 2000 was about the same as it was in 1970. Historians have remarked not about how much ARC accomplished, but how little. "If the 1965 act was so successful," two scholars ask, "why does poverty persist in Appalachia?"[29]

One reason might be that ARC regarded Appalachia as an underdeveloped country in need of foreign direct investment. The highways built under ARC made millions of acres accessible for mountaintop-removal mining, though extraction on that scale buries towns, poisons watersheds, and creates a landscape that looks more like the surface of Mercury than West Virginia—all this in order to return dividends to shareholders who would never see the effects of their investments. As the historian Paul Salstrom concludes, "To sacrifice a region's economic base for short-term gains reveals a tragically deficient conception of the economy, conjoined in this case with almost total outside control." Another reason simply comes down to an overreliance on a single volatile commodity. Coal has never delivered and will never deliver stability. The people who mine it and sell it will always feel every bump and plunge in its price. ARC did nothing to change Appalachia's dependence on coal. On the contrary, its economic vision steadfastly refused to look beyond it.[30]

IN RECENT YEARS, INDICTMENTS of extractive industry have come from those who have felt its slow violence. The sadness of West Virginia, its dead-last or worst-as-first ranking among the states, stems from the utter defeat its people suffered in the twentieth century, resulting in their astonishing lack of control over their environment. Political leaders continually menace West Virginians with a false choice: health or jobs. Julian Martin spent his childhood in hollows and glades surrounded by coal mining. He assailed the vicious destruction of his home and the lies he had been told for decades when he addressed a public hearing on a proposed strip-mining project in 1988:

> All my life I've watched the destruction of my native state. When I was a little boy 40 years ago, I used to walk up Bull Creek over on Coal River. Bull Creek's not there anymore. It's gone. My Uncle Ken used to work timber up in the head of that hollow with a mule, and he did the least amount of destruction you possibly

could do. That place was beautiful. It's not there anymore. It's just simply gone. It's been destroyed by a strip mine . . . The first time I saw a strip mine it absolutely stunned me into silence. I was sad and I was sick. I couldn't believe what people could do with a bulldozer to land that used to be beautiful.

Is it wrong to love beauty; is it wrong to love nature? Is it wrong to say that we have only one earth and it will never be reclaimed—you can't reclaim a destroyed mountain—you can put something back there but you can't put that topsoil back on—just try it. You never, never can walk through that little glade where the ferns are growing . . .

And if you think strip mining is going to bring jobs, look where they've got strip mining in West Virginia and look where they've got the most unemployment. Mingo County. McDowell County. You go to the counties where they have strip mining—that's where they have the worst of everything. They've got the worst roads; they've got the worst schools; they've got the highest unemployment rate. Everything is wrong with those counties. Is that what you want this beautiful place to become? My daddy was a coal miner, and I understand being out of work, okay? I've been down that road myself. And I know you've got to provide for your family. But I'm saying they're only giving us two options. They're saying, "Either starve—or destroy West Virginia." And surely to God there must be another option.[31]

Citizens of West Virginia confronted that false choice once again on January 9, 2014. A chemical known as MCHM drained from a rusted tank owned by Freedom Industries into the Elk and Kanawha Rivers. Within hours it had entered an intake that fed drinking water to 300,000 people in nine counties. Residents of Charleston and other cities and towns in the valley reported a licorice smell coming from their taps. The spill did not turn into a major public health emergency. No one reported feeling sick; no one went to the hospital. Its significance lies in its ordinariness, in its illustration of the routine powerlessness and defeatism that characterizes extractive economies.

Investors had created Freedom Industries just weeks before, after folding four smaller firms into one. The corporate weave involved other companies owned or managed by Cliff Forrest, including Chemstream and Rosebud Mining, both located in Pennsylvania.[32] The storage tanks that contained the MCHM were sixty years old, suggesting a long-standing industrial site that had changed hands over and over again without much thought for safety. Nothing could be more ordinary than the licorice-smelling substance itself, 4-Methylcyclohexanemethanol. It's an alcohol used in froth flotation. It creates bubbles that bring fine particles to the surface where they can be captured. In a sense, froth flotation created the minerals industry by enabling companies to mine low-quality veins at a profit.

But no one had analyzed the toxicity of MCHM in humans. Eastman, the manufacturer, performed the only study in 1998. They found some evidence of liver and kidney damage in rats at relatively low levels, concluding a low toxicity. (All the test rats died after consuming higher levels.) But Eastman's scientists didn't follow the surviving rats for more than six weeks. The study says nothing about the chemical's chronic effects, but we know something about these risks from other lingering sources of disease—like radiation and DDT. The implications for public health years after exposure (or after years of continual exposure) are what matter.[33]

The irony of the rusted tank is that its contents would have entered the environment anyway, though at a slower rate and lower concentrations. After its job is done, MCHM ends up in decant ponds where it seeps into rivers and aquifers. Coal mining is intimate with its environment, although companies repeatedly deny that their catchment systems fail (even after spectacular failures). In 1972, a slurry dam on Buffalo Creek owned by Pittston Coal Company released a thirty-foot-high magma-like wall of coal sludge that killed 125 people, injured over 1,000, and left 4,000 homeless. Another slurry pond, owned by the Kingston Fossil Plant on the Clinch River in Tennessee, broke its dike in 2008, releasing 1.1 billion gallons of toxic ash. The Environmental Protection Agency lists ninety-five Superfund Sites in the state, but a never-to-be-known number of obscure seepages and furtive leaks have saturated the public with untested chemicals. Said one lawyer who filed a class-action suit in federal court against the companies involved in the 2014 spill, "There are so many chemicals out there that are not properly characterized. It's only after they dump it in our water and it smells like licorice that we know about it."[34]

"Surely to God," said Julian Martin, "there must be another option." But West Virginia's political leadership is unlikely to come up with one. During his last term in office, Senator Jay Rockefeller of West Virginia made his irrelevance irrefutable when he whimpered to National Public Radio a month after the spill, "Industries win, people lose. It's an old formula."[35] If a U.S. senator admits his helplessness to discipline or regulate the coal industry, then the people have no representation. A year earlier, the state's three-member House delegation clarified their constituency. They introduced the Coal Residuals Reuse and Management Act of 2013. The bill purported to regulate highly toxic slurry ponds and coal ash impoundment toward the "protection of health and environment." But its true purpose was to prevent the Environmental Protection Agency from managing these very sites. Before she became a U.S. senator, Representative Shelley Moore Capito claimed to have saved citizens from the octopus of government. "Many West Virginians have already been laid off as a result of the EPA's burdensome regulations, and this legislation will play a key role in preventing further job loss." But the bill makes no mention of jobs, and there's no reason to think that it would have generated employment. It was a gift to industry parading as reform. It passed in the House but failed in the Senate.[36]

Another abdication of leadership followed the Freedom Industries leak. In 2014, the West Virginia House of Delegates passed a law giving the secretary of environmental protection authority to regulate chemical holding tanks. The law does not set standards but gives that authority to the Department of Environmental Protection. It does set penalties, including a fine of $25,000 for every day that the owner of a chemical tank does not comply. The coal industry assailed the law. A year later, after meetings with industry attorneys, the House of Delegates scaled it back. The Senate passed its own version, and the governor signed the final bill. The new law lowers safety standards for certain tanks, denies the public information about what's inside the tanks, and reduces the number of inspections. It exempts 36,000 tanks from regulation altogether. Five Republicans in the

House of Delegates voted in opposition to the bill, along with sixteen Democrats. With some exceptions, West Virginia's elected representatives have shown a striking refusal to legislate for the good and welfare of their citizens.[37]

West Virginia's congressional delegation is equally concerned about their poorest and most vulnerable citizens. Concerned, that is, that the United States spends too much on them. In 2013, Congress approved a farm bill that included an $8.7 billion reduction in the Subsidized Nutrition Assistance Program. That year, 16 percent of West Virginia households received SNAP benefits, a rate higher than the national average. All three members of the House voted in favor. Evan Jenkins, a Republican elected in 2015 from the third district (which includes McDowell County), voted to repeal the Affordable Care Act and weaken clean-air regulations. Whose interests do these positions serve? Not those of the state's struggling families. After all, what does West Virginia have to show for the political influence of coal mining throughout the last century? The worst of everything. That's how Julian Martin described it. The worst schools, roads, health, environment, and unemployment.[38]

Another lifelong resident delivered a jeremiad to those members of Congress and their peers in the House of Delegates. Eric Waggoner teaches English at West Virginia Wesleyan University. In response to the Freedom Industries spill, he published an article in *The Huffington Post*.

> To hell with every greedhead operator who flocked here throughout history because you wanted what we had, but wanted us to go underground and get it for you. To hell with you for . . . treating the people you found here like just another material resource— suitable for exploiting and using up, and discarding when they'd outlived their usefulness. To hell with you for rigging the game so that those wages were paid in currency that was worthless everywhere but at the company store, so that all you did was let the workers hold it for a while, before they went into debt they couldn't get out of.
>
> To hell with you all for continuing, as coal became chemical, to exploit the lax, poorly-enforced safety regulations here, so that you

could do your business in the cheapest manner possible by short-cutting the health and quality of life not only of your workers, but of everybody who lives here. To hell with every operator who ever referred to West Virginians as "our neighbors."

To hell with every single screwjob elected official and politico under whose watch it all went on, who helped write those lax regulations and then turned away when even those weren't followed. To hell with you all, who were supposed to be stewards of the public interest, and who sold us out for money, for political power. To hell with every one of you who decided that making life convenient for business meant making life dangerous for us.

And, as long as I'm roundhouse damning everyone . . . To hell with all of my fellow West Virginians who bought so deeply into the idea of avoidable personal risk and constant sacrifice as an honorable condition under which to live, that they turned that condition into a culture of perverted, twisted pride and self-righteousness, to be celebrated and defended against outsiders. To hell with that insular, xenophobic pathology. To hell with everyone whose only take-away from every story about every explosion, every leak, every mine collapse, is some vague and idiotic vanity in the continued endurance of West Virginians under adverse, sometimes killing circumstances. To hell with everyone everywhere who ever mistook suffering for honor, and who ever taught that to their kids. There's nothing honorable about suffering. Nothing.[39]

Waggoner implies a connection between a culture of self-sacrifice and elected officials with contempt for the people. As long as West Virginians continue to blame themselves for everything and yield their power as citizens, nothing will improve.

A new formula is needed. During President Barack Obama's two terms in office, supporters of the coal industry accused him of waging a "war on coal." They were right, at least in one sense. Obama thought of coal as an egregious source of atmospheric carbon dioxide and an insecure basis for the economy of Appalachia. He listened to scientists and activists who argued that fossilized carbon must remain buried to prevent rising sea levels, extraordinary drought, and disrupted agriculture, leading to the forced migration of millions of people. In 2015, Obama announced that the EPA would regulate carbon dioxide emissions. The United States pledged reductions in its greenhouse gas emissions as part of the international agreement reached by 196 countries meeting in Paris during the United Nations Climate Change Conference in 2016.

Regulation does affect the profitability of the coal industry. But coal is in decline for other reasons. Natural gas emits about half the carbon dioxide as coal. It's less expensive, easier to extract, and can be moved around for a lower cost. By 2035, gas will have overtaken coal as the dominant fuel for generating electricity. The greatest job killers in coal country are the mining companies themselves. Their changeover to mountaintop removal resulted in thousands of unemployed workers.[40] But even by slashing labor costs, the industry cannot save itself. Alpha Natural Resources, the nation's second-largest coal company, filed for federal protection against creditors in 2015. It has shed 6,500 employees and closed eighty mines since 2011. Of the top thirteen most productive mines in the United States, not one is located in Appalachia. West Virginia delivered about 113 million tons in 2013, down 6 percent in one year. Between 2012 and 2015, deliveries fell by 18 percent.[41]

Coal companies can walk away from their gutted wastes and reorganize or rebrand themselves as natural gas drillers. Unemployed coal miners have fewer options. Some made seventy thousand dollars a year toward the end of their employment, the result of fewer and more highly skilled jobs. Some will find jobs in fracking, others in county maintenance crews, and others in big-box retail. The implosion of coal has emptied towns of small businesses. A few years ago, in Bluefield, West Virginia, I found no locally owned restaurants. The largest business in town was a pawnshop. The shelves in the grocery store were sparse. The majority of counties bracing eastern Kentucky, western Virginia, and southern West Virginia qualify as food deserts— where markets that sell fresh fruits and vegetables are more than twenty miles away or where residents lack the means to travel ten miles to go shopping. Even big-box retailers might not survive. In 2016, the Walmart in McDowell closed. One hundred forty people lost their jobs, but that's not the worst of it. Walmart contributed to a food pantry that fed eleven thousand people.[42]

Ghost towns dot the state. Since 1950, the number of people living in West Virginia has fallen 40 percent. Without income from property taxes, county governments cannot survive, but in the poorest places these small bureaucracies are often the largest employers. When they cease to function, so do essential services like garbage collection, police protection, fire and rescue, and county hospitals. In parts of West Virginia, 20 percent of the population lives in poverty. Over 30 percent of African-Americans survive below that line, as do 30 percent of children under the age of five. Just as stunning, 8 percent of West Virginians *with paying jobs* might not eat three times a day or have an adequate place to live. The median household in the United States earns about $50,000 a year. In more than half of West Virginia's fifty-five counties, households report incomes under the national median. A typical family of four in Marion County lives on $22,000.[43]

What could happen? The pessimistic scenario is not difficult to imagine. There is little reason to believe that Apple or Intel or any other tech company will emerge as a savior. Even at the existing minimum wage, American workers are more expensive than the Chinese or Vietnamese laborers who earn a few dollars a day. Their political representatives will fail them, to the highest office, promising them greater economic security but delivering only retail jobs with inferior health insurance. People will leave the mountains, as they always have. Maybe no one should waste much time thinking about what the unemployed will do to survive. They'll just go south. But like Scotts Run circa 1932, there will be thousands who lack the cash to pay for a moving van or a tank of gas. They'll be destitute, stuck in place. This is already happening.

Optimism always requires greater effort. If our sense of the possible doesn't contain an element of the unlikely, then it's only a compromise with what is. There can be no improvement without a viable political identity. This would require the white working class of the southern mountains to stop identifying their interests with those of the rich and powerful, a position that leaves them poorer and more powerless than they have ever been. They should also consider abandoning false and imploding racial distinctions. Instead of telling a story about themselves that separates them from African-Americans, American Indians, and all those who have been dispossessed, they could tell a story about their common predicament. They could organize for true democracy, as they once did. Nearly everything that the industrial workers of Appalachia have ever gained (the eight-hour workday, the Wagner Act, health and retirement benefits, and higher wages) came from collective politics. It came, in other words, from people who refused to be divided by imaginary differences.

It is difficult to find anything Appalachians have gained by voting for Republicans. Yet a majority in every county in West Virginia voted for Donald Trump in 2016. His promise to revitalize the coal industry lacks a footing in reality. Sensing this, one voter gave him a desperate endorsement, saying, "He's the only shot we got." If Trump studies West Virginia's congressional delegation, he might conclude that he doesn't need to do very much. But the people can do better than that. They can make their representatives justify the trust placed in them. They can demand more of their government. They can assert a right to land and livelihood and reparations from the corporations that used and abused them for so long. Maybe that can be the basis for a positive political identity.[44]

I favor democratic socialism and a reinvention of the nation-state as a conduit for meeting human needs rather than for accumulating capital. I also favor a realm of democratic autonomy, and that might have more political traction. If Congress and the president can cooperate, such a realm can exist as a function of the United States itself. But it can also exist outside of centralized government, sponsored by West Virginia or Kentucky or Tennessee. Or people can do it themselves, by squatting on abandoned land and defending their right to the commons.[45]

There is talk and some action regarding returning land. Various organizations have held public meetings to elicit policies directly from citizens. Even Congress is thinking along these lines. In 2016, Representative Harold Rogers, a Kentucky Republican, introduced the Reclaim Act. The law would empower the Department of the Interior to distribute funds to states and Indian nations aimed at developing land in communities "adversely affected by coal mining." I would push this thinking toward creating a reconstituted commons. What if people who wished to do so lived by hunting and gardening as part of a social project that encouraged political participation? What if citizens possessed use-rights over a sustaining landscape?

Historians don't often write legislation. My attempt is consistent with the argument of this book. Consider it more a thought experiment than a ready-made policy. Any actual solution would require the knowledge of people who live in the mountains and the sponsorship of organizations and activists working on these questions. The following owes something to the New Deal economist Milburn Wilson, the geographer J. Russell Smith, the historian Lewis Cecil Gray, the Kentucky farmer and writer Wendell Berry, and also to Mahatma Gandhi, Lewis Mumford, and E. F. Schumacher.[46] I call it . . .

THE COMMONS COMMUNITIES ACT

Whereas coal mining is diminishing in the southern mountains, leaving thousands unemployed, and *whereas* coal contributes to climate change and the disruption of human societies all over the world; *whereas* a rural policy should incorporate ecological principles with food production on a small scale, and *whereas* the United States once included millions of households engaged in production for subsistence and exchange; *whereas* when people take care of landscapes, landscapes take care of them,

SECTION 1. The United States shall create a series of commons communities, each designed to include a specified number of households within a larger landscape that will be managed by them, the residents. This landscape will provide the ecological base for hunting and gathering, cattle grazing, timber harvesting, vegetable gardening, and farming. The ecological base will be owned as a conservation easement or land trust under the authority of the states and/or counties where each community resides.

SECTION 2. Commons communities would be organized according to the design principles developed by the economist Elinor Ostrom, who was awarded the Nobel Prize in Economic Sciences in 2009 for her work on the economic governance of common resources. Each community shall include well-defined boundaries and members. Each will devise rules for appropriation suitable to the environment, along with sanctions and penalties for those who violate the rules and take too much or otherwise abuse the resource. Each must establish a means of conflict resolution and governance. In the event that residents need to sue the community or other residents, they would use the county, state, or federal courts.[47]

SECTION 3. Commons communities will not be limited to Appalachia but could be established anywhere a sufficient ecological base exists, including the outskirts of cities and suburbs. This law must not be construed to favor one location or ethnic group.

SECTION 4. Social services and education will be paid for by an income tax on the top 1 percent of household incomes in the United States and an Industrial Abandonment Tax, attached to any corporation that closed its operations in any city or region of the United States within the last twenty years of the date of this Act and moved elsewhere, leaving behind toxic waste and poverty.

SECTION 5. Resident households with incomes under $50,000 a year will pay no federal income tax. Residents will own their own homes, paying for them with low-interest mortgages and a $1.00 down payment.

SECTION 6. No nonresident, trust, or corporation is permitted to purchase property in a commons community.

SECTION 7. The organization of commons communities will proceed through the Department of Agriculture. The Department will initiate the identification of suitable lands for condemnation by eminent domain or land already owned by counties, states, or the United States. The Department will determine how much land is needed to sustain a given number of residents.

SECTION 8. Allied Programs.

> SUB-SECTION A. Income tax incentives will encourage teachers and medical doctors to live in commons communities and work in the schools and nearby hospitals.

SUB-SECTION B. College-age members of any commons household may apply for free tuition at their state university. Tuition shall be paid for by the Industrial Abandonment Tax.

SUB-SECTION C. Commons communities will receive special programs intended to link them to the Internet. Cooperation between communities will incorporate schools, artists and writers in residence, and scientists engaged in the study of the environment. This Act provides funds for the publication of a journal or magazine of commons life to be written and published by the residents of the various communities.

SUB-SECTION D. Another program will link gardeners with markets for their produce, including grocery stores and restaurants. Proceeds from this Market Garden Initiative will not be subject to state or federal income tax.

SUB-SECTION E. University experiment stations in every state where commons communities exist will send representatives to teach the latest methods of garden production, with the approval and consent of residents.

SECTION 9. If the members of a commons community no longer wish to be associated with the federal government, they may become independent at any time with a majority vote consisting of two-thirds of adult residents, at which time all federal programs associated with this Act will cease. Ownership of the commons would not change and residents would keep their homes.

The act might look like Arthurdale and the Division of Subsistence Homesteads all over again. But it has no factory, no originating debt, and no presumption that people must subsist entirely from gardens. It emphasizes scientific conservation, cultural expression, entrepreneurship, and democracy. It would not prevent any resident from earning money in any job or profession. Some within Appalachia might object to the participation of the federal government. But government can do things that communities cannot by themselves, like purchase land, relieve taxes on citizens and levy them on corporations, advance citizen participation, and pay for college. Government can help the residents of commons communities remain connected to the wider world of economic opportunity and political participation. But the act allows for its own dissolution. Residents would have the authority to end the government's participation and keep their gains.[48]

The act seeks to preserve and encourage a makeshift economy that has been practiced for two centuries among mountain farmers, as well as among people in other parts of the United States. Readers in New York, Chicago, or Los Angeles might not appreciate the extent to which rural Americans depend on forests and other environments for food and cash. In the 1980s, Timothy Lee Barnwell photographed and interviewed Appalachians who practiced agrarian economy. Charlie Thomas of Bush Creek, North Carolina, said, "Even when I was growing up we raised almost everything we ate. You'd buy a little coffee if you wanted it, but we never drank it, and buy or trade for what sugar you needed, and we used honey for that. We've always kept bees for our own honey." A series of interviews conducted in southern West Virginia during the 1990s is now part of the Library of Congress. "People around here . . . on Coal River, just about every one of them does the same thing," explained Dave Baily. "They pick the grains, they pick the black berries, they fish, they hunt . . . they get the molly moochers [the morchella or morel mushroom] . . . They do that, their kids is going to do it, their grandkids is going to do it, and that's the way it is on Coal River." Others interviewed detailed their extensive knowledge of trees and plants. None of these West Virginians need the Commons Communities Act to continue living as they always have, from whatever forested commons they can still find. The act is meant to promote this social ecology. By combining land and livelihood—by fostering possession against a history of dispossession—it would reconnect communities and landscapes in a structure for sustaining both.[49]

The political economy of the act combines private and communal property. Residents may buy and sell their homes, pass them to the next generation, and do anything else with them permitted by local law. They would act differently in their role as managers of common woods and waters. Economists have rarely understood the logic of collective use. The most common argument says that every user has an incentive to cut every last tree, shoot every last large-bodied mammal, and let his cattle graze every last acre of wild meadow, leaving nothing for anyone else. The forest is reduced to stumps; the high meadow is overrun with thistle. This is the misleading parable of the "Tragedy of the Commons," most famously described by the biologist Garrett Hardin in 1968.[50]

Hardin based his model on a self-serving conception of human nature. His essay has nothing to do with how actual people govern actual shared resources, cases that Hardin seems to have known little about. His first mistake was to think that a commons is a free-for-all. No such set of resources is open to everyone, but only to members, defined in various ways. Consider the forests of New England in the nineteenth century. Colonial towns owned them and controlled access, allowing some to cut trees and others to hunt and fish with permission. Lobster fishermen in Maine operate according to their own rules and institutions, with little government involvement, resulting in one of the most successful fisheries in the world. But they decide who can and cannot benefit. Thus everyone who depends on common property has an incentive to maintain it. This is not to say that everyone is always satisfied. Community management requires governance to mediate disagreement and limit the consequences of conflict. The point is that it's simply not true that common property always degenerates into scarcity.[51]

But Hardin cannot be dismissed altogether. His fable reasonably describes resources that no group can manage, like the open ocean and the atmosphere. And not all collective uses of land have succeeded. (In fact, we know very little about how the functional forest commons fared in West Virginia, how well users governed themselves.) Without regulations and penalties, without clear borders and firm institutions, they can result in devastation. This is why Elinor Ostrom studied them—to figure out why some failed and others thrived.[52]

We all live in communities. In a sense, no one really lives in the United States but in neighborhoods, towns, and counties. Strengthening those bonds within environments that allow for economic autonomy seems like a way of creating space between people and the nation-state. It might also offer a way to endure during times of climate disruption, when the United States might not be capable of compensating for any number of possible disasters. The Commons Communities Act proposes land reform and collective governance. It proposes nothing new, but rather something very old, a sense of ownership without the enclosure and the abuse of power characteristic of private property.[53]

And yet, I have my own objections to the Commons Communities Act. Small-scale development programs appeared decades ago, with mixed results. The same reformers and intellectuals who rediscovered the small town and the Indian pueblo during the New Deal urged communitarian approaches all over the world. But these schemes harbored certain false assumptions, well described by the historian Daniel Immerwahr. Development agencies believed that the members of a village acted from shared principles and that local elites would fairly apportion money entrusted to them. But villages in the Philippines and India turned out to be more complicated—and divided—than the sanguine Americans had thought. Immerwahr suggests another problem. When a nation-state invests in a community, where does its influence end? What role would the United States play in a commons community?[54]

The act might also be criticized for shunting the problem of industrial abandonment onto the poor, just like the Division of Subsistence Homesteads. In this way, it seems like a neoliberal policy intended to reduce the cost of state services and lower taxes on the rich. And while under the act the corporations that caused so much human and ecological ruin would be required to pay for houses and schools, this doesn't change or challenge a political economy in which humans and environments serve as inputs in the circulation of capital. For corporations, compensating for social destruction is merely part of the cost of doing business. Eliminating these contradictions so that citizens benefit would require a government and a set of laws dedicated to human welfare.

The act includes scholarships so that the children of Appalachian households might attend college, but it does not come close to addressing the larger cultural problem of why high school kids in Appalachia often don't apply. In *Hillbilly Elegy* (2016), J. D. Vance eloquently explains why it's so difficult for Appalachians to find a way out of unemployment and improve the quality of their lives. Some see themselves as different from those outside their families or counties. People in other parts of the country view them harshly, with many of the same racialized stereotypes present a century ago. All of this makes geographic and social mobility difficult. Vance's own story suggests that a strong mentor with the capacity to see beyond limited local opportunities can overcome self-defeat. Vance's mentor was his grandmother. "She didn't just preach and cuss and demand. She showed me what was possible . . . and made sure I knew how to get there." Her home provided Vance stability and peace, "not just a short-term haven but also hope for a better life."

Vance got out. He graduated from Ohio State University, the Marines, and Yale Law School before joining a Silicon Valley investment firm. But his very success implies the depth of the problem he confronted. The most unsettling currents in *Hillbilly Elegy* lie in the necessity of leaving and in its emphasis on a strong and uncompromising grandmother. If meaningful work and a decent occupation only exist elsewhere, then most Appalachians will be abandoned. If escape depends on someone who rises above despair and abuse, then most will be stuck. The role of public policy and a political solution to poverty is to attempt to help everyone in the same situation rather than rely on extraordinary circumstance and plain luck to produce successful individuals. Vance's book is inspiring as a memoir, but it might be construed as saying that the tragedy of Appalachia is the sum of its individual failings or the insularity of its families. Domestic violence, drug abuse, and hopelessness on such a scale have social causes. They require solutions that do not place the burden on the sufferers themselves to transcend their circumstances.[55]

AT THE END OF THIS long account of dispossession we find the past reflected in the present. Historians emphasize the distinctiveness of the stories they tell. They tend to make few observations across places and times. But one of the arguments of this book has been that capitalism tells a certain story about people who hunt or garden outside the circuit of capital or who buy and sell into markets on their own terms. Capitalism must expand geographically in order to survive. It must find new people and new funds of stuff from environments in order to combine them into new commodities, which then perpetuate the circulation of capital. In just the same way, the history of capitalism breaches national, spatial, and temporal borders.

The simple narrative that so many have told since the seventeenth century stresses the world-historical progress of wealth, measured in material stages. From the point of view of those who have benefited by it, to be brought into the realm of capital's creation, even unwillingly, is to join the flow of history. In 1675, the English political economist Roger Coke asserted that no man or nation would ever succeed "against the Nature and Order of things." He meant that the laws of capitalist motion encompass everyone and everything and that these laws come from the cosmos, not from prime ministers, central bankers, or chief executive officers. Capitalism is not nailed to the roof of heaven, but the perception that it is brought the existence of household hunters and farmers into question.[56]

Enclosure, more than any other of capitalism's defining practices, embodies its historical patterns and enabling assumptions. Enclosure is not past but present, especially throughout Africa. Since 2008, corporations, governments, and international development agencies have looked anew at territory that agrarians have occupied for centuries without formal ownership. Private property doesn't exist in most of the fifty-four countries on the continent. Just as the Parliament of Great Britain invented that unprecedented right and gave it to lords, some African governments now do the same for foreign corporations. "Across Africa and the developing world," reported *The New York Times* in 2010, "a new global land rush is gobbling up large expanses of arable land. Despite their ageless traditions, stunned villagers are discovering that African governments typically own their land and have been leasing it, often at bargain prices." So as a contemporary point of reference for enclosure in England circa 1600 and West Virginia circa 1900, I offer the case of Mali, circa 2000. Africa raises questions crucial to the purpose of this book. Who is served by development and what is its relationship to capital?

In 1999, the United States Agency for International Development decided that the arid plains along the Niger River in Mali would be ideal for growing sugarcane. The Americans targeted a peasant commune called Markala, consisting of around thirty villages near the city of Ségou, all located within the Office du Niger, an administrative region established during French colonization. A South African sugar company expressed interest and formed a subsidiary, the Société Sucrière de Markala, known as Sosumar. Seventeen lenders tossed $600 million into the project, including the African Development Bank, the Korea Eximbank, the Islamic Development Bank, and Saudi and Kuwaiti investors. The government of Mali solidified its involvement in 2007 by writing leases for 17,000 hectares to Sosumar for fifty years. Sosumar agreed to establish two hundred pivot-irrigated cane fields along with a mill.

They organized everything just perfectly except for one thing. Thousands of people planted millet, beans, corn, rice, and peanuts on those 17,000 hectares. The agencies started planning and the capital started flowing, the government drew up papers and the corporation spun off Sosumar, all before anyone informed the peasants. But unlike British lords, Sosumar did not (or could not) evict the farmers and destroy their villages. The project took place within an international context much more transparent, including advocates for the rights of peasants. The African Development Bank, for one, demanded that the villagers be treated with respect. In response, Sosumar offered to give each household a slice of irrigated land. Smallholders would produce 40 percent of the company's cane by contract. Everyone involved seems to have known that specialization is dispossession in slow motion. The company agreed to establish "a floor price" that would protect growers from market adversity. Smallholders would also cultivate their own food between the rows of cane, further securing them against the vagaries of events and institutions beyond their control.[57]

Sosumar needed someone to front the project by mediating among the parties. Mima Nedelcovych arrived in 2010. Nedelcovych advocates for private investment as the most effective means of generating economic development. Once in Mali, he moved fluidly between government ministries, meetings with bankers, construction sites, and village councils. When Nedelcovych talks about dispossession as social progress, he sounds more like Bill Clinton than James Steuart. The "straight land grab," he said, "will not last." Nedelcovych believed that Sosumar would save the villagers from themselves. They grew food and commodities just as they did three centuries ago. "There is no change . . . bringing the small farmer[s] into the value chain is giving them a reason to produce more than what they eat." Take their land, goes this thinking, but make them into commercial farmers. Usher them into history itself by making their labor take the form of commodities and Mali's GDP would increase, the company would make billions of dollars, and everyone would win.

Two filmmakers, Hugo Berkeley and Osvalde Lewat, interviewed Nedelcovych along with the residents of two villages for *Land Rush* (2012). The people of one village, Tain, expressed interest in Sosumar. A farmer named Massa spoke: "Our harvests have not improved in eighteen years. That's why we agreed to stop growing millet and do something new. We want to change." Representatives of Tain knew that the government had already leased their land to the corporation. Some argued that change might be good for them. One man said, "No one here eats three meals a day." Anything that promised more money would give them a higher standard of living. "When I learned about Sosumar," said a woman, "I saw that women have a lot to gain. Any woman who wants work will be able to work all year round."

The residents of the other village, Soungo, were opposed. A farmer named Kassoum spoke of his farm as a legacy. "Everyone in my family works together on the same farm. We have about thirty hectares of land . . . We considered the sugarcane project, and we have no interest in it." Then he added, "Even if they give us lots of money, it will run out. But the land never runs out." Others at a subsequent meeting acknowledged that they sometimes went hungry, sometimes had to "make do." But they preferred a known unknown to an unknown unknown. "Destroying a village is like destroying a whole country," said another. Kassoum added that no one in the company or the government had presented the members of the village with a choice, but rather a thinly disguised ultimatum.

The village debates replayed the kinds of unrecorded discussions that must have taken place among English peasants of the seventeenth and eighteenth centuries calculating how they might survive enclosure. Households and kin in the southern mountains must have had the same conversations, with some anticipating schools and roads and others worried about giving up woods and hunting. All of them must have talked about the benefits of money from outside their means and methods of exchange and whether money would take care of them or run out and leave them with nothing. One skein of the Sosumar debate addressed land grabbing in general. An activist involved with the villages, Ibrahim Coulibaly, told those assembled at another meeting not to be swayed by money. "Don't pick up guns or knives, but do something, or else you'll disappear, 1,000 square kilometers at a time."[58]

No peasants ended up taking the deal and none lost their land because Sosumar never planted a hectare of cane or sold a pound of sugar. In 2012, Islamist Tuareg fighters attempted to cleave away Mali's northern region for an independent state. The ensuing political storm and escalating violence shattered the relative stability that followed a prodemocracy movement in 1992. Foreign direct investment pulled out, and Sosumar might never go forward.

Like the story at the center of this book, the meaning of Sosumar depends on whose interests we think with. We can trace the land rush in West Africa and other "undervalued" regions to the food crisis of 2008. Prices spiked, not because of a scarcity of rice, but because speculation in commodities markets drove them up. This led corporations to view agriculture as profitable, prompting them to invest in so-called idle lands. The governments of host countries welcomed the foreign money. They could increase national income by leasing the only abundant resource they controlled. And though these interests did not fit hand in glove then or now, they allowed "transactions to be concluded."[59] What do the peasants of West Africa want? By their own standards, the farmers of Markala are not thriving. Mali lands 179th out of 188 countries in the United Nations Human Development Index. Average life expectancy is fifty-eight years. Should they have gone along with Sosumar? Should they have trusted an enormous amalgamation of capital and political power, assuming that they had been given a meaningful choice?[60]

The villages of Markala are around one thousand years old. They have endured drought, colonization, and war. Sosumar, however, wanted more from them than even French colonizers demanded. The company wanted them to give up their only hold and stake in the world for a set of promises. Its managers proposed they become full-time commodity producers and cast their fate upon a market that includes state-supported competitors in

Brazil, India, Mexico, Thailand, and Pakistan, as well as Hawaii and Texas. Sosumar offered to maintain contract farmers in the event of low prices, but no one knows if they would have. No government agency or international court exists that could have compelled the company to follow through. But even with assurances, the risks of planting an inedible commodity on a small plot of land with no control over the conditions of production, trade policy, or final sale would have been substantial.

Nedelcovych sought the agreement of the villagers in what looked like an open process of deliberation. Was it? The financial power he represented preceded him. One elder quoted a local official connected to Sosumar who reportedly said, "Whether you like it or not, we're taking your land. This land belongs to the state so we can take it." A number of those interviewed mentioned a radio campaign funded by Sosumar. Those opposed did not have the same access to make their arguments known. Kassoum threw up his hands at the thought of Sosumar. "We want them to leave our land to us. We pray to God that they do." How sincere was the process Nedelcovych pursued? Would Sosumar have disbanded and returned $600 million to investors had a few hundred peasants decided not to cooperate? Perhaps. But when Kassoum placed his faith and fate with God, he might have been thinking of the village of Kolongo.

Muammar Gaddafi came to the government of Mali asking for land in 2008. The government leased 100,000 hectares to a corporation Gaddafi controlled, including the water rights, without asking for anything in return. Gaddafi only needed to extend the irrigation infrastructure. It took two years and tens of millions of dollars for Libya to reach an agreement with a Chinese construction company. Unknown to the residents of Kolongo, however, the Chinese company designed the main canal to run right through the middle of their village. We do not know what the residents were told in advance. We do know that bulldozers destroyed their houses while armed thugs held them off. "They fired tear gas at us," said one woman. "Afterwards, they came with their electric batons. They hit me and pushed me over. Then they took us away." The woman told of arriving at another location, where she was ordered to lie facedown on the ground. "After that, they hit us." The construction company even gutted the cemetery. A visitor from an international aid organization reported seeing human remains strewn all over the construction site. An outraged man pointed to the exhumed graves of his ancestors, shaking with anger at the violation, "As if we're not citizens of Mali."[61]

Should we consider the dispossession of Kolongo an example of economic development? To call it that would be unfair to all the agricultural specialists and well-intentioned administrators in organizations like the United Nations and the World Bank who are dedicated to improving the lives of the global poor. It would be an insult to representatives of the African Development Bank who pursue a peaceful transition from subsistence economy to commercial relations for African peasants. Clearly, no legitimate agency would endorse the violent removal of people from their land. And yet, in their ends, if not their means, Sosumar's plans for Markala and Gaddafi's destruction of Kolongo share certain qualities.

In both cases, corporations cut a deal with the government without first securing the consent of the people who would be forced out. In both cases, the intention was to turn fields of millet into spaces that generate global commodities and billions of dollars in profit, not food for the people. According to Oxfam, "More than 60 percent of crops grown on land bought by foreign investors in developing countries are intended for export." As reported in *The New York Times*, an economist with the United Nations Development Programme in Mali spoke broadly of the effects of corporate enclosure. "The land is a natural resource that 70 percent of the population uses to survive . . . You cannot just push 70 percent of the population off the land, nor can you say they can just become agriculture workers." Yet this is the logical conclusion of land grabbing in Africa *regardless of who is doing it*, though it might not be possible for decades.[62]

The difference, of course, is that Gaddafi made no pretense to improving anyone's life but his own. But while Sosumar insisted that it would do right by the people, it had no obligation to any group other than its shareholders. This is a problem with corporate-financed economic development. The product's only purpose is to return a profit. The chief information officer for a private equity firm that acquires land in Africa rejected any suggestion of humanitarianism: "We are not investing money to grow food or help people in Africa—we are investing to return capital to our clients.

But a consequence of our investment is the production of food and increased food security." The equity firm's policy would be a fair parallel to Sosumar's except for one thing: Sosumar would not have improved Mali's food security at all.[63]

It is important to keep something else in mind. Development often means *transformation*, by which is meant village to city, mutuality to individuality, subsistence to wage. The World Bank has recently offered an updated description of its role. Apparently, development does not consist merely of "the quantitative accumulation of national capital" and crude economic growth. "Development is also the qualitative transformation of a whole society, a shift to new ways of thinking, and, correspondingly, to new relations and new methods of production." Transformation qualifies as social progress, "only if it benefits most people—improves their quality of life and gives them more control over their destinies." The World Bank wants universal education, the reduction of child mortality, and the elimination of AIDS and malaria. These are all admirable ends. But why does meeting a people's basic human needs require that they shift to new ways of thinking? Two economists also insist on transformation as salvation: "For economic development to succeed in Africa in the next 50 years, African agriculture will have to change beyond recognition. Production will have to have increased massively, but also labour productivity, requiring a vast reduction in the proportion of the population engaged in agriculture and a large move out of rural areas." Why do people need to leave everything they know for new social relations in order to have food and education?[64]

The Sosumar project inadvertently highlighted an indigenous method of making money from the ecological base. But rather than encourage it, the plan was to destroy it. Under the company's vision for Markala, irrigated cane fields would have replaced thousands of shea trees on the savannah of the Office du Niger. Women harvest the fruits and remove the nuts, roast them in pots, and then grind them. From this they make a creamy butter. The butter is used as cooking oil and made into soap in Africa. Europeans and Americans like it as a skin moisturizer. Shea brings in cash in much the same way as rubber tapping does for the rice planters of Kalimantan and whiskey did for the settlers of western Pennsylvania. It connects the villages of Markala to the distant realm of exchange, where money and opportunity are abundant. More than that, it offers a social ritual exclusively for women and girls. "Shea is our livelihood," said one woman to the filmmakers. "We don't want our trees cut down."[65]

Shea is not some obscure West African product. The United Nations Development Programme estimates that 3 million women produce it, including fifteen thousand who sell it to the cosmetics company L'Occitane. The Global Shea Alliance works with women's groups, manufacturing companies, and nongovernmental organizations to create demand for shea butter. So if the government of Mali and international lenders wanted the people of Markala to make more money, they could have helped them to sell more shea butter instead of asking them to hand over their land to Sosumar. Sosumar would have excised women and men from socially embedded ways of creating commodities, generational patterns of work, and beloved landscapes. For people around the world who lack government protection, who are subject to capital, with no social welfare system to see them through unemployment, *an income detached from a subsistence livelihood does not provide economic security.*[66]

An essential critique of land grabbing comes from Olivier De Schutter, a Belgian professor of human rights law who served as United Nations special rapporteur on food security. De Schutter reveals the contradictions and false premises involved in leasing peasant land to corporations. If we view these deals without the history of the people involved, we will fail to see them for what they are. Like the smallholders of the southern mountains circa 1890, African farmers face challenges to their occupancy, having already endured a narrowing of their subsistence stability by previous acts of coercion that "relegated [them] to soils that are arid, hilly, or without irrigation." They work for wages on plantations to replace food and cash incomes they once created for themselves. Employment brings a better life only when no other better life is possible. The hardships that flow from prior events allowed Nedelcovych to evoke an ideology of progress identical to capitalist premises. He could argue that poor farmers had nothing to lose. But step out of that ideology, and this is what it looks like: For mere speculation in commodities, for the sake of profit, the basis of life for millions of people is recast as an alienable asset.

We should not be fooled when a benevolent purpose is read backward into these motives.[67]

Capitalism generates a blanket of protective assumptions that ties it to nature or the order of things. Compounding interest became the material proof of progress, a value easily projected onto society, so that what is good for capital must be good for the world. As Karl Polanyi observed decades ago, the capitalist sees utopia just ahead or else continually undermined by timid constitutionalists or delusional socialists, regardless of the actual consequences of actual policies. The ideology filters out data that contradict it. If corporations pursuing their objectives through free trade over the last one hundred years really spread wealth wherever they went, there would be no Global Slum of 1 billion people and growing—no Dharavi in Mumbai, no Neza-Chalco-Itza in Mexico City. The truth is that the spatial manifestation of capital in the twenty-first century is not a functioning city with a sanitation infrastructure and a responsible civil service, but an archipelago of misery that is the mirror image of the wealth created by dispossession.

Writes De Schutter, "If it is to be truly responsible, agricultural investment must be investment that benefits the poor in the South, rather than leading to a transfer of resources to the rich in the North. It must be investment that truly reduces hunger and malnutrition, rather than aggravating them." He offers his own set of principles intended to limit and govern land grabbing. They include accepting existing rights to land and natural resources, transparency and mutuality in all transactions, estimating environmental impacts, and—most of all—deploying money in order to enhance food security and social stability. De Schutter calls these *minimum requirements*, meaning that even if a corporate scheme satisfies them, the project in question might still be objectionable. One reason Sosumar or another corporation might fail the humanitarian test has to do with the economic vulnerability that lies behind minimum requirements. African governments have only limited capacities to compensate for downturns and unemployment. If villagers become wageworkers or contract farmers, what happens when the bottom falls out of the international market or a company pivots its interests and closes down?[68]

Something like Sosumar will come to fruition (if it hasn't already).

Peasants will leave their villages. Some of the profit will go to education and infrastructure. Workers will move into houses with electric lights and send their daughters to school. When that happens, we should not look away. Any recession in the importing countries, any financial bubble in New York or London or Beijing, can cause tenuous incomes and fragile institutions to evaporate. A commonly asked question about the spectacular ascent of Chinese production and urban migration is whether China can handle its own Great Depression. Yet China has a series of social welfare policies, including unemployment insurance, universal healthcare, and pension funds. It also has enormous stockpiles of foreign currency. African governments have none of these things. When a crisis leaves sugar mills to rust, workers who traded their ecological base for wages will be hungrier than they ever were before.

All of this should give us pause. It isn't clear that subsistence wages are preferable to subsistence gardens. Maybe agrarians are better off being agrarians. They still feed one-third of the world. According to the United Nations International Fund for Agricultural Development, 500 million smallholds sustain 2 billion people, producing 80 percent of the food consumed in Asia and sub-Saharan Africa. Oxfam and the World Bank agree about at least one thing: "Measures to improve smallholder farmers' capacity to increase food production and productivity, as well as to link to markets, will . . . contribute to global food security."[69] The way forward is to stop thinking of peasants as categorically poor but to ask what they need to do better. Just because a family has little money, limiting their consumption of store-bought goods, does not mean that they cry out to be moved away. As long as people have access to land, control over their own labor, and freedom from debt, they are unlikely to feel wanting.

"The first step towards reimagining a world gone terribly wrong would be to stop the annihilation of those who have a different imagination," writes Arundhati Roy.[70] Privileging the needs of peasants, campesinos, and smallholders over those of capitalists means acting averse to some of our closely held assumptions. It means accepting the limitations of agrarians without viewing money spent on their betterment as a financial investment. The brutality of enclosure will only cease when we cease to regard people and landscapes as instruments of wealth. Freedom, in order to have any meaning, must include the freedom to live in a village and farm as a household, with all its uncertainty. The question we need to ask of every migration from country to city is whether it originated from a government scheme or corporate gambit that so degraded a people's autonomy as to give them no choice. We need to know history in order to make policy. Otherwise, we might allow an old story to think for us, a story told for centuries that has never told the truth.

NOTES

Preface

1. Census of the United States (1940), Union District, Monongahela County, West Virginia, Schedules 31–38 and 31–15.
2. Census of the United States (1900), Union District, Monongahela County, West Virginia, Sheet 288.

1. Contemporary Ancestors

1. This book relies on some of the most important recent scholarship on the history of Appalachia. I benefited especially from Billings and Blee, *The Road to Poverty*; Dunaway, *The First American Frontier*; Eller, *Miners, Millhands, and Mountaineers*; Salstrom, *Appalachia's Path to Dependency*; Shapiro, *Appalachia on Our Mind*; Gaventa, *Power and Powerlessness*; Hsiung, *Two Worlds in the Tennessee Mountains*; Lewis, *Transforming the Appalachian Countryside*; Newfont, *Blue Ridge Commons*; Pudup, "The Limits of Subsistence"; Pudup, Billings, and Waller,

Appalachia in the Making; Sachs, *Home Rule*; Weise, *Grasping at Independence*; Williams, *Appalachia: A History*; and other books in the notes and bibliography.

2. The entire range of the Appalachian Mountains runs northeast from Georgia. Just above New York City it makes a hard left turn due north along the Hudson River. It embraces the Green Mountains of Vermont and the White Mountains of New Hampshire before heading northeast again into Maine.

3. The more specific definition has 165 counties, compared to the 406 in the wider view. To the extent that this book relies on any geographical definition, it uses the narrower one. See Williams, *Appalachia*, 12–14, and Fernow, *The Great Timber Belt*, 5.

4. For this and the previous paragraph: Huntington, Williams, and Van Valkenburg, *Economic and Social Geography*, 170. Another report noted, "The Mountains and the Bluegrass were settled by people of the same racial stock." Quoted in Billings and Blee, *Road to Poverty*, 29. *The Oxford English Dictionary* gives an instance of *Appalachian* used to describe the people of the region from 1888, but the term did not enter common usage until at least the 1970s. John Alexander Williams thinks of Appalachia as "a zone where diverse groups have interacted with one another and with a set of regional and subregional environments over time." Williams, *Appalachia*, 12. The government report is Marschner, *Rural Population Density in the Southern Appalachians*, 1.

5. I am thinking of Immanuel Wallerstein, Fernand Braudel, André Gunder Frank, Raúl Prebisch, David Harvey, and Raymond Williams. Each of them followed a similar intellectual evolution, from the influence of markets to the political economy of societies organized by capital. In Wallerstein's thinking, the world-system is "an integrated zone of activity and institutions which obey certain systemic rules." Wallerstein formulated the world-system with (or against) the evidence and arguments of historians of capitalism like Fernand Braudel, Paul Sweezy, and Karl Polanyi. He added in David Ricardo's comparative advantages and Karl Marx's observation that history can be understood as the perpetual transformation of modes of production. The terms *core* and *periphery* came from the National Economic Commission for Latin America. Most of all, Wallerstein took the global division of labor from the economist Prebisch. Wallerstein, *World-Systems Analysis*; Harvey, *Social Justice and the City*; Williams, *The Country and the City*; Braudel, *Civilization and Capitalism* (three volumes); Frank, "The Development of Underdevelopment." For a narrative describing Chicago and North America, see Cronon, *Nature's Metropolis*.

6. In *The First American Frontier*, Wilma Dunaway argues that Appalachia became part of the world-system in the eighteenth century. She further argues that subsistence production (in the limited way she defines it) ended at that point. In my argument, subsistence production and exchange are not mutually exclusive. In fact, the one has rarely existed without the other.

7. Abraham Lincoln, speech at New Salem, Illinois, March 9, 1832, *Abraham Lincoln: A Documentary Portrait*, 31.

8. The judge and merchant was Richard Henderson.

9. Ferguson's proclamation of October 1, 1780, quoted in McCrady, *History of South Carolina in the Revolution*, 778. For an account, see *Virginia Gazette*, October 21, 1780.

10. Thwaites and Kellogg, *Documentary History of Dunmore's War*, 371. Dunmore referred to the Watauga Association, a frontier government in eastern Tennessee created in 1772. See Williams, "The Admission of Tennessee into the Union," 291; Rush, "Account of the Progress of Population," in *Essays*, 215; Crèvecoeur, *Letters from an American Farmer, quoted in American Georgics*, 24. James Madison also agonized over them. "Our own people nursed and reared in these habits and tastes," he propounded to an audience of lowland planters, "easily slide into those of the savage and are rarely reclaimed to civilized society with their own consent." Madison, "Address Before the Agricultural Society of Albemarle."

11. Absentee landowners are discussed in chapters 3 and 4.

12. Ioor, *Independence; Or Which Do You like Best, the Peer, or the Farmer?*

13. Faulkner, *The Speech of Charles Jas. Faulkner (of Berkeley) in the House of Delegates of Virginia*, 9; Benton, "Speech of Mr. Benton, of Missouri, on the Oregon Question," 30.

14. Woodbury, "Speech of Senator Levi Woodbury," 92.

15. *The Knickerbocker; or New York Monthly Magazine*, August 1839, 2, 14.

16. For this and the previous paragraph: Hill, *Daniel Boone*, 11, 229–30; Aron, *How the West Was Lost*, 78–84; Faragher, *Daniel Boone*, 242–50.

17. Hill, *Daniel Boone*, 229–30. Also see Hale, *Trans-Allegheny Pioneers*, 158.

18. Faulkner, *Speech upon the Mineral and Agricultural Resources of the State of West Virginia*, 10, 12, 15, 23–24.

19. Taylor, *Alleghania*, 23–24; *New York Times*, November 6, 1862; June 19, 1861; October 24, 1861.

20. Pollard, *The Virginia Tourist*, 28–30. Also see Mayer, "A June Jaunt," *Harper's Magazine*, April 1857, 592–612. "Everything seems to be the property of the wilderness—a wilderness incapable of yielding to any mastery but that of an engineer."

21. Harney, "A Strange Land and a Peculiar People," 431–32.

22. The quotation is by George E. Vincent, quoted in Turner, *The Frontier in American History*, 35. Hsiung, *Two Worlds in the Tennessee Mountains*, 187–88. On nineteenth-century social science, see Wallerstein, "Societal Development, or Development of World-System?" in *Unthinking Social Science*, 78, 81.

23. Frost, "University Extension in Kentucky." On Frost and his thoughts about Appalachian otherness, see Shapiro, *Appalachia on Our Mind*, 115–22. On Roosevelt and Turner, see Slotkin, *Gunfighter Nation*, 29–42. The phrase "barbarian virtues" comes from the book of that title by Mathew Frye Jacobson.

24. Semple, "Anglo-Saxons of the Kentucky Mountains," 1–7. The Daughters of the American Revolution dates to October 11, 1890. Congress chartered the National Society of the DAR in 1896 at the peak of immigration from eastern and southern Europe. William R. Grace was elected the first Irish (and Catholic) mayor of New York City in 1880. Hugh O'Brian became the first Irish mayor of Boston in 1884.

25. On the claim for Chaucer and Shakespeare in mountain dialect, see Frost, "University Extension in Kentucky"; Semple, "Anglo-Saxons of the Kentucky Mountains," 1–7; Graffenried, "The Georgia Cracker in the Cotton Mills," 497; Fox, *Blue-grass and Rhododendron*, 15; Pinchot, *Breaking New Ground*, 62. The best piece debunking the idea is Montgomery, "In the Appalachians They Speak Like Shakespeare," passim. On the general subject of mistaken origins, I benefited from Keesing, *Ethnohistory of Northern Luzon*, passim, and Roth, "Notes on the Ethnohistory of Northern Luzon," 374–75. "Learn me how to lose a winning match," *Romeo and Juliet*, III.ii.12.

26. Huntington, Williams, and Van Valkenburg, "Climate, Health, and the Distribution of Human Progress," in *Economic and Social Geography*, 118.

27. Jones, *A Dreadful Deceit*, xi.

28. Allen, *The Blue-Grass Region of Kentucky*, 273–76. The historian David Hsiung suggests *connectedness* as a more accurate description. It accounts for remoteness but emphasizes the linkages that people forged and maintained. Hsiung, *Two Worlds in the Tennessee Mountains*, 10–11, 69–70. Frank Owsley, *Plain Folk of the Old South*, vii–viii, quoted in Otto, "Southern 'Plain Folk' Agriculture," 29; Allen, "Mountain Passes of the Cumberland," *Harper's Magazine*, September 1890, 561. For many examples and an analysis of this literature, see Shapiro, *Appalachia on Our Minds*, 157. Appalachian Regional Commission, *Network Appalachia: Access to Global Opportunity*, www.arc.gov/noindex/programs/transp/intermodal /NetworkAppalachiaAccesstoGlobalOpportunity-Chap1.pdf.

29. Scott, *The Art of Not Being Governed*, 327; Nourse, "The Place of Agriculture in Modern Industrial Society II," 561–77; Fitzgerald, *Every Farm a Factory*, 28.

30. *New York Journal*, April 23, 1900, quoted in Harkins, *Hillbilly*, 7; Fowler, "Social and Industrial Conditions in the Pocahontas Coal Fields," 387; Allen, "Mountain Passes of the Cumberland," 575–76; Nixon, *Slow Violence and the Environmentalism of the Poor*, 19.

31. Robinson, "Anecdotes of the Mountain Folk," 930–32.

32. Lewis Cass, "Removal of the Indians" (January 1830), quoted in Perdue and Green, *The Cherokee Removal*, 115–20.

33. Jackson made these remarks in his State of the Union Address of December 6, 1830 (Perdue and Green, *The Cherokee Removal*, 125) and in a circular to the Cherokee dated March 16, 1835 (www.gilderlehrman.org/sites/default/files/content -images/07377p1.jpg). The removal cannot be separated from the politics of land and slavery that intensified after the Missouri Compromise, which outlawed

slavery in the Louisiana Territory north of 36°30′. Planters wanted every last corner of Georgia (and Alabama and Mississippi) to employ their slaves. A decade later, they needed still more, and that is when they made their next major gambit for Texas. Letters and firsthand accounts of the removal may be found in Perdue and Green, *The Cherokee Removal*, 171–76.

34. I refer here to *Worcester v. Georgia* (1832), in which Chief John Marshall upheld Cherokee sovereignty from the laws of Georgia but stated that the federal government maintained jurisdiction over all Indian nations. See Perdue and Green, *The Cherokee Removal*, 81.

35. As James C. Scott writes of the mountains of Southeast Asia, "Neglected and seemingly useless territories to which stateless peoples had been relegated were suddenly of great value to the economies of mature capitalism." See Scott, *The Art of Not Being Governed*, 11; White, *Backcountry and the City*, 31–35; and Nixon, *Slow Violence and the Environmentalism of the Poor*, 150–51.

36. Kwashiorkor is caused by protein deficiency.

37. Holmberg, *Nomads of the Longbow*, 8, 11, 44, 77, 96. See Mann, *1491*, chap. 1.

38. According to the anthropologist Barry Isaac, this representation of the Sirionó as "man in the raw state of nature" amounts to a vicious conception of hunter-gatherers. "And so long as the Hobbesian view prevailed, Holmberg's description of the Sirionó—with their desperate food quest, short life span, quarrels about food, etc.—did not seem odd." Isaac, "The Siriono of Eastern Bolivia: A Reexamination," *Human Ecology*, 137–54 (Isaac does not accent the last vowel). I also used William Balée's entry on the Sirionó in *The Cambridge Encyclopedia of Hunters and Gatherers*. Another early study that differs in substantial ways from Holmberg's is Stig Rydén, *A Study of the Sirionó Indians*. I also read Allyn MacLean Stearman's restudy of the Sirionó, *No Longer Nomads*. And see Mann, *1491*, 10.

39. Baumol and Blinder, *Economics: Principles and Policy*, 811.

40. For this chain and other similar cycles, see Wallerstein, *Unthinking the Social Sciences*; Samson, *A Way of Life That Does Not Exist*, 96–101. Frank quoted in Wallerstein, "The Rise and Future Demise of the World Capitalist System," *The Capitalist World Economy*, 7.

41. Ronald L. Lewis first made the argument that the destruction of the Appalachian forest led to dependency in *Transforming the Appalachian Countryside*. He does not use the term *ecological base*. Among the first uses of that phrase comes from Radhakamal Mukerjee, *Man and His Habitation: A Study in Social Ecology* (1940). For other references to the ecological base, see Merchant, *Ecological Revolutions*, 87, and Gudeman, *Anthropology of Economy*, 134. Mike Davis makes a distinction between economic and ecological poverty, which I see as the same distinction between makeshift economy with and without a viable ecological base. See Davis, *Late Victorian Holocausts*, 310.

42. Williams, *The Country and the City*, 37.

43. Toynbee, *A Study of History*, 570.

44. Ibid., 148–49.

45. Idleman, *History of the Mt. Storm Community*. For other firsthand accounts, see Shackelford, Weinberg, and Anderson, *Our Appalachia*. John Alexander Williams gave a similar lament: "What went wrong? What was done, or not done, to guarantee the failure of West Virginians' aspirations for their proportionate share of the national wealth?" Williams, *West Virginia and the Captains of Industry*, 2.

2. Provision Grounds

1. The theory of stages is pervasive in political economy. Steuart, *An Inquiry into the Principles of Political Economy*, book I, chaps. 4, 14, 28. Newton, *Report of the Commissioner of Agriculture for the Year 1862* ("In its rudest state men subsist, for the most part, upon the chase, or such roots, fruits, and grains as are easily gathered. In its second stage men follow the pastoral life, wherein as nomadic tribes, inhabiting hilly countries or table-lands, they depend chiefly upon flocks and herds for food, raiment, and locomotion"). Hamilton, *Federalist*, No. 30; World Bank, *Rural Development: Sector Policy Paper*; Rostow, *The Stages of Economic Growth*; Adams, *Curious Thoughts on the History of Man*; Kames, *Sketches of the History of Man*, 83–84. For a discussion, see Michael Perelman, *The Invention of Capitalism*, 124–25.

2. There are many examples. "Civilization, therefore, is an improved condition of man, resulting from the establishment of social order in place of the individual independence and lawlessness of a savage or barbarous mode of life." Cartée, *Elements of Physical and Political Geography*, 218. The complete isolation and cultural otherness of hunters and foragers seemed so obvious by the twentieth century that an anthropologist could instruct children in 1948, "A man who spends his whole life following animals just to kill them and eat, or moving from one berry patch to another, is really living just like an animal himself." Braidwood, *Prehistoric Men*, 86–87.

3. A. S. Kline, trans., *Virgil: The Eclogues*, Eclogue IX, www.poetryintranslation.com /PITBR/Latin/VirgilEclogues.htm; Williams, *Country and the City*, 16–17.

4. The entire series is in the collection of the New-York Historical Society. Paine, *Agrarian Justice*.

5. Kames made a remarkable statement about the relationship between population and production that, while it lacked any data, was more accurate than anything uttered by Malthus: "In fact, the greatest quantities of corn and of cattle are commonly produced in the most populous districts, where each family has its proportion of land." Kames, *Sketches of the History of Man*, 83–84. Ester Boserup would lend fieldwork and anthropological insight to the same idea in *The Conditions of Agricultural Growth*. Also see Smith lecture, March 29, 1763, in *Lectures on Jurisprudence*, vol. 5, 297. Adams, "Society and Civilization," 83–85.

6. The Scots sometimes referred to it as a *conjectural* narrative, in the words of Smith's friend Dugald Stewart. In other words, they acknowledged that they had no direct evidence of the distant past. Instead, they theorized that civilization must have appeared in stages. While many societies did change from hunting to farming, they did so for complex reasons, not because the latter represented progress over the former. See Brewer, "Adam Smith's Stages of History." Marx, *The German Ideology*, in Tucker, ed., *The Marx-Engels Reader*, 156; Turner, *Frontier in American History*, 35; Sachs, *Commonwealth: Economics for a Crowded Planet*, 220.

7. Wallerstein, *Capitalist World Economy*, 3; Trouillot, "The Otherwise Modern," 225; Sauer, *Seeds, Spades, Hearths, and Herds*, 3.

8. Adams, *Curious Thoughts on the History of Man*, 2. As the historian Michael Perelman has stated, "For much of classical political economy, self-provisioning was nothing more than a residue of a savage past." Perelman, *The Invention of Capitalism*, 124–25. Other political economists who noted this include Steuart, *Principles of Political Economy*, chap. 28, and Drayton, *Nature's Government*, 54.

9. Some anthropologists believe that the separate tasks of male and female sapiens allowed them to survive scarcities of game that drove their Neanderthal cousins to extinction. Sapiens separated hunting and gathering by sex, while Neanderthals appear to have all hunted, forgoing the benefits of gathering. Kuhn and Stiner, "What's a Mother to Do?," 953–81. Another example is the division that exists between people who live in different environments. People who have hides and furs can trade them to people who have metals. See Smith, *Wealth of Nations*, 11, and Marx, *Capital*, vol. 1, 474–77.

10. Smith, *Wealth of Nations*, 987. Smith worried about social inequality. See the same source, 132–33, 1064–65.

11. Williams, *Lectures on Political Principles*, 85. Urquhart, *Familiar Words*, 119. Urquhart founded the Free Press in 1856. Marx quotes the same sentence quoted here in chap. 4 of *Capital*. Also see Monboddo, *Ancient Metaphysics*, vol. 5, 27, 71; Davis, "Eleventh Anniversary Address," 1–29; and Emerson, "American Scholar," 54.

12. As the French economist Jean-Baptiste Say recognized, "Agriculture does not allow of one person being continually employed in the same operation." Say, *Treatise on Political Economy*, 96.

13. I thank Colin A. M. Duncan for this insight.

14. For a discussion of labor organizations and political clubs, many of which appeared after Smith wrote, see Thompson, *Making of the English Working Class*.

15. Smith, *Wealth of Nations*, 12–13.

16. For the best work on James Steuart, see Perelman, *The Invention of Capitalism*.

17. "Hence I conclude," Steuart wrote, "that the best way of binding a free society together is by multiplying reciprocal obligations, and creating a general dependence

between all its members. This cannot be better effected, than by appropriating a certain number of inhabitants, for the production of the quantity of food required for all, and by distributing the remainder into proper classes for supplying every other want. I say farther, that this distribution is not only the most rational, but that mankind fall naturally into it." Steuart, *Principles of Political Economy*, 116. Steuart was by no means the first or only person to make these arguments. They date to the end of the English Civil War and the onset of enclosure in the seventeenth century. See Appleby, *Economic Thought and Ideology in Seventeenth-Century England*, 149. Every critic of peasants and settlers echoed Edward Chamberlayne, who urged Britons in 1668 to make the most of their resources, saying, "It is the Interest of the Common-wealth, that every Subject should make a right use of his own Estate," even suggesting that "a Guardian should be set over the Person and Estate, not only of Mad-men, but of all prodigal Persons." Edward Chamberlayne, *England's Wants*, 14. And see Hartlib, *The Reformed Husbandman*, 2–4, and Hartlib, *Samuel Hartlib His Legacy of Husbandry*. Drayton, *Nature's Government*, 54.

18. This and the previous paragraph: Townsend, *Dissertation on the Poor Laws*, 35–36. Colquhoun, *Treatise on the Wealth, Power, and Resources of the British Empire*, 110 (emphasis in original); Temple from a pamphlet of 1739, quoted in Mintz, *Sweetness and Power*, 253; Paine, *Rights of Man*, part II, 56; More, "The Shepherd of Salisbury Plain," in *The Works of Hannah More*, 192–93.

19. List, *National System of Political Economy*, 170–73. Turgot, Reflections 11 and 12 in *Reflections on the Formation and Distribution of Wealth*. Jean-Baptiste Say echoed all those who said that while farming might have made civilization possible, it no longer did. Manufacturing had inherited that mantle. Not an abundance of grain but the output of factories "marks the distinction between a civilized community, and a tribe of savages." Say, *A Treatise on Political Economy*, 64.

20. Marx, *The Eighteenth Brumaire of Louis Napoleon*, chap. 7; Marx, *Communist Manifesto*, 224; Marx, *Capital*, vol. 3, 945. The argument that idiocy is mistranslated comes from Hal Draper's *The Annotated Communist Manifesto*. Draper's long footnote is reproduced here: https://linguisticcapital.wordpress.com/2011/09/27 /mistranslating-marx-the-idiocy-of-rural-life/.

21. Trouillot, "North Atlantic Universals: Analytic Fictions, 1492–1945," 850; World Bank, *Rural Development: Sector Policy Paper*; Polanyi, *Great Transformation*, 88–89.

22. Merrill, "Putting Capitalism in Its Place," 317–18. I have benefited especially from Wood, *The Origin of Capitalism*.

23. Langland, *Piers Plowman*, Passus 8, lines 310–40. The feast was recorded by John Leland around 1506 from what he described as a paper roll. *Joannis Lelandi: Antiquarii De Rebus Britannicis Collectanea*, vol. 6, 10. There is no direct evidence of the feast. Sutton and Hammond, *Coronation of Richard III*, 286, 294–95.

24. For this and the previous paragraph, see Giovanni Boccaccio, quoted in Aberth, ed., *The Black Death*, 78–79; Braudel, *Mediterranean World*, 62; Hurst, *Sheep in the Cotswolds*, chap. 4.

25. Steve Muhlberger, ed., *Tales from Froissart*, quoted from www.nipissingu.ca/department /history/muhlberger/froissart/tales.htm.

26. Quoted in Kulikoff, *British Peasants to Colonial American Farmers*, 11–16.

27. Le Roy Ladurie calls this cycle of food and famine a bellows in *Peasants of Languedoc*, 150–55 and conclusion. Behringer, *Cultural History of Climate*, 109– 13. The reason the two should be understood together is that epidemic plague played a part in causing a colder climate. So many people died all over the world (including the Amerindian epidemics) that trees returned to millions of acres of farmland, absorbing enough CO_2 to cause a fall in temperatures. CO_2 fell by 10 parts per million during this period, a number that has no purely geological explanation. See Ruddiman, *Plows, Plagues, and Petroleum*.

28. Some have seen centralizing nation-states under monarchical authority, like the rational totalitarian kingdom propounded by Thomas Hobbes in *Leviathan* (1651), as a response, not only to the slaughter that went on between Protestants and Catholics and the English Civil War, but to Europe's three hundred years of subsistence crisis. Behringer, *Cultural History of Climate*, 109–13.

29. On common lands there are a number of useful sources. I benefited from New-font, *Blue Ridge Commons*, 15–16, and Ostrom, *Governing the Commons*.

30. For a very useful primer on land in the everyday life of a medieval woman, see Bennett, *A Medieval Life: Cecilia Penifader of Brigstock*, 87, 97. The best description of tenures and estates I found is Overton, *Agricultural Revolution in England*, 31–36.

31. For a complete discussion of the transition of the aristocracy and many of these ideas, see Wood, *Origin of Capitalism*, 97–100.

32. Hurst, *Sheep in the Cotswolds*, chap. 4. For more about what improving farmers called "convertible husbandry," see Stoll, *Larding the Lean Earth*.

33. This and the previous paragraph derive from Overton, *Agricultural Revolution in England*, 156–63, and Kerridge, *Agrarian Problems in the Sixteenth Century and After*. I especially learned from Joan Thirsk's "Enclosing and Engrossing," in *The Agrarian History of England and Wales*, vol. IV, 99–106, 200–55. A work of history that flushes out all the dimensions of this process, neither squarely of one interpretation or the other, is Keith Wrightson's *Earthly Necessities*. It includes a penetrating description of enclosure as proceeding by fits and starts, over centuries not decades, sometimes by negotiation, and with plenty of protest and condemnation. Historians now regard the seventeenth century as the most vigorous period of enclosure. Twenty-four percent of England was enclosed in that century, 2 percent in the sixteenth, 13 percent in the eighteenth, and 11 percent in the nineteenth. Overton, *Agricultural Revolution*, 148.

34. Overton, *Agricultural Revolution in England*, 158–59. Wrightson gives this account

of Sedgemoor, a region of fens: "The draining of the eastern fens, initiated with crown support, was represented as a project which would bring a barren and unprofitable wasteland into cultivation . . . The fact that the area was already occupied by thousands of fenlanders who derived a poor but independent living from its numerous resources was overlooked, and the formidable resistance to drainage which they sustained for three decades was gradually worn down." Wrightson, *Earthly Necessities*, 211.

35. Kulikoff, *From British Peasants to Colonial American Farmers*, 18–19; Tawney, *The Agrarian Problem in the Sixteenth Century*, 64–66. Spufford, *Contrasting Communities*, 149.

36. The fields were known as Hooknorton and Southrop. "Petition of the Owners and Proprietors of . . . Hooknorton and Southrop," *Journals of the House of Commons*, vol. 34, 65. John Locke aided the lords by elevating greed to principle. He managed to turn an argument about the God-given earth into one for enclosing. According to Locke, since land in private hands produced more of everything, everyone benefited, even those without land.

37. Winstanley, *A DECLARATION FROM THE Poor oppressed People OF ENGLAND*; Kennedy, *Diggers, Levellers, and Agrarian Capitalism*, 107; Overton, *Agricultural Revolution in England*, 150, 155, 204; documents relating to the Newton rebellion may be found here: www.newtonrebels.org.uk/rebels/history.htm. On Locke, see *Second Treatise of Government*, chap. 4.

38. Wolf, *Europe and the Peoples Without History*, 77. Wood, *Origin of Capitalism*, 96. Price summed up the effect: "Upon the whole, the circumstances of the lower ranks of men are altered in almost every respect for the worse. From little occupiers of land, they are reduced to the state of day-labourers and hirelings." Price, *Observations on Reversionary Payments*, quoted in Marx, *Capital*, vol. 1, 888. Also see Marx, *Grundrisse*, 505–507, and Perelman, *The Invention of Capitalism*, 14.

39. Thomas More published *Utopia* in 1516, writing that sheep "may be said now to devour men and unpeople, not only villages, but towns." More, *Utopia*, 16. Davies, *The Case of Labourers in Husbandry*, 50–54.

40. Goldsmith, *The Deserted Village*. Mavis Batey reconstructed the village's location and gives wonderful detail in "Nuneham Courtenay: An Oxfordshire 18th Century Deserted Village." Engels, *The Condition of the Working Class in England*, 284–88. Polanyi, *Great Transformation*, 88–89.

41. Statistics for the previous paragraph from Overton, *Agricultural Revolution in England*, 77; Wrightson, *Earthly Necessities*, 317–19; Fogel, *Escape from Hunger and Premature Death*, 10–12; and Perelman, *Invention of Capitalism*. Intellectuals asked how poverty could continue amid wealth. Bentham, Burke, Malthus, James Mill, J. S. Mill, Owen, Ricardo, Senior, and Marx, as well as hundreds of lesser writers, recognized that by tearing down traditional customs and social norms, capitalism

challenged centuries of received wisdom about the survival of human communities. On the poor laws and enclosure, see Wrightson's *Earthly Necessities*, 215–20. Wrightson explains that the poor laws came about for more than one reason, among them food crises that afflicted England before the last famine in 1624 but also to aid "labouring persons not able to live off their labour." Also see Appleby, *Economic Thought*, 162–64. On enclosure as a revolution, see Thirsk, "Enclosing and Engrossing," in *The Agrarian History of England and Wales*, 255. Young quoted in Williams, *The Country and the City*, 67.

42. Hydén, *Beyond Ujamaa in Tanzania*, 16; Hydén, *No Shortcuts to Progress*, 7.

43. Estates became both capital and ecological base, money and legacy. As Gudeman puts it, "The European estate and the hacienda may be exchanged for cash only at the expense of losing the patrimony, of severing the continuity of a community." Gudeman, *Anthropology of Economy*, 33.

44. Stead, "Mobility of English Tenant Farmers," 173–89. The tripartite system of lords, tenants, and laborers is simplified and exaggerated. The subject of fluctuating rents and the antipathy between tenants and landowners is the central relationship in Brenner's "Agrarian Class Structure and Economic Development in Pre-Industrial Europe." Historians of early modern Britain take every possible exception to Brenner's conclusions. Most ignore him altogether. Wrightson, *Earthly Necessities*, 74, 134–35, 186.

45. This is the circuit or pathway of capital. Marx, *Capital*, vol. 1, 247.

46. *Chattel* applied to slaves dates to 1649 when Milton referred to slaves owned by a king. *The Oxford English Dictionary* implies that the term was meant rhetorically or perhaps as a metaphor to point out the irony and injustice of owning a person.

47. Braudel, *Wheels of Commerce*, 21, 232–34, 428–30; *Oxford English Dictionary*; Smith, *Wealth of Nations*, 353–55.

48. For this and the previous paragraphs, see Braudel, *The Perspective of the World*, 623, and *Wheels of Commerce*, 21, 230, 428–30. For an analysis of this idea, see Wallerstein, "Braudel on Capitalism, or Everything Upside Down," in *Unthinking Social Science*, 207–17.

49. Polanyi, *The Great Transformation*, 136. By *autonomy* I do not mean independence from all relationships and institutions of power. I mean a sufficient material wherewithal to choose whether to earn wages or not. Autonomy, as I mean it, is freedom from the direct control of capital, not necessarily political autonomy from states or state power, though it can mean that too.

50. There are all sorts of distinctions implied here. Medievalists claim a highly specific definition for *peasant*, but a peasant can be any country person. *Smallholder* often refers to an intensive form of agriculture, in which a household owns its land. Netting would not use the term to describe mountain farmers in West Virginia who made extensive use of the forest. I will use the term to describe

them nonetheless. On peasants, see Scott, *Moral Economy of the Peasant*, Netting, *Smallholders, Householders*, 3–6. *Chinampas* are fields or garden plots constructed within a shallow lake. They are made by layering mud, silt, and composted organic matter until the structures rise above water level. Aztec farmers invented the *chinampa* in the twelfth century.

51. Netting, *Smallholders, Householders*, 59, 240–43; Shanin, "The Peasantry as a Political Factor," 8–9; Attwood, *Raising Cane*, 17. My use of the household does not open up all the conflict and tension that existed within families. I prefer to regard the household as an economic unit. See Sachs, *Home Rule*, 147.

52. For a discussion of subsistence and some of its meanings, see Trouillot, *Peasants and Capital*, 155–57. For more on surplus and poverty, see Mayer, *Articulated Peasant*, 321.

53. Netting, *Smallholders, Householders*, 270, 329–30.

54. Scott, *Moral Economy of the Peasant*, 13; Marx, *Capital*, vol. 1, 200.

55. Criticism of Chayanov is abundant. He described a certain peasantry at a certain time. He was right in some essential ways, but peasants have been known to break some of his rules. Chayanov, *On the Theory of Non-Capitalist Economic Systems*, 7. I have also benefited from Boserup, *Conditions of Agricultural Growth*, passim; Wrightson, *Earthly Necessities*, 51–55; Netting, *Smallholders, Householders*, 1–13; Kulikoff, *From British Peasants to Colonial American Farmers*; Neth, *Preserving the Family Farm*; Mayer, *The Articulated Peasant*; Scott, *The Moral Economy of the Peasant*; Dove, *The Banana Tree at the Gate*. Industrial agriculture functions on entirely different assumptions. Its key metric is labor efficiency.

56. Netting, *Smallholders, Householders*, 130–33. The ratio takes all energy into consideration, the calories expended by animals and humans, the diesel fuel in the tractor and the electricity used to manufacture fertilizers. There are some problems with these numbers. For one thing, the pull power of oxen and fossil fuels are commensurate only in the sense that both can be converted into the same units. They have entirely different origins. And while a harvesting and threshing machine is made for one specific crop (wheat or corn), oxen apply their energy to lots of possible products and tasks. It would make more sense to ask the energy budget of the entire peasant farm. If rice demands more energy than the rice contains, something growing in another field might make up for it. It is also true that gasoline and diesel engines are increasingly efficient. Nonetheless, this is a useful measure. Also see Pimentel, "Energy Inputs in Food Crop Production in Developing and Developed Nations."

57. Netting, *Smallholders, Householders*, 9, 107–108; Boserup, *Conditions of Agricultural Growth*, passim.

58. Colman, *The Agriculture and Rural Economy of France*, 8, 296; Candler, *Brief Notices of Hayti*, 38, 143–44.

59. Steuart, *Principles of Political Economy*, chap. 28. Netting, *Smallholders, House-holders*, 10–15, 270, 298, 329–30. Among historians of Appalachia who understand these distinctions, Lewis writes, "a common misconception that has skewed the interpretation of the region's history is that *subsistence* and *market* are dichotomous, antagonistic forms of economic relations," *Transforming the Appalachian Countryside*, 23, and "Self-sufficiency was not inconsistent with production for exchange, and most farmers engaged in both modes of production," "Beyond Isolation and Homogeneity," 26. Salstrom, *Appalachia's Path to Dependency*, chap. 1. Chayanov, *Theory of Peasant Economy*, 48–49, 92. Chayanov hated the idea of romanticizing or idealizing peasants. "No peasant would refuse either a good roast beef, or a gramophone, or even a block of Shell Oil Company shares." Daniel Thorner, "Chayanov's Concept of Peasant Economy," in Chayanov, *Theory of Peasant Economy*, xv–xix; Sahlins, *Stone Age Economics*, 86–87; Netting, *Smallholders, Householders*, 318–20; Boserup, *Conditions of Agricultural Growth*, 63. Kulikoff writes of North America, "Yeomen . . . participated in commodity markets with regularity—but only to sustain noncommercial neighborhood networks." Kulikoff, *The Agrarian Origins of American Capitalism*, 36. Chevalier, "There Is Nothing Simple About Simple Commodity Production," 118.

60. Mayer, *The Articulated Peasant*, 45, 218–19. On separate "accounts," Gudeman writes of the Kekchi Maya of southern Belize, "Even when a man has an important source of cash income through trade or market cropping, he raises corn for the house." Gudeman, *Anthropology of Economy*, 27, 44, and *The Demise of a Rural Economy*, 33. On articulation theory, see Dore, *Myths of Modernity*, 20.

61. Dove, *The Banana Tree at the Gate*, 169–80; Dove, "Hybrid Histories and Indigenous Knowledge Among Asian Rubber Smallholders," 349–59; Dove, "Rice-Eating Rubber and People-Eating Governments," 33–63.

62. Dove, *The Banana Tree at the Gate*, 6. Of all the innovations of the smallholders, writes Dove, the most important "may have been the development of a mechanism for rationalising the combination of market-oriented cash-cropping and subsistence-oriented food production." Hydén, *Beyond Ujamaa in Tanzania*, 4. Also Gudeman, *The Demise of a Rural Economy*, 33, and Waters, *The Persistence of Subsistence Agriculture*.

63. See Gudeman, *The Demise of a Rural Economy*, 130.

64. Tocqueville, "A Fortnight in the Wilderness," published in *Memoirs, Letters, and Remains*, 159. Michael Merrill was the first to break through the "this or that" duality that still plagues the way most Americans think about noncapitalist modes of production. I owe a great debt to Merrill's "Cash Is Good to Eat," 42–71. Crèvecoeur, *Letters from an American Farmer*, Letter III.

65. The number of emigrants is estimated to have been thirteen to twenty thousand.

Kulikoff, *From British Peasants to Colonial American Farmers*, 40–41, 53–59, 65. Shepard, *God's Plot*, 57.

66. On ghost acres, see Pomeranz, *The Great Divergence*, 275.

67. Richards, *Unending Frontier*, 1–5; Cunliffe, *Europe Between the Oceans*, 110.

68. On the dispossession of the Acadians and the quotation, see Faragher, *A Great and Noble Scheme*, 333.

69. Dublin, *Farm to Factory*, 15; Donahue, *The Great Meadow*, 102, 166, 209.

70. This and the previous paragraph are based on Prude, *The Coming of Industrial Order*, and Clark, *Roots of Rural Capitalism*.

71. On the transition to capitalism in New England, I benefited from Henretta, *Origins of American Capitalism*, chaps. 6 and 7; Clark, *Roots of Rural Capitalism*; Kulikoff, *Agrarian Origins of American Capitalism*; Merrill, "The Anti-Capitalist Origins of the United States"; Agnew, "The Threshold of Exchange," 115; Prude, *The Coming of Industrial Order*.

72. Donahue, *The Great Meadow*, 102, 166, 209. The Great Meadow was not a common after 1653. But even after the town divided it into private property, it retained many elements of common management. Richard Judd's *Common Lands, Common People* is about the continued management of the ecological base in northern New England.

73. See Kennedy, *Mr. Jefferson's Lost Cause*, 208; Jefferson, *Notes on the State of Virginia*, 176; Letter to John Taylor, May 1, 1794, and letter to Benjamin Hawkins, February 18, 1819, both in the Thomas Jefferson Papers (www.loc.gov/collections /thomas-jefferson-papers/about-this-collection/). Robin Blackburn notes that slavery became rooted in the Louisiana country for many reasons, but Jefferson's silence on the question was among them. "Jefferson was the only man who could have prevented that outcome." Quoted in Kennedy, *Mr. Jefferson's Lost Cause*, 81. For Jefferson's hope for the diminution of slavery and the settlement of the Mississippi near New Orleans, see Rothman, *Slave Country*.

74. Crèvecoeur, *Letters from an American Farmer*, Letter II, quoted in *American Georgics*, 17. The letters appeared first in London and then in Philadelphia in 1793. The parenthetical quotation two paragraphs down comes from Letter III.

75. Agrarian thought among whites does not have an impressive record of insisting upon the equal rights of African-Americans. For an example of abolitionist argument wrapped in an implicitly racist free-soil philosophy, see Julian, "Speech Before Congress on the Homestead Bill," in *Speeches on Political Questions*, 52. Crèvecoeur, *Letters from an American Farmer*, Letter IX, in *American Georgics*, 26.

76. On slave gardens, one traveler observed: "But the number that are permitted to labor at all for such purposes [their own gardens] is very small . . . the great object of the master is to derive the greatest possible profit, at the least possible

expense, provided that he does not endanger the life, and health, and value of his slaves." Parsons, *Inside View of Slavery*, 155. And see Schlotterbeck, "The Internal Economy of Slavery in Rural Piedmont Virginia," 173; Westmacott, *African-American Gardens and Yards*, 90; and Genovese, *Roll, Jordan, Roll*, 154. On black agrarianism, see Smith, "Black Agrarianism and the Foundations of Black Environmental Thought," and the following sources quoted therein: "Narrative of Williams Wells Brown, A Fugitive Slave"; Solomon Northup, "Twelve Years a Slave: Narrative of Solomon Northup"; "The Life of Josiah Henson"; and Frederick Douglass, "An Address to the Colored People of the United States." David Omowalé Franklyn captures the sense of a fugitive existence in the Caribbean. Franklyn, "Grenada, Naipaul, and Ground Provision," 70–71.

77. King, *The Great South*, 274. The best discussion that I have seen of post-emancipation land policies and attempts to recapture black labor is Foner, *Nothing but Freedom*, 30–35.

78. Julian, "Speech on the Homestead Bill," *American Georgics*, 90–95. Popular sovereignty had been written into the Compromise of 1850. Residents of Utah Territory and New Mexico Territory were to decide themselves if slavery would be allowed.

79. Flagg, "Agricultural Progress," *American Georgics*, 82.

80. Jordan and Kaups, *The American Backwoods Frontier*, 38–58. See Lewis C. Gray, *History of Agriculture in the Southern United States*, vol. 1, 122.

81. For this and the previous paragraph, see Van Ruyvan, "Appendix 5. Received 28 January, 1656. Secret," *Pennsylvania Archives*, vol. 5, 248–49; "Deduction of Clear and Precise Account of the Condition of the South River . . . Received 28 January 1656," *Pennsylvania Archives*, vol. 5, 236. Outrages committed by the Swedes went back to 1646. Also see Sachs, *Home Rule*, 104.

3. The Rye Rebellion

1. Chernow, *Alexander Hamilton*, 475.

2. Washington quoted in Cayton, *Frontier Republic*, 7; Lear quoted in Slaughter, *Whiskey Rebellion*, 30, 190; Bouton, "A Road Closed," 855.

3. White, *The Backcountry and the City*, 2. Slaughter refers to the Rebellion as "frontier epilogue" in *Whiskey Rebellion*. Here is an example of how two historians writing in 1967 dismissed the Rebellion: "The Whiskey Rebellion was an early, violent expression of the unease, discontent, and rebellious spirit which disturbed the American scene for two decades before the War of 1812 brought the nation relief from internal tensions." Hyneman and Carey, eds., *A Second Federalist*, 282. Agrarian insurrection continued beyond 1800, including the New York Anti-Rent War of the 1830s and the Farmers' Alliance of the 1870s–1890s. See Catherine M. Stock, *Rural Radicals*, and Reeve Huston, *Land and Freedom*.

4. Nevins and Commager, *A Short History of the United States*, 151, 156; White, *The Backcountry and the City*, 2, 210; Braudel, *The Wheels of Commerce*, 255.

5. My argument owes a debt to Cayton, who writes, "The Federalists wanted to fully integrate the Ohio Country into the Atlantic cultural and commercial community . . . they sought interdependence not independence." *Frontier Republic*, 21. I saw Sartre's *Critique of Dialectical Reason* ("Critique of Critical Investigation," "3. Totality and Totalisation") quoted by White in *Backcountry and the City*, 31. The other word for identifying people with labels and collective identities is *seriality*. Jefferson and Hamilton had a disagreement about this. They both believed in seriality, but Jefferson's was unbound (meaning looser identities like American or settler) while Hamilton's was more bound (defined and numerated, like tax rolls and the census).

6. Williams, *Appalachia*, 118–19; Bonsteel Tachau, "The Whiskey Rebellion in Kentucky," 240; Wiley, *History of Monongalia County, West Virginia*, chap. X; Slaughter, *The Whiskey Rebellion*, 90.

7. Keith Tribe uses the term *governing economy* a little differently. To him it refers to the German school of political economy of the eighteenth and nineteenth centuries. See Tribe, *Governing Economy*, and Hamilton, *Report on Manufacturers*, 199.

8. Smith, *Inquiry into the Nature and Causes of the Wealth of Nations*, 1126. Hamilton is often said to have been deeply influenced by Smith, who wrote in the *Wealth of Nations*, 1193, "Sugar, rum, and tobacco are commodities which are nowhere necessaries of life, which are become objects of almost universal consumption, and which are therefore extremely proper subjects of taxation."

9. "The Spirit of the Times, Addressing the People of Massachusetts," *Massachusetts Centinel*, October 25, 1787. This passage is often quoted and misquoted but rarely attributed to its source. Its author is sometimes cited as "Old Plough Jogger," but that is incorrect. The unnamed author of the article paraphrases a conversation he had with "an old plough jogger" and a young man.

10. Hamilton appears to support an act of the New York Legislature to relieve debtors by releasing them from jail. Hamilton to Hugh Seton (January 1, 1785), *The Papers of Alexander Hamilton*, vol. 3, 592–93.

11. Hamilton, *Federalist*, Nos. 12, 21, 30. He said on a number of occasions that he didn't really believe in any such thing as a lack of currency. "It is said there is a scarcity of money in the community," proclaiming before the New York Ratifying Convention in 1788, "I do not believe this scarcity to be so great." Money might hide away, "it may be retained by its holders," but "nothing more than stability and confidence in the government is requisite to draw it into circulation." In 1792, he had "no evidence to satisfy his mind, that a real scarcity of money will be found on experiment a serious impediment to the payment of the tax." New York Ratifying Convention. Third speech of June 28, 1788 (Francis

Childs's version), *Papers of Alexander Hamilton*, vol. 5, 114–25. Hamilton to Washington (August 5, 1794), *Papers of George Washington*, vol. 16, 478–508; "Report on the Difficulties in the Execution of the Act Laying Duties on Distilled Spirits" (March 5, 1792), *Papers of Alexander Hamilton*, vol. 11, 77–106.

12. United States Congress, *An Act repealing . . . duties heretofore laid upon distilled spirits imported from abroad, and laying others in their stead; and also upon Spirits distilled within the United States, and for appropriating the same*; Brackenridge, 14; Hamilton, Letter to George Washington (August 2, 1794), in Hamilton, *Writings*, 823.

13. Hamilton to Washington (September 1, 1792) in *Works of Alexander Hamilton*, vol. 4, 285; Chernow, *Alexander Hamilton*, 468–70; Slaughter, *Whiskey Rebellion*, 3, 11–13; Brackenridge, *Western Insurrection*, 6–11; Ferguson, *Early Western Pennsylvania Politics*, 127.

14. Hamilton, *Federalist*, No. 12; Brissot de Warville, *New Travels in the United States of America*, 186. Adam Smith writes in detail about excise, with reference to the Scottish malt tax, in Book 5, chap. 2, of *Wealth of Nations*, in which he notes, "Fermented liquors brewed, and spirituous liquors distilled, not for sale, but for private use, are not in Great Britain liable to any duties of excise. This exemption, of which the object is to save private families from the odious visit and examination of the tax-gatherer, occasions the burden of those duties to fall frequently much lighter upon the rich than upon the poor." *Wealth of Nations*, 1126.

15. Schöpf, *Travels in the Confederation*, 238–39.

16. Dunaway, "Speculators and Settler Capitalists," in *Appalachia in the Making*, 52–53; Gates, *Landlords and Tenants*, 17; *Washington-Crawford Letters* (September 21, 1767).

17. This piece of Washington's western Virginia land lies on the northern side of the river at the present location of Saint Albans, West Virginia (38°22′49″N and 81°49′11″W). Samuel Lewis [the cartographer and perhaps assistant surveyor], *Copy of a survey . . . for George Washington 2950 acres of land . . . lying in the county of Botetourt on the n.e. side of the Great Kanhaway about a mile and half above the mouth of Cole River . . . Novemr. 6th, 1774*. Williams, *Appalachia*, 11, 109. Also see Lewis, *Transforming the Appalachian Countryside*.

18. Fernow, *The Great Timber Belt*, 5; Cunliffe, *Europe Between the Oceans*, 98.

19. For the first written use of squatting, see Winthrop Sargent to Timothy Pickering (March 1, 1800), in Rowland, ed., *Mississippi Territorial Archives*, vol. 1, 212. In the words of John C. Weaver, "The very idea of a pre-emptive occupation prior to petitioning for a grant or in advance of an organized sale was dismissive of central authority." Weaver, *The Great Land Rush*, 264–65. And I learned from Williams, *Appalachia*, 53, 92, 113; Williams, *West Virginia*, 13; and Dunaway, "Speculators and Settler Capitalists," in *Appalachia in the Making*, 50. The quotation is from

Rothert, "John D. Shane's Interview with Pioneer John Hedge, Bourbon County," 177–78. On the common uses of private land, Newfont, *Blue Ridge Commons*, 3.

20. An example of case law relating to adverse possession is *Lessee of Ewing v. Burnet* (1837). On cases of ejectment, see Harper, *The Transformation of Western Pennsylvania*, 10. One case I read included a number of households, all attempting to acquire farms adversely. *McClure v. Maitland*, 561.

21. Washington, *Diary of George Washington* (September 1784), 28–31; Achenbach, *The Grand Idea*, 98–99. The squatter who told the story was a member of the Reed family, either John or David Reed.

22. Thomas Smith to George Washington (February 9, 1785), George Washington Papers (www.loc.gov/collections/george-washington-papers/about-this-collection/). Washington offered them a consolation. They could stay if they started to pay him rent, and he would not charge them for twelve years of illegal occupation. The squatters moved on rather than pay him anything. Achenbach, *The Grand Idea*, 147–50; Harper, *The Transformation of Western Pennsylvania*, 78. Honor Sachs argues that one reason for resistance to speculators and absentee owners was the threat they posed to male heads of households. The engrossment of land made it more difficult to establish households, which threatened male authority. "Ordinary settlers stood to lose their personal status, their very identities as independent men." See *Home Rule*, 30–35.

23. People and figures from "Census of Westmoreland County–1783," in *Pennsylvania Archives*, vol. 22, 419–30. Only twenty-eight people in the Springhill Township owned nothing, and most of them were unmarried sons who had left, though their names remained on the tax rolls. The assessment described them as "single, gone." This number is substantially lower than that of the four southeastern counties of western Pennsylvania. See Harper, *The Transformation of Western Pennsylvania*, 25–28, 248–50.

24. Sachs, *Home Rule*, 45–46.

25. One who saw them passing through Illinois said that they "still hold negroes in the utmost contempt; not allowing them to be of the same species of themselves, but look on *negers*, as they call them, and Indians, as an inferior race of beings, and treat them as such." Faragher, *Sugar Creek*, 48–50. Kulikoff, *From British Peasants to Colonial American Farmers*, 215. Wood, *Two Year's Residence*, 245.

26. Jordan and Kaups, *American Backwoods Frontier*, 100–105. For more on swidden, see Otto, "Forest Fallowing in the Southern Appalachian Mountains"; Conklin, *Hanunóo Agriculture*; and Dove, *The Banana Tree at the Gate*.

27. Debar, *West Virginia Hand-Book*, 83–85.

28. Jordan and Kaups, *American Backwoods Frontier*, 114–15; Lorain, *Nature and Reason*, 332–33. Even still, a twentieth-century researcher described farms in eastern Kentucky as "permanent peninsulas of cultivated land, with changing margins . . .

Everywhere, the forest encroaches on the cultivated fields, in places retreating before the advance of agriculture, again advancing and repossessing the area from which it has been forced to retreat temporarily." Davis, *Geography of the Mountains of Eastern Kentucky*, 61.

29. Doddridge, *Notes on the Settlement and Indian Wars of the Western Parts of Virginia and Pennsylvania*, 84.

30. Davis, *Geography of the Mountains of Eastern Kentucky*, 60–61; Otto, "Forest Fallowing in the Southern Appalachian Mountains," 56–58; Harper, *Transformation*, 24–26, 28–29, 42; Boserup, *Conditions of Agricultural Growth*, 35–36; "Census of Westmoreland County–1783," in *Pennsylvania Archives*, vol. 22, 419–30. Data on labor and field size comes from Netting, *Smallholder, Householder*, 148. It refers to India in the 1970s—certainly far removed in time and space from Appalachia, but the figures are only intended to be suggestive.

31. Zohary and Hopf, *Domestication of Plants in the Old World*, 64–73. On the hardiness of rye and wheat compared to corn, see Lorain, *Nature and Reason*, 284, 343. Rye's fate was to fade away as a relic. Total U.S. imports of rye for the year ending May 1, 2007, came to zero. The nation exported 49,500 metric tons of wheat. http://www.fas.usda.gov/export-sales/myfimay.htm. By the 1950s rye had been industrialized into a series of new strains developed by experiment stations in the 1940s. The old rye held on mostly as a hay and silage crop. USDA, *Growing Rye*, Farmers' Bulletin No. 2145, 1–9, and Leighty, "The Place of Rye in American Agriculture," 169–84.

32. Wiley, *History of Monongalia County*, www.wvculture.org/history/settlement /whiskeyrebellion01.html; Strickland, *Observations on the Agriculture of the United States of America*, 47; Victor, *History of American Conspiracies*, 204–205.

33. The quotation in the previous paragraph is from Bouton, "A Road Closed," 858. Soltow, "Distribution of Income in the United States in 1798," 181–85.

34. Buck and Buck, *The Planting of Civilization in Western Pennsylvania*, 248; Humphrey, "Barter and Economic Disintegration," 48.

35. Marshall, *Practical Introduction to Arithmetic*, 38. James Steuart was right when he wrote, "When reciprocal wants are supplied by barter, there is not the smallest occasion for money." Steuart, *Principles of Political Economy*, vol. 1, 177.

36. Nimrod Warden daybook (January 24, 1806), Warden Ledger Collection, SC# 5023, James Madison University, Special Collections. 1,200 shillings = £60; Lucy Kennerly Gump, "Amis Ledger D (1794–1801), Interpretive Transcription of an East Tennessee Business Record Book," manuscript (1997). Such transactions did not result in profit. Braudel cites a passage in Clavière and Brissot, *De la France et des Etats-Unis*, that indicates the conversion into coin to make up for a discrepancy after a barter exchange, calling this the "eulogy of barter," but this is how people had exchanged for centuries. See Braudel, *The Structures of Everyday Life*, 447.

37. One economist came up with the nonsensical notion that bartering takes more time than using money. He writes, "The movement from a barter to a money economy therefore frees up some of the transaction time, which people can use in other ways." But there is no actual comparison in this foolish assertion. Exchanges in currency took time, too, and maybe even more time, since the value of currencies from different states or counties needed to be evaluated and agreed upon. The economist thought of none of these things, though; he simply wanted to call barter primitive, or what is the same thing for most economists, inefficient. Arnold, *Economics*, 272. I also consulted Toulmin, *The Western Country in 1793*, 114, 124; Perkins, "The Consumer Frontier," 488–92; Martin, *Buying into the World of Goods*, 2–3; Buck and Buck, *The Planting of Civilization in Western Pennsylvania*, 248.

38. Steuart, *An Inquiry into the Principles of Political Economy*, vol. 2, 147.

39. For Hamilton's reliance on James Steuart, see his 1791 *Report on the Establishment of a Mint*. I found this introductory note especially helpful, "Introductory Note: Report on the Establishment of a Mint [January 28, 1791]," *Papers of Alexander Hamilton*, vol. 7, 462–73, founders.archives.gov. For quotations from Steuart, see *Principles of Political Economy*, vol. 1, 11, 178, 225, 395, 508.

40. Hamilton, "Communicated to the Speaker of the House of Representatives, at Philadelphia" (March 6, 1792), quoted in Whitten, "An Economic Inquiry into the Whiskey Rebellion of 1794," 496–98. Whitten made a comprehensive study of whiskey prices, rye harvests, and the onset of the tax. He concluded that whiskey prices spiked in 1792 when distillers passed on the cost of the tax to buyers, rising 16.4 cents per gallon over pretax prices. Prices fell in 1793, possibly the effect of a strong rye crop or an increase in production as new distillers tried to profit from high prices. The insurrection followed, causing prices to spike again—17 cents over pretax prices. This time, the increase probably came from a pullback in supply, as distillers called off the business for a little while. They might not have planted as much rye as they had in previous years, or they might have diverted it to other uses. Whiskey production returned to something like normal in 1796. Whitten concludes that a "cash-loss burden" did not cause the Whiskey Rebellion. Whitten isolates whiskey's price at market without considering it as part of household economy in the backcountry. Whitten, "Economic Inquiry," 500–504.

41. Jardine, *Letter from Pennsylvania to a Friend in England*, 21; Asbury, *Journal of the Rev. Francis Asbury* (July 10, 1788), 36.

42. Harper, *The Transformation of Western Pennsylvania*, 10–15, 55; Perkins, "Consumer Frontier," 488–92. In no case did the poor own more than 2 percent of the wealth throughout the region. Ninety percent of the non-landowning set owned no more than two horses and three head of cattle. Pennsylvania had an inconsistent state property tax. One author maintains that the tax was not collected during the 1790s. Howe, "Historical Evolution of State and Local Tax Systems," 6.

43. "Petition of the Inhabitants of Westmoreland County—Excise on Liquors—1790," in *Pennsylvania Archives*, vol. 11, 671; Harper, *The Transformation of Western Pennsylvania*, 248, *n*22; Kulikoff, *British Peasants*, 205–206.

44. *Pennsylvania Archives*, 2nd ser., vol. 4, 20–22; Gudeman, *Anthropology of Economy*, 128–29.

45. Victor, *History of American Conspiracies*, 204–205; Bouton, "A Road Closed," 855.

46. Anderson, *Imagined Communities*, 19. Scott, *The Art of Not Being Governed*, 10–11.

47. Madison uses the word *empire* in *Federalist*, No. 19, but in reference to Germany, not the United States. See Hamilton, No. 13.

48. Peter Onuf, quoted in Slaughter, *Whiskey Rebellion*, 34. For Hamilton on sovereignty, see New York Ratifying Convention, third speech of June 28, 1788 (Francis Childs's version), *Papers of Alexander Hamilton*, vol. 5, 114–25. For yeoman farmers, writes Allan Kulikoff, the phrase "sovereignty of the people" "suggested a democracy of property holders in which their views would be paramount." If legislatures ignored their interests, "yeomen could resort to other means to assert their will." Kulikoff, *Agrarian Origins of Capitalism*, 136.

49. Thompson, "Moral Economy of the English Crowd"; Tilly, "Food Riot as a Form of Political Conflict in France"; Scott, *Moral Economy of the Peasant*, 14. Scott makes reference to Chayanov on the relationship between crafts and trades and available land.

50. Hamilton to Washington (September 1, 1792), in *Works of Alexander Hamilton*, vol. 4, 285; "Spirits, Foreign and Domestic" (March 6, 1992), in *Works of Alexander Hamilton*, vol. 3, 305.

51. Rush, *Essays*, 201–25, 227.

52. Hamilton, "Communicated to the House of Representatives, March 6, 1792," in *Works of Hamilton*, vol. 3, 304–306; Hamilton, *Report on Manufactures*, in *Works of Hamilton*, vol. 3, 193–96; Hamilton, "Tully No. III," in *Hamilton Writings* (Library of America), 831. In *Federalist*, No. 12, he wrote, "The often-agitated question between agriculture and commerce has, from indubitable experience, received a decision which has silenced the rivalship that once subsisted between them, and has proved, to the satisfaction of their friends, that their interests are intimately blended and interwoven." Hamilton, *Federalist*, Nos. 12, 21, 30, and 31. Hamilton thought like Adam Smith that every factor of production generated money in characteristic form. In Smith's words, "Whoever derives his revenue from a fund which is his own, must draw it either from his labour, from his stock, or from his land . . . All taxes, and all the revenue which is founded upon them . . . are ultimately derived from some one or other of those three original sources of revenue." Smith further said in the same paragraph, "To him [the farmer], land is only the instrument which enables him to earn the wages of this labour, and to make the profits of this stock." *Wealth of Nations*, 75. Also see Steuart, *Principles of Political Economy*, vol. 1, 50.

53. These two paragraphs owe a debt to Graeber's *Debt*, 50–51. The head tax is also known as a *poll tax*. Some assume that *poll* refers to voting, but *poll* is a Middle English word that means "head." *Polling* really means "head count." Colonial officials imposed direct taxes in Natal, South Africa, 1848; Nyasaland, 1891; Gambia and Sierra Leone, 1890s; and Nyanza Province, Kenya, 1900. In Kenya, the occupier of each hut paid two or three rupees per year. Direct taxes, by hut and later by head, created colonies as independent economic entities, less dependent on London. Evidence suggests that rural Kenyans paid a higher rate of their incomes than urban workers and sought wage labor in order to obtain the currency to pay that tax. Gardner, *Taxing Colonial Africa*, 50–57. Forstater, "Taxation and Primitive Accumulation," 57–60. Another French governor, of Ivory Coast, said "the payment of taxation . . . would stimulate them to produce for export," quoted in Migdal, *Strong Societies and Weak States*, 70.

54. Hamilton to Morris (April 30, 1781), *Papers of Alexander Hamilton*, vol. 2, 604–35.

55. Coxe, "A Plan for Encouraging Agriculture, and Increasing the Value of Farms in the Midland and More Western Counties of Pennsylvania," in *View of the United States of America*, 384–404. Emphasis in original. Coxe would have agreed with Fernand Braudel, who said that every town "*generalizes* the market into a widespread phenomenon." Braudel, *Structures of Everyday Life*, 479–81.

56. "Report on the Difficulties in the Execution of the Act Laying Duties on Distilled Spirits" (March 5, 1792), *Papers of Alexander Hamilton*, vol. 11, 77–106. Hamilton sneered that surplus money "will sensibly foster the industry of the parties concerned, if they avail themselves of it under the guidance of a spirit of œconomy and exertion."

57. Slaughter, *Whiskey Rebellion*, 220–21.

58. Ibid., 226–27.

4. Mountaineers Are Always Free

1. Scott, *The Art of Not Being Governed*, preface and 178. Johnson traveled with James Boswell in 1773. Johnson, *A Journey to the Western Islands of Scotland*, 56–61, 111. Writing in 1857, Friedrich Engels argued against Prussia's impending invasion of Switzerland on similar grounds. "Military men will recite the names of a dozen mountain passes and defiles, where a handful of men might easily and successfully oppose a couple of thousands of the best soldiers." Engels, "Mountain Warfare in the Past and Present," *New York Daily Tribune*, January 27, 1857.

2. William Preston, "Diary: Sandy Creek Expedition February–March 1756," Draper Manuscripts, State Historical Society of Wisconsin, Madison, http://www.as .wvu.edu/WVHistory/documents/003.pdf; Williams, *West Virginia*, 96; Dunmore, *Documentary History of Dunmore's War* (letter of 1774), 371.

3. Eicher, *Civil War High Commands*, 482; Williams, *Appalachia*, 171–78.
4. Breckinridge, *The Civil War*, 641.
5. Seavoy, *An Economic History of the United States from 1607 to the Present*, 163.
6. Eller, *Millers, Millhands, and Mountaineers*, 50; Davis, *The Wilson Carey Nicholas Survey*.
7. *Oil-Dorado of West Virginia*, 3, 32; *Prospectus of the West Virginia Iron Mining and Manufacturing Company* (emphasis in original); Dodge, *West Virginia*, 220–25; Faulkner, *Speech upon the Mineral and Agricultural Resources of the State of West Virginia . . . April 10, 1876*, 10, 6.
8. I thank Elizabeth Blackmar for pointing this out to me.
9. *Report on the Manufacturers of the United States at the Tenth Census* (1880), 10. On railroads and the lumber business, see Lewis, *Transforming the Appalachian Countryside*.
10. Boreman, *Inaugural Address*. The entire state of Virginia counted 500,000 slaves in 1860. Willey, *An Inside View of the Formation of the State of West Virginia*, 9–11.
11. Dunaway, *Slavery in the American Mountain South*, 25–31.
12. Williams, *Appalachia*, 165–67. According to Barbara Rasmussen, "Neither eastern planters nor northern industrialists could accommodate the needs of the West without undermining their own security." Rasmussen, *Absentee Landowning and Exploitation in West Virginia*, 62, 72.
13. *West Virginia Iron Mining and Manufacturing Company* (1837); *Prospectus of the West Virginia Iron Mining and Manufacturing Company*; *Oil-Dorado of West Virginia*, 3; Boreman, *Inaugural Address*; Eller, *Miners, Millhands, and Mountaineers*, 44, 46–47.
14. The fifty counties that became West Virginia voted 34,677 to 19,121 to remain in the Union. Curry, *A House Divided*, 141–47. See Dunaway on slaves in manufacturing (*Slavery in the American Mountain South*, 120–26, and *First American Frontier*, 109). "Unionism was confined largely to twenty-four Northwestern counties along the banks of the Ohio River, the Pennsylvania border, and the lines of the Baltimore and Ohio Railroad . . . But at least twenty-four West Virginia counties, forming nearly two-thirds of the total area of this state and containing 145,000 white inhabitants, were unquestionably Confederate in outlook and opposed to the dismemberment of the Old Dominion." Curry, *A House Divided*, 6–8; Lewis, *How West Virginia Was Made*. There was one exception to the nonparticipation of mountaineers. Waitman T. Willey, who presented the petition to Congress for the creation of West Virginia and was one of its first U.S. senators, was born in a log cabin not far from Morgantown.
15. For more on the world internal to households, see Honor Sachs, *Home Rule*. To what extent was this insularity a recent adaptation or something brought with them from the formation of Scots-Irish kinship? Tony Waters notes, "Subsistence

groups often fear and distrust those beyond the immediate kin-group." Waters, *The Persistence of Subsistence Agriculture*, 39.

16. For this and the previous paragraph: Billings and Blee, *The Road to Poverty*, 304–13, 331, 417. Billings and Blee write about Clay County, Kentucky, but the same conclusions hold for West Virginia. They also detail the continuing legacy of patronage into the 1980s and 1990s. More than 450 films produced between 1904 and 1927 told stories about mountaineers, and 92 of them were about feuding. See Williamson, *Southern Mountains in Silent Films*.

17. *Acts of the Legislature of West Virginia* (1866), 141–269.

18. I learned about Dillon's Rule from Paul Salstrom. For a critical essay on Dillon's Rule, see Ben Price, National Organizing Director of the Community Environmental Legal Defense Fund, "A (Very) Brief History of 'Dillon's Rule,'" www.celdf.org/downloads/A_(Very)_Brief_History_of_Dillons_Rule.pdf. Dillon quoted in *City of Clinton v. The Cedar Rapids and Missouri River Railroad Company* in *Reports of Cases in Law and Equity*, 3 (June Term, 1868), 475. Emphasis in original document. The case decided by the Supreme Court of the United States was *Merrill v. Monticello* (1891).

19. Smith, *The Spirit of American Government*, 289. This book appears to be popular among the "home rule" movement in the United States today. The legislature of West Virginia abolished Dillon's Rule in 1969. Richardson, Gough, and Puentes, *Is Home Rule the Answer? Clarifying the Influence of Dillon's Rule on Growth Management*, 21.

20. Williams, *West Virginia*, 92; *New York Times*, August 15, 1872, July 25, 1876; *Constitution of West Virginia, as Adopted in 1872*. There were two justices of the peace and one president (also a judge). All three were elected positions.

21. This and the following paragraphs owe their detail to the spectacular research of John Alexander Williams, in *West Virginia and the Captains of Industry*, 16, 109, 148–53, 161–64.

22. Williams, *West Virginia and the Captains of Industry*, 148–53, 161–64; Gaventa, *Power and Powerlessness*, 91–92.

23. Lewis, *Transforming the Appalachian Countryside*, 110–16.

24. West Virginia voted for Democrat Grover Cleveland in the election of 1892. William MacCorkle, "Inaugural Address" (1893), in *Public Papers of Governor William A. MacCorkle, of West Virginia*, 297. On the Farmers' Alliance in West Virginia, see Barns, *West Virginia State Grange*, 71–73.

25. MacCorkle once refused to send in military forces to put down a strike, apparently telling one mining corporation that he would not merely act in their interests when the miners were not a threat to public order. MacCorkle, *Recollections of Fifty Years of West Virginia*, 480–85.

26. See Graeber, "In Regulation Nation," *Harper's Magazine*, March 2015. On how local elites and those in positions of political power interacted over the indus-

trial transition, see Billings and Blee, *Road to Poverty*; Bailey, *Matewan Before the Massacre*; and Weise, *Grasping at Independence*. A painting by George Caleb Bingham, *The Country Politician* (1849), suggests a meeting between a politician, a merchant, and a farmer in Missouri.

27. Bartram quoted in Williams, *Homeplace*, 24. Blankets and curtains created separate spaces, which could then be taken down for dancing. Visitors described beds near the back wall and the table placed near the hearth. Williams, *Homeplace*, 48–52.

28. Sohn, *Appalachian Home Cooking*, 42: "Mountaineers don't look for the greenest, straightest, cleanest beans. In some cases it seems that the worst looking, most mottled beans are the old varieties that have the best flavor."

29. For this and the previous paragraph I used census data. In the census, it is not clear whether "unimproved" included land once cultivated but left to fallow or never cultivated. Taking the category at face value, I set up a ratio of acres of *improved land in farms* to acres of *unimproved land in farms* for various Virginia counties according to the tabulated census returns of 1860. These ratios apply mostly to the higher elevations. *Agriculture of the United States in 1860 . . . Eight Census*, 158. Newfont reports that Blue Ridge farmers kept between 60 and 90 percent of their overall holdings in forest as late as 1900. Newfont, *Blue Ridge Commons*, 30–31. Waller also finds that cleared spaces were about 10 percent of total land owned or claimed. Waller, *Feud*, 22–23. Also see Billings and Blee, *Road to Poverty*, 180–81.

30. West Virginia Department of Agriculture, *Old-Fashioned Cookbook* [n.d.], www .agriculture.wv.gov/divisions/comm/Documents/Publications%20Print/Old%20 Fashioned%20Cookbook%20WEB.pdf.

31. Newfont, *Blue Ridge Commons*, 5.

32. Warman, *Corn and Capitalism*, 117. Farmers in Nebraska harvested thirty to eighty bushels per acre. Nebraska State Board of Agriculture, *Annual Report for the Year 1888* (1889), 243. On corn and yields, see Otto, "Forest Fallowing in the Southern Appalachian Mountains," 55–56, and Debar, *West Virginia Hand-Book*, 57–60. Mountaineers produced a regional average of thirty-seven bushels per capita, according to Gray and Thompson, *History of Agriculture in the Southern United States*, 876, 884. "Planting more corn than was needed for one's own annual consumption was also a calculated way of ensuring family survival." Davis, Colten, Nelson, and Allen, *Southern United States*, 145. By *labor-days* I mean the number of days worked per individual laborer in order to produce a given commodity.

33. Olmsted, *A Journey in the Back Country*, 228–32; Anonymous, "Poor White Trash," *The Living Age* 153, June 17, 1882, 688–91; King, *The Great South*, 503. Two New Englanders recounted being served, in one meal, pork, potatoes, cornbread, applesauce, blackberries, buckwheat cakes with maple syrup, pies, and wheat biscuits.

"A Farming Experiment in West Virginia. (Concluded)," *Catholic World* 41 (August 1885), 627. And see the first part, "A Farming Experiment in West Virginia," *Catholic World* 41 (July 1885).

34. Previous paragraph, Pollard, *The Virginia Tourist*, 165–69. "Prior to the arrival of railroads, once or twice a year mountain farmers drove their stock to regional gathering points, where large herds were purchased and driven to distant markets by professional drovers." Lewis, "Railroads, Deforestation, and the Transformation of Agriculture in the West Virginia Back Counties," 310. L. C. Gray collected this data, comparing the mountains and the Shenandoah Valley by livestock per capita. The mountains outproduced the valley in cattle, 1.9 to .81. See Gray and Thompson, *History of Agriculture in the Southern United States to 1860*, 876. Roger Kennedy notes that the annual value of Southern livestock (not limited to the mountains) was one and a half times the value of cotton in 1860. *Mr. Jefferson's Lost Cause*, 57. During the 1850s, raising a steer to the age of three cost around $8 in West Virginia, compared to $24 in New York and Ohio. See Debar, *West Virginia Hand-Book*, 83–85; Lanman, *Letters from the Alleghany Mountains*, 123; and Pollard, *Virginia Tourist*, 165–69.

35. The practice of not feeding cattle in winter was well observed. Olmsted, *Journey in the Back Country*, 224; Debar, *West Virginia Hand-Book*, 83–85; Dodge, *West Virginia*, 43. Henry M. Price of Nicholas Court House, Virginia, explained the custom of the country: "Cattle command the chief attention of our farmers. They are chiefly raised by 'browsing,' having little attention given them besides regularly salting during the summer . . . The fall before the cattle are four years old, they are usually sold and driven off to other counties to be grain fed. The usual price is from $17 to $20." *Report of the Commissioner of Patents for the Year 1853: Agriculture*, 8, 19. A correspondent for the Missouri State Board of Agriculture wrote this of the method: "I have no doubt but one-half of the entire neat cattle of this country with horses, mules, sheep and hogs go through the winter season with no more food than would be required to feed them well two weeks." Quoted in Vance, *Human Geography of the South*, 149. Lanman said, "his beast subsists upon whatever it may happen to glean in its forest rambles, and, when the first supply of his own provisions is exhausted, he usually contents himself with wild game." Lanman, *Letters from the Alleghany Mountains*, 49.

36. Debar, *West Virginia Hand-Book*, 57–60; Olmsted, *Journey in the Back Country*, 222. Otto, "Southern 'Plain Folk' Agriculture," 31. Pinchot, *Breaking New Ground*, 61; *Report of the Commissioner of Patents for the Year 1853: Agriculture*, 58.

37. In 1820, one cattleman said, "This plan has been proved here for forty years," quoted in MacMaster, "The Cattle Trade in Western Virginia," 143.

38. He sometimes spelled his name *Vandivier*. Census of the United States (1870), Halberstam County; Bonner, "Profile of a Late Ante-Bellum Community," 664 (note); Lanman, *Letters from the Alleghany Mountains*, 40–43. Billy's tenants prob-

ably included members of his extended family, whom he referred to as his "boys." He likely charged them little, accepting food or labor in exchange for a field and garden. But he also might have taken a portion of their crop and sold it, adding to his own accumulated wealth. Pollard, *Virginia Tourist*, 170. Two New Englanders in West Virginia said the same: "They neither know poverty nor riches, the well-to-do living about the same as their poorer neighbors." See "A Farming Experiment in West Virginia. (Concluded)," *Catholic World* 41 (August 1885).

39. Zinn's mother attended Rector College and studied by firelight. Zinn, *The Story of Woodbine Farm*, 1–12, 37.

40. Census of the United States (1870). Another way to reveal the presence of improved cattle is improved meadow. In 1880, one-third of all West Virginia counties had fewer than 10,000 acres of improved meadow. McDowell had 265. Boone had 616. Census of the United States (1880). In 1899, the State Board of Agriculture began to advise ranchers on how to improve. "The 'come-and-go-easy' methods together with the 'pennyroyal cow' and the 'razor-back hog' are rapidly becoming a thing of the past." The same institution had little advice for the majority striving to stay in place and make a few dollars. *Fifth Biennial Report of the West Virginia State Board of Agriculture*, vol. 5 (1900), 8.

41. Brenner, "The Social Basis of Economic Development," 23–28. The crucial distinction is not how many head of cattle households sold or the manufactured commodities they bought, write Dwight Billings and Kathleen Blee, "but rather to what extent agrarian households were able structurally to reproduce themselves independently of these exchanges." Billings and Blee, *Road to Poverty*, 164; Pruitt, "Self-Sufficiency and the Agricultural Economy," 335. Generally, the mountaineers of the nineteenth century did not exchange wages for work. In 1870, West Virginians disbursed the lowest annual wages of any state in the country—$48 per farm. By comparison, Minnesotans shelled out twice that ($95) and Californians almost ten times as much ($437, an average composed of tiny sums paid to armies of harvesters on thousand-acre wheat farms). In Mercer County, households paid an average of $3 for all the work they hired out in a year. In Wyoming County, they paid 29¢. In Logan and Nicholas counties, they paid nothing at all. Calhoun County represented the mean at $33 per farm in annual wages paid. Historical Census Browser (https://mapserver.lib.virginia.edu).

42. Harper, *The Transformation of Western Pennsylvania*, 13. Only 2.6 percent of men, women, and children worked in manufacturing in 1870, and that number was still just 3.4 percent in 1900. The number of people employed in manufacturing did not include the number employed as miners or loggers. Numbers that refer to the Plateau come from Salstrom, *Appalachia's Path to Dependency*, 21, and "Agricultural Origins of Economic Dependency," 270. Mary Beth Pudup notes, "Emigration was relatively small in amount, and this, coupled with the rapid

increase in population, forced an increase in the number of farms, largely by the process of subdivision." Pudup, "The Limits of Subsistence," 59. The hidden defect in any estimate of cleared or improved land has to do with uses and quality. Statistics from "Farms and Farm Property," Census of the United States (1920), 41, 47. The census does not tell us what improved land looked like—thriving in maize or ravaged by erosion. One researcher found that 30 to 40 acres of "improved" land in farms that averaged 144 consisted of old field and pasture—not very productive. Davis, *Geography of the Mountains of Eastern Kentucky*, 52–60.

43. Ross, "Pocketed Americans," 171.

44. "If population is increasing in communities of this type a change directly to annual cropping or multi-cropping imposes itself." Boserup, *Conditions of Agricultural Growth*, 41, 44, 64. For Netting's take on this, see *Smallholders, Householders*, 263–65, 270. For other observations of population and density in the southern mountains, see Gray, "Economic Conditions and Tendencies in the Southern Appalachians," 7–12.

45. See "The Five-Acre Farm," in Seymour, *The Self-Sufficient Life and How to Live It*, 35–36.

46. Davis, *Geography of the Mountains of Eastern Kentucky*, 61.

47. West Virginia had the lowest number of mortgaged farms of any state in 1920. This might seem like farmers had escaped the debt trap so common in other regions. But that's not what it means. No bank thought farm property in most parts of the state valuable enough to loan against. It meant that farmers could not borrow a portion of the value of their land to buy or improve anything. *Fourteenth Census of the United States Taken in the Year 1920, Volume V, Agriculture*, 481.

48. Smith, "Farming Appalachia," 333.

49. Salstrom, "Agricultural Origins of Economic Dependency," 275. We will consider W. Arthur Lewis's "dual-sector" model in another section. Census of the United States (1890).

50. I have heavily paraphrased Paul Wallace Gates in this paragraph, taken from *The Farmer's Age*, 404–405. On merchant credit and farmer debt in Floyd County, Kentucky, see Weise, *Grasping at Independence*, 110–12. On the barter and borrow system, see Salstrom, *Appalachia's Path to Dependency*, chap. 3.

51. "[Twelfth Census of the United States]." *Special Reports: Mines and Quarries: 1902*, 701–702.

52. "In the Supreme Court of Appeals of West Virginia, Charleston. Major Henry Totten [son of T. K. Totten] vs. Pocahontas Coal and Coke Company" (1908), typescript in the West Virginia State Archives.

53. Works of environmental history that consider different kinds of appropriative and communal use-rights include White, *The Roots of Dependency*; Judd, *Common*

Lands, Common People; McEvoy, The Fisherman's Problem; and Jacoby, Crimes Against Nature. And see Warren, "Owning Nature," 398.

54. Marshall, History of Kentucky, vol. 1, 150, quoted in Gates, Landlords and Tenants, 14–15.

55. Blackmar, "A Speculative Essay on the History of American Land Speculation," 4–7; Gates, History of Public Land Law, 124, quoted in Blackmar, "A Speculative Essay," 7; Rappleye, Robert Morris, 507–10. On the China trade, see Fichter, So Great a Profit. Speculators acquired millions of acres by purchasing from grantees. Rasmussen, Absentee Landowning and Exploitation, 35. No one knows exactly how much land Nicholas and Morris owned. Some mountain families ended up with grants themselves, especially in the 1860s, perhaps for military service during the Civil War.

56. One of the best explanations comes from the opinion of Judge James Keith in Harman v. Stearns (July 22, 1897), Report of Cases in the Supreme Court of Appeals of Virginia, 58–69. The case concerns one parcel of 1,500 acres but it encapsulates much of the history of Morris's lands.

57. Elkhorn Creek flows into Tug Fork, which meets Levisa Fork in Kentucky to form the Big Sandy, which drains into the Ohio River. Patents for William Belcher, Jr., are listed in the online catalog of the Library of Virginia: http://lva1 .hosted.exlibrisgroup.com/F/4EMDAM5K45STV47M1JTUU8XDQA4YNCBD IEHV5G12L4R6F759AY-37502?func=find-acc&acc_sequence=004638778. William Floyd Belcher, Sr., lived between 1785 and 1869. He died in Big Four, West Virginia. "Pleas at the Court House of the County of Logan before the Circuit Superior Court of Law and Chancery for said County on the 13th day of October, 1846," Pocahontas Land Company Papers. Also see Reports of Cases Decided in the Supreme Court of Appeals of Virginia (1857), 794. I don't know if the younger Belcher secured title by adverse possession on forfeited land (meaning no senior patent) or if he paid for it.

58. "An act to prevent future conflictions in claims to land," Journal of the House of Representatives of the Commonwealth of Kentucky (1826), 314.

59. For the first law I could find, see Code of Virginia (1849), 449. I also used Philbin v. Carr (1920), quoted in Phipps, "Note and Comment," 191–92. Furthermore, "the adverse possessor holding under color of title has prima facie a valid title, though in fact he has no title at all." Senior patent holders had a simple way of taking back full possession. All they needed to do was reoccupy part of the land by putting up a house or planting a field. Doing this extinguished any adverse claim as a whole. Sims, "The Constructive Possession of a Claimant by Adverse Possession," 569. The state of West Virginia adopted color of title in its second constitution (1872), in Article 13. In Cook et al. v. Raleigh Lumber Co., argued before the Supreme Court of West Virginia (June 16, 1914), the holder of a junior patent was sued for collecting firewood outside of boundaries that marked the

senior patent held by the lumber company. *Southern Reporter . . . Containing all the Decisions of . . .* , vol. 82, 327. For an early reference of color of title by the Supreme Court of the United States, see *Taylor v. Walton and Hundly, Reports of Cases Argued and Adjudged in the Supreme Court of the United States. February Term, 1816,* vol. 1, 141. The state of Kentucky committed itself to "confirm existing interest" by controlling adverse possession claims in "An act to prevent future conflictions in claims to land," *Journal of the House of Representatives of the Commonwealth of Kentucky* (1826), 314.

60. For an early reference to mineral rights, see Hitchins, *History of Cornwall*, 305. Rasmussen, *Absentee Landowning*, 56–68. On Edwards and the incorporation of his company, see *Journal of the House of Delegates of the Commonwealth of Virginia . . . 1849–1850*, 415. Cody Dickens interview on October 3, 1996, Coal River Folklife Collection of the Library of Congress (AFC 1999/008, http://hdl.loc.gov/loc.afc /afccmns.141006). Mayer, "A June Jaunt," *Harper's Magazine*, April 1857, 592–612.

61. Weise, *Grasping at Independence*, 259.

62. G. W. Duhring (manager) to E. W. Clark (president), February 1, 1889, Pocahontas Land Company Papers, Eastern Regional Coal Archives. Byrne, "Pocahontas-Flat Top Coalfield," 33. The company was also known as the Flat Top Land Association, also known as the Trans-Flat Top Land Association and later the Pocahontas Land Corporation. I will call it the Flat Top Land Trust for simplicity. It amassed around 300,000 acres in McDowell and Mercer counties. *Annual Report of the Board of Managers of the Flat Top Coal Land Association.*

63. "Note 1–Redemptions," in General Letters (August 20, 1887, to July 2, 1889) and "List of Surveys Within the Maitland Davis Survey . . . February 1887," Flat Top Land Association Papers. Here is more evidence from surveyor's notes: "On the waters of Laurel Creek . . . Edmond Lester claims 97 acres. I could not find any record of a survey or grant, in Virginia or West Virginia, to answer the local description." "On the waters of Burke and Buzzard Creeks, near the Indian Ridge . . . John T. Belcher claims several tracts, could not find any description. He claims as heir of Samuel Lambert." I also used "List of Landowners and Letter From M.A. Miller" (1888), Pocahontas Land Company Papers. Billings and Blee make the point that mountain people created legal documents and kept records of their exchanges. *Road to Poverty*, 270–75.

64. Grantee Index to Deeds, 1868–1969, McDowell County, West Virginia, West Virginia State Archives. Eller, *Miners, Millhands, and Mountaineers*, 56. Billings and Blee, *Road to Poverty*, 270. Weise, *Grasping at Independence*, 226–27.

65. Letter from John C. Belcher to M. A. Miller (February 12, 1883), Letters, 1883–1885, Pocahontas Land Company Papers.

66. I edited the letter to make it more readable. Here is the original text: "Inclosed you will find leases of Hill H. Cecil. Cecil is on your land in a House he built some time ago had left it and another man had taken possession and sold his

improvements to a Mr Edords. Mr Edords wonts Cecil to give him posession you will have to decide between them." Letter from G. W. Belcher to J. W. Davis, January 11, 1884. The author asked Davis about an important case regarding West Virginia land, in which the state repossessed delinquent land and gave it to the schools of Wyoming County for sale. The author wrote, "Please let me know what has been done with McClure vs. Maitland about the Wyoming [County] School land in the Court of appeals." These letters are included in letters from G. W. Duhring to E. W. Clark (January 11, 1884, and January 31, 1884), Flat Top Land Trust Papers.

67. Letters from G. W. Belcher to J. W. Davis (January 11 and 31, 1884), Letters, 1883–1885, Flat Top Land Trust Papers. Another Belcher wanted to buy one hundred or two hundred acres from Davis. On July 16, 1885, John T. Belcher wrote, "I have signed your lease and would have been glad to have seen you as I have 2 tracts of land lying parallel with each other and you own a string between them . . . I would like to buy yours if you will sell it."

68. An engineer and surveyor testified that he had "followed the occupation" of the land in question for twenty years. Deposition of J. E. Wagner, civil engineer for the company and land surveyor, in *Major Henry Totten vs. Pocahontas Coal and Coke Company*, 117.

69. Letter from Duhring to Clark (January 1888 and January 23, 1888), Flat Top Land Trust Papers. In the 1930s, William Zinn recalled clearing land with his father in the 1870s. "One-third of the timber which we destroyed, if standing there today, would be valued at more than the land is worth." Zinn, *The Story of Woodbine Farm*, 10.

70. One of the last parcels of land belonged to Hiram Christian and his son Maston, detailed in this letter: E. W. Clark to G. W. Duhring, January 23, 1888, Flat Top Land Association Papers. Part of this land is detailed here: http://image.lva.virginia.gov/cgi-bin/drawer?retrieve_image=LONN&dir=/LONN/LO-7/180/180&image_number=0047&offset=%2B33&name=Grants+No.114++1857-1858&dbl_pgs=no&round=. The company announced its unbroken ownership in an internal report of February 1, 1889, and in a published report, *Annual Report of the Board of Managers of the Flat Top Coal Land Association . . . December 31st, 1889*, 10. "[Twelfth Census of the United States]." *Special Reports: Mines and Quarries: 1902*, 701–702.

71. For more, see Lewis, *Transforming the Appalachian Countryside*. On fire and mountain logging, see Roosevelt, *Message from the President of the United States*, and Bush, *Dorie: Woman of the Mountains*, 132–33.

72. Eller, *Miners, Millhands, and Mountaineers*, 89–91; Fox, *Blue-grass and Rhododendron*, 63.

73. The personalities and events of the feud are far too complicated to detail here. These three paragraphs depend on Altina L. Waller's *Feud: Hatfields, McCoys, and Social*

Change in Appalachia, 1860–1900. Waller uncovers the motives behind the events with great skill. Waller, *Feud*, 43, 80–83, 166–70, 185, 204–205.

74. Lewis, *Transforming the Appalachian Countryside*, 46–47, 60–61. The average yearly inflation rate of the U.S. dollar was 2.57 percent between 1889 and 2013.

75. My argument here owes a debt to Lewis, *Transforming the Appalachian Countryside*, but also to Salstrom, *Appalachia's Path to Dependency.* Also see Dunaway, *The First American Frontier*; Simon, "Uneven Development and the Case of West Virginia."

76. A board foot is one square foot, one inch thick. Fernow, *The Great Timber Belt*, 5, 10.

77. *Wheeling Register*, quoted in Lewis, *Transforming the Appalachian Countryside*, 58; Hall, *The Rending of Virginia*, 615–19.

78. Summers, *The Mountain State*, 28, 97–98; Williams, *Americans and Their Forests*, 357–60; Otto, "Forest Fallowing in the Southern Appalachian Mountains," 33. "Financial Statement for the Year 1908," Elk River Coal and Lumber Company Collection, West Virginia State Archives. In 1908 alone, the Crescent Lumber Company sent 240 carloads of lumber to market, amounting to 2.4 million board feet. The estimate is based on 10,000 board feet per carload. Brooks, "Forestry and Wood Industries," 44–46. Lumber manager quoted in Kephart, *Our Southern Highlanders*, 383–84. Market logic drove the depletion of forests. James Watt Raine observed, "The best timber was cut long ago. As the price of lumber rises, and the sawmills pay more for logs, another swath still farther off may be cut." See Raine, *The Land of Saddle-Bags*, 226–27.

79. "Timber Famine Due in 20 Years," *New York Times*, November 5, 1907; Gregg, *Managing the Mountains*, 4, 86–87.

80. Otto, "The Present Condition of West Virginia Forest"; Brooks, *Forestry and Wood Industries*, 33. A biography of Brooks and his map of 1910 are available here: www .wvforestry.com/conservation.cfm?menu2call=conserve.

81. Gregg, *Managing the Mountains*, 16–17.

82. McNeill, "The Last Camp Fire," in *The Last Forest*, 122–54. Among the first literary writers to notice the scale and scope of the taking and to account for the psychological loss was Francis Courtenay Baylor. See Baylor, *Behind the Blue Ridge*, 16–19. On powerlessness in Appalachia, see Gaventa, *Power and Powerlessness*, 20–25.

83. Dorie Woodruff Cope recalled this from her childhood: "It was common practice for men to be paid by the company to live in cabins on land the company was claiming through legal occupancy. Most of the lumber companies used this method to secure thousands of acres of land for timber cutting." Bush, *Dorie: Woman of the Mountains*, 131. The annual reports of the Elk River Coal and Lumber Company contain substantial evidence of these leases. "The leases are, therefore, made to protect your title rather than as a source of income." I looked at financial statements for the years 1908 to 1912. Elk River Coal and

Lumber Company Collection, West Virginia State Archives. For the founding of Elk River Coal and Lumber Company, see Lewis, *Transforming the Appalachian Countryside*, 74. James Lane Allen also noticed these tenants: "The buying up of the mountain lands has of course unsettled a large part of these strange people. Already there has been formed among them a class of tenants paying rent and living in their old homes." Allen, "Mountain Passes of the Cumberland," 561. And see Fox, "The Future Kentucky's Feuds," 14. King, *The Great South*, 503.

84. Skidmore, *I Will Lift Up Mine Eyes*, 105, 116; Bush, *Dorie: Woman of the Mountains*, 107–108, 220–21. John Gaventa notes of the first wages, "The industrial order was introduced to the mountaineers' society by conspicuous consumption, with an exaggerated demonstration of its benefits." Gaventa, *Power and Powerlessness*, 63. Horace Kephart said of the same people after a few years of a cash income, "They can get only the lowest wages, which are quickly dissipated in rent and in foods that formerly they raised for themselves." Kephart, *Our Southern Highlanders*, 383–84.

85. Brooks, "Forestry and Wood Industries," 44–46; Pruitt, "Self-Sufficiency," 335; Fox, "The Future [of] Kentucky's Feuds," 14; Fowler, "Social and Industrial Conditions," 387; Allen, "Mountain Passes of the Cumberland," 575–76. Gregg, *Managing the Mountains*, 18.

86. Fowler, "Social and Industrial Conditions," 387; Allen, "Mountain Passes of the Cumberland," 575–76. "Even before the coal operators came to the region," wrote the union organizer Jim Garland, "mountain society had begun to disintegrate." Julia S. Ardery (*Welcome the Traveler Home: Jim Gardland's Story of the Kentucky Mountains*), quoted in Salstrom, *Appalachia's Path to Dependency*, xxvi; *Economic and Social Problems and Conditions of the Southern Appalachians*, 43–46. In the words of Arturo Escobar, "Massive poverty in the modern sense appeared only when the spread of the market economy broke down community ties and deprived millions of people from access to land, water, and other resources. With the consolidation of capitalism, synthetic pauperization became inevitable." Escobar, *Encountering Development*, 22.

5. Interlude: Agrarian Twilight

1. Land in farms increased from 408 million acres to 839 million acres. *Fourteenth Census of the United States, Taken in the Year 1920, Volume V, Agriculture*, 80–83. *Report on the Productions of Agriculture . . . Tenth Census*, 27–28. By small farms I mean all farms in that category, owned, rented, and on shares.

2. The Indian Appropriation Act (March 3, 1871), quoted in Walker, *The Indian Question*, 5. "Hereafter no Indian nation or tribe within the territory of the United States shall be acknowledged or recognized as an independent nation, tribe, or power, with whom the United States may contract by treaty."

3. Ostler, *The Plains Sioux*, 84. For a discussion about enclosure and its historical specificity, see Greer, "Commons and Enclosure in the Colonization of North America."

4. *Annual Report of the Commissioner of Indian Affairs* (1878), 1.

5. Edward P. Smith, quoted in Greenwald, *Reconfiguring the Reservation*, 20–21.

6. Otis, *The Dawes Act and the Allotment of Indian Lands*, 5–6. Originally published in 1934. The Nez Percé lost 88 percent of their reservation in the ensuing rush, but they did not stoically accept dispossession, nor were they helpless. According to Emily Greenwald, the Nez Percé selected allotments in the bottoms of canyons, where they could cluster them together, blurring the separation of households at the core of the policy. They planned their spaces to reflect recognized kinship groups and familiar social structures, and generally preserved the same economic practices they had always known. Greenwald, *Reconfiguring the Reservation*, 147–49.

7. "Kansas Farmers and Illinois Dairymen," *Atlantic Monthly* 44, December 1879, 717–25; Mock, "Drought and Precipitation Fluctuations in the Great Plains During the Late Nineteenth Century," 37.

8. Fite, *The Farmers' Frontier*, 104–105.

9. The *Iowa State Register*, quoted in Ostler, *Prairie Populism*, 27; Veblen, "The Price of Wheat Since 1867," graph I; Fite, *The Farmers' Frontier*, 106–108. The grade in this example was No. 2 spring wheat.

10. *Fifth Biennial Report of the Bureau of Labor of the State of Minnesota* (St. Paul, 1895–1896), 121–31. On short-term mortgages and drought, see Ostler, *Prairie Populism*, 18–19. On falling prices and general conditions on the Plains, see Hargreaves, *Dry Farming on the Northern Great Plains*, 4, 9–10. Polk, *Agricultural Depression. Its Causes—the Remedy*, 10–11.

11. Fite, *The Farmers' Frontier*, 110–11.

12. Davis, *Late Victorian Holocausts*, 7–9; Norris, *The Pit*, 129.

13. Kellie, "Stand Up for Nebraska," in Kellie, *A Prairie Populist*, 129. Kellie's emphasis. The Homestead Act institutionalized sweat equity, but populists wanted the idea extended to farmers in debt. For anger over the demise of small farms, see Polk, *Agricultural Depression. Its Causes—the Remedy*, 21.

14. Sanders, *Roots of Reform*, 7–8.

15. Wells says: "As a further part of such a system, it is claimed that the farm must be devoted to a specialty or a few specialties, on the ground that it would be almost as fatal to success to admit mixed farming as it would be to attempt the production of several kinds of diverse manufactures under one roof and establishment." Wells, *Recent Economic Changes*, 462. The number of farms over 1,000 acres in Kansas increased 349 percent between 1880 and 1890 and 237 percent in the next decade. *Fourteenth Census of the United States Taken in the Year 1920, Volume V, Agriculture*, 82.

16. Van Dyke, "The Red River of the North," 806; Dondlinger, *The Book of Wheat*, 75–77, 89, 99; Wells, *Recent Economic Changes*, 462. Additional sources: Fargo Board of Trade, *Green Pastures and Vast Wheat Fields*; White, "The Business of a Wheat Farm."

17. This and the previous paragraph depend on Rose, *Rehearsal for Reconstruction*, especially C. Van Woodward's forward; Special Field Order, No. 15 (January 16, 1865); *New York Times*, October 8, 1862, Trinkley and Hacker, "Archeological Manifestations of the 'Port Royal Experiment' at Mitchelville, Hilton Head Island, South Carolina." On African-American farmers after the Civil War, I consulted Smith, "Black Agrarianism and the Foundations of Black Environmental Thought"; Franklin, "Grendada, Naipaul, and Ground Provision," 71; Foner, *Nothing But Freedom*, 25, 40–45; Hahn, *Roots of Southern Populism*, 241; Schlotterbeck, "The Internal Economy of Slavery in Rural Piedmont Virginia"; Stewart, *"What Nature Suffers to Groe,"* 93.

18. The prevalence of planting in small spaces among freed people showed up on the first page of *Harper's Weekly* (May 21, 1870) in an illustration of freed people planting a garden in front of a cabin, "A Spring Scene Near Richmond, Virginia."

19. Andrews, *The South Since the War*, 100; Otto, "Reconsidering the Southern 'Hillbilly,'" 325; Petty, *Standing Their Ground*, 35–36, 41.

20. A Georgia landowner said, "The stock law will divide the people . . . into classes similar to the patricians and plebeians of ancient Rome." This quotation and others in the present and previous paragraphs I owe to Hahn, *The Roots of Southern Populism*, 241, 248–50. "An Act to Better Protect the Lands and Farming Interests of the 741st District, G. M., Known as Reynolds District of Georgia, Taylor County, and for other purposes," 315. Andrews, *The South Since the War*, 100, 206–207.

21. Most of this paragraph is derived from Fraser, *The Age of Acquiescence*, 50–51. *Second Annual Report of the Commissioner of Labor, 1886*, 31.

22. "Given the litany of disadvantages they confronted," writes the historian Adrienne Monteith Petty about North Carolina, "it is a wonder that there was growth in the number of small farm owners at all." Petty, *Standing Their Ground*, 41. Also see Taylor, *In Search of the Racial Frontier*, 138–41.

23. Thoreau, *Walden*, 3–4, 58–59, 170–75; Marx, *Economic and Philosophic Manuscripts of 1844*, 50–51. Both quoted the same passage from the Gospel of Matthew (6:19). "Lay not up for yourselves treasures upon earth, where moth and rust doth corrupt, and where thieves break through and steal."

24. Thoreau, *Walden*, 214–15; Gross, "The Great Bean Field Hoax," 495–96.

25. Emerson, "Farming," *Complete Works of Ralph Waldo Emerson*, vol. 7, 135; "Wealth," *Works of Ralph Waldo Emerson*, vol. 5, 67.

26. Emerson, "American Scholar," *Complete Works of Ralph Waldo Emerson*, vol. 1, 83. Emerson's emphasis.

27. Emerson, "Wealth," 122.

28. George Inness, *Short Cut, Watchung Station, New Jersey* (1883), Philadelphia Museum of Art.

29. Marx, *Machine in the Garden*, 9. For an example and a critique of this book, see Noble, *Death of a Nation*.

30. Interpretations of *Lackawanna Valley* are abundant. See Marx, *Machine in the Garden*, 220, and Novak, *Nature and Culture*, 149. (Novak calls it "one of the most puzzling pictures in American art . . . a shocking picture.") Williams, *Deforesting the Earth*, 264.

31. Shapiro, *Appalachia on Our Mind*; Farland, "Modernist Versions of Pastoral," 907; Dugdale, *The Jukes*.

32. Allen, "Mountain Passes of the Cumberland," 569. For another description, see Graffenried, "The Georgia Cracker in the Cotton Mills."

33. Allen quoted in Shapiro, *Appalachia on Our Minds*, 27–29.

34. Farland, "Modernist Versions of Pastoral," passim. I learned of all the sources in this paragraph from Farland's remarkable article.

35. Among the only anthropological studies of consanguinity in Appalachia—a survey of 140 years of marriage records taken from four counties in eastern Kentucky—concludes that rates of marriage between people of the same last name "do not seem extreme enough to justify labeling intermarriage as something unique or particularly common to the region." (Incest has not been particularly characteristic of the poor or ignorant. DNA taken from the mummies of Egypt's eighteenth dynasty reveals that the parents of King Tutankhamun were siblings.) Marriage between first cousins is not considered incest and is legal in twenty states, including California, Massachusetts, Vermont, and New York. It is illegal in West Virginia. Some still slander Appalachia as inbred. In 2008, Vice President Dick Cheney said before the National Press Club that his maternal grandmother descended from someone named Cheney, "So we had Cheneys on both sides of the family—and we don't even live in West Virginia." See Tincher, "Night Comes to the Chromosomes"; Lapidos, "How the Mountain State Got a Reputation for Inbreeding"; DeMause, "The Universality of Incest," 123–64; and Dugdale, *The Jukes*, 12–14. On incest among royal Egyptians, see Wawass, "King Tut's DNA." Life on the periphery of the urban core was replete with domestic violence. For a scholarly treatment, see Daniels and Kennedy, eds., *Over the Threshold, Intimate Violence in Early America*.

36. The region includes portions of Passaic, Bergen, and Morris counties in New Jersey. One of the only journalistic accounts of the Ramapo people is "A Community of Outcasts," *Appleton's Journal* 7 (March 23, 1872), 325. Also see Cohen, *The Ramapo Mountain People*.

37. Henry George, *Progress and Poverty* (1879), intro.; George Inness, remarks at "The George Dinner: The Great Banquet at the Metropolitan Hotel," *The Standard*

(January 22, 1890), quoted in Bell, *George Inness: Writings and Reflections on Art and Philosophy*, 136.

38. All the paintings mentioned can be viewed at www.the-athenaeum.org. Quick, *George Inness: A Catalogue Raisonné*, 11. Inness made one written statement about *Short Cut*. In 1889, the painting belonged to the American Art Association, which entered it in the International Exposition in Paris without informing Inness. It won a gold medal, but that did not seem to impress the artist: "I positively refused to be represented by a single picture which is not fairly representative of my present work." Bell, *George Inness*, 134.

39. The editor and novelist Abraham Cahan noticed the same immigrants leaving their garden homes and flowing toward city work. Eisenberg, *Jewish Agricultural Colonies in New Jersey*, chap. 6; Cahan, "The Russian Jew in America," 135; "History of Montclair," www.montclairnjusa.org; Census of the United States (1870 and 1880); Inness, Jr., *Life, Art, and Letters of George Inness*, 183.

40. "The Virginia Vendetta," *New York Times*, November 2, 1889. In the same source, see "Deputy Sheriff Shot: Lawlessness in West Virginia," February 1, 1891, and "West Virginia Moonshiners Arrested," May 3, 1893. The urban press accused striking workers in 1877 of "savage cruelty," comparing them to the Lakota, Northern Cheyenne, and Arapaho who destroyed the forces led by George Armstrong Custer in the Battle of the Little Bighorn. Richard Slotkin explains the metaphorical use of Indians as enemies in stories about the streets of New York and Chicago, with capital and the police on one side and workers as Indians. See Slotkin, *The Fatal Environment*, 480–83. Waller, *Feud*, 185, 204–205.

41. Fox, *A Mountain Europa*; Fox, *Blue-grass and Rhododendron*, 8–10. In the latter essay, he writes, "Unaffected by other human influences; having no incentive to change, no wish for it, and remaining therefore unchanged . . . the Southern mountaineer is thus practically the pioneer of the Revolution, the living ancestor of the Modern West." This paragraph benefited from Wilson, "Felicitous Convergence of Mythmaking and Capital," 5–31.

42. Wilson, "Felicitous Convergence of Mythmaking and Capital," 5–31.

43. *The Kentuckians*, quoted in Shapiro, *Appalachia on Our Minds*, 74–77. I am in debt to Shapiro for the kernel of this paragraph.

44. USDA Economic Research Service, "Farms, Land in Farms, and Average Acres Per Farm, 1850–2012," www.ers.usda.gov/data-products/chart-gallery.aspx.

45. Rölvaag, *Giants in the Earth*, 416, 338–39, 453.

46. Wilder, *Little House in the Big Woods* (1932), 199. Tony Waters writes of the *Little House* series, "The descriptions of Wilder's parents in *Little House on the Prairie* resonated particularly well with the peasants I observed in Tanzania who would feed themselves, build houses, hunt, raise animals, and doctor their own illnesses." Waters, *The Persistence of Subsistence Agriculture*, 22.

47. Johnson, *Now in November*, 76. Neth, *Preserving the Family Farm*, 124–27.

48. The phrase "Get big or get out" is usually attributed to Butz, but it might have come from a farmer describing the policies of Secretary of Agriculture Ezra Taft Benson or from Benson himself. See *New York Times*, October 19, 1958. For recent news on subsidies, see Krotz, "Small Farms and the Farm Subsidies Scandal," *Huffington Post*, February 3, 2011, www.huffingtonpost.com/daniel-krotz /small-farms-and-the-farm-_b_817869.html. Between 1995 and 2008 farmers in Carroll County, Arkansas, received $8.22 million. Seventy-seven percent of farmers received no money at all. Eighty percent received just $250 a year. Where did it all go? Half of it went to 10 percent of farmers in the country. See James B. Stewart, "Richer Farmers, Bigger Subsidies," *New York Times*, July 19, 2013.

49. Ann Marie Lipinski, "A Farming Legacy Wiped Out," *Chicago Tribune*, December 11, 1985; Keith Schneider, "Rash of Suicides in Oklahoma Shows That the Crisis on the Farm Goes On," *New York Times*, August 17, 1987.

6. The Captured Garden

1. Letter from an anonymous miner in Davy, West Virginia, to the management of the Pocahontas Coal Company (March 11, 1907), in Justus Collins Papers. Bliss, "Coal Industry," *Encyclopedia of Social Reform*; Raine, *The Land of Saddle-Bags*, 237. On the Battle of Blair Mountain, between an army of coal miners and the United States military, see *New York Times*, September 3, 1921.

2. Raine, *The Land of Saddle-Bags*, 230, 237, 241.

3. Non-wage work and the role of the household in subsidizing capital is well understood by scholars. Immanuel Wallerstein observes, "Somewhere in a remote village at this moment a non-wageworker is producing a surplus in which, via multiple intermediaries, each one of us is partaking, if to different degrees. But this particular transfer of surplus is well hidden from view because its traces are swallowed up, in the obscure facts of the life cycle of the non-wageworker's cousin, the wageworker of the peripheral areas." Wallerstein, *Unthinking Social Science*, 164, and *Capitalist World Economy*, 127–29. Wilma Dunaway elaborates in "The Centrality of the Household to the Modern World-System," 1–2. And see Von Werhof, "Production Relations Without Wage Labor and Labor Division by Sex," and Arrighi and Saul, "Socialism and Economic Development in Tropical Africa," 149. Mintz, "Was the Plantation Slave a Proletarian?" and "Slavery and the Rise of Peasantries."

4. Smith, *Wealth of Nations*, 33–35, 161–62. Raine, *The Land of Saddle-Bags*, 237.

5. Medick, "The Proto-Industrial Family Economy," 297–300. Medick writes, "The origin of modern capitalism is not in any case to be separated from the specific function, which the 'ganze Haus' [entire household] of the small peasant household carried out in the final, critical phase of its development which was at the same time the period of its demise." Cohen, *Women's Work*, 36, quoted in

Salstrom, *Appalachia's Path to Dependency*, 64. The historian Elizabeth Dore observes of Nicaraguan peasants that their means of livelihood endured in the capitalist periphery, "because it bore most of the costs of survival." Dore, *Myths of Modernity*, 20–23. This is a little different from the family wage that Marx describes in *Capital*. Marx, *Capital*, vol. I, 518–19, 717–18. For more on the household in the world economy, see Wallerstein and Smith, "Households as an Institution of the World-Economy," in Smith and Wallerstein, eds., *Creating and Transforming Households*, 21.

6. One lord is quoted as saying, "The management of his little plot, cheerfully and profitably occupies all the leisure hours of the poor man, his wife and family." Dawson, *Spade Husbandry*, 33. Sinclair, *Observations on the Means of Enabling a Cottager to Keep a Cow*. Emphasis added. Dunaway notes that the cottar relationship existed in Appalachia outside of mining camps in *First American Frontier*, 104.

7. Kane, *Industrial Resources of Ireland*, 378; Naper, *Suggestions for the More Scientific and General Employment of Agricultural Labourers*, 22–23; Henry Fawcett, *Manual of Political Economy*, 118. "In every crop of potatoes, it may be expected that some will prove too small for the purposes of cooking . . . and thus after every meal there will be some little refuse for the trough," cited in "The Poor Man's Garden," 178.

8. For early examples of cottars in Pennsylvania, see Clemens and Simler, "Rural Labor and the Farm Household in Chester County, Pennsylvania, 1750–1820," in *Work and Labor in Early America*, 106–108, quoted in Henretta, *Origins of American Capitalism*, 257. All sorts of workers' movements and organizations appeared to fight land monopoly. For the Anti-Rent War in the Hudson River Valley, see Huston, *Land and Freedom*. On the National Reform Association, see Lause, *Young America*. One of the founders of the NRA was Thomas Ainge Devyr, a former British Chartist.

9. On Malthus, Marx, and the working class, see Foster, *Marx's Ecology*, chap. 3.

10. Owen, "On Spade Husbandry," 75–77. Also see Dawson, *Spade Husbandry*, 24. Young, *Annals of Agriculture*, vol. 1, 60. Owen's notion took actual form as allotment gardens. According to Jeremy Burchardt, allotments became viable during the Napoleonic wars as a response to food shortages and starvation among the poor. Burchardt, *The Allotment Movement in England*, 15–16.

11. Still, *River of Earth*, 50–51. Still spent most of his life on the Dead Mare branch of Little Carr Creek, Knott County, Kentucky.

12. Still, *River of Earth*, 7–10.

13. Description and quotations from Weise, *Grasping at Independence*, 216. Miles, "The Common Lot," 145. "There is no economic independence for women . . . Unless a young woman has a father unusually prosperous, she must get married.

It is the only economic position open to her." See Raine, *The Land of Saddle-Bags*, 226.

14. Letters from Justus Collins to Glen Jean (July 20 and 22, 1905), Justus Collins Papers; Bert Wright, diary (August 16, 1898); Fowler, "Social and Industrial Conditions in the Pocahontas Coal Fields," 387; American Constitutional Association, *Life in a West Virginia Coal Field*, 27. The miners had contracted to be paid by the car, but then the company brought in larger cars, thus lowering the cost to the company by reducing the number of cars workers could load in a day. Jones, *Autobiography of Mother Jones*, 9. Notes the historian Ronald Eller, "By ignoring work schedules, mining routines, and other innovations which worked at cross-purposes with their traditional way of life, they sought to maintain their individualism and freedom from authority." Eller, *Miners, Millhands, and Mountaineers*, 167.

15. The term *Hungarians* for foreign workers seems to have been common. See "From Sewell [West Virginia]," *United Mine Workers Journal*, June 12, 1902. The quotation from the sociologist comes from "Coal Industry," *Encyclopedia of Social Reform*, 303.

16. Referring to a strike among mine workers throughout the bituminous coal regions of Virginia, West Virginia, Ohio, Indiana, and Illinois, one observer explained, "The causes which led up to the strike were various; but at bottom it was due to one,–the constant reduction in wages through several years, which had brought the miners and their families to the verge of starvation." Wages per week ran from $3.00 to $4.00. Rent on company house: $2.00 to $2.50 per month. One coal company reported paying 39 men a total of $228.98 for two weeks, or $2.87 per man, per week. See George, "The Coal Miners' Strike of 1897," 186–208. Letters from Justus Collins to Glen Jean (July 20 and 22, 1905), Justus Collins Papers. Fowler, "Social and Industrial Conditions in the Pocahontas Coal Fields," 108.

17. Graeber, "In Regulation Nation," 11–16. There are many other examples and abundant cases in which county officials promoted "reform" that actually gave more power to companies. Bailey, *Matewan Before the Massacre*, 90. Emmet, *Labor Relations in the Fairmont, West Virginia, Bituminous Coal Field*, 6, 74.

18. Managers probably would have agreed with Karl Marx that wages represented a sliver of the value workers created, which workers handed back to management for food in order to "reproduce the muscles, nerves, bones and brains of existing workers, and to bring new workers into existence." Marx, *Capital*, 717–18. "Persuasion by Starvation," *United Mine Workers Journal*, June 12, 1902. Companies attempted to force miners to use only company stores: "When men are paid a little money they are watched, and if they are seen going into any other store than the one owned by the company for which they work, they as a rule

are discharged." A. B. Smoot, quoted in *United Mine Workers Journal*, June 4, 1896.

19. O'Toole, "Colliery Yards and Gardens." The Board of Agriculture drew attention to the invisible value of household gardens in general, without specific mention of miners' gardens: "If an accurate computation of the actual value of these kitchen gardens could be made the magnitude of the figures would astonish most of us." Quoted in Atkeson, "Horticulture in West Virginia," 352. The report of the American Constitutional Association is *Life in a West Virginia Coal Field*, 54. Company interest is well illustrated in their own publications: "The Garden Contest," *Our Own People*, October 1918; "Gardens and Playgrounds in Mining Towns," *Coal Age* 2 (1912): 336–37; Frederick W. Whiteside, "Beautifying a Coal Mining Camp," *Coal Age* 2 (1912): 549; "Frick Coke Co.'s Welfare Work," *Coal Age* 2 (1912): 470. In 1924, the West Virginia Coal Association estimated that 50 percent of the state's miners planted vegetables and kept some livestock. Corbin estimates that vegetables accounted for between 10 and 20 percent of household income. See Corbin, *Life, Work, and Rebellion in the Coal Fields*, 33–34, 123. On money transfers between companies and banks, see Salstrom, *Appalachia's Path to Dependency*, 30–34.

20. "Gardens and Playgrounds in Mining Towns," *Coal Age* 2 (1912): 336–37. Nettie McGill investigated mining communities in West Virginia in order to evaluate the quality of life for children. She reported that 70 percent of residents planted at least beans, corn, potatoes, tomatoes, and cabbages. McGill found that residents who managed to live outside coal camps felt more strongly about their autonomy and had larger and more robust gardens. McGill, *Welfare of Children in Bituminous Coal Mining Communities in West Virginia*, 53, 75.

21. Marx put the contradiction like this: "The consumption of food by a beast of burden does not become any less a necessary aspect of the production process because the beast enjoys what it eats." Marx, *Capital*, 718. The conversation between Ex-Secretary P. McBryde and Tom Farry is recorded in "West Virginia," *United Mine Workers Journal* (June 4, 1896). Paul Saltrom notes of the subsistence economy, "By continuing alongside outside-controlled industrialization, the continuing networks of mutual aid served to reduce wage demands and thus to transfer Appalachia's wealth (in the form of labor's products) outside the region." Salstrom, *Appalachia's Path to Dependency*, 127. Letters from Justus Collins to Glen Jean (July 20 and 22, 1905), Justus Collins Papers.

22. Gaventa, *Power and Powerlessness*, 89.

23. Brown, *Constitutional Government Overthrown in West Virginia*, 7. The "master and servant" decision is attributed to Judge Samuel C. Burdett, but I could not find it. I found mention of it in a hearing before the Senate Committee on Education and Labor held in 1921. *West Virginia Coal Fields, Hearings*, 94.

24. Of course, that is not the end of the story. At that point, the miners called in their

own reinforcements—kin and other allies from other counties described in the press as "backwoods-men." *United Mine Workers Journal*, July 11, 1912; "Terror Reigns in West Virginia," *United Mine Workers Journal*, August 1, 1912. Congress concluded that any workingman constantly robbed of his wages by the company store, subject to rents he must pay in every season, whether working or not, and under the gun of hired security guards, "is virtually a chattel of the operator." Quoted in "Coal Industry," *Encyclopedia of Social Reform* (New York, 1897), 303. Lynch, "The West Virginia Coal Strike," 630–37.

25. Corbin, *Life, Work, and Rebellion*, 33–34. Kenny Lively interviewed by John Flynn, September 28, 1995, River Folklife Project collection (AFC 1999/008), American Folklife Center, Library of Congress, http://hdl.loc.gov/loc.afc/afccmns .068002.

26. *Fourteenth Census of the United States Taken in the Year 1920, Volume XI, Mines and Quarries*, 256. *Thirteenth Census of the United States Taken in the Year 1910. Volume XI, Mines and Quarries*, 171. *Fifteenth Census of the United States, Mines and Quarries: 1929*, 255. "[Twelfth Census of the United States]." *Special Reports: Mines and Quarries: 1902*, 701–702; Malcolm Ross, "Permanent Part-Time," *Survey Graphic* 22 (1933), 268.

27. United States Department of the Interior, Division of Subsistence Homesteads, General Information Concerning the Purposes and Policies of the Division of Subsistence Homesteads, 4; *Quaker Relief Efforts in Europe, 1914–1922* (a visual collection at Swarthmore College), www.swarthmore.edu/library/friends /AFSC/lanternslides.htm.

28. Committee for Economic Recovery, *Arthurdale: A Partial Pattern for the New American Way of Life*; Rice, "Footnote on Arthurdale," 441; United States Department of the Interior, Division of Subsistence Homesteads, General Information Concerning the Purposes and Policies of the Division of Subsistence Homesteads, 4; Tate, "Possibilities and Limitations of Subsistence Homesteads," 530.

29. Clark, "Will Back to the Land Help?," 456. Clark held various positions in the experiment station at the University of Wisconsin. Wilson, "The Place of Subsistence Homesteads in Our National Economy," 73–84; Committee for Economic Recovery, *Arthurdale: A Partial Pattern for the New American Way of Life*; United States Department of the Interior, Division of Subsistence Homesteads, General Information Concerning the Purposes and Policies of the Division of Subsistence Homesteads, 4.

30. Roosevelt, "Subsistence Farmsteads," 199–201.

31. Arthurdale, along with the more than thirty other subsistence communities (in Minnesota, Alabama, Iowa, Ohio, and California), lessened the suffering of approximately one thousand people. It says something that many residents considered the years they spent at Arthurdale the best and most privileged of their lives. For a positive view of the Division of Subsistence Homesteads, see Garvey,

"The Duluth Homesteads"; Lord and Johnstone, *A Place on Earth*, 49, 177–85; and Ware and Powell, "Planning for Permanent Poverty," 517.

32. Lord and Johnstone, *A Place on Earth*, 49, 177–85; Ware and Powell, "Planning for Permanent Poverty," 517. Congress held hearings on the problems of the homestead plan on January 24, 1934. The residents who complained, in this example, lived in Cumberland Homesteads in Tennessee. The Division of Subsistence Homesteads moved from the Department of the Interior to the Resettlement Administration and then to the Department of Agriculture.

33. Ware and Powell reported that the government sought people whose suffering "could be attributed to the depression," as opposed to those who were destitute before, calling into question the homesteads as genuine economic relief. No African-Americans were admitted regardless of their qualifications or need. Looked at from these flaws, Arthurdale hardly presented a bold social experiment. Ware and Powell, "Planning for Permanent Poverty," 513–24; Davis, "A Black Inventory of the New Deal," 141–42. Harold Ware lived between 1889 and 1935 and was the Communist Party's top expert in agriculture. He died in an automobile accident. In 1952, Whittaker Chambers accused Ware of being a Soviet spy.

34. Drucker, "The Industrial Revolution Hits the Farmer." Philip La Follette, former governor of Wisconsin, returned from a tour of Germany in 1933 and despaired of the families he had seen "digging their living out of the soil in the primitive fashion of our ancestors centuries ago." "What have they left behind them?" he pleaded, "the taxes, the rent, the mortgages, stores, factories and farms . . . they are leaving behind them the economic system." A representative of the American Engineering Council worried that society would collapse if people grew their own food for their own needs, writing, "Subsistence farming is not possible unless we are willing to destroy practically everything that we now call desirable in our present civilization . . . Farmers must be able to pay taxes and to purchase clothing and other necessary manufactured products which they are not now capable of producing." The engineer and La Follette quoted in Clark, "Will Back to the Land Help?," 456.

35. "Stirred Up by Henry Ford's 'Shotgun Gardens.'" I also used Kile, *The New Agriculture*, 151, and Zeuch, "The Subsistence Homestead Problem from the Viewpoint of an Economist," 711. And see *Business Week*, September 2, 1931, 23. For articles by industrialists, see Harriman, "Factory and Farm in Double Harness," and Crowther, *A Basis for Stability*, chap. 13.

36. Daniel, "The Metamorphosis of Slavery, 1865–1900," 90.

37. Westmacott, *African-American Gardens and Yards*, 23–24; Reynolds, *Black Farmers in America*, 4.

38. Ochiltree, "Mastering the Sharecroppers," 42. There were pure croppers who owned nothing but their labor and owed every possession to the landowner and

tenants who paid rent in cotton and then offered the remaining cotton to furnishing merchants as a crop lien. Most sharecroppers were of the second kind. Taylor, *An Introduction of the Study of Agricultural Economics*, 350–54. Sharecropping appealed to Edward Gibbon Wakefield, the British political economist of imperialism. "There are other ways in which there may be slavery in fact without the name. The freed negroes, and their descendants, of some of the states of North America . . . are virtually a sort of slaves [*sic*], by means of their extreme degradation in the midst of the whites." Wakefield, *A View of the Art of Colonization*, 175. "Report of President's Committee on Farm Tenancy," *Handbook of Labor Statistics*, 232–34; Taylor, *An Introduction to the Study of Agricultural Economics*, 252. The remaining 15 percent of African-Americans worked as laborers without access to land, and a few owned their own farms.

39. Graeber, *Debt*, 120–22. Vance, *Human Geography of the South*, 328–29.
40. Shaw and Rosengarten, *All God's Dangers*, 488, 190–92, 281, 488. Tenants also exerted influence over their owners. One landlord called it the "copartnership mode of farming" and spoke against it. "It makes the laborer too independent; he becomes a partner, and has a right to be consulted." Alston, "The Wages System—Grasses," 317.
41. Shaw and Rosengarten, *All God's Dangers*, 190–92, 281, 488.
42. Wallerstein, *Unthinking Social Science*, 164–65, and *The Capitalist World-Economy*, 12; Dore, *Myths of Modernity*, 20. Rosa Luxemburg wrote in 1913, "Capitalism depends in all respects on non-capitalist strata and social organizations existing side by side with it." Luxemburg, *The Accumulation of Capital*, 365.
43. On conservation and waste, see Hays, *Conservation and the Gospel of Efficiency*. For a critique of conservation and the way it limited access to commons, see Jacoby, *Crimes Against Nature*.
44. Shea, "Our Pappies Burned the Woods." One informant, in a different source, described the process of "clearing it off for a crop": "They'd send one of us old boys out and invite everybody in the whole community to come to the working." The description suggests that a community did this work, not scattered individuals or households. Shackelford, Weinberg, and Anderson, *Our Appalachia*, 19–20. For a more empathetic assessment of swidden, see Scott, *The Romance of Savage Life*. I also consulted Campbell, *Southern Highlander and His Homeland*, 231–33; Hatch, "Delivering the Goods," 7; Peck, Frank, and Eke, *Economic Utilization of Marginal Lands in Nicholas and Webster Counties, West Virginia*; and Peck, "Farm or Forest in the West Virginia Appalachians?" For the best argument and account of national parks as landscapes of dispossession, see Spence, *Dispossessing the Wilderness*, passim. On the subject of national parks and the coming of tourism, I consulted Gregg, *Managing the Mountains*.
45. Albright, *The Birth of the National Park Service*, 167; Gregg, *Managing the Mountains*, 105–35.

46. Albright and Willis, quoted in Gregg, *Managing the Mountains*, 105–35. The picture of Cliser is on p. 135 of *Managing the Mountains*. Sources spell Cliser's first name more than one way. Some use the spelling Melanchthon.

47. Ross, *Machine Age in the Hills*, 40–42. Johnston, *West Virginia, "The Switzerland of America"*; Anderson, *A Popular School History of the United States*, 324. Vermont sometimes used the same slogan.

48. The USDA report, for which Gray wrote the introduction, is *Economic and Social Problems and Conditions of the Southern Appalachians*. He also wrote an article summarizing key findings published as "Economic Conditions and Tendencies in the Southern Appalachians as Indicated by the Cooperative Survey," in *Mountain Life and Work*. For statistics from the USDA report cited here, see 4–5, 55, and 143–49. The number of self-sufficing households was the same as it was in 1860, but population in the region was vastly greater.

49. Campbell, *The Southern Highlander and His Homeland*, 231–33; Hatch, "Delivering the Goods," 7. Private and church schools make the school attendance rate higher. Illiteracy was as high as 7 percent in some Kentucky counties. Illiteracy figures describe children between the ages of ten and twenty. Gray, *Economic and Social Problems*, 99–101.

50. Gray, *Economic and Social Problems*, 9. A farmer was defined as a male at least fifteen years old.

51. Monroe Quillen, quoted in Shackelford, Weinberg, and Anderson, *Our Appalachia*, 238–39. Another study presents a different picture of the farm on the outskirts of the mining town. Nettie McGill's *The Welfare of Children in Bituminous Coal Mining Communities in West Virginia* is based on fieldwork. Of the families she contacted near mining camps and towns, 70 percent kept gardens. They lived better than those who remained in more distant hollows. Almost all the families had fresh vegetables on the table in late summer. Beans, corn, potatoes, tomatoes, and cabbage were common; beets, onions, lettuce, and carrots less so. Half the families had fruits like cantaloupes, raspberries, rhubarb, and apples. "The possibility of having more land to cultivate was frequently given as one of the great advantages of living outside the mining towns." But McGill also argued in favor of the camps. Shanties often had electric lights rather than kerosene lamps. Some companies installed central water systems. One advantage of hollows: a lower danger of disease from unsanitary conditions. One advantage of camps: nearby doctors. McGill, *Welfare of Children*, 75.

52. For this and the previous paragraph: Gray, "Economic Conditions and Tendencies in the Southern Appalachians," 4–5; Gray, *Economic and Social Problems*, 39.

53. Sherman and Henry, *Hollow Folk*, 5–10.

54. Nancy Parezo, quoted in Dilworth, "'Handmade by an American Indian' Souvenirs and the Cultural Economy of Southwestern Tourism," 106. Jane S. Becker writes, "Fascination with traditional ways expressed middle-class Americans' ambivalence

toward industrialism, which might offer material comforts but denied the human values they perceived in 'simpler' cultures." Becker, *Selling Tradition*, 16. Batteau, *The Invention of Appalachia*, 13–15, 84.

55. Williams, *Appalachia*, 313–20.

7. Negotiated Settlements

1. United Nations, *World Urban Prospects*, 8; Rochester, *Why Farmers Are Poor*, 68–69. Edward Shils defined modernity as consisting of very particular things: democratic institutions, welfare states, and government-supported industry. " 'Modern,' " Shils wrote in the 1950s, "means being western . . . It is the model of the West detached in some way from its geographical origins and locus." Shils, draft of "Political Development in the New States," 1, quoted in Gilman, *Mandarins of the Future*, 2–7. A quotation attributed to the French writer André Siegfried says it best: "The United States is presiding at a general reorganization of the ways of living throughout the world." André Siegfried quoted in Potter, *People of Plenty*, and Lerner, *The Passing of Traditional Society*. Ferguson, *The Anti-Politics Machine*, 281. *Proceedings and Documents of the United Nations Monetary and Financial Conference, Bretton Woods, New Hampshire, July 1–22, 1944*, vol. 1, 166.

2. Zimmerman, "Discussion," 84; Fels, "Planning for Purchasing Power," 202.

3. Kains, *Five Acres and Independence*; Hall, *Three Acres and Liberty*; Borsodi, *Flight from the City*.

4. Zimmerman, "Discussion," 84; Borsodi, *Flight from the City*, 1–4.

5. Indians had their own Subsistence Homestead Authority, established in 1934 and managed by the Department of the Interior. Collier attempted a compassionate paternalism, allowing Indians to hold their dances and manage their own affairs, but he also imposed the government in the slaughter of Navajo sheep and goats, part of a misguided effort at range management. See Collier, "The Fate of the Navajos: What Will Oil Money Do to the Greatest of Indian Tribes?," *Sunset Magazine*, January 1924, quoted in Weisiger, *Dreaming of Sheep in Navajo Country*, 23. Twelve Southerners, *I'll Take My Stand: The South and the Agrarian Tradition*, xlii–xlv, l–liii.

6. Nearing and Nearing, *The Good Life*, intro. and chap. 2, quoted in *American Georgics*, 316–19.

7. *Wickard v. Filburn*, vol. 317, U.S. Reports, 111 (1942). The case is usually cited as establishing precedent for widening the constitutional power of the United States to regulate interstate commerce. The case continues to anger those who favor restricted government powers, though libertarians never seem to recognize capitalism as a distinct force that acts through government. See the Filburn Foundation, http://thefilburnfoundation.com/index.html.

8. Lewis, "Economic Development with Unlimited Supplies of Labor," 181.

9. Rosenstein-Rodan quoted in Cullather, *Hungry World*, 147.

10. Sauer, *Agricultural Origins and Dispersals*, 2.

11. Grove, *Green Imperialism*, 181–85; "Col. Chappell's Address," *Papers Published by Order of the Agricultural Society of South Carolina*, 6–8, 12–17. For reaction to swidden in the United States, see Stoll, *Larding the Lean Earth*, 128–30.

12. "Even within anthropology, the discipline most oriented towards non-western societies," notes Michael Dove, "traditional agriculture had been dismissed as being of minor relevance or importance." See Dove's essay on Conklin: http://cseas.yale.edu/sites/default/files/files/Harold%20C%20Conklin_Michael%20Dove_AAA%202016.pdf.

13. For this and the previous paragraph, I used Conklin, *Hanunóo Agriculture*, 152–55; Cullather, "Miracles of Modernization: The Green Revolution and the Apotheosis of Technology," 233, 238–39. And see Hill, "The Human Factor in Economic Development," and Brzezinski, "The Politics of Underdevelopment," 57–59, both cited by Cullather. I used the FAO's crop statistics database and converted hectograms to U.S. tons per hectare: www.fao.org/faostat/en/#data/QC. For yields per hectare in Kalimantan, Indonesia, I used Dove's number of about 1,500 liters per hectare. I then converted volume to weight, using uncooked brown rice (1 liter = 1.76 pounds). This gave me 2,640 pounds per hectare, or 1.3 U.S. short tons. Dove, *Swidden Agriculture in Indonesia*, 289.

14. The cultural anthropologist Renato Rosaldo writes of Conklin and his accomplishment: "The ethnographer emerges as an advocate for the Hanunóo and as a critic of dominant national policy . . . The tacit implications of his article reflect a politics grounded in notions of human well-being and ecological concern." Rosaldo, *Culture and Truth*, 185–86.

15. Schultz, *Transforming Traditional Agriculture*, 53–66. Schultz quotes the Chicago economist Jacob Viner: "I find it impossible to conceive of a farm of any kind on which . . . it would not be possible, by known methods, to obtain some addition to the crop by using additional labor." Schultz, *Transforming Traditional Agriculture*, 60. Netting ignores the "zero-value" doctrine and Schultz. Instead, he focuses on the ways that agrarian people allocate labor in differing population conditions. See Netting, *Smallholder, Householder*, 108–10.

16. Schultz, *Transforming Traditional Agriculture*, 33–35.

17. Sahlins's argument might apply to hunter-gatherer societies during the warm and stable Holocene, but not to earlier epochs. Life during the Ice Age and the Younger Dryas was extraordinarily hard. For a description of these and other climate events and how they affected early humans, see Brooke, *Climate Change and the Course of Global History*.

18. Grant, "Marginal Men," 121. Grant was best known for his term as the third director of the United Nations International Children's Emergency Fund, or UNICEF. President Bill Clinton presented him with the Presidential Medal of Freedom in 1994.

19. Ibid., 115–19.
20. Williams, *Appalachia*, 253.
21. Rochester, *Why Farmers Are Poor*, 68–69.
22. "Moonshiners Kill Second Dry Raider, Hold Off Big Posse," *New York Times*, December 11, 1922. "The Mountain Moonshiner," *Forest and Stream*, November 10, 1906.
23. Black, Mather, and Sanders, "Standards of Living in Appalachia."
24. Caudill, *Night Comes to the Cumberlands*, 12–13, 27, 103–107, 306, 311. Williams, *Appalachia*, 325. Caudill quoted in *New York Times*, October 20, 1963. For a less sympathetic view, see Homer Bigart, "Kentucky Miners: A Grim Winter," *New York Times*, October 20, 1963. Also see *Look Magazine*, August 9, 1962.
25. Homer Bigart, "U.S. Reveals Plan to Fight Appalachian Poverty," *New York Times*, November 13, 1963. On the volunteers and ARC, see Kiffmeyer, *Reformers to Radicals*.
26. Appalachian Regional Commission, *Report*, 4–7.
27. Gaventa and Horton, "Land Ownership Patterns and Their Impacts on Appalachian Communities," 164–65.
28. Gaventa, *Power and Powerlessness*, 163–64, 210–11.
29. Appalachian Regional Commission, *Performance and Accountability Report*; Ziliak, "The Appalachian Regional Development Act and Economic Change," 16–18; Fickey and Samers, "Developing Appalachia," 124.
30. Salstrom, "More About 'The Impact of Limited Economic Imagination' on Appalachia's Development," 10.
31. Julian Martin, from his website: http://wildwonderfulwv.us/julian/. I have altered the punctuation in a few places.
32. Steven Mufson, "New Owner of Freedom Industries Must Face Fallout of West Virginia Chemical Spill," *Washington Post*, January 17, 2014, www.washingtonpost .com/business/economy/new-owner-of-freedom-industries-must-face-fallout-of -west-virginia-chemical-spill/2014/01/17/77b1a572-7df2-11e3-93c1-0e888170b723 _story.html?utm_term=.61e5fd34d0dc.
33. "No metallurgical process developed in the 20th century compares with that of froth flotation and the profound effect it had on the mineral industry." Fuerstenau, "A Century of Developments in the Chemistry of Flotation Processing," 3. Blum, "Our Toxicity Experiment in West Virginia." Occupational Health Guidelines, www.cdc.gov/niosh/docs/81-123/pdfs/0407.pdf.
34. Mufson, "New Owner of Freedom Industries Must Face Fallout of West Virginia Chemical Spill," *Washington Post*, January 17, 2014. Lottermoser, *Mine Wastes*, 207.
35. Interview with Senator Jay Rockefeller, National Public Radio (February 10, 2014). Shelley Moore Capito (R), a member of the House in 2014, was elected that year to replace Rockefeller, who is also a former governor of West Virginia.

36. "HR2218 Fails to Protect Health and Safety," earthjustice.org; "HR2218," govtrack.us.

37. *Aboveground Storage Tank Act*. West Virginia Senate Bill No. 373. Passed March 8, 2014. *Amending Aboveground Storage Tank Act*. West Virginia Senate Bill No. 423. Passed March 14, 2015. www.dep.wv.gov/WWE/abovegroundstoragetanks /Documents/WVCode2230.pdf. Ward, "Chemical Tank Safety Rollback Passes House."

38. Resnikoff, "Congress Passes $8.7 Billion Food Stamp Cut," MSNBC, February 4, 2013, www.msnbc.com/msnbc/congress-passes-farm-bill-food-stamp-cuts#50092. The report referring to 2017 comes from the *International Business Times*, May 16, 2016, www.ibtimes.com/paul-ryan-gop-eye-23b-food-stamp-cuts-2017-budget -2369301. In the Senate, Joe Manchin (D) voted in favor of the Agriculture Reform, Food, and Jobs Act of 2013. Jay Rockefeller (D) did not vote. www.senate.gov/legislative /LIS/roll_call_lists/roll_call_vote_cfm.cfm?congress=113&session=2&vote =00020#name. For the percentages of households receiving SNAP benefits, see www.governing.com/gov-data/food-stamp-snap-benefits-enrollment-participation -totals-map.html.

39. Waggoner, "I'm from West Virginia and I've Got Something to Say About the Chemical Spill"; Martin quoted in Salstrom, "Cash Is a Four-Letter Word," 242–44.

40. Anthracite emits 228.6 pounds of CO_2 per million British thermal units. Bituminous emits 205.7. Natural gas emits 117. www.eia.gov/tools/faqs/faq.cfm?id =73&t=11. "Coal-to-Gas Plant Conversions in the U.S." www.power-eng.com /articles/print/volume-119/issue-6/features/coal-to-gas-plant-conversions-in-the -u-s.html.

41. Wyoming delivered 390 million tons in the same year, but its production is also declining. See Nathan Vardi, "U.S. Coal Company Alpha Natural Resources Files for Bankruptcy," *Forbes*, August 3, 2015: www.forbes.com/sites/nathanvardi/2015 /08/03/u-s-coal-company-alpha-natural-resources-files-for-bankruptcy/. National employment in the coal industry fell by 10 percent between 2012 and 2013. U.S. Energy Information Administration, "Annual Coal Report, Table 1. Coal Production and Number of Mines . . . 2013 and 2012," December 1, 2015: www.eia.gov /coal/annual/index.cfm.

42. On the state's population, see West Virginia Health Statistics Center, Statistical Brief Number 8, www.wvdhhr.org/bph/hsc/pubs/briefs/008/default.htm. On Walmart, see Lilly and Todd, "What Happens When Walmart Closes in One Coal Community?" On food deserts, see Lilly and Todd, "What Would You Do If Your Grocery Store Disappeared?"; Walsh, "Alienated and Angry, Coal Miners See Donald Trump as Their Only Choice."

43. Amy Arnett, "On the Map: West Virginia's Largest Employers by County," *West Virginia Executive*, November 21, 2014: www.wvexecutive.com/west

-virginias-largest-employers; Census of the United States (2010); "Number of Poor West Virginians Remains High," www.wvpolicy.org/number-of-poor-west -virginians-remains-high-increase-in-children-living-in-poverty; Dennis Sadowski, "Despite Long Mining History Poverty Straps Many in West Virginia, *National Catholic Reporter*, November 4, 2014: www.ncronline.org/blogs/eco-catholic /despite-long-mining-history-poverty-straps-many-west-virginia; "State of American Well-Being," Gallo-Healthways Well-Being Index, www.well-being.com.

44. For an argument in favor of collective identities in the service of an ethical politics, see Critchley, *Infinitely Demanding*. I have especially learned from David Whisnant's "Developments in the Appalachian Identity Movement," which though published in 1980 still resonates. "At its worst . . . regional identification is an isolationist impulse." He deconstructs an essentialist mountain identity. And yet, "The political value of regional identity lies in its usefulness as a basis for broad solidarity and coalition."

45. In the words of two historians, "Making visible activities that neoliberalism renders invisible expands the range of ideas for producing social livelihoods and economic development." Fickey and Samers, "Developing Appalachia," 123.

46. Appalachian Voices is one such organization. The Reclaim Act is H.R. 4456, 114th Congress. Introduced in the House in February 2016.

47. Ostrom (1933–2012) shared the Nobel Prize with Oliver E. Williamson. The act would rely on Ostrom's *Governing the Commons*. For design principles, see pages 90–101.

48. On corporate subsidies, Niraj Chokshi, "The United States of Subsidies," *Washington Post*, March 18, 2015: www.washingtonpost.com/blogs/govbeat/wp/2015 /03/17/the-united-states-of-subsidies-the-biggest-corporate-winners-in-each-state /?utm_term=.314361798972.

49. Barnwell, *The Face of Appalachia*, 121, 122, 126. The project is Tending the Commons: Folklife and Landscape in Southern West Virginia in cooperation with the Coal River Folklife Project and the American Folklife Center at the Library of Congress. Dave Baily interviewed by Mary Hufford on April 12, 1996 (AFC 1999/008), http://hdl.loc.gov/loc.afc/afccmns.104007; Virgil Jarrell interviewed by Mary Hufford on May 23, 1996 (AFC 1999/008), http://hdl.loc.gov/loc.afc/afccmns.117004.

50. Hardin, "Tragedy of the Commons."

51. According to Richard Judd, "These local common resource regimes established two central principles for the emerging New England conservation tradition: communities bore collective responsibility for managing their resources in a productive fashion, and they were to allocate these resources equitably." Judd, *Common Lands, Common People*, 7–8, 41–45; Acheson, *Capturing the Commons*, 206; Greer, "Commons and Enclosure in the Colonization of North America."

52. Newfont, *Blue Ridge Commons*, 276.

53. Ibid.

54. Immerwahr, *Thinking Small*.
55. Vance, *Hillbilly Elegy*, 148–49, 206.
56. Roger Coke, *England's Improvements*, quoted in Appleby, *Economic Thought and Ideology*, 253.
57. United Nations Food and Agriculture Organization, Bioenergy and Food Security Criteria and Indicators, "Markala Sugar Project," www.fao.org/bioenergy /31530-0af3706e7240fe92a72ca083cf834cce5.pdf.
58. Quoted in Berkeley and Lewat, *Land Rush*.
59. De Schutter, "How Not to Think of Land-Grabbing," 252.
60. On speculation as to the cause of the food crisis of 2008, see Kaufman, "The Food Bubble."
61. Chris Arsenault, "Mali's Land Deal with the Devil—Letter from Markala," Pulitzer Center on Crisis Reporting, May 14, 2015, http://pulitzercenter.org/reporting /malis-land-deal-devil-letter-markala. Dispossessed woman quoted in Berkeley and Lewat, *Land Rush*. NGO's statement and account from Brautigam, *Will Africa Feed China?*, 87.
62. Berkeley and Lewat, *Land Rush*; MacFarquhar, "African Farmers Displaced as Investors Move In," *New York Times*, December 21, 2010.
63. The quotation is from Des Sheehy, chief information officer at Duxton, a private equity fund. Ann White, "African Farming Is the New Frontier for Brave Investors," *The Telegraph*, June 14, 2014, www.telegraph.co.uk/finance/economics/10901154 /African-farming-is-the-new-frontier-for-brave-investors.html. Duxton also buys and sells water.
64. "Development Goals and Strategies," www.worldbank.org/depweb/english/beyond /beyondco/beg_17.pdf, 123.
65. In an interview for *Land Rush*, Nedelcovych notes that the shea trees would have been replanted in new locations. But young trees don't fruit for a number of years, creating a lapse in income.
66. Moudio, "Shea Butter Nourishes Opportunities for African Women." For the Global Shea Alliance, see www.globalshea.com. Joan Martinez-Alier explains it this way: "Economic security refers, in the first instance, to the livelihood or subsistence of humans. While in many past societies material provisioning was secured outside the market, in today's society income earned in the market appears to be the main means of acquisition of the essentials for human livelihood." Martinez-Alier, "The Environmentalism of the Poor," 42.
67. De Schutter served from 2008 to 2014. At this writing, he teaches at Columbia University.
68. For this and the previous paragraph, see De Schutter, "How Not to Think of Land-Grabbing," 254–57.
69. Nwanze, "Viewpoint: Smallholders Can Feed the World." Wegner and Zwart, *Who Will Feed the World*, Oxfam Research Report, April 2011. According to a

World Bank report, "Seventy-five percent of the world's poor are rural, and most are engaged in farming. The need for more and better investment in agriculture to reduce poverty, increase economic growth, and promote environmental sustainability was already clear when there were 'only' 830 million hungry people before the food price rise." World Bank, *Rising Global Interest in Farmland: Can It Yield Sustainable and Equitable Benefits?* (2011).

70. Roy, *Walking with the Comrades*, 214.

BIBLIOGRAPHY

Manuscripts

Eastern Regional Coal Archives, Craft Memorial Library, Bluefield, West Virginia
    Bert Wright Diary.
    Flat Top Land Trust Association and Pocahontas Coal Company Papers.
        Annual Reports of the Board of Managers of the Flat Top Coal Land Association.
        General Letters, August 20, 1887–July 2, 1889.
        John C. Belcher and J. W. Belcher Letters, 1883–1885.
        List of Surveys within the Maitland Davis Survey . . . February 1887.
        Pocahontas Coal Company, Letters, 1883–1885.
        "Pleas at the Court House of the County of Logan before the Circuit Superior
        Court of Law and Chancery for Said County on the 13th Day of October, 1846."
James Madison University, Special Collections
    Nimrod Warden daybook, Warden Ledger Collection (https://mdid.lib.jmu.edu
    /viewers/presentationviewer/11274/?sessionid=2cb4622fbb694ef8f9164a6f7ff3ad).

Library of Congress
  Alexander Hamilton Papers (www.loc.gov/item/mm81024612/).
  Lewis, Samuel [cartographer]. Copy of a survey . . . for George Washington 2950 acres of land . . . lying in the county of Botetourt on the n.e. side of the Great Kanhaway about a mile and [a] half above the mouth of Cole River . . . Novemr. 6th, 1774 (www.loc.gov/item/75693269/).
  Thomas Jefferson Papers (www.loc.gov/collections/thomas-jefferson-papers/about-this-collection/).
  Vinckeboons, Joan. *Caert vande Svydt Rivier in Niew Nederland.* 1639. (www.loc.gov/item/2003623407).
West Virginia State Archives, Charleston, West Virginia
  Elk River and Lumber Company Papers.
  Grantee Index to Deeds, 1868–1969, McDowell County, West Virginia.
West Virginia University Library
  Justus Collins Papers.

Journals and Newspapers

Annals of Agriculture
Appleton's Journal
Atlantic Monthly
Catholic World
Charleston Gazette-Mail
Coal Age
Economist
Forest and Stream
Harper's Magazine
Knickerbocker; or New York Monthly Magazine
Literary Digest
Mountain Life and Work
New York Daily Tribune
New York Times
Our Own People (Davis Coal and Coke Company)
Southern Literary Messenger
United Mine Workers Journal
Virginia Free Press
Washington Post
West Virginia Farm Journal
West Virginia Journal
Western Farmer and Gardener
Wheeling Daily Intelligencer
Wheeling Register

Government Documents

State and Local

Commonwealth of Kentucky. "An act to prevent future conflictions in claims to land." *Journal of the House of Representatives of the Commonwealth of Kentucky.* 1826.

Commonwealth of Virginia. *Journal of the House of Delegates of the Commonwealth of Virginia . . . 1849.* 1849.

———. Supreme Court of Appeals. *Report of Cases in the Supreme Court of Appeals of Virginia.* 1857.

———. Supreme Court of Appeals. *Report of Cases in the Supreme Court of Appeals of Virginia.* 1897.

Dakota Territory. Fargo Board of Trade. *Green Pastures and Vast Wheat Fields: A Sketch, Historical, Descriptive and Statistical. The County of Cass and the City of Fargo.* 1888.

Georgia. "An Act to Better Protect the Lands and Farming Interests of the 741st District, G. M., Known as Reynolds District of Georgia, Taylor County, and for other purposes." *Acts and Resolutions of the General Assembly of the State of Georgia,* Part III. 1888.

Minnesota. *Fifth Biennial Report of the Bureau of Labor of the State of Minnesota.* 1895–1896.

Nebraska State Board of Agriculture. *Annual Report for the Year 1888.* 1889.

Pennsylvania General Assembly, House of Representatives. *Votes and Proceedings of the House of Representatives of the Province of Pennsylvania Beginning the Fourteenth Day of October, 1767.* 1767.

Tennessee State Geological Survey. *The Resources of Tennessee.* Nashville: Tennessee State Geological Survey, 1911.

West Virginia Commissioner of Immigration. *Annual Report of the Commissioner of Immigration of the State of West Virginia for the Year 1869.* 1870.

West Virginia Commissioner of Labor. *Report of the Commissioner of Labor of the State of West Virginia, 1897–1898.* 1898.

West Virginia Department of Agriculture. *Old-Fashioned Cookbook.* [n.d.].

West Virginia Historical Records Survey. *Calendar of Wills in West Virginia,* No. 49, Upshur County (Buckhannon). Charleston, 1941.

West Virginia Legislature. *Acts of the Legislature of West Virginia.* 1866.

———. *Acts of the Legislature of West Virginia.* 1870.

West Virginia State Board of Agriculture. *Fifth Biennial Report of the West Virginia State Board of Agriculture.* Charleston, 1900.

———. *Report of the West Virginia State Board of Agriculture: Forestry.* Charleston, 1908.

———. *West Virginia, "The Switzerland of America": A Brief Guide for Tourists to Some of Its Many Scenic and Historic Places.* Bulletin of the West Virginia Department of Agriculture. Issue 66. 1926.

West Virginia Supreme Court of Appeals. *Reports of Cases Decided in the Supreme Court of Appeals of West Virginia.* Edited by John Marshall Hagans. Vol. 2. 1868.

——. *McClure v. Maitland.* Decided September 20, 1884. *Reports of Cases Argued and Determined in the Supreme Court of Appeals of West Virginia.* Vol. 24. 1884.

——. *Major Henry Totten V. Pocahontas Coal and Coke Company.* Decided May 17, 1910. *Reports of Cases Argued and Determined in the Supreme Court of Appeals of West Virginia.* Vol. 67. Charleston, 1910.

National and International

Appalachian Regional Commission. *Performance and Accountability Report.* 2009. www .arc.gov/publications/FY2009PerformanceandAccountabilityReport.asp.

——. *Network Appalachia: Access to Global Opportunity.* www.arc.gov/noindex/programs /transp/intermodal/NetworkAppalachiaAccesstoGlobalOpportunity-Chap1.pdf.

Bercaw, Louise O., A. M. Hannay, and Esther M. Colvin. *Bibliography on Land Settlement, with Particular Reference to Small Holdings and Subsistence Homesteads.* Washington, D.C.: United States Department of Agriculture, 1934.

Committee for Economic Recovery. *Arthurdale: A Partial Pattern for the New American Way of Life.* Washington, D.C.: Government Printing Office, 1937.

Dimitri, Carolyn, Anne Effland, and Neilson Conklin. *The 20th Century Transformation of U.S. Agriculture and Farm Policy.* Washington, D.C.: United States Department of Agriculture, 2005.

Emmet, Boris. *Labor Relations in the Fairmont, West Virginia, Bituminous Coal Field.* United States Department of Labor. Bureau of Labor Statistics. Bulletin No. 361. Washington, D.C.: Government Printing Office, 1924.

Fuglie, Keith O., James M. MacDonald, and Eldon Ball. *Productivity Growth in U.S. Agriculture.* United States Department of Agriculture Economic Research Service. Economic Brief No. 9. Washington, D.C.: USDA, 2007.

House of Commons [Great Britain]. "Petition of the Owners and Proprietors of . . . Hooknorton and Southrop." January 26, 1773. *Journals of the House of Commons.* Vol. 34. 1804.

House of Lords [Great Britain]. *Journals of the House of Lords.* Vol. 34: 1772–1774. 1804.

Lord, Russell, and Paul H. Johnstone, eds. *A Place on Earth: A Critical Appraisal of Subsistence Homesteads.* Washington, D.C.: United States Bureau of Agricultural Economics, 1942.

Marschner, F. J. *Rural Population Density in the Southern Appalachians.* Washington, D.C.: Government Printing Office, 1940.

——. *Land Use and Its Pattern in the United States.* Washington, D.C.: United States Department of Agriculture, 1959.

McGill, Nettie P. *The Welfare of Children in Bituminous Coal Mining Communities in West Virginia.* Washington, D.C.: United States Department of Labor, Children's Bureau, 1923.

Nwanze, Kanayo F. "Viewpoint: Smallholders Can Feed the World." United Nations International Fund for Agricultural Development. 2011. www.ifad.org/documents /10180/ca86ab2d-74f0-42a5-b4b6-5e476d321619.

Peck, Millard, Bernard Frank, and Paul A. Eke. *Economic Utilization of Marginal Lands in Nicholas and Webster Counties, West Virginia.* Washington, D.C.: United States Department of Agriculture, 1932.

President's Committee on Farm Tenancy. *Report of President's Committee on Farm Tenancy.* 1937.

Reynolds, Bruce J. *Black Farmers in America, 1865–2000: The Pursuit of Independent Farming and the Role of Cooperatives.* USDA Rural Business Cooperative Service. Research Report 194. Washington, D.C.: USDA, 2002.

Roosevelt, Theodore. *Message from the President of the United States Transmitting a Report of the Secretary of Agriculture in Relation to the Forests, Rivers, and Mountains of the Southern Appalachian Region.* Washington, D.C.: Government Printing Office, 1902.

Sherman, William Tecumseh. Special Field Order, No. 15. January 16, 1865.

United Nations. Food and Agriculture Organization. *Calorie Requirements. Report of the Committee on Calorie Requirements.* FAO Nutritional Studies No. 5. Rome: FAO, 1950.

——. *FAO Statistical Yearbook.* Rome: FAO, 2011.

United States Bureau of the Census. "[Twelfth Census of the United States]." *Special Reports: Mines and Quarries: 1902.* Washington, D.C.: Government Printing Office, 1905.

——. *Thirteenth Census of the United States Taken in the Year 1910, Volume XI, Mines and Quarries.* Washington, D.C.: Government Printing Office, 1913.

——. *Fourteenth Census of the United States Taken in the Year 1920, Volume XI, Mines and Quarries.* Washington, D.C.: Government Printing Office, 1922.

——. *Fifteenth Census of the United States, Mines and Quarries: 1929.* Washington, D.C.: Government Printing Office, 1933.

——. Union District, Monongahela County, West Virginia. 1900.

——. Union District, Monongahela County, West Virginia. 1940.

United States Bureau of Indian Affairs. *Annual Report of the Commissioner of the Bureau of Indian Affairs.* Washington, D.C.: Government Printing Office, 1878.

United States Bureau of Labor. *Second Annual Report of the Commissioner of Labor, 1886. Convict Labor.* Washington, D.C.: Government Printing Office, 1887.

United States Commissioner of Patents. *Report of the Commissioner of Patents for the Year 1853: Agriculture.* Washington, D.C.: Government Printing Office, 1854.

United States Congress. *An Act repealing . . . duties heretofore laid upon distilled spirits imported from abroad, and laying others in their stead; and also upon Spirits distilled within the United States, and for appropriating the same.* First Congress, Sess. 3. 1791.

——. *American State Papers: Documents, Legislative and Executive of the Congress of the United States.* Class 3. Finance. Vol. 1. 1832.

——. *An Act to Provide for the Allotment of Lands in Severalty to Indians on the Various Reservations (General Allotment Act or Dawes Act), Statutes at Large* 24. Forty-Ninth Congress, Sess. 2. 1887.

——. Senate Committee on Education and Labor. *Conditions in the Paint Creek District, West Virginia: Hearings Before a Subcommittee of the Committee on Education and Labor.* Washington, D.C.: Government Printing Office, 1912.

——. Senate Committee on Education and Labor, Sixty-Seventh Congress, *West Virginia Coal Fields, Hearings . . . Pursuant to Senate Resolution 80.* Vol. 1. Washington, D.C.: Government Printing Office, 1921.

United States Department of Agriculture. *Report of the Commissioner of Agriculture.* Washington, D.C.: USDA, 1862.

——. *Conditions of the Southern Appalachian Mountains. Report of the Secretary of Agriculture on the Southern Appalachian and White Mountain Watersheds.* Washington, D.C.: USDA, 1908.

——. "The Place of Rye in American Agriculture." *Yearbook of the United States Department of Agriculture.* Washington, D.C.: Government Printing Office, 1918, 169–84.

——. *Economic and Social Problems and Conditions of the Southern Appalachians.* Misc. Pub. No. 205. Washington, D.C.: Government Printing Office, January 1935.

——. *Growing Rye.* Farmers' Bulletin No. 2145. Washington, D.C.: Government Printing Office, 1959.

——. Economic Research Service. Farms, Land in Farms, and Average Acres per Farm, 1850–2012. www.ers.usda.gov/data-products/chart-gallery.aspx.

United States Department of the Interior. *Agriculture of the United States in 1860; Compiled from the Original Returns of the Eighth Census.* Washington, D.C.: Government Printing Office, 1864.

——. *Manufactures of the United States in 1860; Compiled from the Original Returns of the Eighth Census.* Washington, D.C.: Government Printing Office, 1865.

——. *Annual Report of the Secretary of the Interior of the United States.* Washington, D.C.: Government Printing Office, 1874.

——. *Report on the Manufacturers of the United States at the Tenth Census.* Washington, D.C.: Government Printing Office, 1880.

——. *Report on the Productions of Agriculture . . . Tenth Census.* Washington, D.C.: Government Printing Office, 1882.

——. *General Information Concerning the Purposes and Policies of the Division of Subsistence Homesteads,* Circ. No. 1. Washington, D.C.: Government Printing Office, 1933.

United States Department of Labor. *Handbook of Labor Statistics, 1941.* Vol. 1. Washington, D.C.: Government Printing Office, 1942.

United States Department of State. *Proceedings and Documents of the United Nations Monetary and Financial Conference, Bretton Woods, New Hampshire, July 1–22, 1944.* Vol. 1. Washington, D.C.: Government Printing Office, 1948.

United States Geological Survey. *West Virginia–Pennsylvania, Morgantown Quadrangle.* 1900. Washington, D.C.: USGS, 1902.

——. *West Virginia, Charleston Quadrangle.* 1907. Washington, D.C.: USGS, 1909.

United States Library of Congress. Coal River Folklife Project Collection (AFC 1999/008), American Folklife Center, Library of Congress. www.loc.gov/collections/folklife-and-landscape-in-southern-west-virginia/about-this-collection/.

United States Supreme Court. *Wickard v. Filburn.* Vol. 317. U.S. Reports, 111. 1942.

University of Virginia Geospatial and Statistical [Census] Data Center. http://mapserver.lib.virginia.edu.

Washington, George. *Proceedings of the Executive of the United States, Respecting the Insurgents. 1794.* 1795.

Wilcox, Walter B. *Planning a Subsistence Homestead.* Washington, D.C.: United States Department of Agriculture, 1934.

World Bank. *Rural Development: Sector Policy Paper.* Washington, D.C.: The World Bank, 1975.

——. *Rising Global Interest in Farmland: Can It Yield Sustainable and Equitable Benefits?* Washington, D.C.: The World Bank, 2011.

Yarnell, Susan L. *The Southern Appalachians: A History of the Landscape.* Washington, D.C.: U.S. Dept. of Agriculture, Forest Service, 1998.

Primary Sources

Aberth, John, ed. *Black Death: The Great Mortality of 1348–1350: A Brief History with Documents.* Boston: Bedford/St. Martin's, 2005.

Adams, Edward Francis. *The Modern Farmer in His Business Relations.* 1899.

Adams, John. *Curious Thoughts on the History of Man.* 1789.

Adams, John Quincy. "Society and Civilization." *The American Review* (July 1845).

Albright, Horace Marden. *The Birth of the National Park Service: The Founding Years, 1913–1933.* Salt Lake City: Howe Brothers, 1985.

Alison, Archibald. *The Principles of Population, and their Connection with Human Happiness.* 1840.

Allen, James Lane. "Mountain Passes of the Cumberland." *Harper's Magazine* (September 1890): 561–76.

——. *The Blue-Grass Region of Kentucky.* 1892.

Alston, William. "The Wages System—Grasses." *Rural Carolinian* 1 (February 1870): 317.

American Constitutional Association. *Life in a West Virginia Coal Field.* 1923.

Anderson, John J. *A Popular School History of the United States.* 1881.

Andrews, Sidney. *The South Since the War, as Shown by Fourteen Weeks of Travel and Observation in Georgia and the Carolinas.* 1866.

Asbury, Francis. *The Journal of the Rev. Francis Asbury, Bishop of the Methodist Episcopal Church.* Vol. 2. 1821.

Austin, Oscar P. *Why Wheat Fell: A Few Facts for Farmers.* 1896.

Barnwell, Tim. *The Face of Appalachia: Portraits from the Mountain Farm.* New York: W. W. Norton, 2003.

Baylor, Francis Courtenay. *Behind the Blue Ridge: A Homely Narrative.* 1887.

Benton, Thomas Hart. "Speech of Mr. Benton, of Missouri, on the Oregon Question . . . May 22, 25, & 28, 1846." *Distant Horizon: Documents from the Nineteenth-Century American West.* Edited by Gary Noy. Lincoln: University of Nebraska Press, 1999.

Bishop, John Leader. *Address to the Freemen of the Agricultural and Manufacturing Interests of Rhode-Island.* 1829.

Blake, John Lauris. *The Modern Farmer.* 1854.

Bliss, William Dwight Porter, ed. *Encyclopedia of Social Reform.* 1897.

Boreman, Arthur I. *Inaugural Address of Governor Arthur I. Boreman, June 20, 1863.* http://www.wvculture.org/history/boremania.html.

Borsodi, Ralph. *Flight from the City: An Experiment in Creative Living on the Land.* [1933]. New York: Harper & Row, 1972.

———. "The Case Against Farming as a Big Business." [1947–1948]. *From the Land.* Edited by Nancy P. Pittman. Washington, D.C.: Island Press, 1988.

Boswell, James. *The Journal of a Tour to the Hebrides with Samuel Johnson.* 1860.

Brackenridge, Hugh Hammond. *Incident of the Western Insurrection.* 1795.

Breckinridge, Robert J. *The Civil War: Its Nature and End.* 1861.

Brissot de Warville, Jacques-Pierre. *New Travels in the United States of America, Performed in 1788.* 1797.

Brooks, Alonza Beecher. "Forestry and Wood Industries." *West Virginia Geological Survey* 5 (1910).

———. "The Present Condition of West Virginia Forest." *West Virginia State Board of Forestry, Quarterly Report . . . 1910* (1911): 30–33.

Brown, John W. *Constitutional Government Overthrown in West Virginia.* 1913.

Brzezinski, Zbigniew. "The Politics of Underdevelopment." *World Politics* 9 (October 1956): 55–75.

Buck, Solon J., and Elizabeth Hawthorn Buck. *The Planting of Civilization in Western Pennsylvania.* Pittsburgh: University of Pittsburgh Press, 1939.

Buckingham, James Silk. *The Slave States of America.* 1842.

Bush, Florence Cope. *Dorie: Woman of the Mountains.* Knoxville: University of Tennessee Press, 1992.

Butterfield, Kenyon L. *Chapters in Rural Progress.* Chicago: University of Chicago Press, 1908.

Byington, Margaret F. *Homestead: The Households of a Mill Town.* New York: Russell Sage Foundation, 1910.

Byrne, George. "Pocahontas-Flat Top Coalfield." *Manufacturers' Record* 52 (July 25, 1907).

Cahan, Abraham. "The Russian Jew in America." *Atlantic Monthly* 82 (July 1898): 128–39.

Campbell, John C. *The Southern Highlander and His Homeland.* New York: Russell Sage Foundation, 1921.

Campbell, Olive D. *The Southern Highlands.* New York: Russell Sage Foundation, 1920.

Candler, John. *Brief Notices of Hayti: With Its Condition, Resources, and Prospects.* 1842.

Carey, Henry C. *Money: A Lecture Delivered before the New York Geographical and Statistical Society.* 1857.

Cartée, Cornelius Soule. *Elements of Physical and Political Geography.* 1855.

"Census of Westmoreland County–1783." Edited by William Henry Egle. *Pennsylvania Archives*. Vol. 22. 1897.

Chamberlayne, Edward. *England's Wants*. 1667.

Chase, Stuart. "This Age of Plenty." *Harper's Magazine* (March 1934).

——. "Our Capacity to Produce." *Harper's Magazine* (February 1935).

Clark, Noble. "Will Back to the Land Help?" *Survey Graphic* 22 (September 1933).

Cobbett, William. *Advice to Young Men and (Incidentally) to Young Women in the Middle and Higher Ranks of Life in a Series of Letters, Addressed to a Youth, a Bachelor, a Lover, a Husband, a Father, a Citizen, or a Subject*. 1829.

——. *Cobbett's Legacy to Parsons; or, Have the Clergy of the Established Church an Equitable Right to the Tithes, or to any Other Thing Called Church Property . . . ?* 1845.

Coffin, Charles Carleton. "Dakota Wheat Fields." *Harper's Magazine* (March 1880).

"Col. Chappell's Address, Delivered on Saturday the 6th of July, to a Large Meeting of the Planters . . . of the Neighborhood of Columbia." *Papers Published by Order of the Agricultural Society of South Carolina*. 1818.

Colman, Henry. *The Agriculture and Rural Economy of France, Belgium, Holland and Switzerland, from Personal Observation*. 1848.

Colquhoun, Patrick. *A Treatise on the Wealth, Power, and Resources of the British Empire: The Rise and Progress of the Funding System Explained*. 1814.

Combs, Josiah Henry. *The Kentucky Highlanders from a Native Mountaineer's Viewpoint*. Lexington, Ky.: J. L. Richardson, 1913.

Cook, D. *Cook's American Arithmetic: Being a System of Decimal Arithmetic, Comporting with the Federal Currency of the United States of America*. 1800.

Cooper, Thomas R. "What Is the Problem of Mountain Agriculture?" *Mountain Life and Work*, July 1927: 13–15.

Cowan, John I. "The Hope of the Little Landers." *World's Work* 23 (November 1912): 96–100.

Coxe, Tench. *Observations on the Agriculture, Manufactures and Commerce of the United States*. 1789.

——. "A Plan for Encouraging Agriculture, and Increasing the Value of Farms in the Midland and More Western Counties of Pennsylvania." *View of the United States of America, in a Series of Papers, Written at Various Times between the Years 1787 and 1794*. 1794.

Creigh, Alfred. *History of Washington County: From Its First Settlement to the Present Time*. 1870.

Crèvecoeur, J. Hector St. John. *Letters from an American Farmer*. 1782.

Cross, Jonathan. *Five Years in the Alleghanies*. 1863.

Crowther, Samuel. *A Basis for Stability*. Boston: Little, Brown, 1932.

Cutright, William Bernard, Hu Maxwell, and Earle Amos Brooks. *The History of Upshur County, West Virginia, from Its Earliest Exploration and Settlement to the Present Time*. W.Va.: 1907.

Davies, David. *The Case of Labourers in Husbandry Stated and Considered, in Three Parts . . . ; Containing a Collection of Accounts, Shewing the Earnings and Expences of Labouring Families in Different Parts of the Kingdom.* 1795.

Davis, Hewitt. *The Effects of the Importation of Wheat upon the Profits of Farming.* 1839.

Davis, J. W. *The Wilson Carey Nicholas Survey, Patented June 25, 1795, 500,000 Acres of Land.* 1871.

Davis, John. "Eleventh Anniversary Address. Delivered Before the Officers, Members, and Friends of the American Institute . . . Oct. 18, 1838." *Journal of the American Institute* 4 (October 1838): 1–29.

Davis, John P. "A Black Inventory of the New Deal." *The Crisis* 42 (May 1935): 141–42.

Dawson, Edmund. *Spade Husbandry; or, an Attempt to Develop the Chief Causes of Pauperism and Distress.* 1833.

Debar, Joseph Hubert Diss. *The West Virginia Hand-Book and Immigrant's Guide.* 1870.

Doddridge, Joseph. *Notes on the Settlement and Indian Wars of the Western Parts of Virginia and Pennsylvania.* 1824. Edited by John S. Ritenour and William T. Lindsey. 1912.

Dodge, J. R. *West Virginia: Its Farms and Forests, Mines and Oil-Wells.* 1865.

Dondlinger, Peter Tracy. *The Book of Wheat, an Economic History and Practical Manual of the Wheat Industry.* Chicago: Orange Judd Company, 1916.

Douglas, Stephen Arnold. *Address of the Hon. Stephen A. Douglas, at the Annual Fair of the New York State Agricultural Society.* 1851.

Drucker, Peter F. "The Industrial Revolution Hits the Farmer." *Harper's Magazine* (November 1939).

Dugdale, Robert L. *The Jukes: A Study in Crime, Pauperism, Disease, and Heredity.* 1877.

Dummeier, Edwin F. *Economics, with Applications to Agriculture.* Ithaca, N.Y.: Cornell University Press, 1934.

Elliot, G. F. Scott. *The Romance of Savage Life: Describing the Life of Primitive Man.* Philadelphia: J. B. Lippincott Company, 1908.

Emerson, Ralph Waldo. "The American Scholar." 1837. *The Complete Works of Ralph Waldo Emerson.* Vol. 1. New York: Houghton, Mifflin, 1904.

——. "Farming." 1858. *The Complete Works of Ralph Waldo Emerson.* Vol. 7. New York: Houghton, Mifflin, 1904.

——. "Wealth." 1876. *The Complete Works of Ralph Waldo Emerson.* Vol. 5. New York: Houghton, Mifflin, 1880.

Engels, Friedrich. *The Condition of the Working Class in England.* 1844. First English edition, 1886. New York: Penguin, 1987.

——. "Mountain Warfare in the Past and Present." *New York Daily Tribune* (January 27, 1857).

——. *The Peasant Question in France and Germany.* 1894.

Erskine, [Emma] Payne. *The Mountain Girl.* 1911.

Everett, Alexander H. *New Ideas on Population: With Remarks on the Theories of Malthus and Godwin.* Boston: Oliver Everett, 1823.

Faulkner, Charles J. *The Speech of Charles Jas. Faulkner (of Berkeley) in the House of Delegates of Virginia.* 1832.

——. *Speech upon the Mineral and Agricultural Resources of the State of West Virginia.* 1876.

Fawcett, Henry. *Manual of Political Economy.* 1863.

Fels, Samuel S. "Planning for Purchasing Power." *Survey Graphic* 22 (April 1933): 197–207.

Fernow, Bernard. *The Great Timber Belt: The Timber of West Virginia.* 1888.

Findley, W. *History of the Insurrection: In the Four Western Counties of Pennsylvania in the Year MDCCXCIV; with a Recital of the Circumstances Specially Connected Therewith, and an Historical Review of the Previous Situation of the Country.* Philadelphia: Samuel Harrison Smith, 1796.

Flat Top Coal Land Association. *Third Annual Report of the Board of Managers of the Flat Top Coal Land Association for the year ending December 31st, 1889.* 1890.

Folck, John. *A Diary Kept by John Folck, Jr.: Containing a Journal of His Travels through the Western Part of the United States.* 1831.

Fortune, Timothy Thomas. *Black and White: Land, Labor, and Politics in the South.* 1884.

Fowler, George L. "Coals and Coal-Mining Methods of the Pocahontas Field." *Engineering Magazine* 27 (May 1904): 217–32.

——. "Social and Industrial Conditions in the Pocahontas Coal Fields." *Engineering Magazine* 27 (June 1904): 383–92.

Fox, John, Jr. *A Mountain Europa.* 1899.

——. *Blue-grass and Rhododendron: Out-doors in Old Kentucky.* New York: Scribner's, 1901.

——. "The Future Kentucky's Feuds." *Colliers* 33 (January 18, 1904): 14–15.

——. *The Heart of the Hills.* New York: Scribner's, 1913.

Franklin, Benjamin. *"Observations Concerning the Increase of Mankind, Peopling of Countries, etc."* 1751.

——. *Narrative of the Late Massacres, in Lancaster County, of a Number of Indians, Friends of this Province, by Persons Unknown.* 1764.

Franklin, James. *The Present State of Hayti (Saint Domingo): With Remarks on Its Agriculture, Commerce, Laws, Religion, Finances and Population, etc. etc.* 1828.

Frost, William Goodell. "University Extension in Kentucky." *Outlook* (September 1898): 72.

——. "Our Contemporary Ancestors in the Southern Mountains." *Atlantic Monthly* (March 1899).

George, J. E. "The Coal Miners' Strike of 1897." *Quarterly Journal of Economics* 12 (January 1898): 186.

Goodrich, Frances Louisa. *Mountain Homespun.* New Haven: Yale University Press, 1931.

Grattan, C. H. "The Vine-Covered Factory Worker." *Harper's Magazine* (January 1946): 67.

Grattan, Peachy R. *Reports of Cases Decided in the Supreme Court of Appeals of Virginia*, 13. 1902.

Gray, L. C. "Economic Conditions and Tendencies in the Southern Appalachians as Indicated by the Cooperative Survey." *Mountain Life and Work* (July 1933): 7–12.

Greeley, Horace. *Essays Designed to Elucidate the Science of Political Economy, while Serving to Explain and Defend the Policy of Protection to Home Industry as a System of National Cooperation for True Elevation of Labor.* 1870.

Guernsey, Alfred H. "Our Farmers." *Harper's Magazine* (November 1860): 835–40.

Gummere, Francis Barton. *Germanic Origins. A Study in Primitive Culture.* New York: C. Scribner's Sons, 1892.

Hacker, Louis M. "Plowing the Farmer Under." *Harper's Magazine* (June 1934).

Hale, John Peter. *Trans-Allegheny Pioneers; Historical Sketches of the First White Settlements West of the Alleghenies.* 1886.

Hall, Bolton. *Three Acres and Liberty.* New York: Macmillan, 1907.

Hall, Granville Davisson. *The Rending of Virginia.* Chicago: Mayer & Miller, 1902.

Hamilton, Alexander. *The Works of Alexander Hamilton: Comprising His Correspondence, and His Political and Official Writings, Exclusive of the Federalist, Civil and Military.* Edited by John C. Hamilton. 1851.

——. *The Papers of Alexander Hamilton.* Edited by Harold C. Syrett. Vols. 2, 5. New York: Columbia University Press, 1962.

——. *Writings.* New York: Library of America, 2001.

Hamilton, Alexander, James Madison, and John Jay. *The Federalist.* 1788.

Haney, William H. *The Mountain People of Kentucky. An Account of Present Conditions with the Attitude of the People Toward Improvement.* Cincinnati, OH: Robert Clark Co., 1906.

Hariot, Thomas. *A Brief and True Report of the New found Land of Virginia.* 1588.

Harney, Will Wallace. "A Strange Land and a Peculiar People." *Lippincott's Magazine* (October 1873): 429–32.

Harriman, Henry I. "Factory and Farm in Double Harness." *New York Times* (October 15, 1933).

Hartlib, Samuel. *The Reformed Husband-man.* 1651.

——. *Samuel Hartlib His Legacy of Husbandry. Wherein are Bequeathed to the Common-Wealth of England.* 1655.

Herskovits, Melville J. *Economic Anthropology: A Study in Comparative Economics.* New York: Alfred A. Knopf, 1952.

Hill, Forrest F. "The Human Factor in Economic Development." *World Politics* 9 (October 14, 1957).

Hill, George Canning. *Daniel Boone: Pioneer of Kentucky.* 1859.

Holmes, George Frederick. "Population and Capital." *De Bow's Review* 21 (September 1856).

Home, Henry (Lord Kames). *Sketches of the History of Man.* New ed. 1813.

Homer, Winslow. *Veteran in a New Field.* 1865. Metropolitan Museum of Art, New York City.

Hovenden, Thomas. *Breaking Home Ties.* 1890. Philadelphia Museum of Art.

Howlett, John. *Enclosures, a Cause of Improved Agriculture, of Plenty and Cheapness of Provisions, of Population, and of both Private and National Wealth.* 1787.

Hoyle, William. *Our National Resources: And How They Are Wasted.* 1871.

Hubbard, William. *A General History of New England.* 1848.

Huntington, Ellsworth, Frank Ernest Williams, and Samuel Van Valkenburg. *Economic and Social Geography.* New York: J. Wiley & Sons, 1933.

Idleman, D. W. *History of the Mt. Storm Community.* 1927.

Imlay, G. *A Topographical Description of the Western Territory of North America Containing a Succinct Account of Its Soil, Climate, Natural History, Population, Agriculture, Manners, and Customs.* 1797.

Inness, George. *Short Cut, Watchung Station, New Jersey.* 1883. Philadelphia Museum of Art.

Inness, George, Jr., *Life, Art, and Letters of George Inness.* New York: Century, 1917.

Institution for Pro-Poor Growth. *Agribusiness Versus Household Farming in the Office Du Niger.* Briefing Paper No. 14. October 2017. www.ippg.org.uk/papers/bp14.pdf.

Ioor, William. *Independence; Or Which Do You Like Best, the Peer, or the Farmer?* 1805.

Irving, Washington. *Knickerbocker.* 1839.

Ise, John. "What Is Rural Economics?" *Quarterly Journal of Economics* 34 (November 1919): 300–12.

Jardine, L. J. *A Letter from Pennsylvania to a Friend in England: Containing Valuable Information with Respect to America.* 1795.

Jefferson, Thomas. *Notes on the State of Virginia.* 1787.

Johnson, Samuel. *A Journey to the Western Islands of Scotland.* 1795.

Jones, Mary Harris. *Autobiography of Mother Jones.* Chicago: 1925.

Julian, George Washington. *Speeches on Political Questions.* 1872.

Kains, Maurice G. *Five Acres and Independence: A Practical Guide to the Selection and Management of the Small Farm.* New York: Greenberg, 1940.

Kane, Robert. *The Industrial Resources of Ireland.* 1845.

Kellie, Luna. "Stand Up for Kansas." *A Prairie Populist: The Memoirs of Luna Kellie.* Edited by Jane Taylor Nelsen. Iowa City: University of Iowa Press, 1992.

Kellogg, Paul Underwood. *The Pittsburgh Survey: Findings in Six Volumes.* New York: Russell Sage Foundation, 1914.

Kephart, Horace. *Our Southern Highlanders.* New York: Outing Publishing Company, 1913.

Kidd, Benjamin. *Social Evolution.* 1894.

——. *The Control of the Tropics.* 1898.

Kile, Orville Merton. *The New Agriculture.* Ithaca, N.Y.: Cornell University Press, 1932.

King, Edward. *The Great South: A Record of Journeys.* 1875.

Lanman, Charles. *Letters from the Alleghany Mountains.* 1849.

La Vía Campesina. "Sustainable Peasant and Family Farm Agriculture Can Feed the World." 2010. http://viacampesina.org/en/index.php/publications-mainmenu-30/1017 -sustainable-peasant-and-family-farm-agriculture-can-feed-the-world.

Leighty, Clyde E. "The Place of Rye in American Agriculture." *Yearbook of the United States Department of Agriculture* (1918), 169–84.

Leland, John. *Joannis Lelandi: Antiquarii De Rebus Britannicis Collectanea.* Vol. 6. Edited by Thomas Hearne. 1774.

Lewis, Virgil A., ed. *How West Virginia Was Made: Proceedings of the First Convention of the People of Northwestern Virginia . . . at Wheeling, May 13, 14 and 15, 1861.* 1909.

Liebig, Justus. *Organic Chemistry in Its Applications to Agriculture and Physiology.* 1840.

Liebig, Justus, and John Gardner. *Familiar Letters on Chemistry, and Its Relation to Commerce, Physiology and Agriculture.* 1843.

Liebig, Justus, and Lyon Playfair. *Chemistry in Its Application to Agriculture and Physiology.* 1842.

Lincoln, Abraham. *Abraham Lincoln: A Documentary Portrait Through His Speeches and Writings.* Edited by Don E. Fehrenbacher. Stanford, Calif.: Stanford University Press, 1964.

Linn, John B., and William H. Egle, eds. "Deduction of Clear and Precise Account of the Condition of the South River . . . Received 28 January 1656." *Pennsylvania Archives.* Vol. 5. 1877.

List, Friedrich. *Speech, Delivered at the Philadelphia Manufacturers' Dinner, Nov. 3 1827.* 1827.

———. *The National System of Political Economy.* 1841.

Lorain, John. *Nature and Reason Harmonized in the Practice of Husbandry.* 1825.

Lynch, Lawrence R. "The West Virginia Coal Strike," *Political Science Quarterly* 29 (1914): 630–37.

MacCorkle, William A. *Biennial Message of Governor William A. MacCorkle, to the Legislature of West Virginia, Session of 1897.* 1897.

———. *Public Papers of Governor William A. MacCorkle, of West Virginia.* 1897.

———. *Recollections of Fifty Years of West Virginia.* 1928.

Madison, James. "Address Before the Agricultural Society of Albemarle" (May 12, 1818).

Malthus, Thomas Robert. *An Essay on the Principle of Population as it Affects the Future Improvement of Society.* 1798.

Mandel, Sherman, and Thomas R. Henry. *Hollow Folk.* New York: Thomas Y. Crowell Company, 1933.

Mandeville, Bernard. *The Fable of the Bees.* 1714.

Marshall, C. *A Practical Introduction to Arithmetic.* 1789.

Martin, Lawrence, and Sylvia Martin. "Four Strong Men and a President: A Central-American Group Portrait." *Harper's Magazine* (September 1942).

Marx, Karl. *Economic and Philosophic Manuscripts of 1844*. Translated by Martin Milligan. New York: Progress Publishers, 1959.

——. *The Eighteenth Brumaire of Louis Napoleon*. 1852.

——. *Capital: A Critique of Political Economy*. Vol. 1. Translated by Ben Fowkes. 1867. New York: Penguin, 1990.

——. *Capital: A Critique of Political Economy*. Vol. 3. Edited by Frederick Engels. Translated by David Fernbach. 1894. New York: Penguin, 1993.

Marx, Karl, and Friedrich Engels. "The Manifesto of the Communist Party." 1848. *The Communist Manifesto*. Translated by Samuel Moore. New York: Penguin Classics, 2002.

Maury, Matthew, and William Morris Fontaine. *Resources of West Virginia*. 1876.

Maury, Matthew Fontaine, and Thomas S. Ridgway. *Map Showing the Economic Minerals Along the Route of the Chesapeake & Ohio Rail Way to Accompany the Geological Report of Thomas S. Ridgway*. 1872. http://hdl.loc.gov/loc.gmd/g3881h.rr003650.

Mayer, Brantz. "A June Jaunt; With Some Wanderings in the Footsteps of Washington, Braddock, and the Early Pioneers." *Harper's Magazine* (April 1857).

McCrady, Edward. *History of South Carolina in the Revolution*. New York: Macmillan Co., 1902.

McNeill, G. D. *The Last Forest: Tales of the Allegheny Woods*. 1940. Parsons, W.Va.: McClain Printing, 1989.

Miles, Emma Bell. "The Common Lot." *Harper's Magazine* (December 1908).

Mitchell, Elisha. *Diary of a Geological Tour by Dr. Elisha Mitchell in 1827 and 1828*. 1905.

Mombert, Jacob I. *An Authentic History of Lancaster County: In the State of Pennsylvania*. 1869.

More, Hannah. *The Works of Hannah More*. 1840.

More, Thomas. *Utopia*. 1551.

Morgan, Arthur E. " 'Group Industries' Problems and Their Solution." 1933.

Morris, Edmund. *Ten Acres Enough: A Practical Experience*. 1864.

Morris, Homer Lawrence. *Plight of the Bituminous Coal Miner*. New York: Oxford University Press, 1934.

Murfee, Mary Noailles [Charles Egbert Craddock]. *In the Tennessee Mountains*. 1885.

Myers, Grace Funk. *"Them Missionary Women," Or Work in the Southern Mountains*. 1911.

Naper, J.L.W. *Suggestions for the More Scientific and General Employment of Agricultural Labourers*. 1844.

Nearing, Helen, and Scott Nearing. *The Good Life: Helen and Scott Nearing's Sixty Years of Self-Sufficient Living*. [1954]. New York: Schocken Books, 1970.

Nicholls, W.D.J., and Z. L. Galloway. "Family Incomes and Land Utilization in Knox County." *Kentucky Agricultural Experiment Station Bulletin*. No. 375. 1937.

Nieboer, H. J. *Slavery as an Industrial System: Ethnological Researches*. The Hague: Martinus Nijhoff, 1900.

Norris, Frank. *The Pit*. New York: Doubleday, Page & Co., 1903.

Nourse, Edwin G. "The Place of Agriculture in Modern Industrial Society II," *Journal of Political Economy* 27 (July 1919): 561–77.

Oil-Dorado of West Virginia: A Full Description of the Great Mineral Resources of West Virginia, the Kanawha Valley, and the Country between the Ohio, the Hughes, and the Kanawha River. 1865.

Olmsted, Frederick Law. *A Journey in the Back Country.* 1861.

O'Sullivan, John L. "Growth of States." *Democratic Review* 22 (May 1848).

O'Toole, Edward. "Colliery Yards and Gardens." *Coal Age* 2 (August 10, 1912).

Owen, Robert. "On Spade Husbandry." *The Economist . . . the New System of Society* (August 18 and 25, 1821).

Paine, Thomas. *Agrarian Justice.* 1797.

Parmelee, Maurice. *Farewell to Poverty.* 1935.

Parsons, Charles Grandison. *Inside View of Slavery; or, A Tour Among the Planters.* 1855.

Peck, Millard. "Farm or Forest in the West Virginia Appalachians?" *Journal of Farm Economics* 11 (July 1929): 422.

Perdue, Theda, and Michael D. Green, eds. *The Cherokee Removal: A Brief History with Documents.* New York: Bedford/St. Martin's, 2005.

Periam, Jonathan. *The Groundswell. A History of the Origin, Aims, and Progress of the Farmers' Movement: Embracing an Authoritative Account of Farmers' Clubs, Granges.* 1874.

Peters, Alfred. "The Depreciation of Farming Land." *Quarterly Journal of Economics* 4 (October 1889): 18–26.

Petition of the Inhabitants of Westmorland County—Excise on Liquors—1790. John B. Linn and William H. Egle, eds. *Pennsylvania Archives.* Vol. 11. 1880.

Pinchot, Gifford. *Breaking New Ground.* New York: Harcourt, Brace and Co., 1947.

Polk, Leonidas L. *Agricultural Depression. Its Causes—the Remedy. Speech of L. L. Polk, President of the National Farmers' Alliance and Industrial Union, Before the Senate Committee on Agriculture and Forestry. April 22, 1890.* 1890.

Pollard, Edward. *The Virginia Tourist: Sketches of the Springs and Mountains of Virginia.* 1870.

"The Poor Man's Garden." *Cottager's Monthly Visitor* 10 (1830): 175–79.

Price, Richard. *Observations on Reversionary Payments.* Vol. 2. 1812.

Prospectus of the West Virginia Iron Mining and Manufacturing Company, Incorporated by the Legislature of Virginia, March 15, 1837. 1837.

Proudhon, Pierre-Joseph. *What Is Property?* 1840. Translated by Benjamin R. Tucker. 1890.

R.E.C. "The Problem of Free Society." *Southern Literary Messenger* (July 1858): 401–18.

Raine, James Watt. *The Land of Saddle-Bags: A Study of the Mountain People of Appalachia.* 1924.

Reeve, James K. "Agriculture as a Profession." *Harper's Magazine* (May 1889).

Rice, Millard Milburn. "Footnote on Arthurdale." *Harper's Magazine* (March 1940).

Rideing, William H. "How New York Is Fed." *Scribner's Monthly* 14 (October 1877).

Robinson, Neil. "Anecdotes of the Mountain Folk." *Coal Age* 4 (December 20, 1913): 930–32.

Rochester, Anna. *Why Farmers Are Poor: The Agricultural Crisis in the United States*. New York: International Publishers, 1940.

Rölvaag, E. O. *Giants in the Earth*. [1927]. New York: HarperCollins, 1991.

Roosevelt, Eleanor. "Subsistence Farmsteads." *Forum* 91 (April 1934): 199–201.

Ross, Edward Alsworth. *What Is America?* New York: The Century Co., 1919.

——. "Pocketed Americans." *New Republic* (January 9 and January 23, 1924).

Ross, Malcolm. *Machine Age in the Hills*. New York: Macmillan Company, 1933.

Rothert, Otto A. "John D. Shane's Interview with Pioneer John Hedge, Bourbon County." *Filson Club Historical Quarterly* 14 (July 1940): 176–81.

Rousseau, Jean-Jacques. *The Social Contract*. 1762.

Rowland, Dunbar, ed. *The Mississippi Territorial Archives, 1798–1803, Executive Journals of Governor Winthrop Sargent and Governor William Charles Cole Claiborne*. Vol. 1. Nashville, Tenn.: Press of Brandon Printing Company, 1905.

Rush, Benjamin. *An Account of the Manners of the German Inhabitants of Pennsylvania*. 1789.

——. *Essays, Literary, Moral & Philosophical*. Philadelphia: 1798.

Saint-Pierre, Bernadin de. *Voyage to the Isle of France, to Isle of Bourbon, and the Cape of Good Hope; with Observations and Reflections upon Nature and Mankind*. 1775.

Savage, James Woodruff. *A Farmer's Life: An Address Delivered at Omaha, September 22, 1880, during the Nebraska State Fair*. 1880.

Say, Jean-Baptiste. *A Treatise on Political Economy: Or, the Production, Distribution, and Consumption of Wealth*. 1880.

Schöpf, Johann David. *Travels in the Confederation [1783–1784]*. Philadelphia: William J. Campbell, 1911.

Semple, Ellen Churchill. *Anglo-Saxons of the Kentucky Mountains: A Study in Anthropogeography*. 1910.

Shaw, Nate [Ned Cobb], and Theodore Rosengarten. *All God's Dangers: The Life of Nate Shaw*. Chicago: University of Chicago Press, 1974.

Shea, John P. "Our Pappies Burned the Woods." *American Forests* 46 (April 1940).

Sherman, Mandel, and Thomas R. Henry. *Hollow Folk*. New York: Thomas Y. Crowell, 1933.

Simms, William Gilmore. *The Sword and the Distaff*. 1853.

Simpson, Stephen. *The Working Man's Manual: A New Theory of Political Economy, on the Principle of Production the Source of Wealth*. 1831.

Sinclair, John. *Specimens of Statistical Reports; Exhibiting the Progress of Political Society, from the Pastoral State, to that of Luxury and Refinement*. 1793.

——. *Observations on the Means of Enabling a Cottager to Keep a Cow: By the Produce of a Small Piece of Land*. 1801.

——. *Essays on Miscellaneous Subjects*. 1802.

Skidmore, Hubert. *I Will Lift Up Mine Eyes*. New York: Doubleday, 1936.

Slater, T. F. *The Rough Notes of a Farmer during an Agricultural Tour through Russia, Prussia, Denmark and Sweden*. 1842.

Smith, Adam. *Lectures on Jurisprudence*. [1763]. Glasgow Edition of the Works of Adam Smith. Vol. 5. Edited by Ronald L. Meek, David Daiches Raphael, and Peter G. Stein. London: Oxford University Press, 1978.

———. *Inquiry into the Nature and Causes of the Wealth of Nations*. [1776]. New York: Bantam, 2003.

Smith, J. Russell. "Farming Appalachia." *The American Review of Reviews* 53 (March 1916): 529–36.

———. *The World's Food Resources*. New York: Henry Holt, 1919.

———. *North America: Its People and the Resources, Development, and Prospects of the Continent as an Agricultural, Industrial, and Commercial Area*. New York: Harcourt, Brace and Company, 1925.

Smith, James Allen. *The Spirit of American Government: A Study of the Constitution: Its Origin, Influence and Relation to Democracy*. New York: Macmillan, 1907.

Steuart, James. *An Inquiry into the Principles of Political Economy*. Vol. 1. [1767]. 1770.

———. *An Inquiry into the Principles of Political Economy*. Vol. 2. 1796.

Still, James. *River of Earth*. New York: Viking Press, 1940.

"Stirred Up by Henry Ford's 'Shotgun Gardens.'" *Literary Digest* (September 12, 1931).

Strickland, W[illiam]. *Journal of a Tour in the United States of America, 1794–1795*. New York Historical Society, 1971.

Strickland, William. *Observations on the Agriculture of the United States*. 1801.

Summers, George W. *The Mountain State: A Description of the Natural Resources of West Virginia*. Board of World's Fair Managers for West Virginia, 1893.

Swann, John S. *Map of the Coal Field of the Great Kanawha Valley West Virginia*. 1867.

Tate, Leland B. "Possibilities and Limitations of Subsistence Homesteads." *Journal of Farm Economics* 15 (July 1934): 530–33.

Taylor, C. F. *Land Question from various Points of View. A Study in Search of the Highest Truth and Best Policy, and Not a Propaganda Print*. 1898.

Taylor, Henry Charles. *An Introduction to the Study of Agricultural Economics*. New York: Macmillan, 1905.

Taylor, James. *Alleghania: A Geographical and Statistical Memoir. Exhibiting the Strength of the Union, and the Weakness of Slavery, in the Mountain Districts of the South*. 1862.

Taylor, Paul Schuster. "Good-by to the Homestead Farm: The Machines Advance in the Corn Belt." *Harper's Magazine* (May 1941): 589–97.

Taylor, Richard Cowling. *Statistics of Coal: The Geographical and Geological Distribution of Mineral Combustibles Or Fossil Fuel, Including, also, Notices and Localities of the various Mineral Bituminous Substances, Employed in Arts and Manufactures . . . Embracing, from Official Reports of the Great Coal-Producing Countries, the Respective Amounts of their Pro-*

duction, Consumption and Commercial Distribution, in all Parts of the World; Together with their Prices, Tariffs, Duties and International Regulations. 1848.

"Terrible Accident at the Midlothian Coal Pits." *Virginia Free Press* (December 25, 1856).

Thompson, C. W. "The Movement of Wheat-Growing: A Study of a Leading State." *Quarterly Journal of Economics* 18 (August 1, 1904).

Thompson, Samuel Hunter. *The Highlanders of the South*. 1910.

Thoreau, Henry David. *Walden*. [1854]. Edited by Jeffrey S. Cramer. New Haven: Yale University Press, 2006.

Thünen, Johann Heinrich Von. *Der Isolierte Staat*. 1826.

Thwaites, Reuben Gold, and Louise Phelps Kellogg, eds. *Documentary History of Dunmore's War, 1774*. Madison: Wisconsin Historical Society, 1905.

Tocqueville, Alexis de. *Democracy in America*. Vol. 1. [1835]. Edited by Harvey C. Mansfield and Delba Winthrop. Chicago: University of Chicago Press, 2000.

——. "A Fortnight in the Wilderness." *Memoirs, Letters, and Remains*. Vol. 1. 1861.

Toulmin, Harry. "The Western Country in 1793: Reports on Kentucky and Virginia." Edited by Godfrey Davies and Marion Tinling. San Marino, Calif.: Huntington Library, 1948.

Townsend, Joseph. *A Dissertation on the Poor Laws*. [1817]. Berkeley: University of California Press, 1971.

Toynbee, Arnold J. *A Study of History, Abridgement of Volumes I–VI*. Edited by D. C. Somervell. New York: Oxford University Press, 1946.

Turgot, Anne Robert Jacques. *Reflections on the Formation and Distribution of Wealth*. London, 1793.

Turner, Frederick Jackson. *The Frontier in American History*. New York: Henry Holt, 1921.

Twelve Southerners. *I'll Take My Stand: The South and the Agrarian Tradition*. [1930]. Baton Rouge: Louisiana State University Press, 2006.

Twiss, Travers. *View of the Progress of Political Economy in Europe since the Sixteenth Century*. 1847.

Urquhart, David. *Familiar Words: The Character of Englishmen and the Fate of England*. 1855.

Van Dyke, Henry, Jr. "The Red River of the North." *Harper's Magazine* (May 1880): 801–18.

Van Ruyvan, Cornelis. "Appendix 5. Received 28 January, 1656. Secret." Edited by John B. Linn and William H. Egle. *Pennsylvania Archives*. Vol. 5. 1877.

Vance, J. D. *Hillbilly Elegy: A Memoir of a Family and Culture in Crisis*. New York: HarperCollins, 2016.

Vance, Rupert Bayless. *Human Geography of the South; A Study in Regional Resources and Human Adequacy*. Chapel Hill: University of North Carolina Press, 1932.

Veblen, Thorstein B. "The Price of Wheat Since 1867." *Journal of Political Economy* 1 (December 1892): 68–103.

Victor, Orville J. *History of American Conspiracies; a Record of Treason, Insurrection, Rebellion, &c., in the United States of America, from 1760 to 1860.* 1863.

Vincent, George E. "A Retarded Frontier." *American Journal of Sociology* 4 (July 1898): 1–20.

Wakefield, Edward Gibbon. *A View of the Art of Colonization, with Present Reference to the British Empire.* 1849.

Walker, Francis Amasa. *The Indian Question.* 1874.

———. *The Wages Question: A Treatise on Wages and the Wages Class.* 1876.

Ware, Harold M., and Webster Powell. "Planning for Permanent Poverty." *Harper's Magazine* (April 1935).

Washington, George. *Washington-Crawford letters. Being the correspondence between George Washington and William Crawford, from 1767 to 1781, concerning western lands . . . containing later letters of Washington on the same subject; and letters from Valentine Crawford to Washington, written in 1774 and 1775.* 1877.

———. *Diaries of George Washington.* Vol. 4. Edited by Donald Jackson and Dorothy Twohig. Charlottesville: University of Virginia Press, 1978.

———. *Papers of George Washington.* Vol. 16. Edited by David R. Hoth and Carol S. Ebel. Charlottesville: University of Virginia Press, 2011.

Wells, David A. *Recent Economic Changes and their Effect on the Production and Distribution of Wealth.* 1899.

West Virginia Mining and Manufacturing Company. *Prospectus of the West Virginia Mining and Manufacturing Company.* 1838.

Weston, George M. *The Poor Whites of the South.* 1856.

Wheaton, Henry, ed. *Taylor v Walton and Hundly. Reports of Cases Argued and Adjudged in the Supreme Court of the United States. February Term, 1816.* Vol. 1. 1816.

White, Edwin Elverton. *Highland Heritage; the Southern Mountains and the Nation.* New York: Friendship Press, 1937.

White, William Allen. "The Business of a Wheat Farm." *Scribner's Magazine* 22 (November 1897).

Wilder, Laura Ingalls. *Little House in the Big Woods.* [1932]. New York: HarperTrophy, 1971.

Wiley, Samuel T. *History of Preston County, West Virginia.* 1882.

———. *History of Monongalia County, West Virginia.* 1883.

Willey, William P. *An Inside View of the Formation of the State of West Virginia.* 1901.

Williams, David. *Lectures on Political Principles.* 1789.

Wilson, M. L. "The Place of Subsistence Homesteads in Our National Economy." *Journal of Farm Economics* 16 (January 1934): 73–84.

Winstanley, Gerrard. *A DECLARATION FROM THE Poor oppressed People OF ENGLAND, DIRECTED To all that call themselves, or are called Lords of Manors, through this NATION; That have begun to cut, or that through fear and covetousness, do intend to cut down the Woods and Trees that grow upon the Commons and Waste Land.* 1649.

Withers, Alexander Scott, William Powers, and William Hacker. *Chronicles of Border Warfare; or, A History of the Settlement by the Whites, of North-Western Virginia and of the Indian Wars and Massacres.* 1831.

Woodbury, Levi. "Speech of Senator Levi Woodbury." *Appendix to the Congressional Globe.* 27th Congress, 3rd Session, January 1843.

Young, Arthur. *Annals of Agriculture.* Vol. 1. 1790.

Zeuch, William E. "The Subsistence Homestead Problem from the Viewpoint of an Economist." *Journal of Farm Economics* 17 (November 1935): 710–20.

Ziliak, James P. "The Appalachian Regional Development Act and Economic Change," unpublished report (University of Kentucky). http://www.irp.wisc.edu/newsevents /workshops/2011/participants/papers/12-Ziliak.pdf.

Zimmerman, Carle C. "Discussion." *Journal of Farm Economics* 16 (January 1934): 84–87.

Zinn, William. *The Story of Woodbine Farm.* Buckhannon, W.Va.: 1931.

Secondary Sources

Achenbach, Joel. *The Grand Idea: George Washington's Potomac and the Race to the West.* New York: Simon & Schuster, 2004.

Acheson, James M. *Capturing the Commons: Devising Institutions to Manage the Maine Lobster Industry.* Hanover, N.H.: University Press of New England, 2003.

Agnew, Jean-Christophe. "The Threshold of Exchange: Speculations on the Market." *Radical History Review* 21 (1980): 99–118.

Anderson, Benedict. *Imagined Communities: Reflections on the Origin and Spread of Nationalism.* Rev. ed. New York: Verso, 2006.

Anglin, Mary K. *Women, Power, and Dissent in the Hills of Carolina.* Urbana: University of Illinois Press, 2002.

Appleby, Joyce Oldham. *Economic Thought and Ideology in Seventeenth-Century England.* [1978]. Los Angeles: Figueroa Press, 2004.

Arnold, David. "Europe, Technology, and Colonialism in the 20th Century." *History and Technology* 21 (2005).

Arnold, Roger A. *Principles of Economics.* New York: Cengage Learning, 2011.

Aron, Stephen. *How the West Was Lost: The Transformation of Kentucky from Daniel Boone to Henry Clay.* Baltimore: Johns Hopkins University Press, 1996.

Arrighi, Giovanni, and John Saul. "Socialism and Economic Development in Tropical Africa." *Journal of Modern African Studies* 6 (August 1968): 141–69.

Attwood, Donald W. *Raising Cane: The Political Economy of Sugar in Western India.* Boulder, Colo.: Westview Press, 1992.

Bailey, Rebecca J. *Matewan Before the Massacre: Politics, Coal, and the Roots of Conflict in a West Virginia Mining Community.* Morgantown: West Virginia University Press, 2008.

Barnett, Barry J. "The U.S. Farm Financial Crisis of the 1980s." *Agricultural History* 74 (Spring 2000), 366–80.

Barns, William D. *The West Virginia State Grange: The First Century, 1873–1973.* Morgantown, W.Va.: Morgantown Printing and Binding, 1973.

Batey, Mavis. "Nuneham Courtenay: An Oxfordshire 18th Century Deserted Village." *Oxoniensia* 33 (1968): 108–24.

Batteau, Allen W. *The Invention of Appalachia.* Tucson: University of Arizona Press, 1990.

Baumol, William J., and Alan S. Blinder. *Economics: Principles and Policy.* 3rd ed. New York: Harcourt Brace Jovanovich, 1985.

Becker, Jane S. *Selling Tradition: Appalachia and the Construction of an American Folk, 1930–1940.* Chapel Hill: University of North Carolina Press, 1998.

Beckwith, Christopher I. *Empires of the Silk Road: Central Eurasia from the Bronze Age to the Present.* Princeton, N.J.: Princeton University Press, 2009.

Behringer, Wolfgang. *Cultural History of Climate.* Translated by Patrick Camiller. Malden, Mass.: Polity, 2010.

Bell, Adrienne Baxter. *George Inness: Writings and Reflections on Art and Philosophy.* New York: George Braziller, 2006.

Bennett, Judith M. *A Medieval Life: Cecilia Penifader of Brigstock.* Boston: McGraw-Hill College, 1999.

Biggers, Jeff. *The United States of Appalachia: How Southern Mountaineers Brought Independence, Culture, and Enlightenment to America.* Berkeley, Calif.: Counterpoint, 2005.

Billings, Dwight B., and Kathleen M. Blee. *The Road to Poverty: The Making of Wealth and Hardship in Appalachia.* New York: Cambridge University Press, 2000.

Bisson, Thomas. *The Crisis of the Twelfth Century: Power, Lordship, and the Origins of European Government.* Princeton, N.J.: Princeton University Press, 2009.

Black, Dan A., Mark Mather, and Seth G. Sanders. "Standards of Living in Appalachia, 1960 to 2000." Appalachian Regional Commission, 2007.

Blackmar, Elizabeth. "A Speculative Essay on the History of American Land Speculation." Manuscript.

Blum, Deborah. "Our Toxicity Experiment in West Virginia." *Wired* (January 18, 2014). http://www.wired.com/wiredscience/2014/01/chemistry-experiments-west -virginia-dont-try-home/.

Bogue, Allan. "The Iowa Claim Clubs: Symbol and Substance." *Mississippi Valley Historical Review* 45 (September 1958): 231–53.

Bonner, James C. "Profile of a Late Ante-Bellum Community." *American Historical Review* 49 (July 1944): 663–80.

Bonsteel Tachau, Mary K. "The Whiskey Rebellion in Kentucky: A Forgotten Episode of Civil Disobedience." *Journal of the Early Republic* 2 (Autumn 1982): 239–59.

Borras, Saturnino M., Jr., Ruth Hall, Ian Scoones, Ben White, and Wendy Wolford. "Towards a Better Understanding of Global Land Grabbing: An Editorial Introduction." *Journal of Peasant Studies* 38 (2011): 209–16.

Boserup, Ester. *The Conditions of Agricultural Growth: The Economics of Agrarian Change Under Population Pressure.* London: Aldine Publishing Company, 1965.

Bouton, Terry. "A Road Closed: Rural Insurgency in Post-Independence Pennsylvania." *Journal of American History* 87 (December 2000): 855–87.

——. *Taming Democracy: "The People," the Founders, and the Troubled Ending of the American Revolution*. New York: Oxford University Press, 2007.

Braidwood, Robert J. *Prehistoric Men*. Chicago: Natural History Museum, 1948.

Braudel, Fernand. *Afterthoughts on Material Civilization and Capitalism*. Baltimore: Johns Hopkins University Press, 1977.

——. *The Structures of Everyday Life: Civilization and Capitalism, 15th–18th Century*. Vol. 1. New York: Harper & Row, 1979.

——. *Civilization and Capitalism*. Vol. 1. *The Structures of Everyday Life*. Translated by Siân Reynolds. Berkeley: University of California Press, 1992.

——. Vol. 2. *The Wheels of Commerce*. Translated by Siân Reynolds. London: Phoenix Press, 2002.

——. Vol. 3. *The Perspective of the World*. Translated by Siân Reynolds. London: Phoenix Press, 2002.

Braund, Kathryn E. Holland. *Deerskins and Duffels: The Creek Indian Trade with Anglo-America, 1685–1815*. Lincoln: University of Nebraska Press, 1993.

Brautigam, Deborah. *Will Africa Feed China?* New York: Oxford University Press, 2015.

Brenner, Robert. "Agrarian Class Structure and Economic Development in Pre-Industrial Europe." *Past and Present* 70 (February 1976): 30–75.

——. "The Social Basis of Economic Development." *Analytical Marxism*. Edited by John Roemer. New York: Cambridge University Press, 1986, 23–53.

Brewer, Anthony. "Adam Smith's Stages of History." Discussion Paper No. 08/601. Department of Economics, University of Bristol. March 2008.

Brooke, John L. *Climate Change and the Course of Global History*. New York: Cambridge University Press, 2014.

Brooks, Alonza B. *Forestry and Wood Industries*. Morgantown, W.Va.: ACME Publishing for the West Virginia Geological Survey, 1910.

Brooks, Sara. *You May Plow Here*. New York: W. W. Norton, 1986.

Buck, Solon, and Elizabeth Buck. *The Planting of Civilization in Western Pennsylvania*. Pittsburgh: University of Pittsburgh Press, 1976.

Bulgakov, Sergei. *Philosophy of Economy: The World as Household*. Translated by Catherine Evtuhov. New Haven, Conn.: Yale University Press, 2000.

Burchardt, Jeremy. *The Allotment Movement in England, 1793–1873*. London: Royal Historical Society, 2002.

Bush, Florence Cope. *Dorie: Woman of the Mountains*. Knoxville: University of Tennessee Press, 1992.

Cahill, Kevin J. "Fertilizing the Weeds: The New Deal's Rural Poverty Program in West Virginia." Ph.D. dissertation, West Virginia University, 1999.

Callahan, Richard J., Jr. *Work and Faith in the Kentucky Coal Fields: Subject to Dust*. Bloomington: Indiana University Press, 2009.

Cammack, Paul. "What the World Bank Means by Poverty Reduction, and Why It Matters." *New Political Economy* 9 (June 2004): 189–211.

Carlyle, Thomas. "Signs of the Times." *A Carlyle Reader.* Edited by G. B. Tennyson. New York: Cambridge University Press, 1984.

Cayton, Andrew R. *The Frontier Republic: Ideology and Politics in the Ohio Country, 1780–1825.* Kent, Ohio: Kent State University Press, 1986.

Chayanov, A. V. *Theory of Peasant Economy.* Translated by Daniel Thorner, Basile Kerblay, and R.E.F. Smith. Madison: University of Wisconsin Press, 1986.

Chernow, Ron. *Alexander Hamilton.* New York: Penguin, 2004.

Chevalier, Jacques M. "There Is Nothing Simple About Simple Commodity Production." *Journal of Peasant Studies* 10 (1983).

Clark, Christopher. *Roots of Rural Capitalism: Western Massachusetts, 1780–1860.* Ithaca, N.Y.: Cornell University Press, 1990.

Clark, Colin, and Margaret Rosary Haswell. *The Economics of Subsistence Agriculture.* New York: Macmillan, 1968.

Clarkson, Roy B. *Tumult on the Mountains: Lumbering in West Virginia, 1770–1920.* Parsons, W.Va.: McClain Printing, 1964.

Clemens, Paul G. E., and Lucy Simler. "Rural Labor and the Farm Household in Chester County, Pennsylvania, 1750–1820." *Work and Labor in Early America.* Edited by Stephen Inness. Chapel Hill: University of North Carolina Press, 1988.

Cohen, David. *The Ramapo Mountain People.* New Brunswick, N.J.: Rutgers University Press, 1974.

Cohen, Marjorie Griffin. *Women's Work, Markets, and Economic Development in Nineteenth-Century Ontario.* Toronto: University of Toronto Press, 1978.

Collier, Paul, and Stefan Dercon. "African Agriculture in 50 Years: Smallholders in a Rapidly Changing World?" Food and Agriculture Organization of the United Nations, 2009.

Collins, Carvel Emerson. "The Literary Tradition of the Southern Mountaineer, 1824–1900." Ph.D. dissertation, University of Chicago, 1945.

Conklin, Harold C. *Hanunóo Agriculture: A Report on an Integral System of Shifting Cultivation in the Philippines.* Rome: Food and Agriculture Organization of the United Nations, 1957.

Corbin, David A. *Life, Work, and Rebellion in the Coal Fields: The Southern West Virginia Miners, 1880–1922.* Urbana: University of Illinois Press, 1989.

Critchley, Simon. *Infinitely Demanding: Ethics of Commitment, Politics of Resistance.* London: Verso, 2012.

Cronon, William. *Nature's Metropolis: Chicago and the Great West.* New York: W. W. Norton, 1991.

Crummy, Joan. "The Subversion of Gleaning in Balzac's *Les Paysans* and in Millet's *Les Glaneuses.*" *Neohelicon* 26 (1999): 9–18.

Cubby, Edwin Albert. "The Transformation of the Tug and Guyandotte Valleys: Economic Development and Social Change in West Virginia, 1888–1924." Ph.D. dissertation, Syracuse University, 1962.

Cullather, Nick. "Miracles of Modernization: The Green Revolution and the Apotheosis of Technology." *Diplomatic History* 28 (April 2004): 235–54.

——. *Hungry World: America's Cold War Battle Against Poverty in Asia*. Cambridge, Mass.: Harvard University Press, 2010.

Cunliffe, Barry W. *Europe Between the Oceans: 9000 BC–AD 1000*. New Haven, Conn.: Yale University Press, 2011.

Curry, Richard Orr. *A House Divided: A Study of Statehood Politics and the Copperhead Movement in West Virginia*. Pittsburgh: University of Pittsburgh Press, 1964.

Danbom, D. B. *Born in the Country: A History of Rural America*. Baltimore: Johns Hopkins University Press, 2006.

Daniel, Pete. "The Metamorphosis of Slavery, 1865–1900." *Journal of American History* 66 (June 1979): 88–99.

Daniels, Christine, and Michael V. Kennedy, eds. *Over the Threshold, Intimate Violence in Early America*. New York: Routledge, 1999.

Darby, H. C. *The Domesday Geography of Eastern England*. New York: Cambridge University Press, 2007.

Davenport, Coral. "Coal Country Is Wary of Hillary Clinton's Pledge to Help." *New York Times* (August 28, 2016).

Davis, Darrell Haug. *Geography of the Mountains of Eastern Kentucky*. Frankfort: Kentucky Geological Survey, 1924.

Davis, Donald E., Craig E. Colten, Megan Kate Nelson, Barbara L. Allen, and Mikko Saikku. *Southern United States: An Environmental History*. Santa Barbara, Calif.: ABC-CLIO, 2006.

Davis, Mike. *Late Victorian Holocausts: El Niño Famines and the Making of the Third World*. New York: Verso, 2001.

——. *Planet of Slums*. New York: Verso, 2006.

DeMause, Lloyd. "The Universality of Incest." *Journal of Psychohistory* 19 (Fall 1991): 123–64.

De Schutter, Olivier. "How Not to Think of Land-Grabbing: Three Critiques of Large-Scale Investments in Farmland." *Journal of Peasant Studies* 23 (2011): 249–79.

Dilworth, Leah. "'Handmade by an American Indian' Souvenirs and the Cultural Economy of Southwestern Tourism." *The Culture of Tourism; The Tourism of Culture: Selling the Past to the Present in the American Southwest*. Edited by Hal K. Rothman. Albuquerque: University of New Mexico Press, 2003.

Donahue, Brian. *The Great Meadow: Farmers and the Land in Colonial Concord*. New Haven: Yale University Press, 2007.

——. "Look from Sanderson's Farm: A Perspective on New England Environmental History and Conservation." *Environmental History* 12 (January 2007): 9–34.

Dore, Elizabeth. *Myths of Modernity: Peonage and Patriarchy in Nicaragua*. Durham, N.C.: Duke University Press, 2006.

Dove, Michael R. "Rice-Eating Rubber and People-Eating Governments: Peasant Versus State Critiques of Rubber Development in Colonial Borneo." *Ethnohistory* 43 (Winter 1996): 33–63.

——. "Hybrid Histories and Indigenous Knowledge Among Asian Rubber Smallholders." *International Social Science Journal* 54 (2002): 349–59.

——. *The Banana Tree at the Gate: A History of Marginal Peoples and Global Markets in Borneo*. New Haven, Conn.: Yale University Press, 2011.

Drayton, Richard Harry. *Nature's Government: Science, Imperial Britain, and the 'Improvement' of the World*. New Haven, Conn.: Yale University Press, 2000.

Dublin, Thomas, ed. *Farm to Factory: Women's Letters, 1830–1860*. New York: Columbia University Press, 1993.

Dudley, Kathryn Marie. *Debt and Dispossession: Farm Loss in America's Heartland*. Chicago: University of Chicago Press, 2000.

Dunaway, Wilma A. "Speculators and Settler Capitalists: Unthinking the Mythology About Appalachian Landholding, 1790–1860." *Appalachia in the Making: The Mountain South in the Nineteenth Century*. Edited by Mary Beth Pudup, Dwight B. Billings, and Altina L. Waller. Chapel Hill: University of North Carolina Press, 1995.

——. *The First American Frontier: Transition to Capitalism in Southern Appalachia, 1700–1860*. Chapel Hill: University of North Carolina Press, 1996.

——. *The African-American Family in Slavery and Emancipation*. Maison des sciences de l'homme/Cambridge University Press, 2003.

——. *Slavery in the American Mountain South*. Cambridge: Cambridge University Press, 2003.

——. "The Centrality of the Household to the Modern World-System." *Routledge Handbook of World-Systems Analysis*. Edited by Salvatore J. Babones and Christopher Chase-Dunn. New York: Routledge, 2012.

Eicher, John H., and David J. Eicher. *Civil War High Commands*. Stanford, Calif.: Stanford University Press, 2001.

Einhorn, Robin L. *American Taxation, American Slavery*. Chicago: University of Chicago Press, 2008.

Eisenberg, Ellen. *Jewish Agricultural Colonies in New Jersey, 1882–1920*. Syracuse: Syracuse University Press, 1995.

Elkins, S. M., and E. McKitrick. *The Age of Federalism*. New York: Oxford University Press, 1995.

Eller, Ronald D. *Miners, Millhands, and Mountaineers: Industrialization of the Appalachian South, 1880–1930*. Knoxville: University of Tennessee Press, 1982.

Eltis, W. A. "Francois Quesnay: A Reinterpretation." *Oxford Economic Papers, New Series* 27 (November 1975): 327–51.

Escobar, Arturo. *Encountering Development: The Making and Unmaking of the Third World*. Princeton, N.J.: Princeton University Press, 1995.

Faragher, John Mack. *Sugar Creek: Life on the Illinois Prairie*. New Haven, Conn.: Yale University Press, 1986.

——. *Daniel Boone: The Life and Legend of an American Pioneer*. New York: Henry Holt, 1992.

——. *A Great and Noble Scheme: The Tragic Story of the Expulsion of the French Acadians from Their American Homeland*. New York: W. W. Norton, 2005.

Farland, Maria. "Modernist Versions of Pastoral: Poetic Inspiration, Scientific Expertise, and the 'Degenerate' Farmer." *American Literary History* 19 (Winter 2007): 905–36.

Febvre, Lucien Paul Victor, and Lionel Bataillon. *A Geographical Introduction to History*. Westport, Conn.: Greenwood Press, 1974.

Ferguson, James. *The Anti-Politics Machine: "Development," Depoliticization, and Bureaucratic Power in Lesotho*. Minneapolis: University of Minnesota Press, 1994.

Fichter, James R. *So Great a Profit: How the East Indies Trade Transformed Anglo-American Capitalism*. Cambridge, Mass.: Harvard University Press, 2010.

Fickey, Amanda L., and Michael Samers. "Developing Appalachia: The Impact of Limited Economic Imagination." *Studying Appalachian Studies: Making the Path by Walking*. Edited by Chad Berry, Phillip J. Obermiller, and Shaunna L. Scott. Urbana: University of Illinois Press, 2015.

Finberg, H.P.R., and Joan Thirsk. *The Agrarian History of England and Wales*. General Editor: H.P.R Finberg. New York: Cambridge University Press, 2000.

Fite, Gilbert C. *The Farmer's Frontier, 1865–1900*. New York: Holt, Rinehart, 1966.

Fletcher, Stevenson Whitcomb. *The Subsistence Farming Period in Pennsylvania Agriculture, 1640–1840*. Philadelphia: University of Pennsylvania Press, 1947.

Foner, Eric. *Nothing but Freedom: Emancipation and Its Legacy*. Baton Rouge: Louisiana State University Press, 1983.

Forstater, Mathew. "Taxation and Primitive Accumulation: The Case of Colonial Africa." *Research in Political Economy* 22 (2005): 51–65.

Foster, George M. "Treasure Tales, and the Image of the Static Economy in a Mexican Peasant Community." *Journal of American Folklore* 77 (January–March 1964): 39–44.

Foster, John Bellamy. *Marx's Ecology: Materialism and Nature*. New York: Monthly Review Press, 2000.

Frank, André Gunder. "The Development of Underdevelopment." *Monthly Review* (September 1966): 17–31.

Franklyn, David Omowalé. "Grenada, Naipaul, and Ground Provision." *Small Axe* 22 (February 2007): 67–75.

Fraser, Steve. *The Age of Acquiescence: The Life and Death of American Resistance to Organized Wealth and Power*. New York: Little, Brown, 2015.

Fuerstenau, Douglass W. "A Century of Developments in the Chemistry of Flotation Processing." *Froth Flotation: A Century of Innovation*. Edited by M. C. Fuerstenau, Graeme Jameson, and Roe-Hoan Yoon. Littleton, Colo.: Society of Mining, Metallurgy, and Exploration, 2007.

Fullilove, Courtney. "The Price of Bread: The New York City Flour Riot and the Paradox of Capitalist Food Systems." *Radical History Review* 118 (2014): 15–41.

Gallup Organization. *Gardens for All: National Gardening Survey Conducted by the Gallup Organization*. 1984.

Gardner, Leigh. *Taxing Colonial Africa: The Political Economy of British Imperialism*. New York: Oxford University Press, 2012.

Garvey, Timothy J. "The Duluth Homesteads, a Successful Experiment in Community Housing." *Minnesota History* 46 (Spring 1978): 2–16.

Gates, Paul Wallace. *The Farmer's Age, 1815–1860*. New York: Harper & Row, 1960.

——. *Landlords and Tenants on the Prairie Frontier*. Ithaca, N.Y.: Cornell University Press, 1973.

——. *History of Public Land Law Development*. 1978. New York: Arno Press, 1979.

Gaventa, John. *Power and Powerlessness: Quiescence and Rebellion in an Appalachian Valley*. Urbana-Champaign: University of Illinois Press, 1980.

Gaventa, John, and Bill Horton. "Land Ownership Patterns and Their Impacts on Appalachian Communities: A Survey of 80 Counties," as submitted to the Appalachian Regional Commission by the Appalachian Land Ownership Task Force. February 1981. Typescript report. Archives of Coal River Mountain Watch (http://files .eric.ed.gov/fulltext/ED325280.pdf).

Genovese, Eugene D. *Roll, Jordan, Roll: The World the Slaves Made*. New York: Pantheon, 1974.

George, Henry. *Progress and Poverty: An Inquiry into the Cause of Industrial Depressions, and of Increase of Want with Increase of Wealth: The Remedy*. New York: 1887.

Gilman, Nils. *Mandarins of the Future: Modernization Theory in Cold War America*. Baltimore: Johns Hopkins University Press, 2003.

Gladwin, Christina H., and John Butler. "Gardening: A Survival Strategy for the Small, Part-Time Florida Farm." *Proceedings of the Florida State Horticultural Society* 95 (1982): 246–68.

Goldman, Michael. *Imperial Nature: The World Bank and Struggles for Social Justice in the Age of Globalization*. New Haven, Conn.: Yale University Press, 2005.

Graeber, David. *Debt: The First 5,000 Years*. Brooklyn, N.Y.: Melville House, 2010.

——. "In Regulation Nation." *Harper's Magazine* (March 2015).

Graffenried, Clare de. "The Georgia Cracker in the Cotton Mills." *Century Magazine* 41 (February 1891): 483–98.

Grant, James P. "Marginal Men: The Global Unemployment Crisis." *Foreign Affairs* 50 (October 1971): 112–24.

Gray, John. *False Dawn: The Delusions of Global Capitalism*. New York: New Press, 2000.

Gray, L. C., and Esther Katherine Thompson. *History of Agriculture in the Southern United States to 1860*. Washington, D.C.: Carnegie Institution, 1933.

Greenwald, Emily. *Reconfiguring the Reservation: The Nez Perces, Jicarilla Apaches, and the Dawes Act*. Albuquerque: University of New Mexico Press, 2002.

Greer, Allan. "Commons and Enclosure in the Colonization of North America." *American Historical Review* 117 (April 2012): 365–86.

Gregg, Sara M. *Managing the Mountains: Land Use Planning, the New Deal, and the Creation of a Federal Landscape in Appalachia*. New Haven, Conn.: Yale University Press, 2010.

Gronewold, Nathanial. "No Shortage of Blame as Haiti Struggles to Feed Itself." *New York Times* (November 19, 2009).

Groover, Mark D. *An Archeological Study of Rural Capitalism and Material Life: The Gibbs Farmstead in Southern Appalachia, 1790–1920*. New York: Springer Press, 2003.

Gross, Robert A. "The Great Bean Field Hoax: Thoreau and the Agricultural Reformers." *Virginia Quarterly Review* 61 (Summer 1985). www.vqronline.org/essay/great-bean-field -hoax-thoreau-and-agricultural-reformers.

Grove, Richard H. *Green Imperialism: Colonial Expansion, Tropical Island Edens and the Origins of Environmentalism, 1600–1860*. Cambridge: Cambridge University Press, 1995.

Gudeman, Stephen. *The Demise of a Rural Economy: From Subsistence to Capitalism in a Latin American Village*. New York: Routledge & Kegan Paul, 1978.

——. *Anthropology of Economy: Community, Market, and Culture*. Malden, Mass.: Blackwell, 2001.

Gump, Lucy K. "Half Pints to Horse Shoes: Meeting the Needs of a Growing 18th Century Appalachian Frontier." Paper Presented to the Appalachian Studies Association, East Tennessee State University [n.d.].

Hagenstein, Edwin C., Sara M. Gregg, and Brian Donahue. *American Georgics: Writings on Farming, Culture, and the Land*. New Haven, Conn.: Yale University Press, 2011.

Hahn, Steven. *The Roots of Southern Populism: Yeoman Farmers and the Transformation of the Georgia Upcountry, 1850–1890*. New York: Oxford University Press, 1983.

Hall, Granville Davisson, and John E. Stealey III. *The Rending of Virginia: A History*. Knoxville: University of Tennessee Press, 2000.

Hall, Van Beck. "The Politics of Appalachian Virginia." *Appalachian Frontiers: Settlement, Society, and Development in the Preindustrial Era*. Edited by Robert D. Mitchell. Lexington: University Press of Kentucky, 1991.

Hardin, Garrett, "The Tragedy of the Commons." *Science* 162 (December 13, 1968): 1243–48.

Hargreaves, Mary W. M. *Dry Farming on the Northern Great Plains: Years of Readjustment, 1920–1990*. Lawrence: University Press of Kansas, 1993.

Harkins, Anthony. *Hillbilly: A Cultural History of an American Icon*. New York: Oxford University Press, 2003.

Harper, R. E. *The Transformation of Western Pennsylvania, 1770–1800*. Pittsburgh: University of Pittsburgh Press, 1991.

Hart, John Fraser. *The Changing Scale of American Agriculture*. Charlottesville: University of Virginia Press, 2003.

Harvey, David. *Social Justice and the City*. Athens: University of Georgia Press, 2009.

Harwood, Jonathan. "Peasant Friendly Plant Breeding and the Early Years of the Green Revolution in Mexico." *Agricultural History* 83 (Summer 2009): 384.

——. "Why Have Green Revolutions So Often Failed to Help Peasant-Farmers?" Conference paper, Colloquium of the Agrarian Studies Program, Yale University, October 9, 2009.

Hatch, Elvin. "Delivering the Goods: Cash, Subsistence Farms, and Identity in a Blue Ridge County in the 1930s." *Journal of Appalachian Studies* 9 (Spring 2003): 6–48.

Hays, Samuel P. *Conservation and the Gospel of Efficiency: The Progressive Conservation Movement, 1890–1920*. Cambridge, Mass.: Harvard University Press, 1959.

Henretta, James A. *Origins of American Capitalism: Collected Essays*. Boston: Northeastern University Press, 1991.

Hilliard, Sam Bowers. *Hog Meat and Hoecake: Food Supply in the Old South, 1840–1860*. Carbondale: Southern Illinois University Press, 1972.

Hitchins, Fortescue. *History of Cornwall, from the Earliest Records and Traditions, to the Present Time*. Vol. 2. 1826.

Hobsbawm, E. J. *Primitive Rebels; Studies in Archaic Forms of Social Movement in the 19th and 20th Centuries*. New York: W. W. Norton, 1959.

Holmberg, Allan R. *Nomads of the Longbow: The Siriono of Eastern Bolivia*. Washington, D.C.: Smithsonian Institution Press, 1950.

Howe, Edward T., and Donald J. Reeb. "The Historical Evolution of State and Local Tax Systems." Lincoln Institute, n.d. www.lincolninst.edu/subcenters/property-valuation -and-taxation-library/dl/howe_reeb.pdf.

Hsiung, David C. "How Isolated Was Appalachia?" *Appalachian Journal* 16 (Summer 1989): 336–49.

——. *Two Worlds in the Tennessee Mountains: Exploring the Origins of Appalachian Stereotypes*. Lexington: University Press of Kentucky, 1997.

Hubbard, Glen R., and William Duggan. *The Aid Trap: Hard Truths About Ending Poverty*. New York: Columbia Business School, 2009.

Humphrey, Caroline. "Barter and Economic Disintegration." *Man* 20 (New Series, March 1985): 48–72.

Huntington, Ellsworth, Frank Ernest Williams, and Samuel Van Valkenburg. *Economic and Social Geography*. New York: J. Wiley & Sons, 1933.

Hurst, Derek. *Sheep in the Cotswolds: The Medieval Wool Trade*. Stroud, Gloucestershire, U.K.: The History Press, 2005.

Hurt, R. Douglass. *The Ohio Frontier: Crucible of the Old Northwest, 1720–1830*. Bloomington: Indiana University Press, 1998.

Huston, Reeve. *Land and Freedom: Rural Society, Popular Protest, and Party Politics in Antebellum New York*. New York: Oxford University Press, 2002.

Hydén, Göran. *Beyond Ujamaa in Tanzania: Underdevelopment and an Uncaptured Peasantry*. Berkeley: University of California Press, 1980.

Hyneman, Charles S., and George W. Carey. *A Second Federalist: Congress Creates a Government*. New York: Meredith Publishing, 1967.

Immerwahr, Daniel. *Thinking Small: The United States and the Lure of Community Development*. Cambridge, Mass.: Harvard University Press, 2015.

Innes, Steven, ed. *Work and Labor in Early America*. Chapel Hill: University of North Carolina Press & the Institute of Early American History & Culture, 1988.

Isaac, Barry L. "The Siriono of Eastern Bolivia: A Reexamination." *Human Ecology* 5 (June 1977): 137–54.

Isenberg, Andrew C. *The Destruction of the Bison*. New York: Cambridge University Press, 2000.

Jacoby, Karl. *Crimes Against Nature: Squatters, Poachers, Thieves, and the Hidden History of American Conservation*. Berkeley: University of California Press, 2001.

Johnson, E. A. "Effect of Farm Woodland Grazing on Watershed Values in the Southern Appalachian Mountains." *Journal of Forestry* 50 (February 1952): 109–13.

Johnson, Josephine Winslow. *Now in November*. New York: Feminist Press at the City University of New York, 1991.

Jones, Ben. *Beyond the State in Rural Uganda*. Edinburgh: Edinburgh University Press, 2008.

Jones, Daniel P. *The Economic and Social Transformation of Rural Rhode Island, 1780–1850*. Boston: Northeastern University Press, 1992.

Jones, Jacqueline. *A Dreadful Deceit: The Myth of Race from the Colonial Era to Obama's America*. New York: Basic Books, 2013.

Jordan, Terry G., and Matti E. Kaups. *The American Backwoods Frontier: An Ethnic and Ecological Interpretation*. Baltimore: Johns Hopkins University Press, 1992.

Joseph, Gilbert, and Daniel Nugent, eds. *Everyday Forms of State Formation: Revolution and the Negotiation of Rule in Modern Mexico*. Durham, N.C.: Duke University Press, 1994.

Judd, Richard William. *Common Lands, Common People: The Origins of Conservation in Northern New England*. Cambridge, Mass.: Harvard University Press, 1997.

Kaufman, Frederick. "The Food Bubble: How Wall Street Starved Millions and Got Away with It." *Harper's Magazine* (July 2010).

Keesing, Feliz Maxwell. *The Ethnohistory of Luzon*. Palo Alto, Calif.: Stanford University Press, 1962.

Kennedy, Roger G. *Mr. Jefferson's Lost Cause: Land, Farms, Slavery, and the Louisiana Purchase*. New York: Oxford University Press, 2003.

Kerridge, Eric. *Agrarian Problems in the Sixteenth Century and After*. New York: Barnes & Noble, 1969.

Kiffmeyer, Thomas. *Reformers to Radicals: The Appalachian Volunteers and the War on Poverty*. Lexington: University Press of Kentucky, 2008.

Kirk-Greene, A. *The Principles of Native Administration in Nigeria: Selected Documents, 1900–1947*. New York: Oxford University Press, 1965.

Kirschenmann, Frederick. "The Current State of Agriculture: Does It Have a Future?"

The Essential Agrarian Reader: The Future of Culture, Community, and the Land. Edited by Norman Wirzba. Lexington: University Press of Kentucky, 2003.

Klooster, Dan. "Campesinos and Mexican Forest Policy During the Twentieth Century." *Latin American Research Review* 38 (2003): 94–126.

Kuhn, Steven L., and Mary C. Stiner. "What's a Mother to Do? The Division of Labor Among Neanderthals and Modern Humans in Eurasia." *Current Anthropology* 47 (December 2006): 953–81.

Kulikoff, Allan. *The Agrarian Origins of American Capitalism.* Charlottesville: University of Virginia Press, 1992.

——. *From British Peasants to Colonial American Farmers.* Chapel Hill: University of North Carolina Press, 2000.

Kuruma, Samezo. *History of Political Economy: An Overview.* Tokyo: Iwanami Shoten, 1954.

Landau, Misia. "Human Evolution as Narrative." *American Scientist* 72 (May–June 1984): 262–68.

Land Rush. Television and Film. Directed by Hugo Berkeley and Osvalde Lewat. London: Normal Life Pictures, 2012.

Langland, William. *Piers Plowman: The C Version: A Verse Translation.* Translated by George Economou. Philadelphia: University of Pennsylvania Press, 1996.

Lapidos, Juliet. "How the Mountain State Got a Reputation for Inbreeding." *Slate* (June 3, 2008).

Latham, Michael. *The Right Kind of Revolution: Modernization, Development, and U.S. Foreign Policy from the Cold War to the Present.* Ithaca, N.Y.: Cornell University Press, 2011.

Lause, Mark A. *Young America: Land, Labor, and the Republican Community.* Urbana-Champaign: University of Illinois Press, 2005.

Lee, Nichols Rose. *Rehearsal for Reconstruction: The Port Royal Experiment.* New York: Oxford University Press, 1964.

Lefebvre, Henri. *The Production of Space.* Hoboken, N.J.: Blackwell, 1991.

Lerner, Daniel. *The Passing of Traditional Society: Modernizing the Middle East.* New York: Free Press of Glencoe, 1958.

Le Roy Ladurie, Emmanuel. *Peasants of Languedoc.* Translated by John Day. Urbana-Champaign University of Illinois Press, 1974.

Lewis, Arthur W. "Economic Development with Unlimited Supplies of Labor." *The Manchester School of Economic and Social Studies* 22 (1954): 139–91.

Lewis, Ronald L. "Railroads, Deforestation, and the Transformation of Agriculture in the West Virginia Back Counties." *Appalachia in the Making: The Mountain South in the Nineteenth Century.* Edited by Mary Beth Pudup, Dwight B. Billings, and Altina L. Waller. Chapel Hill: University of North Carolina Press, 1995.

——. *Transforming the Appalachian Countryside: Railroads, Deforestation, and Social Change in West Virginia, 1880–1920.* Chapel Hill: University of North Carolina Press, 1998.

——. "Beyond Isolation and Homogeneity: Diversity and the History of Appalachia." *Back Talk from Appalachia: Confronting Stereotypes*. Edited by Dwight B. Billings, Gurney Norman, and Katherine Ledford. Lexington: University Press of Kentucky, 1999.

Lilly, Jessica, and Roxy Todd. "What Would You Do If Your Grocery Store Disappeared?" West Virginia Public Broadcasting (July 10, 2015). http://wvpublic .org/post/inside-appalachia-what-would-you-do-if-your-grocery-store-disappeared.

——. "What Happens When Walmart Closes in One Coal Community?" West Virginia Public Broadcasting (August 26, 2016). http://wvpublic.org/post/what-happens-when -walmart-closes-one-coal-community.

Lord, Russell. *The Wallaces of Iowa*. Boston: Houghton, Mifflin, 1947.

Lottermoser, Bernard G. *Mine Wastes*. New York: Springer Heidelberg, 2010.

Luden, David. *Early Capitalism and Local History in South India*. Princeton, N.J.: Princeton University Press, 2005.

Luxemburg, Rosa. *The Accumulation of Capital*. New Haven, Conn.: Yale University Press, 1951.

Lynch, Lawrence R. "The West Virginia Coal Strike." *Political Science Quarterly* 29 (1914): 630–37.

MacFarquhar, Neil. "African Farmers Displaced as Investors Move In." *New York Times* (December 21, 2010).

MacMaster, Richard K. "The Cattle Trade in Western Virginia, 1760–1830." *Appalachian Frontiers: Settlement, Society, and Development in the Preindustrial Era*. Edited by Robert D. Mitchell. Lexington: University Press of Kentucky, 1991.

Mann, Charles C. *1491: New Revelations of the Americas Before Columbus*. New York: Vintage, 2006.

Mann, Ralph. "Mountains, Land, and Kin Networks: Burkes Garden, Virginia, in the 1840s and 1850s." *Journal of Southern History* 58 (August 1992): 411–34.

Mann, Susan, and James Dickinson. "Obstacles to the Development of Capitalist Agriculture." *Journal of Peasant Studies* 5 (July 1978): 466–81.

Martin, Ann Smart. *Buying into the World of Goods: Early Consumers in Backcountry Virginia*. Baltimore: Johns Hopkins University Press, 2008.

Martinez-Alier, Joan. "The Environmentalism of the Poor." Prepared for the Conference on Political Economy of Sustainable Development (August 2002). http://www .unrisd.org.

Marx, Leo. *The Machine in the Garden: Technology and the Pastoral Ideal in America*. New York: Oxford University Press, 1964.

Mayer, Enrique. *The Articulated Peasant: Household Economies in the Andes*. Boulder, Colo.: Westview Press, 2002.

McCrady, Edward. *History of South Carolina in the Revolution, 1780–1783*. New York: Macmillan, 1902.

McDowell, H. C. "Adversary Possession, or the Open Question in Virginia." *Virginia Law Register* 4 (May 1898): 1–11.

McEvoy, Arthur F. *The Fisherman's Problem: Ecology and Law in the California Fisheries, 1850–1980.* New York: Cambridge University Press, 1986.

McMichael, Philip. "Peasants Make Their Own History, but Not Just as They Please. . . ." *Journal of Agrarian Change* 8 (April and July 2008): 205–28.

McWhiney, Grady. *Cracker Culture: Celtic Ways in the Old South.* Tuscaloosa: University of Alabama Press, 1988.

Medick, Hans. "The Proto-Industrial Family Economy: The Structural Function of Household and Family During the Transition from Peasant Society to Industrial Capitalism." *Social History* 1 (1976): 297–300.

Meggison, W. J. *African American Life in South Carolina's Upper Piedmont, 1780–1900.* Columbia: University of South Carolina Press, 2006.

Merrill, Michael. "Cash Is Good to Eat: Self-Sufficiency and Exchange in the Rural Economy of the United States." *Radical History Review* (Winter 1977): 42–71.

——. "The Anti-Capitalist Origins of the United States." *Review: The Journal of the Fernand Braudel Center* 13 (1990): 465–97.

——. "Putting 'Capitalism' in Its Place: A Review of Recent Literature." *William and Mary Quarterly* 52 (April 1995): 315–26.

Migdal, Joel S. *Strong Societies and Weak States: State-Society Relations and State Capabilities in the Third World.* Princeton, N.J.: Princeton University Press, 1988.

Mintz, Sidney. "Was the Plantation Slave a Proletarian?" *Review* 2 (1978): 81–98.

——. "Slavery and the Rise of Peasantries." *Historical Reflections* (Summer 1979): 213–53.

——. *Sweetness and Power: The Place of Sugar in Modern History.* New York: Penguin Books, 1985.

——. "Can Haiti Change?" *Foreign Affairs* 74 (January–February 1995): 73–86.

Mithen, Steven. *After the Ice: A Global Human History, 20,000–5,000 BC.* Cambridge, Mass.: Harvard University Press, 2003.

Mitman, Gregg, and Paul Erickson. "Latex and Blood: Science, Markets, and American Empire." *Radical History Review* 107 (2010): 45–73.

Mock, C. J. "Drought and Precipitation Fluctuations in the Great Plains During the Late Nineteenth Century." *Great Plains Research* 1 (1991): 26–57.

Montgomery, Michael. "In the Appalachians They Speak Like Shakespeare." *Language Myths.* Edited by Laurie Bauer and Peter Trudgill. New York: Penguin Books, 1998.

Moudio, Rebecca. "Shea Butter Nourishes Opportunities for African Women." *Africa Renewal Online* (August 2013). www.un.org/africarenewal/magazine/august-2013/shea-butter-nourishes-opportunities-african-women.

Munger, Donna Bingham. *Pennsylvania Land Records: A History and Guide for Research.* New York: Rowman & Littlefield, 1993.

Munn, Robert F. *The Southern Appalachians: A Bibliography and Guide to Studies.* Morgantown: West Virginia University Library, 1961.

Ndalilah, Joseph W. "Colonial Capitalism and the Making of Wage Labour in Kimilili, Kenya: 1900–1963." *International Journal of Humanities and Social Science* 2 (December 2012): 282–90.

Neth, Mary. *Preserving the Family Farm: Women, Community and the Foundations of Agribusiness in the Midwest, 1900–1940.* Baltimore: Johns Hopkins University Press, 1995.

Netting, Robert McC. *Smallholders, Householders: Farm Families and the Ecology of Intensive, Sustainable Agriculture.* Palo Alto, Calif.: Stanford University Press, 1993.

Nevins, Allan, and Henry Steele Commager. *A Short History of the United States.* New York: The Modern Library, 1945.

Newfont, Kathryn. *Blue Ridge Commons: Environmental Activism and Forest History in Western North Carolina.* Athens: University of Georgia Press, 2012.

Nixon, Rob. *Slow Violence and the Environmentalism of the Poor.* Cambridge, Mass.: Harvard University Press, 2011.

Noble, David W. *Death of a Nation: American Culture and the End of Exceptionalism.* Minneapolis: University of Minnesota Press, 2002.

Norona, Delf, ed. *West Virginia Imprints, 1790–1863; A Checklist of Books, Newspapers, Periodicals, and Broadsides.* Moundsville: West Virginia Library Association, 1959.

Novak, Barbara. *Nature and Culture: American Landscape Painting, 1825–1875.* 3rd ed. New York: Oxford University Press, 2007.

Novak, William J. "The Myth of the Weak American State." *American Historical Review* 113 (June 2008): 752–72.

Obermiller, Phillip J. "Historical Sources on Appalachian Migration and Urban Appalachians, 1870–1999: A Selectively Annotated Bibliography." http://uacvoice.org /pdf/Historical%20Sources%20on%20Appalachian%20Migration.pdf.

Ochiltree, Ian. "Mastering the Sharecroppers: Land, Labour and the Search for Independence in the US South and South Africa." *Journal of Southern African Studies* 30 (March 2004): 41–61.

Ostler, Jeffrey. *Prairie Populism: The Fate of Agrarian Radicalism in Kansas, Nebraska, and Iowa, 1880–1892.* Lawrence: University Press of Kansas, 1993.

———. *The Plains Sioux and U.S. Colonialism from Lewis and Clark to Wounded Knee.* New York: Cambridge University Press, 2004.

Ostrom, Elinor. *Governing the Commons: The Evolution of Institutions for Collective Action.* Cambridge: Cambridge University Press, 1990.

Otis, Delos Sacket. *The Dawes Act and the Allotment of Indian Lands.* Edited by Francis Paul Prucha. Norman: University of Oklahoma Press, 1973.

Otto, John Solomon. "The Decline of Forest Farming in Southern Appalachia." *Forest History* 27 (January 1983): 18–27.

———. "Southern 'Plain Folk' Agriculture." *Plantation Society in the Americas* 2 (April 1983): 29–31.

——. "Forest Fallowing in the Southern Appalachian Mountains: A Problem in Comparative Agricultural History." *Proceedings of the American Philosophical Society* 133 (March 1989): 51–63.

Overton, Mark. *Agricultural Revolution in England: The Transformation of the Agrarian Economy 1500–1850.* London: Cambridge University Press, 1996.

Peck, Gunther. "The Nature of Labor: Fault Lines and Common Ground in Environmental and Labor History." *Environmental History* 11 (April 2006): 212–38.

Peña, Devon G. "Farmers Feeding Families: Agroecology in South Central Los Angeles." Lecture presented to the Environmental Science, Policy, and Management Colloquium, University of California, Berkeley. October 10, 2005.

Perelman, Michael. *The Invention of Capitalism: Classical Political Economy and the Secret History of Primitive Accumulation.* Durham, N.C.: Duke University Press, 2000.

Perkins, Elizabeth A. "The Consumer Frontier: Household Consumption in Early Kentucky." *Journal of American History* 78 (September 1991): 486–510.

Petty, Adrienne Monteith. *Standing Their Ground: Small Farmers in North Carolina Since the Civil War.* New York: Oxford University Press, 2013.

Phipps, Charles A. "Note and Comment." *Oregon Law Review* 22 (1943): 191–92.

Pimentel, David. "Energy Inputs in Food Crop Production in Developing and Developed Nations." *Energies* 2 (2009): 1–24.

Platt, Colin. *King Death: The Black Death and Its Aftermath in Late-Medieval England.* Toronto: University of Toronto Press, 1996.

Polanyi, Karl. *The Great Transformation: The Political and Economic Origins of Our Time.* [1944]. Boston: Beacon Press, 2001.

Pomeranz, Kenneth. *The Great Divergence: China, Europe, and the Making of the Modern World Economy.* Princeton, N.J.: Princeton University Press, 2000.

——. "Political Economy and Ecology on the Eve of Industrialization: Europe, China, and the Global Conjuncture." *American Historical Review* 107 (April 2002): 425–46.

Post, Charles. "The Agrarian Origins of U.S. Capitalism: The Transformation of the Northern Countryside Before the Civil War." *Journal of Peasant Studies* 22 (April 1995): 389–445.

Potter, David. *People of Plenty: Economic Abundance and the American Character.* Chicago: University of Chicago Press, 1954.

Price, Ben. *A (Very) Brief History of "Dillon's Rule."* Community Environmental Legal Defense Fund, 2011(?). www.freedomforallseasons.org/RuralCleansing/2011 -09-05%20A%20(Very)%20Brief%20History%20of%20Dillons%20Rule.pdf.

Prude, Jonathan. *The Coming of Industrial Order: Town and Factory Life in Rural Massachusetts, 1810–1860.* Amherst: University of Massachusetts Press, 1999.

Pruitt, Bettye Hobbs. "Self-Sufficiency and the Agricultural Economy of Eighteenth-Century Massachusetts." *William and Mary Quarterly* 41 (July 1984): 333–64.

Pudup, Mary Beth. "The Limits of Subsistence: Agriculture and Industry in Central Appalachia." *Agricultural History* 64 (Winter 1990): 61–89.

Pudup, Mary Beth, Dwight B. Billings, and Altina L. Waller. *Appalachia in the Making: The Mountain South in the Nineteenth Century.* Chapel Hill: University of North Carolina Press, 1995.

Quick, Michael. *George Inness: A Catalogue Raisonné.* New Brunswick, N.J.: Rutgers University Press, 2007.

Raper, Arthur F., and Ira De A. Reid. *Sharecroppers All.* Chapel Hill: University of North Carolina Press, 1941.

Rappleye, Charles. *Robert Morris: Financier of the American Revolution.* New York: Simon & Schuster, 2010.

Rasmussen, Barbara. *Absentee Landowning and Exploitation in West Virginia, 1760–1920.* Lexington: University Press of Kentucky, 1994.

Resnikoff, Ned. "Congress Passes $8.7 Billion Food Stamp Cut." *MSNBC* (February 4, 2013). www.msnbc.com/msnbc/congress-passes-farm-bill-food-stamp-cuts#50092.

Richards, John F. *Unending Frontier: An Environmental History of the Early Modern World.* Berkeley: University of California Press, 2001.

Richardson, Jesse, Meghan Zimmerman Gough, and Robert Puentes, *Is Home Rule the Answer? Clarifying the Influence of Dillon's Rule on Growth Management.* Washington, D.C.: Brookings Institution, 2003.

Rochester, Anna. *Why Farmers Are Poor: The Agricultural Crisis in the United States.* New York: International Publishers, 1940.

Rojas, Carlos Antonio Aguirre. "Between Marx and Braudel: Making History, Knowing History." *Review* 15 (Spring 1992): 175–219.

Rosaldo, Renato. *Culture and Truth: The Remaking of Social Analysis.* Boston: Beacon Press, 1989.

Rosenthal, Elisabeth. "Rush to Use Crops as Fuel Raises Food Prices and Hunger Fears." *New York Times* (April, 7, 2011).

——. "As Biofuel Demand Grows, So Do Guatemala's Hunger Pangs." *New York Times* (January 6, 2013).

Rothman, Adam. *Slave Country: American Expansion and the Origins of the Deep South.* Cambridge, Mass.: Harvard University Press, 2005.

Roy, Arundhati. *Walking with the Comrades.* New York: Penguin Books, 2011.

Rubin, James A. "Farmers in Crisis." *New York Times* (February 26, 1987).

Ruddiman, William F. *Plows, Plagues, and Petroleum: How Humans Took Control of Climate.* Princeton, N.J.: Princeton University Press, 2005.

Rydén, Stig. *A Study of the Sirionó Indians.* Göteborg: Humanistic Foundation of Sweden, 1941.

Sachs, Honor. *Home Rule: Households, Manhood, and National Expansion on the Eighteenth-Century Kentucky Frontier.* New Haven, Conn.: Yale University Press, 2015.

Sachs, Jeffrey D. *Commonwealth: Economics for a Crowded Planet*. New York: Penguin, 2009.

Sahlins, Marshall. *Stone Age Economics*. New York: Routledge, 1972.

Salstrom, Paul. "Cash Is a Four-Letter Word." *Appalachian Journal* 16 (Spring 1989): 242–44.

——."Agricultural Origins of Economic Dependency." *Appalachian Frontiers: Settlement, Society, and Development in the Preindustrial Era*. Edited by Robert D. Mitchell. Lexington: University Press of Kentucky, 1991.

——. *Appalachia's Path to Dependency: Rethinking a Region's Economic History, 1730–1940*. Lexington: University Press of Kentucky, 1994.

Samson, Colin. *A Way of Life That Does Not Exist: Canada and the Extinguishment of Innu*. New York: Verso, 2003.

Sanders, Elizabeth. *Roots of Reform: Farmers, Workers, and the American State, 1877–1917*. Chicago: University of Chicago Press, 1999.

Sauer, Carl Ortwin. *Agricultural Origins and Dispersals*. New York: American Geographical Society, 1952.

——. *Seeds, Spades, Hearths, and Herds*. Cambridge, MA: MIT Press, 1972.

Sauer, Carl Ortwin, and John Leighly. *Land and Life: A Selection from the Writings of Carl Ortwin Sauer*. Berkeley: University of California Press, 1963.

Schimizzi, Sandra Wolk, and Valeria Sofranko Wolk. *Norvelt: A New Deal Subsistence Homestead*. Mount Pleasant, S.C.: Arcadia Publishing, 2010.

Schlotterbeck, John T. "The Internal Economy of Slavery in Rural Piedmont Virginia." *The Slaves' Economy: Independent Production by Slaves in the Americas*. Edited by Ira Berlin, Philip D. Morgan, and Frank Cass. London: Frank Cass, 1991.

Schultz, Theodore W. *Transforming Traditional Agriculture*. Chicago: University of Chicago Press, 1964.

Schust, Alex P. *Gary Hollow: A History of the Largest Coal Mining Operation in the World*. Harwood, Md.: Two Mule Publications, 2005.

Schuyler, David. *Sanctified Landscape: Writers, Artists, and the Hudson River Valley, 1820–1909*. Ithaca, N.Y.: Cornell University Press, 2011.

Scott, Hamilton Kennedy. Dir. *The Garden*. Black Valley Films, 2008.

Scott, James C. *The Moral Economy of the Peasant: Rebellion and Subsistence in Southeast Asia*. New Haven, Conn.: Yale University Press, 1976.

——. *The Art of Not Being Governed: An Anarchist History of Upland Southeast Asia*. New Haven, Conn.: Yale University Press, 2009.

Seavoy, Ronald E. *An Economic History of the United States from 1607 to the Present*. New York: Routledge, 2006.

Sellers, Charles. *The Market Revolution: Jacksonian America, 1815–1846*. New York: Oxford University Press, 1991.

Seymour, John. *The Self-Sufficient Life and How to Live It: The Complete Back-to-Basics Guide*. London: DK Publishing, 2009.

Shackelford, Laurel, Bill Weinberg, and Donald R. Anderson. *Our Appalachia: An Oral History.* New York: Hill and Wang, 1977.

Shanin, Teodor. "The Peasantry as a Political Factor." *Sociologial Review* 14 (March 1966): 5–27.

Shapiro, Henry D. *Appalachia on Our Mind: The Southern Mountains and Mountaineers in the American Consciousness, 1870–1920.* Chapel Hill: University of North Carolina Press, 1978.

Shapiro, K. A. *A New South Rebellion: The Battle Against Convict Labor in the Tennessee Coalfields, 1871–1896.* Chapel Hill: University of North Carolina Press, 1998.

Shepard, Thomas. *God's Plot: Puritan Spirituality in Thomas Shepard's Cambridge.* Edited by Michael McGiffert. Amherst: University of Massachusetts Press, 1994.

Sills, Vaughn, *Places for the Spirit: Traditional African American Gardens.* San Antonio, Tex.: Trinity University Press, 2010.

Simon, Richard. "Uneven Development and the Case of West Virginia: Going Beyond the Colonialism Model." *Appalachian Journal* 8 (Spring 1981): 164–86.

Sims, F. W. "The Constructive Possession of a Claimant by Adverse Possession." *Virginia Law Register* 4 (January 1899), 557–71.

Slaughter, Thomas P. *The Whiskey Rebellion: Frontier Epilogue to the American Revolution.* New York: Oxford University Press, 1988.

Slotkin, Richard. *The Fatal Environment: The Myth of the Frontier in the Age of Industrialization.* New York: Atheneum, 1985.

——. *Gunfighter Nation: The Myth of the Frontier in Twentieth-Century America.* Norman: University of Oklahoma Press, 1998.

Smith, Joan, and Immanuel Wallerstein. *Creating and Transforming Households: The Constraints of the World-Economy.* New York: Cambridge University Press, 1992.

Smith, Kimberly. "Black Agrarianism and the Foundations of Black Environmental Thought." *Environmental Ethics* 26 (Fall 2004): 267–86.

Sohn, Mark F. *Appalachian Home Cooking: History, Culture, & Recipes.* Lexington: University Press of Kentucky, 2005.

Soltow, Lee. "Distribution of Wealth and Income in the United States in 1798: Estimates Based on the Federal Housing Inventory." *Review of Economics and Statistics* 69 (February 1987): 181–85.

Spence, Mark David. *Dispossessing the Wilderness: Indian Removal and the Making of the National Parks.* New York: Oxford University Press, 1999.

Spufford, Margaret. *Contrasting Communities: English Villagers in the Sixteenth and Seventeenth Centuries.* New York: Cambridge University Press, 1974.

Stead, David. R. "Mobility of English Tenant Farmers." *Agricultural History Review* 51 (2003): 173–89.

Stearman, Allyn MacLean. *No Longer Nomads: The Sirionó Revisited.* Lanham, Md.: Hamilton Press, 1987.

Stewart, Mart A. *"What Nature Suffers to Groe": Life, Labor, and Landscape on the Georgia Coast, 1680–1920*. Athens: University of Georgia Press, 2002.

Stock, Catherine McNicol. *Rural Radicals: Righteous Rage in the American Grain*. Ithaca, N.Y.: Cornell University Press, 1996.

Stoll, Steven. *Larding the Lean Earth: Soil and Society in Nineteenth-Century America*. New York: Hill and Wang, 2002.

——. *The Great Delusion: A Mad Inventor, Death in the Tropics, and the Utopian Origins of Economic Growth*. New York: Hill and Wang, 2008.

——. "Nowhere, Fast: George Inness's *Short Cut* and Agrarian Dispossession." *Environmental History* 18 (October 2013): 786–94.

——. "The Captured Garden: The Political Ecology of Subsistence Under Capitalism." *International Labor and Working-Class History* 85 (Spring 2014): 75–96.

Sutter, Paul, and Christopher J. Manganiello. *Environmental History and the American South: A Reader*. Athens: University of Georgia Press, 2009.

Sutton, Ann F., and P. W. Hammond, eds. *The Coronation of Richard III: The Extant Documents*. New York: St. Martin's Press, 1983.

Sweet, Timothy. *American Georgics*. Philadelphia: University of Pennsylvania Press, 2002.

Tams, W.P.J. *The Smokeless Coal Fields of West Virginia: A Brief History*. Morgantown: West Virginia University Library, 1963.

Tawney, R. H. *The Agrarian Problem in the Sixteenth Century*. New York: B. Franklin, 1961.

Taylor, Quintard. *In Search of the Racial Frontier: African Americans in the American West, 1528–1990*. New York: W. W. Norton, 1998.

Thompson, E. P. *The Making of the English Working Class*. New York: Pantheon, 1963.

——. "The Moral Economy of the English Crowd in the Eighteenth Century." *Past and Present* 50 (1971): 76–136.

Tilly, Louise A. "The Food Riot as a Form of Political Conflict in France." *Journal of Interdisciplinary History* 2 (Summer 1971): 23–57.

Timmer, C. P. *Agriculture and the State: Growth, Employment, and Poverty in Developing Countries*. Ithaca, N.Y.: Cornell University Press, 1991.

Tincher, Robert B. "Night Comes to the Chromosomes: Inbreeding and Population Genetics in Southern Appalachia." *Central Issues in Anthropology* 2 (1980): 27–49.

Tribe, Keith. *Governing Economy: The Reformation of German Economic Discourse, 1750–1840*. New York: Cambridge University Press, 1988.

Trinkley, Michael, and Debi Hacker. *Archeological Manifestations of the 'Port Royal Experiment' at Mitchelville, Hilton Head Island, South Carolina*. Columbia, S.C.: Chicora Foundation. Research Contribution 14 (1987).

Trouillot, Michel-Rolph. *Peasants and Capitalists: Dominica in the World Economy*. Baltimore: Johns Hopkins University Press, 1988.

——. "North Atlantic Universals: Analytical Fictions, 1492–1945." *South Atlantic Quarterly* 101 (Fall 2002): 839–58.

——. "The Otherwise Modern: Caribbean Lessons from the Savage Slot." *Modern Alternatives, Alterities, Anthropologies*. Edited by Bruce M. Knauft. Bloomington: Indiana University Press, 2002.

Van Atta, John R. "'A Lawless Rabble': Henry Clay and the Cultural Politics of Squatters' Rights, 1832–1841." *Journal of the Early Republic* 28 (2008): 337–78.

Van Tassel, Kristin. "Nineteenth-Century American Antebellum Literature: The Yeoman Becomes a Country Bumpkin." *American Studies* 43 (Spring 2002): 51–73.

——. "The Yeoman in Nineteenth- and Twentieth-Century American Literature: Resisting, Reviving, and Revising the Agrarian Myth." Ph.D. dissertation, University of Kansas, 2003.

Von Werlhof, Claudia. "Production Relations Without Wage Labor and Labor Division by Sex." *Review* 7 (Fall 1983): 315–59.

Wager, Paul Woodford. *One Foot on the Soil, a Study of Subsistence Homesteads in Alabama*. Bureau of Public Administration: University of Alabama, 1945.

Waggoner, Eric. "I'm from West Virginia and I've Got Something to Say About the Chemical Spill." *Huffington Post* (January 14, 2014).

Waller, Altina L. *Feud: Hatfields, McCoys, and Social Change in Appalachia, 1860–1900*. Chapel Hill: University of North Carolina Press, 1988.

Wallerstein, Immanuel. *The Modern World-System I: Capitalist Agriculture and the Origins of the European World-Economy in the Sixteenth Century*. Cambridge, Mass.: Academic Press, 1974.

——. *The Capitalist World-Economy: Essays*. New York: New York: Cambridge University Press, 1978.

——. *Unthinking Social Science: The Limits of Nineteenth-Century Paradigms*. Philadelphia: Temple University Press, 1991.

Walsh, Declan. "Alienated and Angry, Coal Miners See Donald Trump as Their Only Choice." *New York Times* (August 19, 2016).

Ward, Barbara. "Vision of Barbara Ward." *Development* 50 (2007): 33–38.

Ward, Ken. "Chemical Tank Safety Rollback Passes House," *Charleston Gazette-Mail* (March 13, 2015). www.wvgazettemail.com/apps/pbcs.dll/article?AID=/20150313/GZ01/150319533/200403023.

Warman, Arturo. *Corn and Capitalism: How a Botanical Bastard Grew to Global Dominance*. Chapel Hill: University of North Carolina Press, 2003.

Warren, Louis S. *The Hunter's Game: Poachers and Conservationists in Twentieth-Century America*. New Haven, Conn.: Yale University Press, 1997.

——. "Owning Nature: Toward an Environmental History of Private Property." *The Oxford Handbook of Environmental History*. Edited by Andrew C. Isenberg. New York: Oxford University Press, 2014.

Waters, Tony. *The Persistence of Subsistence Agriculture: Life Beneath the Level of the Marketplace*. Lanham, Md.: Lexington Books, 2007.

Wawass Zahi. "King Tut's DNA." *National Geographic* (September 2010). http://ngm
.nationalgeographic.com/2010/09/tut-dna/hawass-text.

Weaver, John C. *The Great Land Rush: And the Making of the Modern World, 1650–1900.*
Montreal: McGill-Queens University Press, 2003.

Wegner, Lucia, and Gine Zwart. *Who Will Feed the World?* Oxfam Research Report
(April 2011). www.oxfam.org/sites/www.oxfam.org/files/file_attachments/who-will
-feed-the-world-rr-260411-en_4.pdf.

Weise, Robert S. *Grasping at Independence: Debt, Male Authority, and Mineral Rights in
Appalachian Kentucky, 1850–1915.* Knoxville: University of Tennessee Press, 2001.

Weisiger, Marsha. *Dreaming of Sheep in Navajo Country.* Seattle: University of Washington Press, 2009.

Westmacott, Richard. *African-American Gardens and Yards in the Rural South.* Knoxville: University of Tennessee Press, 1992.

Whisnant, David E. "Developments in the Appalachian Identity Movement: All Is
Process." *Appalachian Journal* 8 (Autumn 1980): 41–47.

——. *Modernizing the Mountaineer: People, Power, and Planning in Appalachia.* Knoxville:
University of Tennessee Press, 1994.

White, Ed. *The Backcountry and the City: Colonization and Conflict in Early America.*
Minneapolis: University of Minnesota Press, 2005.

White, Richard. *The Roots of Dependency: Subsistence, Environment, and Social Change
Among the Choctaws, Pawnees, and Navajos.* Lincoln: University of Nebraska Press,
1983.

Whitten, David O. "An Economic Inquiry into the Whiskey Rebellion of 1794." *Agricultural History* 49 (July 1975): 491–504.

Wilhelm, Gene, Jr. "The Mullein: Plant Piscicide of the Mountain Folk Culture." *Geographical Review* 64 (April 1974): 235–52.

——. "Appalachian Isolation: Fact or Fiction." *An Appalachian Symposium: Essays in
Honor of Cratis D. Williams.* Edited by J. W. Williamson. Boone, N.C.: Appalachian
State University Press, 1977: 77–91.

——. "Folk Settlements in the Blue Ridge Mountains." *Appalachian Journal* 5 (Winter
1978): 204–45.

Williams, John Alexander. *West Virginia: A History.* New York: W. W. Norton, 1976.

——. *Appalachia: A History.* Chapel Hill: University of North Carolina Press, 2002.

——. *West Virginia and the Captains of Industry.* Morgantown: West Virginia University
Press, 2003.

Williams, Michael. *Americans and Their Forests: A Historical Geography.* New York:
Cambridge University Press, 1992.

——. *Deforesting the Earth: From Prehistory to Global Crisis.* Chicago: University of Chicago Press, 2003.

Williams, Michael Ann. *Homeplace: The Social Use and Meaning of Folk Dwelling in
Southwestern North Carolina.* Charlottesville: University of Virginia Press, 1991.

Williams, Raymond. *The Country and the City*. New York: Oxford University Press, 1973.

Williams, Samuel Cole. "The Admission of Tennessee into the Union." *Tennessee Historical Quarterly* 4 (December 1945), 291–319.

Williamson, J. W. *Southern Mountains in Silent Films: Plot Synopses of Movies About Moonshining, Feuding, and Other Mountain Topics, 1904–1929*. Jefferson, N.C.: McFarland, 1994.

Wilson, Darlene. "The Felicitous Convergence of Mythmaking and Capital." *Journal of Appalachian Studies* 1 (Fall 1995): 5–31.

Wolf, Eric R. *Europe and the People Without History*. Berkeley: University of California Press, 1982.

Wood, Allan. *The Groundnut Affair*. London: The Bodley Head, 1950.

Wood, Ellen Meiksins. *The Origin of Capitalism: A Long View*. London: Verso, 2002.

Wrightson, Keith. *Earthly Necessities: Economic Lives in Early Modern Britain*. New Haven, Conn.: Yale University Press, 2002.

Zohary, Daniel, and Maria Hopf. *Domestication of Plants in the Old World: The Origin and Spread of Domesticated Plants in Southwest Asia, Europe, and the Mediterranean Basin*. New York: Oxford University Press, 2012.

ACKNOWLEDGMENTS

RAMP HOLLOW WOULD NOT HAVE BEEN POSSIBLE without the scholarship of those who came before me. Historians of Appalachia whose work I read and admire include Allen Batteau, David Whisnant, David C. Hsiung, Dwight Billings, Henry Shapiro, Honor Sachs, John Alexander Williams, Kathleen Blee, Kathryn Newfont, Mary Beth Pudup, Paul Salstrom, Rebecca J. Bailey, Ronald Eller, Ronald L. Lewis, Robert S. Weise, Sarah Gregg, Stephen Aron, and Wilma A. Dunaway. My less proximate inspirations are just as important to this book. They include Barry Cunliffe, Charles Sellers, Christopher Hitchens, David Graeber, David Harvey, E. P. Thompson, Ellen Meiksins Wood, Eric Wolf, Ester Boserup, Fernand Braudel, Immanuel Wallerstein, Joan Martinez-Alier, John Bellamy Foster, J. B. Jackson, John Gaventa, Marshall Sahlins, Michael

Merrill, Michael Watts, Mike Davis, Raymond Williams, Robert McC. Netting, Wendell Berry, Adam Smith, and Karl Marx. I take them wherever I go. They've taught me to look for hidden histories, obscured relationships, and organizing powers.

I have learned from remarkable teachers. Gunter Barth (1925–2004) taught me how to think and write about history. My many other teachers have included Ann Fabian, Carolyn Merchant, David Montgomery (1927–2011), Donald Worster, Enrique Mayer, Herman Daly, Howard Lamar, Jackson Lears, Jack Temple Kirby (1938–2009), James Scott, John Demos, John Mack Faragher, Ken Jowitt, Michael Dove, Michael Perelman, Paul Groth, Paul Salstrom, Pierce Lewis, Robert Wokler (1942–2006), Robin Winks (1930–2003), Roger Kennedy (1926–2011), Robert Middlekauf, William Bouwsma (1932–2004), and William Cronon.

Ann Fabian and Jackson Lears accepted me as a senior fellow at the Rutgers Center for Historical Analysis during 2007–2008. The remarkable members of the RCHA seminar helped me to think at an early stage in my writing. They included Toby Jones, Michael Adas, Paul Clemens, and Alastair Bonnet. Michael Perelman guided me with his deep knowledge of political economy and inspired me to think more deeply. Tony Waters read early chapter fragments and offered important suggestions. This book benefited from the insights and encouragement of Elizabeth Blackmar and Andrew Sartori as part of a seminar sponsored by the O'Connell Initiative on the Global History of Capitalism, hosted by Fordham University in the spring of 2016. Betsy gave me detailed comments on every chapter, for which I am deeply grateful. Harold Forsythe commented during the same seminar, read all the text, and directed me to useful sources. My generous and spirited colleagues Rosemary Wakeman, Christopher Dietrich, David Hamlin, and Silvana Patriarca also commented. Thanks to Stephen Leccese for his help with the bibliography and to Tobias Hrynick for tracking down medieval sources.

Thanks also to the scholars and editors who helped me sharpen my thinking and who published my work: Jennifer Klein, Kate Brown and Thomas Kluboch (*International Labor and Working-Class History*), Cynthia Ott (*Environmental History*), and Andrew Isenberg (*The Oxford Handbook of Environmental History*). Thanks also to Thomas Thurston, Daniel Lanpher, Jonathan Freiman, and Andrew Weise. Mark Fiege commented on an early version of the third chapter. John Mack Faragher and Doron Ben-Atar read a later version of the same. Participants in the Agrarian Studies Colloquium at Yale University read the fourth chapter. I offered an early version of the same to the New York Metro Environmental History Seminar organized by Neil Maher in 2012. Maria Farland gave me a very helpful reading of the fifth chapter. I relied on Maria's terrific scholarship, especially her formulation of rural degeneracy. Brian Donahue read the entire manuscript, instructed me on many points, and corrected a number of errors. Sara Rushing shared her terrific library of political theory. Lisa Adams, my agent at the Garamond Agency, never forgot about me, though it took me more than a decade to send her a draft. Back in 2005, Thomas LeBien took a risk on a vague idea and drew up a contract. By the time I finished, Alex Star had become editor of Hill and Wang at Farrar, Straus and Giroux. I am unbelievably fortunate to have worked with Alex on the final form of this book. Scott Borchert, also at FSG, also gave the manuscript a terrific reading.

I am grateful to Fordham University for a Faculty Fellowship in 2014. H.R. Scott of the West Virginia University Agriculture Extension Service drove me to just about every hollow and ridge top in Monongalia County with great hospitality. Charles and Whitney Hunter showed me their beautiful farm and allowed me to spend all the time I wanted tramping around the Hoard and Stewart cabins. I wish to thank the helpful staff members of the West Virginia History Collection at West Virginia University, the West Virginia State Archives, and the Eastern Regional Coal Archives in Bluefield. Paul Salstrom's contribution to this book goes beyond that of a generous colleague. I asked Paul for a little advice after reading *Appalachia's Path to Dependency* (1994). He gave me much more than that. Paul mailed me article after article, twice read the entire manuscript, alerted me to things I had never heard of, and responded calmly to my confusion and angst. Paul is a great scholar and one of the most generous colleagues I have known.

I wrote this book over several years and through many changes. My wife, Leslie, helped me hone the ideas in *Ramp Hollow* from the day we met. She asked questions that often sent me to rethink a position or revise a conclusion. Our children—Batsheva, Elijah, Elise, Jacob, Jaden, and Katya—mostly experienced my work on this book at the dinner table, when I would tell them about something I found or was thinking about. Maybe one day they'll open it and find that it's about families working together in abundance and hardship, love of place, and perseverance.

INDEX

Numbers in *italics* refer to maps or notes.

Acadians, 78, 81
Adams, Henry, 205
Adams, John Quincy, 40
Affluent Society, The (Galbraith), 255
Affordable Care Act (2010), 267
Africa, xviii, 60, 77, 244, 278, 282,
    287–88; slaves from, 20, 31, 65, 75,
    83, 216; *see also specific nations*
African-Americans, 5, 16, 83, 107,
    270, 304*n75*, 308*n25*, 333*n33*; in
    coal fields, 221, 223; degeneracy
    attributed to, 199; dispossession of,
    211; enclosure to prevent land
    ownership by, 187–88; in Port Royal
    Experiment, 185–87; sharecropping
    by, xiii, 334*n38*; among Sirionó,
    30–31; tenant farming by, 231–34;
    Western migration of, 185, 189;
    see also slaves
African Development Bank, 280, 284
Agrarian Justice (Paine), 39, 256
Agricultural Adjustment Administration,
    209, 248
Agricultural Depression (Polk), 176
Agriculture, U.S. Department of
    (USDA), 130, 152, 208, 229, 238–40,
    248, 273, 333*n32*, 335*n48*
Agriculture Reform, Food, and Jobs Act
    (2013), 339*n38*
Alabama, 5, 23, 159, 233–34, 239, 240,
    295*n33*, 332*n31*
Albanians, 35

Albright, Horace, 237
Alger, Horatio, Jr., 177
Allegheny Front, 100
Allegheny Mountains, 4, 12, 91
Allen, James Lane, 21–22, 197–98, 203,
    323*n83*
Alpha Natural Resources, 269
Alston, William, 334*n40*
Amazonia, 143
American Art Association, 327*n38*
American Constitutional Association,
    223
American Engineering Council, 333*n34*
American Friends Service Committee,
    226
American Revolution, *see* Revolutionary
    War
"American Scholar, The" (Emerson), 193
Anatolia, 109
Anderson, Benedict, 118
Andes, 71–72
Anglican Church, 77
Anglo-Saxons, 17, 18, 20
Anshutz, Thomas, 186–87
Antietam, Battle of, 4, 130
Apache nation, 178
Appalachian Plateau, 4, 22, 132–33, 143,
    149, 152–53, 157, 317*n42*
Appalachian Regional Commission
    (ARC), 7, 22, 123, 260–63
Appleton's Journal, 199
Arapaho nation, 327*n40*

Arcadia, 38–39, 100, 150, 185, 193
Archer Daniels Midland Company, 210
Arkansas, 64, 328*n48*
Armco, 243
Arthurdale (West Virginia), 227–31, 259, 274, 332*n31*, 333*n33*
Associated Presbyterian Church, 104–105
Astor family, 18
Atlantic Charter, 244–45
Atlantic Monthly, The, 181
Australia, 181
Azerbaijan, 51
Aztecs, 302*n50*

Back Allegheny Mountain, 4
Bacon's Rebellion, 92
Bailey, Liberty Hyde, 198
Baily, Dave, 275
Baltimore, 15, 22, 138
Baltimore and Ohio Railroad, 131, 167, 313*n14*
Barbados, 83
Barnwell, Timothy Lee, 275
barter, 68, 111–13, 117, 153, 239, 309*nn35, 36*, 310*n37*
Bartram, William, 141
Batey, Mavis, 300*n40*
Baylor, Francis Courtenay, 322*n82*
Becker, Jane S., 335–36*n54*
Bee, Kathleen M., 314*n16*, 317*n41*, 320*n63*
Beijing, 288
Belcher family, 153, 157–58, 161–65, 168, 319*n57*, 320*n63*, 321*nn66, 67*
Belize, 303*n60*
Benedict, Ruth, 251
Benson, Ezra Taft, 328*n48*
Bentham, Jeremy, 300*n41*
Benton, Thomas Hart, 11, 12
Berea College, 213
Berkeley, Hugo, 281

Bernardino of Siena, Saint, 63
Berry, Wendell, 234, 272
Big Black, 262
Big Sandy River, 128, 130, 319*n57*
Billings, Dwight B., 314*n16*, 317*n41*, 320*n63*
Bingham, George Caleb, 315*n26*
Blackburn, Robin, 304*n73*
Black Death, 51, 52, 62
Blountville, Battle of, 128
Blue-grass and Rhododendron (Fox), 205, 327*n41*
Boas, Franz, 251
Blue Ridge region, 4, 7, 8, 11, 22, 81, 239, 315*n29*; diversity of species of, 143; land ownership west of, 103, 133; livestock of, 144, 146; swidden agriculture in, 235–37; timber industry in, 168–69; tourism in, 237–38, 240; watershed of, 132
Boccaccio, Giovanni, 51
Bohemian immigrants, 180
Bolivia, 30
Bonaparte, Louis-Napoléon, 48
Bonaparte, Napoleon, 63, 118
Boone, Daniel, 8, 13–14, 23, 28, 39, 76, 86, 88
Boreman, Arthur I., 132
Borneo, 72–73, 285, 337*n13*
Borsodi, Ralph, 246
Boserup, Ester, 150, 152, 254, 296*n5*
Boston, 18, 191, 294*n24*
Boswell, James, 312*n1*
Brackenridge, Hugh Hammond, 99
Braidwood, Robert J., 296*n2*
Brasilia, 123
Braudel, Fernand, 63–65, 92, 292*n5*, 309*n36*, 312*n55*
Brazil, 78, 183, 283
Breaking Home Ties (Hovenden), 177, 207
Brenner, Robert, 148, 301*n44*
Bretton Woods Agreement, 245

Brisbane, Albert, 190
Britain, 12, 99, 118, 147, 214, 280, 301*n44*, 307*n14*; capitalism in, 49–50, 53–54, 60, 62–63, 154, 214, 215, 279; coal and iron production in, 15; colonies of, 78, 87, 183, 91; in North American Indian wars, 8, 78; Proclamation Line established by, 11, 92; Revolutionary War against, 81; *see also* England; Scotland; Wales
Bronze Age, 109
Brooks, Alonza Beecher, 170, 174–75
Brown, William Wells, 83
Buffalo Creek, 265
Buffett, Warren, 64
Bull Creek, 263
Burchardt, Jeremy, 329*n8*
Bureau of Indian Affairs, 179, 246
Burke, Edmund, 300*n41*
Burr, Dale, 210
Bush, Florence Cope, 35
Butz, Earl, 209, 328*n48*

Cahan, Abraham, 327*n39*
California, xiv, 12, 86, 177, 207, 262, 317*n41*, 326*n35*, 332*n31*
Camden, Johnson, 138
Campbell, John C., 235, 239
campesinos, xiv–xv, 28, 65, 68, 72, 76, 288
Canada, 78, 91, 181
Candler, John, 70
Canterbury, archbishop of, 52
Cape Hatteras, 119
Capito, Shelley Moore, 266, 338*n35*
captured gardens, 214–35; of African-Americans, 231–34; British, 214–18; on coal company lands, 218–25; during Great Depression, 225–31
Carey, George W., 305*n3*
Carey, Henry, 41
Cargill, Inc., 210

Cartée, Cornelius Soule, 296*n2*
Cass, Lewis, 26
Cather, Willa, 207
Catholics, 294*n24*, 299*n28*
cattle, 27, 38, 78, 98, 142–48, 235, 260, 296*n5*, 317*n40*; commercial production of, 133, 134, 146–48, 151–53, 177, 207; corn for feeding, 143, 146; dairy, 181, 182; in division of labor, 44–45; ecological base for, 80, 174, 272; forest grazing, xiv, 33, 69, 107, 142, 276, 316*n35*; as form of property, 63, 97, 310*n42*; impact of industrialization on, 139, 170, 172; on lands of absentee owners, 9, 103; as market commodities, 22, 95, 241, 317*n41*; *see also* livestock
Caudill, Harry, 259–61
Cayton, Andrew R., 306*n5*
Cecil, Hill H., 162, 320–21*n66*
censuses, xvi, xvii, 9, 144, 147–48, 240, 308*n23*, 315*n29*, 317*n40*, 318*n42*, 323*n1*
Chamberlayne, Edward, 298*n17*
Chambers, Whittaker, 333*n33*
Charles I, King of England, 56
Charles II, King of England, 88
Charleston (South Carolina), 10, 83, 186, 187
Charleston (West Virginia), 150, 158, 269, 238, 264
Chattanooga, Battle of, 128
Chaucer, Geoffrey, 18
Chayanov, Alexander Vasilevich, 68–69, 71, 256, 302*n55*, 303*n59*, 311*n49*
Cheat Mountain, 4; battle of, 128
Cheat River, 104
Chemstream, 265
Cheney, Dick, 326*n35*
Cherokee nation, xiii, 5, 24–28, 60, 65, 142, 211, 294*nn33, 34*
Cherokee War, 78

Chesapeake and Ohio Railroad, 131, 167
Chesapeake Bay, 167
Cheyenne nation, 178, 327*n40*
Chicago, 275, 327*n40*
Chickasaw nation, 24, 25, 27
China, 19, 244, 257, 270, 283, 288
Choctaw nation, 24, 25
Christian family, 321*n70*
Christianity, 25, 26, 186, 260
Church, Frederick, 198
Cincinnati, 3, 243
Civil Disobedience (Thoreau), 192
civilization, 14, 169, 195, 197, 237, 246, 256, 296*n2*, 333*n34*; farming as catalyst of, 11, 40, 217, 298*n19*; impact of division of labor on, 43–44; Indians viewed as incompatible with, 27, 30; mountains as impediment to, 128, 144, 201–202, 205, 259–60, 293*n10*; stages of, 35–38, 41–42; taxation seen as educational force in, 121, 122; wealth as source of, 47, 115
Civil War, 4, 29, 124, 132, 147, 151, 160, 208, 319*n55*; African-American smallholders during, 185–86; guerrilla tactics in, 128–29; Indian wars in aftermath of, 178; industrialization during and after, 129, 165; livestock markets at end of, 144; Western migration following, 189; West Virginia in, 15, 133, 134
Clark, Noble, 332*n29*
Clark, William, 94
Cleft's War, 78
Cleveland, Grover, 314*n24*
Clinch River, 265
Clinton, Bill, 280, 337*n18*
Cliser, Melanchton, 238, 335*n47*
Coal Age magazine, 223
Coal Residuals Reuse and Management Act (2013), 266

Coal River, 130, 263, 275
Cobb, Ned, 234
Coke, Roger, 279
Cold War, 249, 252
Cole, Thomas, 38–39, 198, 296*n4*
Collier, John, 246, 336*n5*
Collins, Justus, 220–21
Colman, Henry, 70
Colorado, 189
Colorado River Reservation, 179
Colquhoun, Patrick, 47
Columbus, Christopher, 77
Comanche nation, 178
Commission on Country Life, 198
"Common Lot, The" (Miles), 35, 219–20
Commons Communities Act, 272–75, 277
Communist Manifesto (Marx and Engels), 48, 298*n20*
Communist Party of the United States, 247, 333*n33*
Comstock Lode, 12
Concord (Massachusetts), 78–80, 96, 189–92
Conditions of Agricultural Growth, The (Boserup), 254
Confederate States of America, 8, 128, 130, 134, 160, 178, 185–86, 247, 313*n14*
Congress, U.S., 14, 186–87, 221, 271, 294*n24*, 332*n24*, 333*n32*; agricultural policies of, 210, 267; conflict over slavery in, 12; and dispossession of Indians, 27, 179; during Great Depression, 209, 229; industrialization supported in, 131, 138; populists elected to, 184; West Virginia admitted to Union by, 134, 313*n14*; Whiskey Tax legislation in, 98, 110, 116; *see also* House of Representatives, U.S.; Senate, U.S.
Conklin, Harold C., 251–53, 255
Connecticut, 142

Conojocular War (Cresap's War), 92
conservationists, 188, 235–37, 240, 253
Constitution, U.S., 25, 92, 117, 118, 132,
    336n7; Thirteenth Amendment, 188;
    Eighteenth Amendment, 259;
    "three-fifths" clause, 132; Twenty-
    First Amendment, 259
Consummation of Empire (Cole), 39
Continental Army, 90, 95, 104
Cook et al. v. Raleigh Lumber Company
    (1874), 319–20n59
Cope, Dorie Woodruff, 166, 174, 322n83
Corbin, D., 331n19
Corn Belt, see Great Plains; specific states
cotton production, 9, 15, 84, 133, 155,
    216, 253, 316n34; for debt payments,
    182; by Indians, 25, 30; for mills, 34,
    129; in Port Royal experiment,
    185–86; slavery and, 12, 27, 39, 81,
    83, 107, 129, 132; by tenant farmers,
    232, 234, 334n38
Coulibaly, Ibrahim, 282
Country and the City, The (Williams), 127
Country Politician, The (Bingham), 315n26
Course of Empire, The (Cole), 38
Coxe, Tench, 122–23, 312n55
Crawford, William, 101
Crazy Horse, 178
Creek nation, xiii, 8, 24, 25, 27, 91
Creek War, 78
Crescent Lumber Company, 322n78
Crèvecoeur, J. Hector St. John de, 3, 9,
    76, 81–84, 190, 234
Crittenden (Fox), 205
Crockett, David, 8
Crow nation, 178
Cumberland Gap, 8, 41, 87, 197, 202
Cumberland Mountains, 16–17, 21
Cumberland Vendetta and Other Stories,
    The (Fox), 205
Cunliffe, Barry, 102
Custer, George Armstrong, 327n40

Dakota Territory, 180–82
Daniel, Pete, 231
Daughters of the American Revolution,
    18, 294n24
Davenport, Charles, 198
Davis, Darrell Haug, 309n28
Davis, Henry, 138
Davis, James W., 162–63, 321n66
Davis, Mike, 183, 295n41
Davis, Richard Harding, 205
Davis Coal and Coke Company, 138
Dawes Act (1887), 179–80, 182, 324n6
DDT, 265
Declaration of Independence, 155
degeneracy, 29, 197–99, 201, 242, 261; as
    racial or ethnic aspersion, 17, 20–21,
    27, 199, 205
Delaware Indians, 5, 8, 19, 87–88, 107,
    124
Delaware River Valley, 86–89, 141
Democratic Party, 137, 139, 184, 267,
    314n24
De Schutter, Olivier, 286, 287, 341n67
Deserted Village, The (Goldsmith), 59
Desolation (Cole), 39
Destruction (Cole), 39
Detroit, 243
development, 122, 130, 238, 279–86,
    288, 328n5; industrial, 133; social,
    61, 244; stages of, 36, 41; see also
    economic development
Devyr, Thomas Ainge, 329n8
Dickens, Cody, 160
Dickerson, William, 133
Dillon's Rule, 136–37, 314nn18, 19
division of labor, 6, 43–44, 67, 113, 119,
    230, 292n5; Hamilton on, 93, 94, 97,
    227; political economists on, 40, 42,
    44–45; social, 64, 98, 193
Division of Subsistence Homesteads,
    U.S., 214, 227, 229–31, 274, 277,
    333n32

Doddridge, Joseph, 108
Donahue, Brian, 80
Dore, Elizabeth, 329*n5*
Dorie: Woman of the Mountains (Bush), 35
Douglass, Frederick, 83–84
Dove, Michael, 72–74, 303*n62*, 337*n12*
Draper, Hal, 298*n20*
Drucker, Peter F., 230
Dugdale, Robert L., 198–99
Dunaway, Wilma, 292*n6*
Dunmore, Lord, 293*n10*
Duplin County (North Carolina)
    Agricultural Society, 187
Durand, Asher B., 198
Dutch, 75, 87–88, 198

Eastman Chemical Company, 265
economic development, xviii, 32, 97,
    236, 237, 244, 277, 340*n45*;
    agricultural, 249–50, 252–54, 257;
    critiques of, 255–57; importance of
    markets in, 113, 122–23; international
    aid organizations and agencies for,
    145, 245, 249, 256–58, 279, 284
    (*see also* World Bank); U.S. domestic
    projects for, 236, 240, 260, 262;
    see also division of labor
Edinburgh, 34
Edwards, William H., 159–60, 162–63
Egypt, 51; ancient, 326n35
Ehrlich, Paul, 256
ejectment, xiv, 21, 46, 125, 168, 177;
    court cases on, 105, 149, 159; of
    Indians, 24–25, 27
Eliot, Jared, 80
Elizabethan English, 19
Elkhorn Creek, 157, 161, 319*n57*
Elkins, Stephen, 138
Elk River, 130, 264
Elk River Coal and Lumber Company,
    172–73, 322–23*n83*
Eller, Ronald, 330*n14*

El Niño oscillations, 183
Emerson, Ralph Waldo, 178, 192–95
enclosure, xiv, 21, 45, 74, 127, 223, 277,
    281, 288; in Africa, 60–61, 279, 284;
    capitalism and, xviii, 48–50, 61, 89,
    250, 279; in England, 45, 46, 49,
    54–61, 76, 154, 178, 214, 298*n17*,
    299*n33*; of Indian hunting lands,
    178–85; logging as method of, 168,
    174; poverty resulting from, 32, 48;
    during Reconstruction, 187–88;
    refugees from, 76, 216, 218; taxation
    and, 113, 125–26
End of the Day, Montclair (Inness), 200
Engels, Friedrich, 59, 312*n1*
England, 54–62, 64, 111, 113, 139, 157,
    158, 160, 216, 279; Appalachian coal
    field investors in, 159–60; Black Death
    in, 51; captured gardens in, 216–17;
    commons in, 53–54; enclosure in, 45,
    49, 54–61, 76, 154, 178, 214, 279,
    299*n33*; excise riots in, 94; famines
    in, 53, 301*n41*; indentures from, 20,
    77; industrialization in, 43, 193;
    peasants in, xiv, 28, 71, 76, 82, 188,
    281; poor laws in, 60; Reformation
    in, 77; settlers from, 76–78, 87, 88,
    223; tenancy in, 61–62, 301*n44*;
    travelers from, 110, 127; *see also*
    Britain; London
English Civil War, 298*n17*, 299*n28*
English language, 19, 63, 66, 67, 70, 143,
    312*n53*
Enlightenment, 251
environmental determinism, 19–20,
    251
Environmental Protection Agency (EPA),
    265, 266, 269
Erie Canal, 208
Ethan Frome (Wharton), 198
expansionism, 12, 23, 25, 29, 41, 78, 87
extractive industries, *see* coal industry,

iron mining, lumber companies, oil
industry

Fairmont Coal Company, 222
Familiar Words (Urquhart), 44
Farland, Maria, 197–98
Farmer and His Son at Harvesting, The
  (Anshutz), 186–87
Farmers' Alliance, 140, 183, 305*n3*
"Farming" (Emerson), 192–93, 195
Faulkner, Charles, 11, 14–15
Fawcett, Henry, 329*n7*
Federal Bureau of Investigation (FBI),
  118
Federalist, The, 90, 96–97, 118, 120,
  311*n20*
Federalists, 9, 25, 89, 91, 102, 119, 124,
  155
Federal Reserve, U.S., 73
Fels, Samuel, 245
Ferguson, Adam, 41
Ferguson, Patrick, 8–9
Fernow, Bernard, 168–69
feudalism, 11, 51–53, 57, 61, 82
Fickey, Amanda L., 340*n45*
Fiji, 255
Filburn, Roscoe, 248
Filipinos, 19
Finnish immigrants, 19, 87, 107
First World War, *see* World War I
Five Acres and Independence (Kains), 246
Flagg, Wilson, 85–86, 184, 193
Flat Top Coal Company/Flat Top Land
  Trust, 130, 161–65, 168, 320*n62*
Flat Top Mountain, 7, 130, 155, 160, 220
Flight from the City (Borsodi), 246
Florida, 5, 186
folk traditions, 22, 236, 237, 242, 246
Ford, Henry, 230–31
Ford Foundation, 249, 252
Fordham University, 64
Foreign Affairs, 256

Forest Farm, 247
Forest Service, U.S., 236
Forrest, Cliff, 265
Fort Sanders, Battle of, 128
Fox, James, 202–203
Fox, John, Jr., 202–207, 327*n41*
France, 31–32, 48, 51–52, 63, 70, 87, 111,
  182; colonization by, 121–22, 280, 282
Frank, André Gunder, 292*n5*
Fredericksburg, Battle of, 130
Freedmen's Bureau Act (1865), 187
Freedom Industries, 264–67
Free Press, 297*n11*
French and Indian War, 8, 11, 81, 101, 103
French and Iroquois War, 78
Frost, Robert, 198
Frost, William Goodell, 17–20
Fuerstenau, Douglass W., 338*n33*
Fulmer, William, xv

Gaddafi, Muammar, 283, 284
Galbraith, John Kenneth, 255
Gallatin, Albert, 156
Gambia, 312*n53*
Gandhi, Mohandas K., 272
Garland, Hamlin, 207
Gaul, 65
Gaventa, John, 224, 261–62
General Allotment Act (1887), *see* Dawes
  Act
General Electric (GE), 228–29
George, Henry, 199, 200
George III, King of England, 87, 101
Georgia, 119, 235, 239, 292*n2*, 295*n33*,
  325*n20*; African-Americans in, 83,
  232; enclosure in, 187, 188; Indians
  in, 5, 24, 25, 91
Germany, 51, 87, 182, 226, 230, 306*n7*,
  311*n47*, 333*n34*
Gettysburg, Battle of, 130
Giants in the Earth (Rölvaag), 207–208
Glasgow, 40, 94–95

Global Shea Alliance, 286
Global Slum, 287
Glover, Uriah, 105
Goddard, Henry, 198
Gold Rush, California, 12
Goldsmith, Oliver, 59
Good Life, The (Nearings), 247
Gordon, Robert Winslow, 246
Gospel of Matthew, 325*n23*
Gossip (Inness), 200
Grace, William R., 294*n24*
Graeber, David, 222, 312*n53*
Grant, James P., 256, 337*n18*
Grant, Ulysses S., 128, 178
Gray, Lewis Cecil, 238–41, 272, 316*n34*,
    335*n48*
Great Appalachian Forest, 165
Great Depression, 207, 209, 225, 243,
    245, 258–61, 288
Great Kanawha Petroleum Coal and
    Lumber Company, 136
Great Kanawha Valley, Title Map of
    Coal Field of, *2*, 3–4, 129, 136
Great Meadow (Concord,
    Massachusetts), 79–80, 304*n72*
Great Plains, 5, 15, 85–87, 128, 153,
    180–85, 207, 216; Indian nations of,
    178–79
Great Smoky Mountains, 166; National
    Park, 143
Green Mountains, 292*n2*
Green Revolution, 249, 252–53
Greenwald, Emily, 324*n6*
Gross, Robert, 190
gross dometic product (GDP), 210
Guatemala, 254
Gudeman, Stephen, 74, 117, 301*n43*,
    303*n60*
Guyandotte River, 155

Hahn, Steven, 187
Haiti, 31–32, 70

Hamilton, Alexander, 46, 110, 118–25,
    127, 306*n10*; economics of, 95–98,
    113–14, 120–24, 131, 225, 227, 306*n8*,
    312*n56*; *Federalist* articles by, 90, 96,
    118, 120, 306*n11*, 311*n52*; rebellions
    against tax policies of, 46, 93, 99–100,
    114–16, 124–25; views on
    governmental power of, 92–95,
    118–19, 306*n5*
Hanunóo people, 251–53, 337*n14*
Hardin, Garrett, 276
Harman v. Stearns (1897), 319*n56*
Harpers Ferry, 4, 167; Battle of, 128
Harper's Magazine, 185, 229, 325*n18*
Harriman, Henry I., 231
Harrison, Benjamin, 138
Harrison, William Henry, 7–8
Hartford Oil and Mining Company, 136
Harvard University, 202
Harvey, David, 292*n5*
Hatch Act (1887), 208
Hatfields, 135, 148, 166–68, 201–202
Hawaii, 255
Heart of the Hills, The (Fox), 205–207
Hebrides, 127
Hell-fer-Sartain and Other Stores (Fox), 205
Henderson, Richard, 293*n9*
Henson, Josiah, 83
Herskovitz, Melville, 255
Highlander Research and Education
    Center, 261
Hill, George Canning, 13–14
Hill-Billies, 23
Hillbilly Elegy (Vance), 277–78
Hillbilly Highway, 243
Hill Folk, The (Davenport), 198
Hills Bank & Trust Company, 210
Hirohito, Emperor of Japan, 230
Hitler, Adolf, 230
Hoard family, xvi
Hobbes, Thomas, 295*n38*, 299*n28*
Hollow Folk (Mandel and Henry), 241–42

Holmberg, Allan, 30–31, 295*n38*
Holocene era, 337*n17*
Home, Henry, *see* Kames, Lord
Homer, Winslow, xvii, 176, 178, 180, 185, 186, 200, 207, 208
Homestead Act (1862), 180, 189, 216, 324*n13*
homesteads, 100, 106, 142, 170, 209, 240, 247; government subsidized, 214, 227–31, 274, 277, 333*nn32, 33*, 336*n5*; on Great Plains, 84–85, 180–82, 216, 324*n13*
Homeward (Inness), 200
Hoover, Herbert, 226, 237–38
Horseshoe Bend, Battle of, 8
Horton, Bill, 261
Hotchkiss, Jedediah, 130, 160
House of Representatives, U.S., 16, 266, 267, 338*n35*; *see also* Congress, U.S.
Houston, Sam, 8
Hovenden, Thomas, xvii, 177, 207
Howells, William Dean, 205
Hsiung, David, 294*n28*
Hudson River, 292*n2*
Huffington Post, 267–68
Humphrey, Caroline, 111
Hungary, 51; immigrants from, 5, 180
Hume, David, 41
Hunter family, xvi–xvii
Huntington, Ellsworth, 20
Huntington and Big Sandy Railroad, 167
Hyneman, Charles Shang, 305*n3*

Idleman, David, 35
Illinois, 5, 87, 153, 258, 308*n25*, 330*n16*
I'll Take My Stand (Twelve Southerners), 246
Immerwahr, Daniel, 277
indenture, 20, 77, 216
Independence (play), 10–11
India, 183, 244, 249, 254, 277, 283, 309*n30*

Indiana, 84, 153, 258, 330*n16*
Indian Appropriation Act (1871), 323*n2*
Indian Citizen Act (1924), 180
Indian Removal Act (1830), 26–27
Indian Reorganization Act (1934), 180, 227
Indians, American, 5, 12, 31, 76, 87, 100, 227, 242; attitudes of whites toward, 9, 29, 34, 94, 246, 308*n25*; dispossession of, xiii, 24–28, 84, 156, 180, 182–83, 237, 270–71, 294*n33*, 324*n6*; New Deal programs for, 277, 336*n5*; South American, 30–31, 295*n38*; wars against, 8, 11, 60, 92, 124–25, 128, 178–80, 327*n40*; Washington's treaties with, 24–25, 91; *see also individual nations*
Indian Territory, 27
Indonesia, 65, 72
Industrial Abandonment Tax, 273, 274
industrialization, *see* coal industry; iron mining; lumber companies; oil industry
Industrial Revolution, xiv, 7, 34
Inness, George, xvii, 195–97, 199–201, 327*n38*
In the Orchard, Milton (Inness), 200
Inquiry into the Principles of Political Economy (Steuart), 45, 113
Interior Department, U.S., 227, 271, 333*n32*, 336*n5*
International Monetary Fund, 245
International Rice Research Institute (IRRI), 252
Interstate Anti-Trust Conference, 221
Iowa, 210, 332*n31*; Supreme Court of, 136–37
Iran, 109
IR-8, 252, 254
Ireland, 51, 87, 139, 159, 215; immigrants from, 8, 18, 221, 294*n24* (*see also* Scots-Irish)

iron mining, 15, 133, 158, 159, 188
Iroquois Confederacy, 118
Irving, Washington, 12
Isaac, Barry, 295*n38*
Ise, John, 207
Islamic Development Bank, 280
Islamists, 282
Italian immigrants, 18, 201
Italian language, 63
Italy, 51
Ivory Coast, 312*n53*
I Will Lift Up Mine Eyes (Skidmore), 35,
    173–74

Jackson, Andrew, 8, 25–27, 294*n33*
Jackson, Robert H., 248
Jackson, Thomas "Stonewall," 8, 130
Jaffa, 51
Jamaica, 60
James I, King of England, 56
Jefferson, Thomas, 25, 81, 93–94, 124,
    156, 304*n73*, 306*n5*
Jenkins, Evan, 267
Jericho, 65
Jersey Land Riots, 92
Jewish immigrants, 18, 201
John Fries' Rebellion, 92
Johnson, Andrew, 187
Johnson, Josephine, 209
Johnson, Samuel, 127–28, 312*n1*
joint-stock companies, xiv, 7, 85, 130,
    133–34
Jones, Jacqueline, 20
Jones, Mary Harris "Mother," 224
Jordan, Terry, 107
Judd, Richard, 340*n51*
Jukes, The (Dugdale), 198–99
Julian, George Washington, 84–86

Kalimantan (Borneo), 72–73, 285, 337*n13*
Kallikak Family, The (Goddard), 198
Kames, Lord, 41, 244, 296*n5*

Kanawha River, 101, 130, 223, 264
Kanawha Valley, 159
Kane, Robert, 215
Kansas, 22, 87, 180, 181, 185, 189, 324*n15*
Kansas-Nebraska Act (1854), 85
Kaups, Matti, 107
Keith, James, 319*n56*
Kekchi Maya, 303*n60*
Kellie, Luna, 183–84
Kennedy, Roger, 316*n34*
Kentuckians, The (Fox), 205–206
Kentucky, 5, 7, 8, 12, 16, 39, 239, 271,
    308–309*n28*, 314*n6*, 319*n57*, 320*n59*,
    326*n35*, 335*n49*; Bluegrass region of,
    144, 166, 202, 292*n4*; in Civil War,
    15, 128; coal industry in, 34, 213,
    240, 269; commerce in, 21–22, 113;
    Fox's novels about, 202–205; land
    ownership in, 9, 13–14, 101, 102, 142,
    158, 159, 219; map of, *x*; settlement of,
    13–14, 18–19, 87, 88; during Whiskey
    Rebellion, 91, 93, 105, 110, 123
Kenya, 312*n53*
King, Martin Luther, Jr., 261
King Philip's War, 78
Kings Mountain, Battle of, 9
Kingston Fossil Plant, 265
Knight of the Cumberland, A (Fox), 205
Korea Eximbank, 280
Kroeber, Alfred, 251
Kulikoff, Allan, 107, 303*n59*, 311*n48*
Kurds, 35
Kuwait, 280

Lackawanna Valley, The (Inness), 196,
    326*n30*
La Follette, Philip, 333*n34*
Lakota nation, 178, 327*n40*
Lambert, Samuel, 320*n63*
Land Rush (film), 281
Land of Saddle Bags, The (Raine), 213
Lanman, Charles, 146–47, 316*n35*

"Last Camp Fire, The" (McNeill), 171
Last Forest, The (McNeill), 35
Lear, Tobias, 91
Lectures on Jurisprudence (Smith), 37
Lee, Robert E., 130
Leland, John, 298*n23*
Lenape nation, 87
Lessee of Ewing v. Burnet (1837), 308*n20*
Letters from an American Farmer
    (Crèvecoeur), 3, 9, 81–83, 234
Lewat, Osvalde, 281
Lewis, Andrew, 128
Lewis, John L., 225
Lewis, Ronald L., 295*n41*
Lewis, William Arthur, 249–50, 253,
    303*n59*, 316*n34*
Library of Congress, 225, 275; Archive of
    American Folk Song, 246
Libya, 283
Lincoln, Abraham, 8, 176
Lippincott's Magazine, 16
List, Friedrich, 47–48
Lithuania, 51
Little Bighorn, Battle of, 327*n40*
Little House series (Wilder), 208, 327*n46*
Little Ice Age, 52, 77
Little Shepherd of Kingdom Come, The
    (Fox), 205
Little Turtle's War, 78, 91, 124–25
Lively, Kenny, 225
livestock, 3, 38, 47, 49–51, 63, 147, 154,
    181, 226, 259; in coal camps, 218,
    225, 331*n19*; enclosure and, 54–56,
    58, 187–88, 214; exchange value of,
    144–46, 148, 316*n34*; during Whiskey
    Rebellion, 105, 115; *see also* cattle
Lloyd, Henry, 221
L'Occitane, 286
Locke, John, 53, 300*n36*
Lodge, Henry Cabot, 205
logging, *see* lumber companies
Lomax, John A., 246

London, 34, 40, 52, 59, 75, 81, 113, 288,
    312*n53*
London School of Economics, 34
Lorain, John, 108
Los Angeles, 275
Los Baños (Philippines), 252
Louisiana, 185
Louisiana Purchase, 12
Louisiana Territory, 295, 304*n73*
Louisville Coal and Coke Company,
    220–21
Lowell family, 18
Lugard, Frederick, 121–22
Luks, George, 205
lumber companies, 68, 188, 171, 172,
    174, 237, 278; depletion of forests by,
    xiv, 131, 165, 168, 170, 322*n78*; land
    ownership by, xiv, 3, 93, 148, 158,
    172, 319–20*n59*, 322*n83*; productivity
    of, 22, 150, 168–69, 322*n78*
Luxemburg, Rosa, 334n42
Luzon, 19

MacCorkle, William, 139, 258, 314*n24*
Machine Age in the Hills (Ross), 238
Machine in the Garden (Marx), 195–96
Madagascar, 121
Madison, James, 293*n10*, 311*n47*
Maine, 79, 168, 247, 276, 292*n2*
makeshift economies, 28, 33–34, 65, 67,
    167, 240, 275; ecological base of, 140,
    165, 174, 295*n41*; exchange
    commodities in, 72, 75–76, 100, 144;
    land ownership practices damaging
    to, 56, 106–107, 124, 131, 153–54;
    New England, 189, 195, 247
Malagasy, 121
Mali, xiv, 136, 279–86
Malthus, Thomas Robert, 70, 79, 150,
    216–17, 228, 296*n5*, 300*n41*
Manchin, Joe, 339*n38*
Manchuria, 78

Marine Corps, U.S., 278

Market Garden Initiative, 274

Marrowbone Oil and Mining Company, 136

Marshall, Humphrey, 102

Marshall, John, 295*n34*

Martin, Julian, 263–65, 267

Martinez-Alier, Joan, 341*n66*

Marx, Karl, 48, 58, 217, 256, 297*n11*, 300*n41*, 329*n5*; historical assumptions of, 40–41, 292*n5*; labor theory of value of, 62, 68, 330*n18*, 331*n21*; similarities of Thoreau and, 190–91, 195

Marx, Leo, 195

Maryland, 87, 90, 239; map, *xi*

Massachusetts, 78–79, 129, 189, 208, 216, 235, 326*n35*; Agricultural Survey of, 70; rebellion in, *see* Shays' Rebellion; witch trials in, 199

Maxwell Land Grant, 138

Mayer, Enrique, 69, 70, 293*n20*

McCormick reapers, 177

McCoys, 135, 166–68, 201–202

McDowell County (Virginia, *later* West Virginia), 16, 148, 151, 155, 160–62, 264, 267, 269, 317*n40*, 320*n62*

McGill, Nettie, 331*n20*, 335*n51*

McGillivray, Alexander, 24–25

MCHM (4-methylcyclohexanemethanol), 264–65

McNeill, G. D., 35, 171, 262

Mead, Margaret, 251

Metacom's War, 78

Medick, Hans, 328–29*n5*

"Mending Wall, The" (Frost), 198

Merrill, Michael, 303*n64*

Merrill v. Monticello (1891), 314*n18*

Merrimack River, 129

Messina (Sicily), 51

metes and bounds, 9, 103, 157

Methodists, 115

Mexican-American War, 12

Mexicans, xiii

Mexican Session, 12

Mexico, 249, 254, 257, 283

Mexico City, 287

Miami nation, 91, 124

Michigan, 26, 153, 230, 231

Milan, 52

Miles, Emma Bell, 35, 219–20, 329–39*n13*

Mill, James, 300*n41*

Mill, John Stuart, 300*n41*

Milton, John, 301*n46*

Mingo nation, 5

Minnesota, 182, 317*n41*, 332*n31*

Mississippi, 5, 185, 295*n33*; Military Division of the, 186

Mississippi River, 25, 91

Mississippi River Valley, 12, 81, 113

Missouri, 11, 14, 209, 316*n35*

Missouri, Department of the, 178

Missouri Compromise, 294–95*n33*

Missouri River, 94, 183

Moby-Dick (Melville), 195

modernity, 29, 37, 42, 44, 234, 245, 247, 336*n1*

modernization, 22, 48–49, 61, 174, 233, 236, 245; agricultural, 22, 249, 253–55, 257

Monacan nation, 237

monetization, 45, 48, 49, 93, 117, 122, 228, 248

Monongahela National Forest, 170

Monongahela River Valley, xvi, 108

Monsanto Company, 210

Montgomery, Michael, 19

More, Hannah, 47

More, Thomas, 300*n39*

Morgantown (Virginia, *later* West Virginia), xv, 7, 93, 133, 226, 313*n14*

Morris, Robert, 122, 155–57, 319*nn55, 56*

Morris Run Coal Company, 247

Mountain Europa, A (Fox), 203–205
Mumford, Lewis, 272
Munsee nation, xiii
Murray, John, Earl of Dunmore, xvi, 8

Napoleonic Wars, 329*n10*
Natchez War, 78
National Folk Festival, 245
National Industrial Recovery Act
 (NIRA; 1933), 227–29
National Park Service, 237
National Public Radio, 266
National Reform Association (NRA),
 329*n8*
National War Garden Commission,
 248
Native Americans, *see* Indians
Natufians, 65
Navajo nation, 246, 336*n5*
Neanderthals, 297*n9*
Nearing, Helen and Scott, 247, 256
Nebraska, 87, 143, 177, 180, 315*n32*
Nedelcovych, Mima, 280–81, 283, 286,
 341*n65*
Netting, Robert McC., 66–68, 301*n50*,
 302*n56*, 309*n30*, 337*n15*
Neville, George, archbishop of York, 50
Neville, John, 99
New Deal, 7, 227, 240, 247, 249, 259, 272,
 277
New England, 78–80, 83, 85, 118, 144,
 156, 189, 193, 195, 216, 276, 340*n51*;
 see also Connecticut; Maine;
 Massachusetts; New Hampshire;
 Vermont
Newfont, Kathryn, 315*n29*
New Hampshire, 12, 79, 282*n2*
New Jersey, 87, 90, 201, 196, 199, 326*n36*
New Mexico, 138
New Mexico Territory, 305*n78*
New Netherland, 88
New Orleans, 22, 81, 91, 113

New Sweden, 88
Newton, Isaac, 53
New York, 5, 12, 130, 198, 306*n10*,
 316*n34*, 326*n35*; Anti-Rent War in,
 305*n3*; farming in, 79, 81–83, 85, 208;
 taxation in, 99, 306*n11*
New York City, 24, 64, 171, 201, 246,
 275, 288, 292*n2*, 327*n40*; coal
 industry and, 3, 34, 159, 202; division
 of labor in, 40; Irish immigrants in,
 18, 294*n24*; during Revolutionary
 War, 81
New York Journal, 23
New York Stock Exchange, 49
New York Times, 15, 201, 260, 279, 284
Nez Percé nation, 324*n6*
Nicholas, Wilson Cary, 155, 157, 319*n55*
Nietzsche, Friedrich, vii
Nigeria, 122
Niger River, 279–80
Night Comes to the Cumberlands (Caudill),
 259–61
Nixon, Richard, 209
Nixon, Rob, 27–28, 212
Nobel Prize, 272, 340*n47*
Nomads of the Longbow (Holmberg), 30
Norfolk and Western Railway, 167–68
Norris, Frank, 183
"North Atlantic Universals" (Trouillot),
 37
North Carolina, 5, 8, 34, 93, 143, 145,
 159, 187, 188, 239, 275, 325*n22*
North Carolina Regulation, 92
Northup, Solomon, 83
Northwest Territory, 92, 118
Norway, 51
"Notes on Liberty and Property" (Tate),
 247
Notes on the State of Virginia (Jefferson),
 81
Novak, Barbara, 326*n30*
Nova Scotia, 78, 258

Now in November (Johnson), 209
Nyasaland, 312*n53*

Obama, Barack, 268–69
O'Brian, Hugh, 294*n24*
Ohio, 5, 132, 133, 153, 248, 316*n34*,
    330*n16*, 332*n31*; Indians in, 91;
    industrialization in, 243; map of, *x*;
    markets in, 22, 144
Ohio River, 7, 87, 92, 101, 119, 124, 128,
    138, 313*n14*, 319*n57*
Ohio State University, 278
Ohio Valley, 124, 138
oil industry, 129–30, 136, 138, 169, 303*n59*
Oklahoma, 27, 210–11
Old Barn, The (Inness), 200
Old Veteran, The (Inness), 200
Olmstead, Fredrick Law, 143–45
Onuf, Peter, 119
"On the Uses and Disadvantages of
    History for Life" (Nietzsche), vii
Ordinance of 1785, 102
Oregon, 5, 12, 87
Ostrom, Elinor, 272, 276, 340*n47*
Ottoman Empire, 51
Owen, Robert, 217, 225–27, 300*n41*,
    329*n10*
Oxfam, 284, 288
Oxford University, 261
Ozark Mountains, 5

Pack, Charles Lathrop, 248
Paine, Thomas, 39, 47, 256
Paint Creek Coal and Iron Mining and
    Manufacturing Company, 159
Paint Creek Strike, 224–25
Pakistan, 283
Palestine, 51
Panic of 1893, 182
Paris Climate Accord, 269
Paris International Exposition, 327*n38*
Parks, Rosa, 261

Parliament, British, 44, 45, 60, 77, 95,
    154, 217–18, 278; Board of
    Agriculture, 55
Pastoral or Arcadian State, The (Cole), 38
Pawnee nation, 178
Paxton Riots, 92
Peasants' Revolt, 52
Peeled Chestnut Gap, 157
Peloponnesian Peninsula, 38
Penn, William, 88
Pennsylvania, xvii, 5, 79, 87–88, 140,
    285, 308*n23*, 313*n14*, 317–18*n42*; coal
    industry in, 225, 226, 265; map of,
    x–xi; oil wells in, 129; tax rebellion
    in, *see* Whiskey Rebellion; University
    of, Wharton School of Business, 247;
    see also Philadelphia; Pittsburgh
People's Party, 184
Pequot War, 78
Perelman, Michael, 297*n8*
Petty, Adrienne Monteith, 325*n22*
Philadelphia, 9, 34, 86, 103, 113, 114,
    130, 156, 159, 160
Philippines, 19, 249, 251–53, 277
Picket, Clarence, 227
Piedmont, 4
Piedmont College, 235
Piers Plowman (Langland), 50
Pinchot, Gifford, 170
Pit, The (Norris), 183
Pittsburgh, 34, 93, 99, 110–11, 114, 116,
    123, 133, 144
Pittston Coal Company, 265
plantations, 12, 101, 132–33, 185–88,
    231, 286, 293*n10*, 313*n12*; in
    developing countries, 30–31, 65, 69,
    73, 285; of European colonialists, 32,
    60, 121; Indian ejection advocated by
    owners of, 24–25, 94; slaves on,
    20–21, 27, 39, 75, 81, 83, 107, 133,
    216, 295*n33*
Plant-Cutter Riots, 92

Plymouth Rock, 18
Pocahontas Coal Company, 212, 220
Polanyi, Karl, 65, 256, 287, 292*n5*
Polish immigrants, 180
Polk, Leonidas L., 176, 182
Pollard, Edward, 15–17
Pontiac's Rebellion, 78
"Poor White Trash" (anonymous), 144
Population Bomb (Ehrlich), 256
Port-au-Prince, 32
Port Royal Experiment, 185–87
Postal Service, U.S., 229
Potomac and Piedmont Coal and
    Railway Company, 138
Powell, Webster, 229–31, 333*n33*
Power and Powerlessness (Gaventa), 262
Prebisch, Raúl, 292*n5*
Price, Ben, 300*n38*
Price, Henry M., 316*n35*
Proclamation Line, 11, 92, 101
Progress and Poverty (George), 199
Prohibition, 259
Protestants, 22, 77, 195, 299*n28*
Prussia, 312*n1*
Pudup, Mary Beth, 317–18*n42*
Puritans, 18, 71, 216
Pythagoras, 38

Quakers, 70, 88, 226–27, 238

Raine, James Watt, 213, 322*n78*
Raketsky, John, xvi
Ramapo Mountains, 199; people of,
    326*n36*
Recent Economic Changes (Wells), 184
Reclaim Act (2016), 271
Reconstruction, 187, 189, 210, 232
Red Cloud, 178
Reed family, 308*n21*
Remington, Frederick, 205
Report on Manufactures (Hamilton),
    121

Republican Party, 137, 266–67, 271
Republicans, Jeffersonian, 124
Resettlement Administration, 333*n32*
Revolutionary War, 24, 88, 122–23,
    327*n41*; agrarian uprisings related to,
    91–92 (*see also* Shays' Rebellion;
    Whiskey Rebellion); economic
    impact on farmers of, 80; land
    ownership by elites of, 9, 13; treaty
    negotiations with Indians following
    end of, 27
Reynolds, John, 56
Rhône Valley, 51
Ricardo, David, 292*n5*, 300*n41*
Richard II, King of England, 51–53
Ridge and Valley, 4
Rights of Man, The (Paine), 47
Ripley and Mill Creek Valley Railroad,
    167
River of Earth (Still), 35, 218–19
Robertson, Susanah, 105
Robinson Crusoe (Defoe), 41
Rochester, Anna, 259
Rockefeller, Jay, 266, 338*n35*, 339*n38*
Rockefeller, John D., 138
Rockefeller Foundation, 249, 252
Rocky Mountains, 11
Rogers, Harold, 271
Rölvaag, Ole, 207–208
Roman Empire, 65, 118, 188
Romeo and Juliet (Shakespeare), 19
Roosevelt, Eleanor, 226–28, 230, 258
Roosevelt, Franklin, 227, 230, 231
Roosevelt, Theodore, 18, 205
Rosaldo, Renato, 337*n14*
Rosebud Mining, 265
Rosengarten, Theodore, 234
Rosenstein-Rodan, Paul N., 250
Ross, Malcolm, 238
Rostow, W. W., 41, 244
Rousseau, Jean-Jacques, vii, 38, 194,
    256

Rowland Land Company, 160
Roy, Arundhati, 244, 288
rubber production, 31, 65, 72–73, 285
Rush, Benjamin, 9, 41, 120
Russia, 63, 68–69, 181

Sachs, Honor, 66–67, 88, 308*n22*
Sachs, Jeffrey, 41
Sahlins, Marshall, 71, 255–56, 337*n17*
St. Clair, Arthur, 125
Saint Johns River, 186
Saint Paul Press, 15
Salstrom, Paul, 263, 331*n21*
Samers, Michael, 340*n45*
Sand Hill and Mud Lick Oil Company,
    136
San Joaquin Valley (California), 86
Santa Fe Ring, 138
Sartre, Jean-Paul, 93
Saudi Arabia, 280
savagery, 14, 37, 38, 48, 123, 225, 245,
    255, 296*n2*; Indians associated with,
    88, 327*n40*; novels depicting, 198,
    199, 204, 206; political economists'
    view of, 37, 38, 42, 112, 193–94, 214,
    297*n8*, 298*n19*; uplanders accused of,
    127, 152, 251, 293*n10*
Savage State, The (Cole), 38, 296*n4*
Savo-Karelians, 87
Say, Jean-Baptiste, 297*n15*, 298*n19*
Scandinavian immigrants, 180
Schultz, Theodore, 253–54
Schumacher, E. F., 272
Scotland, 51, 71, 78, 94, 127, 223
Scots-Irish, xiv, 19, 65, 87, 211, 237,
    314*n15*; degeneracy attributed to, 20,
    27, 199, 205; whiskey tax opposed by,
    100, 109–10
Scott, H.R., xv–xvi
Scott, James C., 68, 118, 295*n35*, 311*n49*
Scottish philosophers, 41, 48
Scotts Run, xv–xvi, 7, 225, 227, 258, 270

Scribner, Charles, 205
Sea Islands, 185–86
Second World War, *see* World War II
self-provisioning, 28, 67, 69, 213–14, 230,
    248, 297*n8*; *see also* captured gardens;
    smallholders
"Self-Reliance" (Emerson), 193
Seminole, 24, 25
Semple, Ellen Churchill, 17–20
Senate, U.S., 138, 266, 339*n38*; *see also*
    Congress, U.S.
serfs, 10, 54, 76, 178, 190, 233
Shakespeare, William, 19
Shanin, Teodor, 29
sharecroppers, 13, 178, 232–34 247, 259,
    333–34*n38*
Sharecroppers' Union, 234
Shawnee nation, xiii, 5, 8, 11, 124, 128,
    156
Shays' Rebellion, 91, 92, 95–96
Shenandoah National Park, 237–38
Shenandoah Valley, 4, 8, 88, 128–30,
    132, 148, 168–69, 178, 316*n34*
Shepard, Thomas, 77
Sheridan, Philip, 128–29, 178–79
Sherman, William Tecumseh, 178, 186,
    187
Shils, Edward, 336*n1*
Short Cut, Watchung Station, New Jersey
    (Inness), 195–97, 199–201, 328*n47*
Shoshone nation, 178
Siegfried, André, 336*n1*
Sierra Leone, 312*n53*
Silicon Valley, 278
Sinclair, John, 215
Sinking Spring Farm, 8
Sioux nation, 60, 128, 178, 182–83
Sirionó people, 30–31, 295*n38*
Skidmore, Hubert, 35, 173–74
slaves, 28, 76, 105, 176, 186, 188, 301*n46*,
    304*n73*, 313*n10*; from Africa, 20, 31,
    65, 75, 83, 216; during Civil War, 129,

132–33, 186; escaped, 83, 102; food raised by, 78, 223, 231, 304–305*n76*; former, discrimination against, 188, 233–34, 334*n38*; freed, xiii, 16, 83–85, 178; Haitian, revolution of, 31–32, 70; Indians as owners of, 25; industrialization involving, 133–34; on plantations, 20–21, 27, 39, 75, 81, 83, 84, 107, 133, 216, 295*n33*; political conflicts over ownership of, 12, 85, 294–95*n33*, 305*n78*; during Whiskey Rebellion, 99–100, 104, 114

Slotkin, Richard, 327*n40*

Slow Violence and the Environmentalism of the Poor (Nixon), 212

smallholders, xiv–xv, 42, 54, 65–68, 76, 183, 232, 301*n50*; capitalism and, 29–30, 52, 68, 214, 288; in developing countries, xiv, 19, 30, 72, 210, 257–58, 280, 286; enclosure and, 58, 74, 188; former slaves as, 70, 185–86; market participation of, 71–74, 208–209, 303*n62*; moralistic views of poverty of, 47; population growth of, 150; sharecroppers compared to, 178; slaveholders versus, 81, 84–85; during Whiskey Rebellion, 114, 125; *see also* makeshift economies; tenant farmers

Smith, Adam, 37, 63, 194, 214, 254, 297*nn6, 10, 15*; on division of labor, 43–45; on taxation, 95, 306*n8*, 307*n14*, 311*n52*; theory of stages as historical assumption of, 40–41, 244

Smith, J. Allen, 137, 314*n19*

Smith, J. Russell, 152, 153, 272

Smith, John, 237

Social Contract, The (Rousseau), vii

Société Sucrière de Markala (Sosumar), 280–87

Sohn, Mark F., 315*n28*

Sosumar, 280–87

Soungo (Mali), 281

South Africa, 280, 312*n53*

South Carolina, 8, 111, 185, 239

South Carolina Greenwood and August Railroad, 188

South Dakota, 177, 181

Southern Highlander and His Homeland, The (Campbell), 235

Southern Pacific Railroad, 262

South Midlands, 57

sovereignty, 96, 118–19, 127–28, 137, 305*n78*, 311*n48*; of Indian nations, 25, 27, 87–88, 180, 295*n34*

Soviet Union, 49, 247

Spain, 19, 51, 76, 91

Special Field Order, No. 15, 186

Spicer, Ross, xv–xvi

Spruce Mountain, 4

stages, theory of, 37–38, 40, 42, 50, 97, 111, 296*n1*

Stages of Economic Growth, The (Rostow), 41, 244

Stalder, Bill, 210–11

Standard Oil, 138

Statistics of Coal (Taylor), 129

Steuart, James, 45–46, 57–58, 71, 84, 113, 225, 250, 280, 297–98*n17*, 309*n35*

Stewart, Dugald, 297*n6*

Stewart, Jessy and Anabelle, xvi–xvii

Still, James, 35, 218–19

Stone Age Economics (Sahlins), 255–56

Story of Woodbine Farm, The (Zinn), 35

Strickland, William, 109–10

Study of History, A (Toynbee), 35

Subsidized Nutrition Assistance Program (SNAP), 267

Subsistence Homestead Authority, 336*n5*

Superfund Sites, 265

Supreme Court, U.S., 25–27, 137, 248, 314*n18*

Susquehanna River Valley, 88, 123

Sweden, 51

Swedish immigrants, 19, 86–88, 107,
305*n81*
Sweezy, Paul, 292*n5*
swidden agriculture, 69, 72, 107–108,
120, 156, 170, 236–37, 251–53, 255
Switzerland, 312*n1*
Syria, 51

Tanzania, 327*n46*
Tate, Allan, 247
Taylor, Richard Cowling, 129
Tecumseh, 8
Teller, Henry, 179–80
Temple, William, 47
tenant farmers, 82, 105, 115, 140, 148–49,
316–17*n38*, 334*n38*; African-
American, 178, 232–34; on coal
company properties, 173, 213, 224,
323*n83*; in England, 54–55, 57–58,
61, 62, 301*n44*; during Whiskey
Rebellion, 103–105, 124, 125
Tennessee, 8, 12, 87, 128, 140, 143, 219,
239, 262, 265, 271, 293*n10*, 333*n32*
Tennessee Valley Authority (TVA), 236,
240
Tenskwatawa, 8
Texas, 12, 207, 295*n33*
Thailand, 283
theory of stages, 37–38, 40, 42, 50, 97,
111, 296*n1*
Thirsk, Joan, 60
Thomas, Charlie, 275
Thoreau, Henry David, 178, 189–92, 195
"three-fifths" clause, 132
Three Acres and Liberty (Bolton), 246
Thünen, Johann Heinrich von, 6
timber industry, *see* lumber companies
Timber Ridge, 8
tobacco, 9, 30, 99, 107, 144, 147, 216,
306*n8*
Tocqueville, Alexis de, 76
Toledo Weekly, xvi

Totten family, 153, 154, 158, 161–65,
168
tourism, 17, 146, 147, 235, 238, 241, 242
Townsend, Joseph, 46–47
Toynbee, Arnold, 34–36, 42
"Tragedy of the Commons, The"
(Hardin), 276
Trail of the Lonesome Pine, The (Fox), 205
Trail of Tears, 24, 27
Transforming Traditional Agriculture
(Schultz), 253–54
Treasury, U.S., 90, 97, 100, 118, 156
treaties, 24–25, 27, 88, 91, 180, 323*n2*
Tresham, Thomas, 56
Tribe, Keith, 306*n7*
Trouillot, Michel-Ralph, 37, 41
Trump, Donald, 271
Tuareg, 282
Tug Fork River, 161, 166, 167, 319*n57*
Turgot, Anne-Robert-Jacques, 48
Turner, Frederick Jackson, 17, 18, 41,
72, 76
Tuscarora War, 78
Tutankhamun, King, 326*n35*
Twelve Southerners (the Agrarians),
246–47
Tyler, Wat, 52

Ulster-Scots, *see* Scots-Irish
Union Pacific Railroad, 177
United Mine Workers of America, 223,
225
United Nations, 150, 245; Children's
Emergency Fund (UNICEF), 337*n18*;
Climate Change Conference, 269;
Development Programme, 284, 286;
Food and Agriculture Organization,
251; Human Development Index,
292; International Fund for
Agricultural Development, 288
United States Agency for International
Development (USAID), 256, 279

United States Chamber of Commerce, 231

Unsettling of America, The (Berry), 234

Urquhart, David, 44, 297*n11*

Utah Territory, 305*n78*

Valley Campaign (1864), 128

Vance, J. D., 277–78

Vanderbilt University, 261

Vandever family, 147–48, 316–17*n38*

Venice, 52

Vermont, 79, 247, 292*n2*, 326*n35*

Vermont insurgency, 92

Veteran in a New Field (Homer), 176, 200, 207–208

Vietnam, 270

Viner, Jacob, 337*n15*

Virgil, 38, 193

Virginia, xvii, 5, 7, 8, 15, 90, 119, 236–39, 330*n16*; cattle in, 146, 316*n35*; in Civil War, 134; coal industry in, 162–63; commerce in, 112, 113; constitution of, 138; farming in, 78, 236–39, 315*n29*; land ownership in, 9, 13, 153, 155–63, 216; map of, *xi;* Tidewater counties of, 60; transport of coal to factories in, 3; travelers' descriptions of backcountry of, 15–16; western, 9, 11–12, 87–88, 101–102, 104, 108, 115, 128, 138–39, 146, 155, 160, 269 (*see also* West Virginia); Whiskey Tax resistance in, 93

Virginia Tourist, The (Pollard), 147

Volga River Valley, 78

Waggoner, Eric, 267–68

Wagner Act (1935), 271

Wakefield, Edward Gibbon, 334*n38*

Walden (Thoreau), 189–92

Wales, 58, 87, 223

Walking with the Comrades (Roy), 244

Waller, Altina, 167, 202, 315*n29*

Wallerstein, Immanuel, 41, 234, 292*n5*, 328*n3*

Walmart, 64, 269

Warden, Nimrod, 112

Ware, Harold, 229–31, 333*n33*

War of 1812, 8, 305*n3*

War on Poverty, 259

Washington, D.C., 4

Washington, George, 24–25, 88, 91, 99, 120; lands owned by, 101–104, 106, 125, 155, 307*n17*, 308*n22*; Whiskey Tax supported by, 90, 93, 110

Washington, University of, 137

Watauga Association, 293*n10*

Waters, Tony, 314*n14*, 327*n46*

Wayne, Anthony, 125

Way They Live, The (Anshutz), 186–87

"Wealth" (Emerson), 192–95

Wealth of Nations, The (Smith), 43, 45, 63, 95

Weaver, John C., 307*n19*

Weeks Act (1911), 170

Weise, Robert, 160

Welch, Isaiah, 160–61, 163–64

Wells, David, 184, 324*n15*

Wenman, Philip, Viscount Wenman of Tuam, 56

West Indies, 70

West Kalimantan (Borneo), 72–73

West Virginia, xvii, 5, 7, 27, 130–41, 238, 276, 296*n45*, 314*n24*, 317*n40*, 319–20*n59*, 326*n35*, 338*n35*; Arthurdale project in, 227–31, 259, 274, 332*n31*, 333*n33*; Board of Agriculture of, 331*n19*; before Civil War, *see* Virginia, western; coal industry in, xv, 33, 34, 130, 136, 138–39, 153–54, 160–65, 205, 212–14, 223–26, 258, 263–71, 320*n62*, 330*n16*, 331*n19*; Coal Mining Institute of, 23–24; constitutions of, 138; corporations chartered in,

West Virginia (*cont.*)
136–38; dialect of English spoken in, 19; ecological base of agrarianism in, 74, 142; enclosure in, 61, 188, 279; feuds in, 166–68, 314*n16*; founding of, 132–36, 313*n14*; House of Delegates of, 266–67; impact of industrialization in, 27, 33–35, 130–31, 140–42; logging in, 168–69, 173, 258, 321*n66*; map of, *x–xi*; mountain farming economy in, 65, 144–46, 150, 184, 275, 301*n50*, 316*n34*, 317*nn38, 41*, 318*n47*; population of, 9, 15, 148–50, 243, 270

West Virginia University, xv, 170

West Virginia Wesleyan University, 267

Wharton, Edith, 198

Wheeling (West Virginia), 133–34, 138, 158, 169

Wheeling, Pittsburgh and Baltimore Railroad, 167

Whiskey Rebellion, 7, 46, 90–125, 127, 305*n3*, 310*n40*; backcountry rebellion context of, 91–92, 95–96; collapse of, 124–26; conflict between woodland culture and land ownership and use patterns preceding, xii, 100–110, 148–49; constitutional powers of government and, 118–24; Federalist versus Jeffersonian approaches to control of region of, 92–94; structure and enforcement of taxes provoking, 96–100, 110–18; Washington and Hamilton lead militia against, 90–91

White, Ed, 91, 306*n5*

White Mountains, 292*n2*

white supremacy, 26, 247

Whitten, David O., 310*n40*

Wickard v. Filburn (1943), 248, 336*n7*

Wilder, Laura Ingalls, 207, 327*n46*

Wilderness Road, 8, 88, 197

Willey, Waitman T., 313*n14*

Wilkinson, James, 91

Willamette Valley (Oregon), 5, 87

William of Orange, 41

Williams, David, 43

Williams, John Alexander, 260, 292*n4*, 296*n45*

Williams, Raymond, 127, 292*n5*

Williamson, Oliver E., 340*n47*

Willis, Lewis, 238

Wilson, Milburn, 228, 272

Winchester and Potomac Railroad, 167

Winstanley, Gerrard, 56–57

Winston Magna, 57

Wisconsin, 153, 208, 235, 333*n34*

Wister, Owen, 205

Wolf, Eric, 58

Woodbury, Levi, 12

Worcester v. Georgia (1832), 295*n34*

World Bank, 48, 245, 250, 257, 262, 284, 285, 288, 342*n69*

world-systems analysis, 41, 139, 183, 292*nn5, 6*

World War I, 226, 247–48, 258

World War II, xvi, 150, 248, 249, 259

Wright, Bert, 220

Wrightson, Keith, 60, 62, 299*n33*, 299–300*n34*, 301*n41*

Wyoming, 339*n41*

Yale Law School, 278

Young, Arthur, 60

Zimmerman, Carle C., 245

Zinn, William, 35, 147–48, 317*n39*, 321*n69*

A NOTE ABOUT THE AUTHOR

Steven Stoll is a professor of history at Fordham University and the author of *The Great Delusion* (Hill and Wang, 2008) and *Larding the Lean Earth* (Hill and Wang, 2002). His writing has appeared in *Harper's Magazine, Lapham's Quarterly*, and the *New Haven Review*.